THE VOICE OF THE CENTURY

The Voice of the Century

The Culture of Italian Bel Canto in Luisa Tetrazzini's Recorded Interpretations

Massimo Zicari

https://www.openbookpublishers.com

© 2022 Massimo Zicari

This work is licensed under an Attribution-NonCommercial 4.0 International (CC BY-NC 4.0). This license allows you to share, copy, distribute and transmit the text; to adapt the text for non-commercial purposes providing attribution is made to the authors (but not in any way that suggests that they endorse you or your use of the work). Attribution should include the following information:

Massimo Zicari, *The Voice of the Century: The Culture of Italian Bel Canto in Luisa Tetrazzini's Recorded Interpretations*. Cambridge, UK: Open Book Publishers, 2022. https://doi.org/10.11647/OBP.0277

In order to access detailed and updated information on the license, please visit https://doi.org/10.11647/OBP.0277#copyright

Further details about Creative Commons licenses are available at http://creativecommons.org/licenses/by-nc/4.0/

All external links were active at the time of publication unless otherwise stated and have been archived via the Internet Archive Wayback Machine at https://archive.org/web

Digital material and resources associated with this volume are available at https://doi.org/10.11647/OBP.0277#resources

Every effort has been made to identify and contact copyright holders and any omission or error will be corrected if notification is made to the publisher.

The Open Access version of this publication was funded by the Swiss National Science Foundation (10BP12_209286/1).

ISBN Paperback: 9781800643321
ISBN Hardback: 9781800643338
ISBN Digital (PDF): 9781800643345
ISBN Digital ebook (EPUB): 9781800643352
ISBN Digital ebook (AZW3): 9781800643369
ISBN Digital ebook (XML): 9781800643376
ISBN Digital ebook (HTML): 9781800646797
DOI: 10.11647/OBP.0277

Cover image: Photograph of Luisa Tetrazzini on the front page of *The San Francisco Call*, 25 December 1910.
Cover design by Anna Gatti.

Contents

Acknowledgements	vii
Introduction	ix
1. The Voice of the Century: Luisa Tetrazzini and Her Discographic Legacy	1
2. The Rossinian Repertoire	15
3. Donizetti's Operas	49
4. Bellini and the New Declamatory Style	73
5. Verdi's Style: The End of Bel Canto?	99
Conclusions	129
Transcriptions	135
List of Illustrations	199
Select Bibliography	203
Index of Names	207

Acknowledgements

The publication of this book was made possible thanks to the support of the Swiss National Science Foundation (10BP12_209286/1).

I owe a debt of gratitude to Michael Aspinall for providing me with great insight into Luisa Tetrazzini's records and discographies, for reviewing an early version of the manuscript and making many valuable suggestions. My thanks also go to all the colleagues and students with whom I have been able to exchange views, experiment with ideas and reflect on the need to have musicians who are better informed about the facts of our musical history.

This book is dedicated to Silvia.

Introduction

> Before leaving the subject of practising I should like to add a word as to the value of the gramophone to the intelligent student. This is, indeed, a truly invaluable adjunct. If to hear the greatest singers is the finest of all experiences for the student, how can it indeed be otherwise? For here in the most convenient manner possible is the means provided for doing this. [...] And he can hear them not only now and again, but as often as ever he likes and by his own fireside. If he happens to be studying some particular rôle he can be "coached" in this most practical and unrivalled manner by all the greatest artists of the day. He can take a particular aria and hear it sung by Caruso again and again until he is familiar with every detail of his rendering—can note his breathing, his phrasing, and every other detail in a manner which would be quite impossible by any other means. And having heard Caruso he can then hear the same number sung by various other great artists if he chooses, and benefit still more by comparing their respective readings—by noting how they resemble one another or how they differ, as the case may be, incidentally learning in the process how widely one interpretation may differ from another and still be of the highest order. [...] Whether it will be so or not remains to be seen. But certainly it may be said that never before have students been so wonderfully helped. I myself have pleasure in testifying that I have derived the greatest benefit as well as delight from the records of Patti, while Mr. John McCormack has similarly acknowledged his indebtedness to the wonderful renderings of Caruso. And I hope in all modesty that students of the present generation may derive similar help in turn from the records which I myself have made.[1]

Were it not for words like 'gramophone' or 'fireside' and the reference to the iconic, but possibly passé figures of Enrico Caruso and Adelina Patti, not to mention the lesser-known John McCormack, we might think that this opinion was expressed by a singing teacher commenting on the plethora of recordings now available from the Internet. Instead, this passage comes from Luisa Tetrazzini's volume *How to Sing*, which was published in 1923. As early as 1908 Tetrazzini, herself a pioneer of audio recordings, admitted to using discs to form an opinion about her colleagues' vocal and interpretative qualities. Having the opportunity to listen to a reference musician again and again, to take notice of his or her breaths, phrasing, use of staccato and, most importantly, to draw a comparison between different interpretations of the same piece must have sounded revolutionary to a generation of musicians who could not have access to other artists, except for those who taught them in local schools or whose performances in municipal theatres and concert venues they could attend in person.

> In my younger days only those dwelling in the great capitals could hope to hear such artists as Patti, Tamagno, Caruso, Battistini, and so forth, and even those only if means permitted, which was not often in the case of poor students. To-day any one can enjoy this priceless privilege, wherever he may happen to reside, for a comparatively small outlay through the agency of the gramophone.[2]

Tetrazzini, like anybody else at that time, did not have access to her colleagues or illustrious predecessors until audio recordings were made commercially available: 'Have I ever heard Patti? Melba? Not until quite recently', she admitted in 1908, 'except through a gramophone, which I listen to frequently'.[3] Although 'so imperfect a musical instrument', Tetrazzini became already familiar with this new technology at the outset of its development, having her voice recorded as early as 1904 for the American Zon-O-Phone.[4] However, it was on the occasion of her

---

1 Luisa Tetrazzini, *How to Sing* (New York: Doran, 1923), pp. 111–14. The same passage can be found at pages 103–05 of the first English edition (London: C. Arthur Pearson, Ltd., 1923).
2 Tetrazzini, *How to Sing*, p. 112 (p. 103 in the English edition).
3 'Making of a Great Singer', *The Sun*, 8 March 1908, p. 6.
4 See Charles Neilson Gattey, Luisa Tetrazzini, *The Florentine Nightingale* (Portland: Amadeus Press, 1995), p. 333.

London début in 1907 that her interest in the gramophone and the fast-evolving discographic market took a new turn. As she recalls, the most interesting of her visitors on the Monday morning following her first appearance at Covent Garden as Violetta 'were the representatives of the numerous gramophone companies which have their offices and works in and around the British capital'.[5] She was approached by, among others, the managers of The Gramophone Company, which she considered the best. Having signed a contract and recorded a number of discs, the gramophone became one of her most trustworthy musical companions from then on.

> Let me say here how astonished I have been by the great improvements made in the gramophone which is now unquestionably capable of exquisitely reproducing high-grade music. I have one in each of my homes in Italy, and I find it a delightful entertainer as well as a very serviceable instructor. I have records by all the well-known artists of every one of the operas and ballads which I sing. I constantly try these records over and listen intently for the faults of the artists, and try to profit by their mistakes. I also try over my own records and find that this practice helps me considerably in the task of keeping my voice in perfect condition.[6]

In a moment when recording technologies were ground-breaking and a new market was arising, Luisa Tetrazzini seems to have been among the first to comprehend how useful a disc could be, not only for entertaining, but also for learning purposes. She immediately understood how valuable a tool a recording could be for analysing the style and technique of other performers. After a century, Tetrazzini's words resonate strongly with any of those among us who have worked on discs, whether new or old, and who have learned how much they can teach us about our past as well as today's boundlessly rich musical present.

What Tetrazzini could not possibly predict was the extent and rapidity of this development and the manner in which recordings would change our musical habits, affect our learning strategies and shape our understanding of music. A hundred years after those words were pronounced, listening to a recorded interpretation has become a simple and inexpensive gesture, with countless audio and video files easily accessible via the Internet, uploaded not only by commercial streaming and media service providers but also countless individuals, eager to share with the rest of the world their private collections of musical memorabilia, even if it means infringing international copyright regulations. More discs are digitised and uploaded to the Internet every day, thus offering us the opportunity not only to cross distant geographical frontiers, but also to travel back into our musical past. It is just a matter of a few clicks and the whole musical world discloses itself, in the form of hundreds and thousands of recordings. Whether a single operatic aria, a solo recital or a fully staged opera, what is most striking in this new soundscape, and for some of us most worrisome, is the diverse quality of these recordings, with international stars being as easily accessible as those many home-made performances by passionate, but sometimes insufficiently trained, music practitioners. This abundance of recordings, however confusing with regard to quality and authoritativeness, gives us the opportunity to put our favourite interpreters and interpretations in perspective. Never before has it been so easy to navigate through generations of performers and compare their renditions, as Tetrazzini envisaged in 1923.

But, if these countless audio and video recordings form an incredibly rich body of evidence that each of us can so effortlessly access, how effectively are we taking advantage of them? Do we listen to them critically? How easy is it for us to decide the merits of recorded interpretations of different quality and value, always excepting those few great masters whose credentials and reputation are undisputed? Does anyone with the necessary competence guide us in the process of familiarising ourselves with past and possibly long-forgotten recordings? And, most importantly, how do we respond to them? As has been suggested, this vast body of phonographic evidence has led to a considerable change in our approach to the canonical compositions of the European concert tradition, and has challenged many of our current interpretative norms and habits.[7] Still, research conducted on responses to recordings suggests that they are often regarded negatively for allegedly stifling artistic originality and

---

5   Luisa Tetrazzini, *My Life of Song* (London, New York, Toronto and Melbourne: Cassell, 1921), p. 214.
6   Ibid., pp. 214–15.
7   Dorottya Fabian, *A Musicology of Performance: Theory and Method Based on Bach's Solos for Violin* (Cambridge: Open Book Publishers, 2015), https://doi.org/10.11647/OBP.0064.

significantly reducing performance individuality and variability.[8] Uninformed listeners and even music students still tend to disregard early recordings and respond with incredulity to the interpretations which they reveal.[9] This is certainly the case for portamento, which was used very liberally by singers like Luisa Tetrazzini, Adelina Patti, Nellie Melba and Marcella Sembrich, but is considered tasteless and inappropriate today, unless used very sparingly.[10] Similarly, the idea of adding unwritten ornamentation and cadenzas into repertoires other than the Baroque may cause many of our colleagues to fall into narrower stylistic prejudices. In recent years scholarly studies in the field of nineteenth-century opera performance practice have made tremendous progress and after long and animated discussions the well-documented practice of adding and substituting for coloratura passages in Italian romantic operas seems to be more generally accepted by both opera conductors and singers.[11] Still, sometimes voice students are forbidden to insert portamentos, to modify tempos or to insert new cadenzas in the arias they are learning, on the grounds of bad taste and improper style. If, on the one hand, it is fair to assume that the habit of learning from recorded performances is extremely common among music practitioners, the likelihood that a young performer will take an early recording as a model is still low. This becomes all the more striking if one considers that, as Robert Philip suggested almost thirty years ago, 'many of the musicians heard on early recordings were trained in the late, or in some cases mid, nineteenth century, and their performing styles can be seen as remnants of nineteenth-century style'.[12] A much stronger case can be made when considering the recorded interpretations left by early twentieth-century composers like Igor Stravinsky, Claude Debussy, Sergei Prokofiev and Benjamin Britten, to name but a few. Should we not consider their recorded interpretations as the strongest evidence of their compositional and interpretative intentions?

Music practitioners are often confronted with a dilemma: even when they come to value the living tradition that discs reveal and make accessible, they are constantly urged to express their originality and define their own creative space, a condition that forces them to steer away from models that are perceived as anachronistic and passé. However authoritative, early recordings are often understood as the remnants of a tradition that has become obsolete and tasteless. To some extent, this helps to explain the paradox behind the commercial success of modern recordings of early music as a consequence of the extraordinary growth of so-called historically informed performance practice (HIPP). The repeated attempts made by performers specialising in a particular genre or period to recreate a musical past which is documented only in text-based sources has led to numerous interpretations that, however different from each other, appeal to a large audience and make a big impact in the discographic market on grounds of novelty and originality rather than historical accuracy or verisimilitude, let alone authenticity.[13] In a way, the lack of aural models has been instrumental in enhancing the interpretative creativity of those who re-invented, say, the Baroque by reading eighteenth-century treatises like Johann Joachim Quantz, Carl Philipp Emanuel Bach and Francesco Geminiani; instead, listening to and using past recordings as a model would cause them to fall into what may be considered a poor imitation or even a bad replica of those

---

8   Georgia Volioti and Aaron Williamon, 'Recordings as Learning and Practising Resources for Performance: Exploring Attitudes and Behaviours of Music Students and Professionals', *Musicae Scientiae*, 21.4 (2017), 499–523.

9   Daniel Leech-Wilkinson, 'Listening and Responding to the Evidence of Early Twentieth-Century Performance', *Journal of the Royal Musical Association*, 135.1 (2010), 45–62.

10 Deborah Kauffman, 'Portamento in Romantic Opera', *Performance Practice Review*, 5.2 (1992), 139–58. https://doi.org/10.5642/perfpr.199205.02.03

11 Philip Gossett, *Divas and Scholars. Performing Italian Opera* (Chicago: Chicago University Press, 2006), p. 264. See also David Lawton, 'Ornamenting Verdi's Arias: The Continuity of a Tradition', in *Verdi in Performance*, ed. by Alison Latham and Roger Parker (Oxford: Oxford University Press, 2001), pp. 49–78; Will Crutchfield, 'Vocal Ornamentation in Verdi: The Phonographic Evidence', *19th-Century Music*, 7.1 (1983), 3–54; Roger Freitas, 'Towards a Verdian Ideal of Singing: Emancipation from Modern Orthodoxy', *Journal of the Royal Musical Association*, 127 (2002), 226–57. Hilary Poriss, *Changing the Score: Arias, Prima Donnas, and the Authority of Performance* (Oxford: Oxford University Press, 2009); Romana Margherita Pugliese, 'The Origins of Lucia di Lammermoor's Cadenza', *Cambridge Opera Journal*, 16.1 (2004), 23–42.

12 Robert Philip, *Early Recordings and Musical Style* (Cambridge: Cambridge University Press, 1992), p. 1.

13 In this regard, Richard Taruskin's idea still holds good, that today's notion of authenticity is more a symptom of commercial propaganda than a description of a historical approach to the past; as he suggests, often 'a thin veneer of historicism clothes a performance style that is completely of our time, and is in fact the most modern style around. Richard Taruskin, 'The Pastness of the Present', in *Authenticity and Early Music*, ed. by Nicholas Kenyon (Oxford: Oxford University Press, 1988), pp. 137–206 (p. 152).

models. No matter how much one values early recordings and the authority of those interpreters, the imperative of originality prevails over any effort to develop a historically informed approach by referring to those recordings. Reviving a style now considered outdated or, even worse, aping the voice of an old but unsurpassed master, would jeopardise a young artist's effort to gain credibility and climb the podium of international recognition.

But, if imitating the voice of one old master would be detrimental to one's creativity, one could safely assume that comparing different models would result in a larger palette of interpretative choices, a more critical understanding of our past and a less idiosyncratic response to the musical contents revealed by these recordings. With this in mind, it should be easier to understand why reconstructing Luisa Tetrazzini's vocal style through the systematic analysis of her recordings is an enterprise worth undertaking. Still, why on earth should anyone embark on such a thankless task as the transcription of the operatic arias a singer may have recorded a century ago? What's the point in wasting endless hours transcribing a recorded voice when one could so easily form an idea by simply playing those very discs? Although the importance of working on sound material from the past in order to understand and reconstruct a performance practice should be more obvious now, the same cannot be said of the necessity of transcribing it in music notation, a task that, as ethnomusicology has long demonstrated, implies an enormous loss of information. Then again, what's the point in listening to a crackling sound recording over and over again with the idea that its transcription will capture something that our ear may have missed?[14] If we assume that music notation by its very nature fails to capture all the details and subtle nuances that make the difference between a music score and its realisation, is there anything we can gain among all that we lose?

In a way, the answer lies in the persisting tyranny of the printed page, that is to say our inclination, whether as music scholars or practitioners, to rely more strongly on texts than any other kind of source. It is not just a question of habit, nor is it a pedantic insistence on the traditional paradigms of historiography. The need for text-based sources, or better, the necessity to turn sound sources into texts, lies in one of the conditions that allow us to study and investigate them: comparability. Historians do not rely on just one source to study an event or a historical process, but on many; they construct their interpretation of the past by collecting and comparing sources. This task becomes much easier if the sources we try to compare lie in front of us in the form of a written document; on the contrary, if we had to listen to one recording after the other and rely uniquely on our memory, the task would become extremely challenging, if not impossible.

There is at least one more good reason why transcribing and comparing may represent a particularly effective way of investigating the recorded interpretations of singers like Luisa Tetrazzini: transcriptions can be especially helpful when it comes to examining a performing tradition in which changing the score was not just a common habit but a stylistic feature endorsed by generations of musicians and distinctive of each individual interpreter. These changes, which included the addition of cadenzas, the use of ornamentation, coloratura passages, small graces, vibrato, portamento and so forth, were considered as expressive devices to be used with taste and consideration, in order to convey the sense of the drama. Each interpreter was encouraged to shape her own stylistic identity by way of a distinctive approach to the repertoire; this involved choosing a set of interpretative devices that worked as a unique and characteristic watermark.

Transcriptions can also be extremely helpful when it comes to comparing the contents of recorded interpretations with what we read and learn from nineteenth- and early twentieth-century singing methods and other text-based source material. By comparing the coloraturas suggested by, say, Manuel García and Mathilde Marchesi with what we hear in early recordings, we form an idea of what the line of continuity may have been, between the nineteenth-century masters who set the paradigms of bel canto and the younger generations of interpreters who inherited that tradition. How this singing culture evolved, or what survived of it at the outset of the twentieth century, may be better understood by analysing the early recordings left by those singers who had been trained in that tradition.

---

14   For a discussion on the necessity for any of us to analyse by comparing see also Nicholas Cook, 'Performance Analysis and Chopin's Mazurkas', *Musicae Scientiae*, 11.2 (2007), 183–207, https://doi.org/10.1177/102986490701100203

Of course, it is hazardous to draw generalisations from the relatively poor evidence we have at our disposal. Can we draw a line between those traits that were distinctive of an individual interpreter and those that were shared among all those who had been trained in the same singing culture? To what extent are these outstanding—and in many ways exceptional—interpretations typical of a broadly shared musical language? To what extent were the tenets of the so-called bel canto still valid at the beginning of the twentieth century? How does Tetrazzini's voice and style compare with those of her contemporary colleagues? What is the relationship between her and those singers whose career and reputation were connected with the modern Italian operas of, say, Giacomo Puccini, Pietro Mascagni and Ruggiero Leoncavallo? Unfortunately, we have no recordings of Romilda Pantaleoni, the first Desdemona in Verdi's *Otello* in 1887 and the first Tigrana in Puccini's *Edgar* in 1889; nor do we know much of Cesira Ferrani, one of the most celebrated interpreters of Puccini at the beginning of the twentieth century, and whose recordings date back to 1903.[15] In other cases, comparisons can be more easily drawn, although with reference to a small number of arias and a select number of interpreters: among them Nellie Melba, Marcella Sembrich, Amelita Galli-Curci, Claudia Muzio and Tetrazzini's protégée Lina Pagliughi, just to name a few, assume special interest.

Although early recordings represent a valuable source and a great opportunity for anyone willing to form an idea of what our musical ancestors' music making sounded like, a few caveats are necessary before we begin. First, compared to modern standards, the sound of acoustic recordings is dramatically poor. This has much to do with the technical constraints and the rudimentary technologies involved in early discs. An accurate description of these is offered by Fred Gaisberg, possibly the first sound engineer ever, the person who literally wrote the history of early recording technologies by recording most of the greatest stars of the time.

> Acoustically recorded sound had reached the limit of progress. The top frequencies were triple high C, 2088 vibrations per second, and the low remained at E, 164 vibrations per second. Voices and instruments, especially stringed instruments, were confined rigidly within these boundaries, although the average human ear perceives from 30 to 15'000 vibrations per second and musical sounds range from 60 to 8'000 vibrations.[16]

As Gaisberg explains, much of what contributes to defining the distinctive quality of each voice or instrument, its timbre, is lost if only a small portion of the acoustic information is captured by the recording medium. This can be easily seen in the following picture, which shows the spectrogram of the opening bars of Tetrazzini's 1908 recording of 'Ah! Fors'è lui' in Verdi's *La traviata* (Figure 1).[17]

The yellow horizontal squiggled lines represent Tetrazzini's unaccompanied voice, with her distinctive vibrato, when pronouncing the words 'È strano! È strano' at the beginning of the scena. The parallel yellow lines are the first and most resonant harmonics in the harmonic series, while the green background represents the whole frequency range which early gramophones could capture. Its upper limit falls around 4'500 Hz and the dark area above it, spanning the frequencies between 4'500 and 15'000 Hz, visualises the amount of acoustic information that has been lost in the process. In a modern recording that area would be colourful, with the upper harmonics contributing to a better definition of the timbral quality of the recorded voice. This is why voices sound thin and reedy in early recordings; they should be understood as a good approximation of what they really sounded like.

Fortissimos and pianissimos were almost impossible to capture, and singers were forced to adapt to awkward restrictions in order to cope with the limited range of dynamics that early phonographs could support. This was the case when in 1905 Fred Gaisberg and his brother Will were sent to Craig-y-Nos, in Wales, to record Adelina Patti's voice. She sang into the small funnel while standing still in one position, and Will had to pull her back when she attacked a high note; in 1906 she was placed on a small, movable platform so that she could be pulled

---

15 All Ferrani's Puccini recordings are included in the 2 CD set *Creators of Verismo*, Marston Records 52062-2. For a review of Puccini's sopranos see Richard Dyer 'Puccini, his sopranos, and some records', *Opera Quarterly*, 2.3 (1984), 62–71, https://doi.org/10.1093/oq/2.3.62

16 Fred W. Gaisberg, *The Music Goes Round* (New York: The Macmillan Company, 1942), p. 86. A detailed account of the early development of the d iscographic industry in Great Britain can be found in Peter Martland, *Recording History, The British Record Industry, 1888-1931* (Lanham, Toronto, P lymouth: The Scarecrow Press, 2013).

17 Sonic Visualiser was used to process the audio track, for which a commercial digital transfer of the original disc was used.

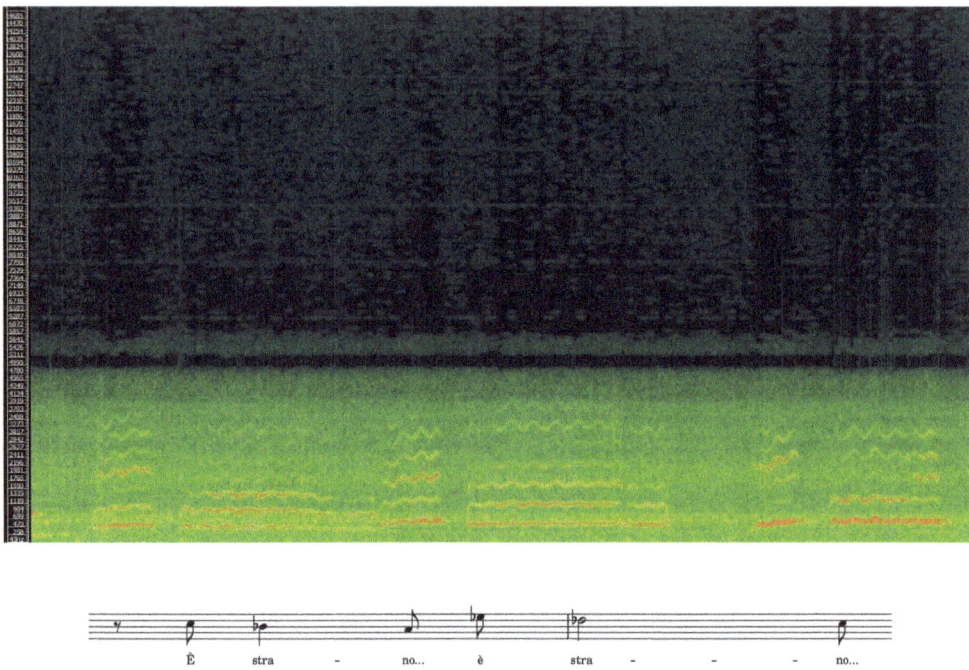

Figure 1 shows the spectrogram of Tetrazzini's 1908 recording of 'Ah! Fors'è lui' in Verdi's *La traviata*.

away from or pushed closer to the horn more easily, depending on the loudness of the passage.[18] Despite these technical limitations, Tetrazzini's *messa di voce* is always distinctively clear in her discs.

A second issue is presented by the use of small instrumental groups instead of real orchestras. As documented by many contemporary accounts and pictures, especially at the beginning of its development, the recording horn could not capture an entire orchestra, even when two funnels were used in combination. As a consequence, orchestras had to be turned into small ensembles with a few instruments representing whole families or substituting for those whose sound did not work well. Again, an account of what was a common practice in early recording studios is provided by Gaisberg.

> The inadequacy of the accompaniments to the lovely vocal records made in the Acoustic Age was their great weakness. There was no pretence of using the composer's score; we had to arrange it for wind instruments entirely. The articulated tuba tone was altogether too insistent. Though marked advances were made in the technique of manufacture which reduced the surface noise on the disc, nevertheless the artist and the selection had invariably to be selected with care so as to cover up all instrumental deficiencies. Only full, even voices of sustained power could be utilized, and all nuances, such as pianissimo effects, were omitted.[19]

String instruments, Gaisberg writes, were often recorded by a subterfuge. A Stroh violin substituted for violins and violas; for a cello they used a bassoon, and a tuba for the double bass.[20] As can be imagined, any pretence of truthfulness, not to talk of philology, should be abandoned when listening to these early discs.

A third limitation was recording time, which in early discs amounted to ca. three to four minutes in total. This raises further questions concerning not only the chosen tempo, but also the cuts and adaptations that were necessary in order to fit the disc length.[21] However, as I have already suggested, even though measuring

---

18 John Frederick Cone, *Adelina Patti: Queen of Hearts* (Portland: Amadeus Press, 1993), pp. 241–48.
19 Gaisberg, *The Music Goes Round*, p. 85.
20 Ibid. The Stroh violin was developed by Augustus Stroh at the beginning of the twentieth century. Its body consisted of a long, narrow piece of wood, the upper surface of which served as the fingerboard. A flexible membrane mounted at one side of the bridge worked as a pick-up and projected the sound to a metal horn. Hugh Davies, 'Stroh violin', *Grove Music Online*. 2001, https://www.oxfordmusiconline.com/grovemusic/view/10.1093/gmo/9781561592630.001.0001/omo-9781561592630-e-0000047635.
21 See also Neal Peres Da Costa, *Off the Record* (Oxford: Oxford University Press, 2012), pp. 3–23.

performance parameters such as duration, amplitude and pitch can be problematic, relative variations in tempo and pitch within a recorded performance are still quite reliable. They can provide us with important information on the use of tempo modifications as a means for dramatic expression.[22]

One last question regards the distance between a studio recording and a live performance. It would be naïve to think of a recording (especially an early one) as evidence of what happened in a fully staged, live performance. Still, the consistency between Tetrazzini's recordings and many contemporary reviews of her interpretations in capital cities like London and New York suggests that once she had learned a role, she remained consistent with her original interpretative idea. As we will see, many contemporary reviews describe in some detail the same roulades and melodic modifications that we find in her recordings.

Of course, there is much more that can be learned from these recordings but, as has been already suggested by Dorottya Fabian, to engage with the richly complex phenomenon represented by a music performance or, even more complicated, a recorded music performance may sound like 'dancing to architecture'.[23] As a matter of fact, any attempt to describe expressive devices like vibrato or portamento, to draw comparisons between tempo variations, or to describe the technical and timbral differences in one's voice may lead to potentially hazardous oversimplifications, or shift the focus to a perceptual level different from the aural. One example is the use of a richly metaphorical language, which again, in the attempt to describe those subtle nuances that make Tetrazzini's interpretations unique, result in a flourished, still pointless piece of scholarly prose. A second form of oversimplification involves the use of descriptive statistics to draw evidence-based generalisations on nineteenth-century performance style, for instance by identifying recurring patterns in the analysis of tempo modifications. However robust the results, performers and mere listeners may find it challenging, if not impossible, to draw sufficient practical insight from complex datasets, no matter how closely related they are to a given interpretative device. It should be added that the jargon used in some articles may sound overwhelmingly challenging to both music practitioners and listeners.

All these difficulties notwithstanding, I will touch on those qualities of Tetrazzini's technique and style that were so greatly appreciated by generations of opera-goers and sound so unfashionable to many of today's music practitioners. In a way, the figure of Luisa Tetrazzini is unique in the early twentieth-century operatic scenario: she epitomises the essence of an Italian *prima donna assoluta* with regard to both her vocal talent and personality, at a time when the glorious history of opera was reaching its conclusion. For instance, in 1888, Nellie Melba who was ten years her senior and one of the most celebrated representatives of bel canto, was found deficient 'in that indescribable something which we call charm' by Hermann Klein of *The Sunday Times*. 'Her accents lacked the ring of true pathos', he continued, and although she possessed admirable intelligence, 'the gift of spontaneous feeling has been denied her'.[24] According to Henry Pleasants, 'she learned to go through the motions with professional aplomb, although these motions were said by her detractors not to have gone beyond the raising of one arm in situations of some intensity and two arms for an outburst'.[25] The distance between Melba and her Italian colleagues was also noted by John Pitts Sanborn from *The Globe*, who heard Tetrazzini and Melba many times throughout their careers.

> Melba sang accurately and with dignity of good workmanship. Her singing was stereotyped without the excitement of the unexpected, the suddenly improvised, the inspiration of the heat and joy of song. Sometimes, as Tetrazzini's harshest critics insist, the soprano injuries the music by the variations she introduces; oftener she lifts it above the clouds. This sort of thing was inherent in the great Italian style as in the Italian temperament. Melba's style was rather mid-century French, the style of *Faust* and *Roméo and Juliette* than that of the older Italian roles, though in many respects she sang those roles so well and so delightfully.[26]

---

22   See Massimo Zicari, 'Expressive Tempo Modifications in Adelina Patti's Recordings: An Integrated Approach', *Empirical Musicology Review*, 12.1–2 (2017), 42–56.
23   Fabian, *A Musicology of Performance*, p. 4, https://doi.org/10.11647/OBP.0064
24   See Henry Pleasants, *The Great Singers from the Dawn of Opera to our own Time* (New York: Simon & Schuster, 1966), pp. 271–72.
25   Ibid., p. 272.
26   Charles Neilson Gattey, *Luisa Tetrazzini. The Florentine Nightingale* (Portland: Amadeus Press, 1995), p. 105.

The aplomb these contemporary critics highlighted can still be heard in Melba's recordings, especially if one focuses on the flawless but slightly inexpressive manner in which she controls the voice and keeps a steady pace. In this regard, the distance between Melba and Tetrazzini could not be more striking, especially if one thinks that they were both described as the personification of bel canto. The same cannot be said of Marcella Sembrich, whose career and vocal qualities very much resemble those of Luisa Tetrazzini; but, Sembrich belonged to that group of nineteenth-century divas who although not Italian, assumed a pivotal role in the development of the Italian operatic tradition. A proficient violinist and pianist, she was appreciated for her intellectual skills, which placed her art on an 'infinitely superior plane to her peers in vocalisation'.[27] Her refined (maybe too refined for an operatic diva?) skills, intelligence and dramatic intensity were noticed also in her interpretation of the Lieder of Robert Schumann, Franz Schubert and Johannes Brahms. Even in the private sphere her figure defies the stereotyped image of a vain, affected and temperamental creature, a woman who constantly changes her mind and entertains dissolute relationships with her *protettori*, with all the sexual implications that this term often carried.[28] Sembrich remained married to Wilhelm Stengel for her entire life and upon his death she withdrew from performing.[29] Other figures like Amelita Galli-Curci and Claudia Muzio made their début when Tetrazzini was at the apex of her career and, one may argue, reached the status of operatic diva in a moment when opera had lost its allure, and cinema was taking over. The careers of singers like Gemma Bellincioni, Rosina Storchio and Cesira Ferrani do not bear comparison with Tetrazzini's: significantly, none of them scored large successes in either London or New York despite their regular tours in Europe. Their singing style was characterised by expression and declamation, two features that were associated with verismo and required bigger voices and more convincing dramatic talents. In Bellincioni's case, her determination to sing roles like Santuzza, which required strong and sustained singing, caused major damage to her voice.

This volume analyses the interpretations of those arias from the so-called bel canto repertoire which Luisa Tetrazzini recorded between 1904 and 1922. In Chapter One I sketch the figure of Luisa Tetrazzini, whom some contemporary commentators described as the voice of the century. In spite of all we know about her public image, professional life and career, not much can be gleaned about her inner thoughts and musical opinions. I put her figure in context and provide a description of those features that were considered typical of bel canto, a notion that needs further consideration.

In Chapters Two to Five I focus on the four composers who are considered the cornerstones of nineteenth-century Italian opera and whose works are still at the core of modern opera singers' professional life: Gioachino Rossini, Gaetano Donizetti, Vincenzo Bellini and Giuseppe Verdi. Select operas from each of these composers were in Tetrazzini's repertoire, together with other Italian and French nineteenth-century works. Although her repertoire was much larger, what she recorded on disc represents a selection of operatic evergreens that were emblematic of a still vibrant operatic tradition. Chapter Two delves into the Rossinian tradition and explores the recordings related to the roles of Rosina and Semiramide, even though Tetrazzini never performed *Semiramide* on stage during her career. Particular attention will be paid to the so-called lesson scene in *Barbiere*, which had already assumed a metatheatrical dimension, breaking the imaginary fourth wall with the audience. Chapter Three focuses on Donizetti's *Lucia di Lammeroor* and *Linda di Chamounix* and addresses, again, the question of the so-called mad scene and the controversial origin of the famous flute cadenza. In Chapter Four, where I deal with Bellini's works, I expand on this issue; Tetrazzini's recordings of Amina's arias from *La sonnambula* see the recording studio transformed into a creative workshop where new and apparently unprecedented cadenzas with obligato instruments originated. Chapter Five elaborates on Verdi's style and the end of bel canto. Tetrazzini's impersonations of Violetta and Gilda were memorable and her recordings are testament to a performing tradition that continued despite Verdi's dramatic treatment of the voice.

---

27   *The Sun*, 14 March 1900, p. 7 cited in Stephen Herx, 'Marcella Sembrich: A Legendary Singer's Career Rediscovered', *The Record Collector*, 44(1) 1999, 2–38 (p. 18).
28   Susan Rutherford, *The Prima Donna and Opera, 1815–1930* (Cambridge: Cambridge University Press, 2006), p. 27.
29   Herx, 'Marcella Sembrich'.

Each chapter tries to reconstruct the phases of the performing tradition to which these composers belonged and focuses on the main characteristics of the arias taken into consideration. Given the much insisted-upon importance of the connection between the dramatic settings and the music, each aria is discussed with regard to the connection between lyrics and musical structure. It is worth remembering that nineteenth-century Italian opera composers worked with a well-established set of conventions in mind (*convenienze*, as they called them), which served as a basis for singers to interact and intervene. The *solita forma* is a case in point: it represents the kind of formal segmentation that is most typically associated with Rossini, Donizetti, Bellini and Verdi. Put in simple terms, a typical set piece, whether a scena and aria, a duet, a trio or even a larger enesemble, involved a first preparatory scena, a *tempo d'attacco*, a *cantabile*, a *tempo di mezzo* and a *stretta* or *cabaletta*.[30] The necessity for a modern interpreter to be familiar with this structure and understand how it worked cannot be sufficiently emphasised since it was, and should be still today, the starting point for the development of different kinds of ornaments, cadenzas and other textual modifications. In fact, the chordal structure typical of a cadenza that singnalled the end of a major section, or the suspended dominant chord accompanied by a *col canto* indication and a fermata sign that preceded the beginning of a repeat, were expected to prompt specific interpretative responses. In a way, by understanding the manner in which music notation and formal segmentation were used, modern interpreters may feel more strongly encouraged to reconstruct the performing practice that was associated with them.

In my analysis of Tetrazzini's recorded interpretations, I will draw attention to those melodic modifications that were typical of the Italian nineteenth-century vocal performance practice and can be found described and exemplified in many contemporary sources. This tradition continued into the twentieth century, to be eradicated soon after the disappearance of the generation of singers to which Tetrazzini belonged. This process, as has long been discussed, was carried out in the name of a much-debated notion of faithfulness to the composers' intentions, of which Arturo Toscanini is considered one of the most emblematic representatives.[31] Much work still needs to be done to bridge the gap between the scholarly knowledge we have amassed on the pre-war performance practice and singers' current approach to this repertoire. Today, we seem to have stripped the training of singers of any memory of that performing practice, and students may find it difficult to understand the manner in which this system of coded information worked. In fact, the concept of *Wecktreue* which still prevails in most of our higher music education institutions contradicts the principles underpinning a tradition that was transmitted orally. Traces of this tradition can be found not only in methods and treatises, but also in recordings, which we should use to complement the sometimes very incomplete instructions offered by a notated score.

For these reasons, this book is aimed not only at scholars but also singers and conductors, in the hope that the overarching discussion regarding nineteenth-century vocal performance practice, together with the many examples and the complete transcriptions of the arias under scrutiny, may guide them in the process of better understanding a century which, in my opinion, still needs to be understood. The book can be seen as a tool to be used in vocal tuition, in a rehearsal room, or when learning a new role. Singers, having read these pages, may feel encouraged to listen to Tetrazzini and her colleagues' recordings again, and to use the transcriptions to find inspiration for more courageous interpretative solutions and ideas. By looking back, they will also look forward.

This book does not embark on a more general discussion on late nineteenth- early twentieth-century operatic divas. Discourses on the prima donna, her role in operatic life, her image, status and condition, can be found in monographs like *The Prima Donna and Opera, 1815–1930* by Susan Rutherford, or *Technology and the Diva*, edited by Karen Henson, to name but two. I refer those readers interested in this different kind of discussion to the above authors, whose contribution and scholarly work prove invaluable.

---

30 See Marco Beghelli, 'The Dramaturgy of the Operas', in Emanuele Senici (ed.), *The Cambridge Companion to Rossini* (Cambridge: Cambridge University Press, 2004), pp. 85–103, and Scott L. Balthazar, 'The Forms of Set Pieces', in *The Cambridge Companion to Verdi*, ed. by Scott L. Balthazar (Cambridge: Cambridge University Press, 2004), pp. 49–68. With regard to Verdi, Balthazar makes a distinction between arias, where the *cantabile* immediately followed the scena, and duets and larger ensembles, where the *tempo d'attacco* connects the scena to the aria.

31 See Robert Philip, *Early Recordings and Musical Style* (Cambridge: Cambridge University Press, 1992), https://doi.org/10.1017/CBO9780511470271

1. The Voice of the Century
Luisa Tetrazzini and Her Discographic Legacy

The discographic career of Luisa Tetrazzini (1871–1940) spans a period of almost twenty years, and includes about 120 recordings, which she realised between 1904 and 1922. She collaborated with two firms: the Gramophone and Typewriter Company, which in 1907 became the Gramophone Company of London, and the Victor Talking Machine of Camden (New Jersey, USA).[1] The composer who features most prominently in her catalogue is Giuseppe Verdi, with eleven arias from five operas, *Traviata, Rigoletto, Trovatore, Un ballo in maschera, Vespri siciliani*, amounting to twenty recordings in total. Donizetti follows suit, with six arias and eight recordings from *Lucia di Lammermoor* and *Linda di Chamounix*; then come Bellini, with four arias and six recordings (*La sonnambula, I puritani*), Rossini with two arias and five recordings (*Barbiere di Siviglia, Semiramide*), Giacomo Meyerbeer (*Dinorah*) and Charles Gounod (*Faust*) with three arias and four recordings each. Mozart (*Don Giovanni, Nozze di Figaro, Flauto magico*) counts for three arias and five recordings and Georges Bizet (*Les pêcheurs de perles, Carmen*) three arias and four recordings. The list includes some more Italian and French opera composers (among them Ambroise Thomas and Léo Delibes), song writers like Gaetano Lama and Ernesto De Curtis, who wrote in the Neapolitan dialect, and figures like Julius Benedict, J. L. Gilbert, Reginald De Koven. Tetrazzini's discography reflects well the repertoire she performed most frequently during a life-long career:

1. *Lucia di Lammermoor* (113 productions)[2]
2. *Rigoletto* (67)
3. *Il Barbiere di Siviglia* (61)
4. *La traviata* (60)
5. *La sonnambula* (37)
6. *I puritani* (21)
7. *Dinorah* (18)
8. *Crispino e la Comare* (17)
9. *Gli ugonotti* (16)
10. *Faust* (13)

As can be seen, Tetrazzini's repertoire features prominently those Italian composers who were long inscribed into the nineteenth-century bel canto tradition, with *Lucia di Lammermoor* occupying a leading position throughout

---

1   The complete discography can be found in Gattey, *Luisa Tetrazzini the Florentine Nightingale*, pp. 333–53. In his discography, Gattey mentions also The Universal Talking Machine Company of New York. However, this company, which issued records under the Zonophone label, was taken over by Victor and the Gramophone & Typewriter Company in 1903; Tetrazzini's Zonophone records were made in New York on 8 September 1904 by Victor. For an account of the history of Zonophone see Allan Sutton, 'The American Zonophone Discography: A History of American Zonophone, 1900–1912', *Discography of American Historical Recordings*, https://adp.library.ucsb.edu/index.php/resources/detail/393

2   The number of individual performances cannot be determined since once a stock opera was mounted, the number of individual performances depended on its success.

her entire career. Years after her début in this role, she remembered that 'no opera could have been selected which gave me a greater opportunity, for Lucia's arias have more possibilities for the prima donna than any of the other operas'.[3]

Two figures hold a prominent position in Tetrazzini's discographic career, the English conductor and composer Percy Pitt (1870–1932) and the American cornet player, conductor and composer Walter B. Rogers (1865–1939). The first was involved in the recordings made by the Gramophone Company of London, while the second was responsible for most of the orchestral arrangements on recordings made for the Victor Talking Machine Company between 1904 and 1916. Pitt studied organ in Leipzig and Munich where he started to familiarise himself with the exigencies of opera productions. In 1907 he was appointed as musical director at Covent Garden where he worked in close contact with Hans Richter. Apparently, having decided not to have Tetrazzini sing in the summer season at Covent Garden in 1907, it was Pitt who persuaded the Directors of the Syndicate to invite her to participate in the autumn season.

> Cleofonte Campanini, her brother-in-law, who had succeeded Mancinelli as Conductor-in-Chief of the Italian opera at Covent Garden, had occasionally mentioned her name and extolled her virtues [Percy Pitt wrote], but it was considered that there was no very great demand for this type of singer, as the operas which served as a vehicle for such musical fireworks had fallen into desuetude, except for two or three well-known examples such as *Rigoletto* and *Traviata*; and as the lady had her own ideas with regard to her value and the fees she should command, ideas which were not shared by the Directors of the Syndicate, it had never been possible to come to an understanding with regard to her appearance in London.[4]

As Pitt suggests, the anachronistic position occupied by Tetrazzini's voice and repertoire represented a challenge that could be won only at the cost of great determination and by means of an extensive 'papering policy', that is to say by giving out a large number of free tickets. As we will see, Tetrazzini's début in London was a great success and all the recordings she would realise for the Gramophone Company were conducted by Pitt himself. Walter Rogers was a cornet player with many years of experience in bands and orchestras. He served as cornet soloist and assistant conductor in John Philip Sousa's Band until 1904, when, tired of travelling, he became music director of the Victor Phonograph Company, a position he held until 1916.[5] Unfortunately, no mention of these musicians can be found in Tetrazzini's autobiography, and one may only speculate as to the role they may have played in her discographic career and artistic development.

After Charles Neilson Gattey's comprehensive reconstruction of Tetrazzini's life and career it would be pointless to delve again into a biographical account of the diva; however, a rapid review of her personality, ideas, attitude and opinions, as she expressed them in her writings, can be worth undertaking. One interesting issue relates to her musical education and the lack of a vocal pedigree. Unlike Nellie Melba, a student of Mathilde Marchesi, and Marcella Sembrich, who moved to Milan in 1876 to study with Giovanni Battista Lamperti and, subsequently, with his eminent father Francesco Lamperti,[6] Tetrazzini was never affiliated with any important school or leading master. During her comparatively short formal training in Florence she studied with Giuseppe Ceccherini (1824–1909), the teacher who had taught her older sister Eva.[7] In *My life of Song* Tetrazzini insists on her innate talent and emphasises more than once that she did not make her voice, since it was there already.[8] When recalling her conservatoire years in Florence (then called the Istituto Musicale) she never mentions one

---

3 Luisa Tetrazzini, *My Life of Song*, p. 74.
4 Daniel Chamier, *Percy Pitt of Covent Garden and the B.B.C.* (London: Edward Arnold, [1938]), p. 113.
5 Ronald W. Holz, 'Rogers, Walter Bowman', *Grove Music Online*, 2 Jun. 2011, https://www.oxfordmusiconline.com/grovemusic/view/10.1093/gmo/9781561592630.001.0001/omo-9781561592630-e-1002103573
6 Sembrich, like Tetrazzini, was saluted as the new Patti, or the Polish Patti, very early on during her career and, like Tetrazzini, her London début launched her towards a career of international acclaim. See Herx, 'Marcella Sembrich'. The New York Public Library—Music Division owns a collection of documents that covers the entirety of Sembrich's professional career from her childhood training to her death, and provides details of parts of her personal and family life (particularly the early years) through correspondence, legal and financial documents, newspaper clippings, and concert programs: http://archives.nypl.org/mus/20137
7 Gattey, *Luisa Tetrazzini*, p. 2.
8 Tetrazzini, *My Life of Song*, p. 34.

particular teacher who may have played a central role in her training and early artistic development; while her *maestri* remain colourless figures in the background, she often insists on the importance of her frequentation of the Florence opera theatre, the Teatro Pagliano, in shaping her musical taste.

Tetrazzini's musical and vocal development is likely to have received an acceleration after her successful début in 1890, when she made her appearance as Inez in Meyerbeer's *L'Africaine*, together with Rosa Caligaris-Marti as Selika.[9] In this regard, the role of the *basso comico* Pietro Cesari, whose touring company she joined soon after her début, cannot be underestimated. Nor should it be forgotten that in the following years she had the opportunity to work with some of the best opera singers of the time: in 1897, when she made her first appearance at St. Petersburg, she worked with Angelo Masini and Mattia Battistini, and appeared with Marcella Sembrich in *Mignon* and *Don Giovanni*. Upon returning to Buenos Aires she collaborated with Francesco Tamagno, Giuseppe Borgatti and Mario Sammarco, not to speak of her lifelong friendship with Enrico Caruso, with whom she sang *Lucia di Lammermoor*, *Un ballo in maschera* and *Bohème* in Russia in the 1899–1900 season. Tetrazzini must have learned a lot from all these masters and evidence of this informal training is to be found in her cadenza notebooks: these were little booklets where the young soprano wrote down the cadenzas passed on to her by experienced teachers. Luisa seems to have given one of them as a gift to the Brazilian soprano Bidu Sayao. Unfortunately, not much is known about these booklets, which have disappeared after her death.[10]

Another important aspect of Tetrazzini's personality is the awareness she manifested of the anachronistic position she occupied in the early twentieth-century operatic firmament. In many pages she suggests how the repertoire she sang and the vocal style connected with that were often stigmatised by music critics as outmoded, trite, and hackneyed, especially when compared to the recent development of modern opera in Italy, France and Germany. Her London début made it clear to her how the operatic world was then divided into two parts, the grave and the gay, as she recalled. The grave part featured the gloomy figure of Richard Wagner, while the gay one was dominated by bel canto Italian composers.[11] Thus, she wondered what the future of coloratura might have been, in a world where, even though people continued to crowd to hear it, composers were no longer interested in this old-fashioned genre and young singers did not even possess the voice to sing it.[12] Although dreaming of a day when a new Donizetti would be born and coloratura music would take a new turn, Tetrazzini must have been well aware that the days of bel canto belonged to a long-gone, golden past.

About her voice comparatively much has been written in past decades, although many questions still remain unanswered. Her vocal compass, as she writes, went from the B below the stave to the E above it and the ease with which she could reach the top notes is confirmed by her recordings: she took the opportunity to show off her wonderful top Es whenever she could, most frequently in the final cadenzas, while she never ventured further down than the D below the stave. Her staccato had a pearly quality which critics did not fail to notice, together with the proverbial agility she showed in the upper register. Of great interest is the question of the uneven quality of her voice, a characteristic that drew the attention of many commentators during her career and is audible also in her recordings; as has already been suggested, this had to do with an expressive method called *voce bianca*, 'white voice' used by high sopranos.[13] Commenting on Tetrazzini's successful début as Violetta in 1908 New York, Sylvester Rowling described in some detail the gap between her very sweet high notes and the childlike quality of her lower register: 'her middle register is luscious. She takes her upper notes with bird-like sweetness. Her lower tones are clean cut even when she falls into an odd utterance that savors somewhat of a

---

9   Gattey, *Luisa Tetrazzini*, p. 4.
10 One of them belonged to Sayao, who seems to have passed it to William Seward. See Aspinall, *Luisa Tetrazzini: The Voice and the Records*, liner notes to *Luisa Tetrazzini—The London Recordings*, EMI, 1992, and Will Crutchfield, 'A Treasury of Voices, from Galli-Curci to Lily Pons', *The New York Times* (Music Notes), 23 June 1985. https://www.nytimes.com/1985/06/23/arts/music-notes-a-treasury-of-voices-from-galli-curci-to-lily-pons.html
11 Tetrazzini, *My life of Song*, p. 177.
12 Ibid., p. 313.
13 Nicholas E. Limansky, 'Luisa Tetrazzini: Coloratura Secrets', *Opera Quarterly*, 20.4 (2004), 540–69.

child's'.[14] Far from being a simple flaw in her technique, the unevenness in the voice resulted in a particularly expressive contrast that, as Tetrazzini would reveal, she adopted in passages where the dramatic situation called for such a richness of shades.

> Too wide a smile often accompanies what is called 'the white voice.' This is a voice production where a head resonance alone is employed, without sufficient of the appoggio or enough of the mouth resonance to give the tone a vital quality. This 'white voice' should be thoroughly understood, and is one of the many shades of tone a singer can use at times, just as the impressionist uses various unusual colors to produce certain atmospheric effects. For instance, in the mad scene in *Lucia*, the use of the 'white voice' suggests the babbling of the mad woman, as the same voice in the last act of *Traviata*, or in the last act of *La Bohème* suggests utter physical exhaustion and the approach of death. An entire voice production on this colorless line, however, would always lack the brilliancy and the vitality which inspires enthusiasm.[15]

She mentions the same device also in the chapter on 'Faults to be corrected', where she adds that 'The "white voice" (voce bianca) is a head voice without deep support and consequently without color; hence its appellation. One can learn to avoid it by practicing with the mouth closed and by taking care to breathe through the nose, which forces the respiration to descend to the abdomen'.[16] It seems clear that Tetrazzini was well aware that the voce bianca should be used sparingly; still, she used it for expressive reasons, especially in her middle- and lower-register.[17] Reviews that were published in a more mature phase of Tetrazzini's career suggest that she had come to master a smoother transition between the lower and the higher notes. Of this vocal feature a detailed description has been provided by Michael Aspinall when referring to the white and open tone coloratura sopranos came to cultivate deliberately during the nineteenth century and Italians called a *bamboleggiante* (baby-doll) voice.[18] In Aspinall's opinion it is plausible that Tetrazzini came to master a better control over the transition between the different voice registers as a response to those critics, especially English and American, who disparaged this effect. Tetrazzini's vocal unevenness can be understood as the remnant of what seems to have been a feature typical of singers from earlier generations. Rossinian interpreters like Maria Malibran were sometimes called contraltos and presented an incredibly wide voice compass, from E above the stave (like Tetrazzini) to the G (or even Eb) below it. Their voice was double, in that it included the soprano and the contralto but at the cost of a remarkably audible timbral difference in the passage from the head to the chest register. A similar characteristic was noted in Giuditta Pasta, Marietta Alboni and, much later, in Guerrina Fabbri (1866–1946) and Elisa Bruno (1869–1942). These last two left a few recordings where the gap between the different registers is clearly audible, causing what may be defined as a yodel effect.[19] What Tetrazzini's recordings have in common with other recordings left by singers trained in the same tradition is a similar timbral gap between lower and higher notes. Of this vocal feature not much seems to have survived in the younger generations of singers, whose vocal quality confirms how important it has become to master a complete timbral evenness and the smoothest possible transition from one register to the other.

Other distinctive features of her voice are the extensive use of portamento, the frequent use of *messa di voce* and a comparatively thick, continuous vibrato. Although now considered tasteless unless used sparingly, Tetrazzini and her contemporary colleagues used portamento as a means to express tender, mournful, or even vigorous feelings, as suggested by García's highly-celebrated school.[20] A case in point is represented by her rendition of 'Ah

---

14 Sylvester Rowling, 'Tetrazzini, Hammerstein's New Prima Donna, Whom London Has Proclaimed the Greatest of Living Singers, Makes Brilliant Debut at Manhattan Opera-House', *The Evening World* (NY), 16 January 1908, p. 3.
15 Tetrazzini, *My life of Song*, p. 314.
16 Tetrazzini, *The Art of Singing*, p. 58.
17 See again Limansky, p. 545.
18 Aspinall, *Luisa Tetrazzini: The Voice and the Records*, p. 23.
19 See Marco Beghelli and Raffaele Talmelli, *Ermafrodite Armoniche, Il contralto nell'Ottocento* (Varese: Zecchini Editore, 2011). It is possible to hear Guerrina Fabbri's and Elisa Bruno's voices on the CD included in the volume.
20 Manuel García, *Scuola di Garcia, Trattato completo dell'arte del canto* (Milan: Ricordi, [1842]), vol. II, pp. 29–30.

non credea' in Bellini's *La sonnambula*, where the mourning of the lost love is the prevalent feeling: portamentos are conspicuously present, especially when compared to modern standards, and a slight continuous vibrato is observable also in those moments where the voice is gliding up or down.[21] Tetrazzini emphasises the dramatic quality of the scene also by slackening the tempo towards the close of the passage (Figure 2).

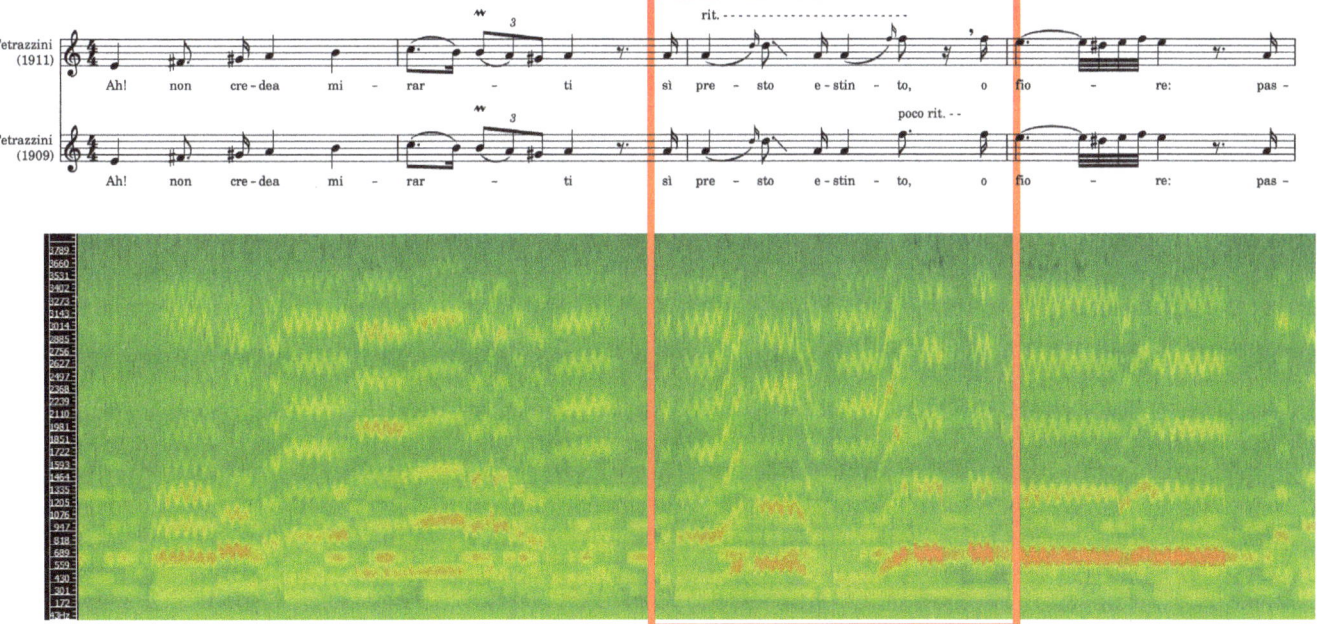

Figure 2 shows the use of vibrato and portamento in Tetrazzini's 1911 recording of 'Ah non credea mirarti'.

A similar pattern can be observed in Adelina Patti's 1906 recording of the same aria, where the strongly pathetic quality of the moment is conveyed by a similar use of portamento. Patti's vibrato is, instead, much thinner, almost inaudible and sometimes unstable, probably due to her age at the time of the recording (Figure 3).

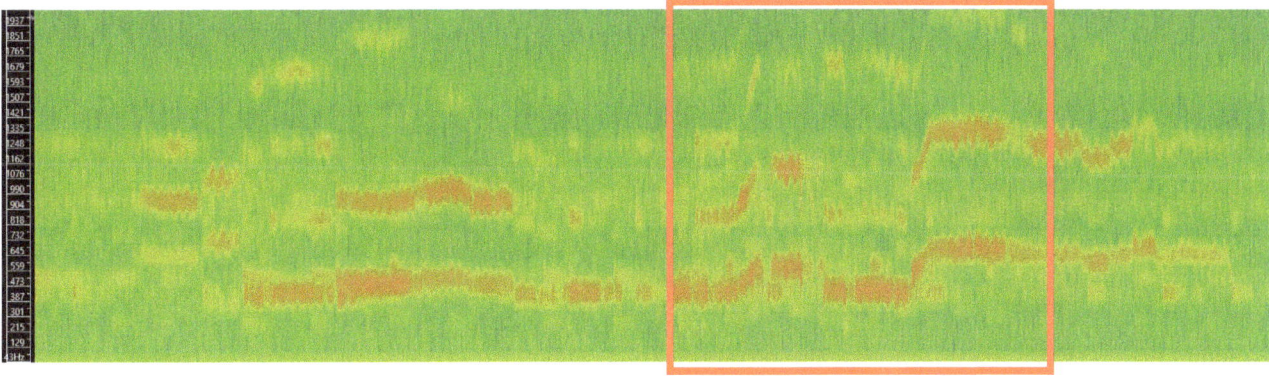

Figure 3 shows Patti's use of portamento in her 1906 recording of 'Ah, non credea mirarti'.

A similar use of portamento and vibrato can be observed in the first measures of 'Ah, fors'è lui' in Verdi's *La traviata*, where again, a sense of hesitant trepidation pervades the scene and the music (Figure 4).

---

21 The following images have been produced using Sonic Visualiser, a program for viewing audio files and extracting data. Chris Cannam, Christian Landone, and Mark Sandler, *Sonic Visualiser: An Open Source Application for Viewing, Analysing, and Annotating Music Audio Files*, in Proceedings of the ACM Multimedia 2010 International Conference.

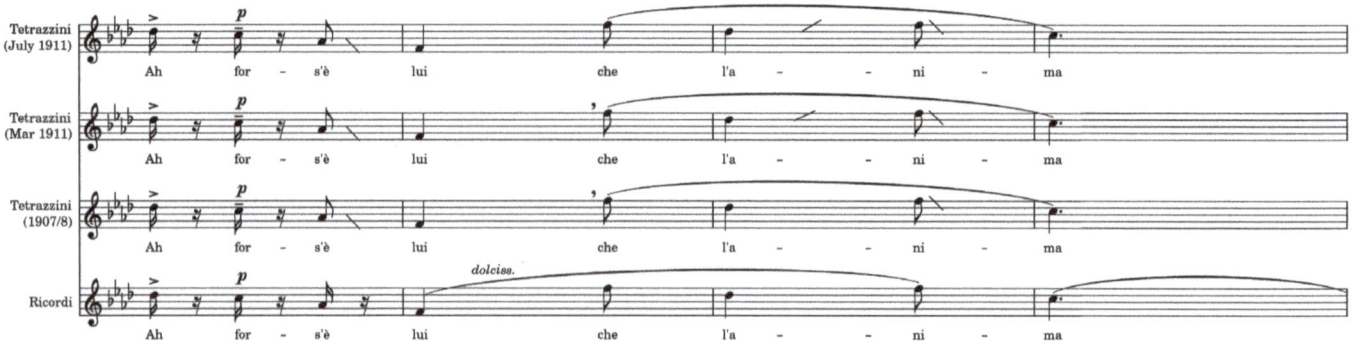

Figure 4 shows the first four measures of Verdi's 'Ah, fors'è lui' in *La traviata* as sung by Tetrazzini.

The spectrogram shows a consistent use of portamento not only between two consecutive notes, but also at the beginning of the phrase, according to a performance practice that would be considered tasteless today. A constant vibrato is present also in the moments where the voice is gliding (Figure 5).

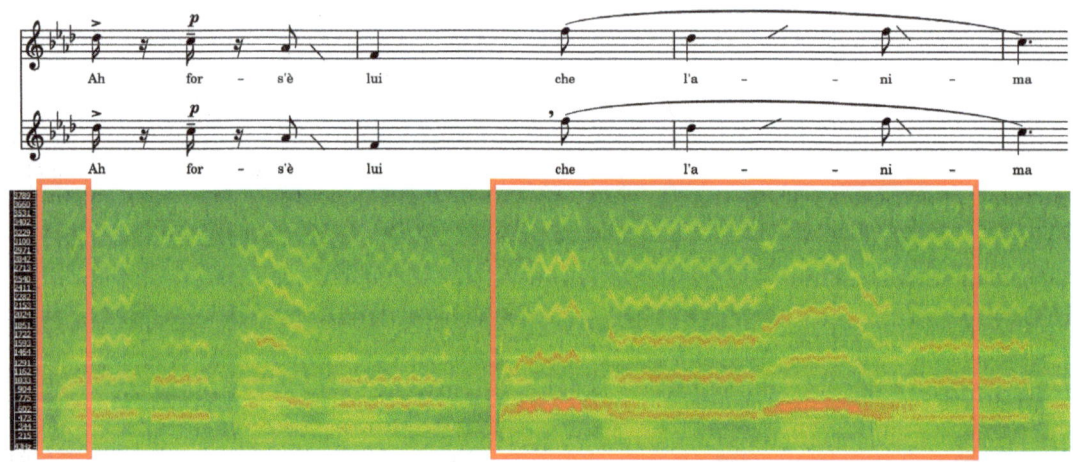

Figure 5 shows Tetrazzini's use of *portamento* in the opening bars of Verdi's 'Ah, fors'è lui', recorded in 1911.

Slightly different is the pattern observable in Marcella Sembrich's rendition recorded in 1904; while she uses the descending portamento in a way similar to Tetrazzini, the upward intervals are taken without any perceivable gliding (Figure 6); her vibrato is also continuous, but thinner than Tetrazzini's.

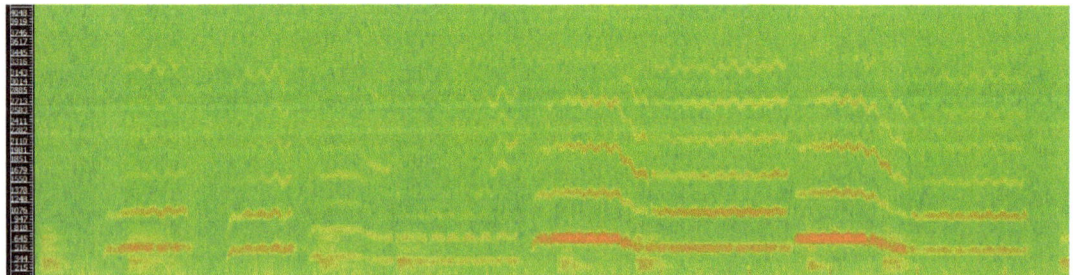

Figure 6 shows Marcella Sembrich's use of *portamento* in the opening bars of Verdi's 'Ah fors'è lui', recorded in 1904.

In her 1904 recording of the same aria Nellie Melba shares with Sembrich a preference for the descending portamento and a thinner vibrato, while the onset of the notes is sometimes prepared by a short but still audible ascending portamento (Figure 7).

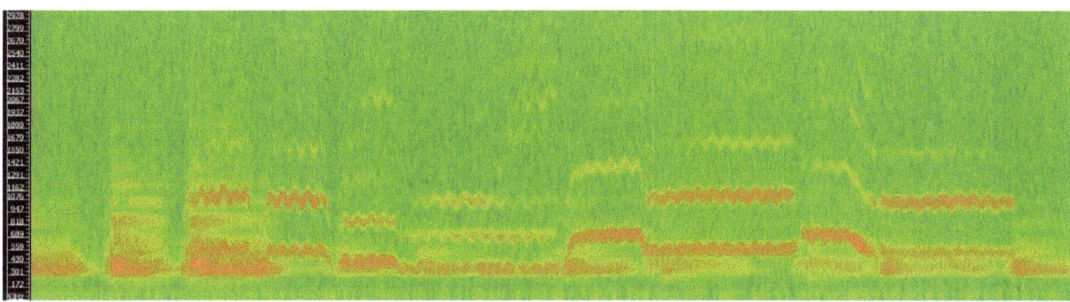

Figure 7 shows Nellie Melba's use of *portamento* in the opening measures of Verdi's 'Ah, fors'è lui', recorded in 1904.

The examples discussed so far suggest that although individual differences could be large, portamento was an expressive device widely used by singers trained in the bel canto tradition. The same can be said of vibrato, which we hear in Tetrazzini's voice and is characteristic of most singers of her generation, used in combination with the *messa di voce* when special emphasis was called for, particularly at the end of a cadenza.

Another long-debated trope suggests that bel canto divas like Luisa Tetrazzini were champions of improvised coloratura and ornamentation. According to Nicholas Limansky, Tetrazzini was above all 'an instinctive performer', a singer for whom 'improvising was of paramount importance'. In his reconstruction of her coloratura secrets, he over-confidently relies on the review the critic of the *Globe-Democrat* wrote of a concert she gave at the Coliseum in Saint Louis, Missouri, on 6 February 1920, which included Julius Benedict's *Carnival of Venice Variations*, to emphasise how she improvised in her performances. 'It seemed' the critic reports 'that Tetrazzini at one time during the rendition was improvising and roulading and trilling ad libitum'.[22] According to the critic, Limansky continues, some of the variations were especially spontaneous. Although similar recollections suggest that Tetrazzini appeared to be composing 'new *cadenzas* at the spur of the moment', one may wonder whether she was really composing extempore, or rather giving the impression of doing so. As I will argue in the course of my analysis, Tetrazzini used to perform a well-prepared set of variations, ornaments and cadenzas, which she delivered with calculated theatricality, thus making the audience believe that she was following the whim of the moment. Whether she collected the train of her gown or added a new roulade to an already richly flourished cadenza, the evidence I have amassed suggests that she was performing a set of gestures that she had long rehearsed and carefully prepared in order to impress the audience. Even in the case reported by Limansky, one may wonder whether the critic of the *Globe-Democrat* was sufficiently knowledgeable about Luisa Tetrazzini's coloratura secrets to draw a line between genuine improvisation and a well-calculated *coup de théâtre*. The *Concert variations on Carnival of Venice arranged for voice and piano by Julius Benedict*, which Tetrazzini sang in 1922, were published in Boston by Oliver Ditson in 1882, with a piano introduction, Andantino, by Jules Schulhoff. Luisa Tetrazzini recorded these variations twice, once on 25 May 1909 with Percy Pitt in London, then again on 16 March 1911 with Walter B. Rogers in Camden. Although the two CDs in which we find the original discs digitised and remastered present the entire piece in one single audio track, each recording consists of two separate takes (matrix 3079f and 3080f form the first, and matrix C10066-1 and C10067-1 the second).[23] The recordings are identical: they present the same cuts and we hear Tetrazzini sing her own cadenzas and passages with not one single note changed, added, or substituted for. Of course, we do not know whether Tetrazzini sang these *Variations* in 1922 in the exact form she had recorded them more than ten years earlier. However, as we will see, some more detailed descriptions of Tetrazzini's live performances in London and New York are consistent with what we hear in her recordings, thus supporting the claim that, once she had learned a piece, she remained true to her first interpretative idea for years.[24] As I will argue, the impression that she was improvising

---

22 Nicholas E. Limansky, 'Luisa Tetrazzini: Coloratura Secrets', *Opera Quarterly*, 20.4 (2004), 540–69 (p. 547).
23 *Luisa Tetrazzini–The London Recordings*, EMI, 1992, and *Tetrazzini*, Prima Voce vol. II, 1999.
24 Massimo Zicari, 'Identità stilistica e capriccio: Luisa Tetrazzini nelle registrazioni discografiche', *Rivista Italiana di Musicologia*, 40 (2020), 153–209.

following the whim of the moment was the result of a well calculated, long rehearsed set of theatrical gestures. The careful attention with which she developed an interpretation extended to the preparation of ornamentation and cadenzas, as is testified by the existence of her cadenza notebooks.

Luisa Tetrazzini is also the author of *How to Sing,* a monograph in which she elaborates on the different aspects related to bel canto and gives advice to prospective singers. She touches upon a number of topics, including the best age to start learning, the qualities needed to become an accomplished singer, the necessity for the sternest self-discipline and the most unremitting application as a condition for success. In the chapter on coloratura singing, she writes that many have asked her how to acquire agility, to which she answers that 'it is simply a case of perseverance and hard work, plus, of course, whatever natural abilities in that direction you may possess'.[25] Scales, she suggests, are the foundation of flexibility and coloratura. She takes a stance in defence of coloratura which, she continues, is so often contemptuously spoken of: 'Coloratura music is false, showy, superficial, unworthy, dramatically unreal, and so on. But what nonsense this is!'[26] Tetrazzini is perfectly consistent with the tradition of which she was one of the best representatives: coloratura, she continues 'should please the ear by its brilliance, but at the same time it should not, and need not, obscure the dramatic significance of what is sung'.[27] As she recalls, music critics 'were all more especially struck by the manner in which I managed, while singing Verdi's florid music brilliantly and effectively in the purely vocal sense, at the same time to make it expressive'.[28] Unfortunately, she does not delve into the topic any further, thus leaving many questions unanswered; among them, the manner in which a coloratura singer should choose the appropriate ornaments, and develop her own cadenzas and roulades. In discussing issues like enunciation, language and so forth, Tetrazzini often mentions illustrious singers and singing teachers like Lilli Lehmann, Francesco Lamperti, Salvatore Fucito and Enrico Caruso; she met many of them in person, collaborated with some and must have read their methods, although no specific reference to them is given in her volume.

As to the issue of style and interpretation, Tetrazzini worked on the assumption that the signs in a score are 'a mere approximation to the composer's complete meaning'. Therefore, '[i]t is the duty of his interpreters to supply what is missing—to breathe the spirit of life into the dry bones and to convert dead printed notes into living human music'.[29] Of course, the singer must possess all the skills necessary to understand and grasp the composer's intention, and, 'the musical taste and knowledge required in order to present it in conformity with the appropriate rules and traditions'.[30] She raises the question of stylistic appropriateness and suggests that every singer 'must be familiar also with the varying needs of the different schools of music, with the historical traditions associated with them'.[31] However, since every repertoire has its own different requirements in terms of both vocal technique and singing style, it is unlikely, if not impossible, she holds, for an artist to excel in all of them. As a consequence, her advice to a young singer is 'to confine himself to the class of work more particularly suited to his talent'.[32] Tetrazzini herself made a clear professional choice and steered away from works that did not fit her vocal skills and artistic personality, even at the cost of harsh criticisms: 'People blame me sometimes, for instance, for confining myself mainly to music of a certain school. But I think I know best as to this, and that I am exercising sound judgment in adopting this course. There is much music which I admire and love, but I do not always try to sing it'.[33] If, on the one hand, she encouraged flexibility as a quality, to push oneself into foreign lands and embrace a repertoire that did not fit one's voice was a completely different and hazardous thing to do. No Italian operatic composer of the verismo generation appears in her discography, not to mention Richard Wagner or Richard Strauss. She provides only one description of how she interprets an aria or a song

---

25 Luisa Tetrazzini, *How to Sing,* p. 73.
26 Ibid., p. 75.
27 Ibid., p. 78.
28 Ibid.
29 Ibid., p. 93.
30 Ibid.
31 Ibid., p. 95
32 Ibid.
33 Ibid.

when talking of the 'Recitative and Polonaise' from the opera *Mignon*, by Ambroise Thomas, but she is more concerned for the manner in which a singer should feel what she sings, than the criteria that lie behind specific interpretative choices, including good taste and appropriate style.

Luisa Tetrazzini's personality was perhaps best described by Kenneth Muir, manager of the Milanese offices of the Gramophone Company, when corresponding with Theo Birnbaum, his colleague from the London headquarters, on 6 November 1907.

> This artiste is undoubtedly as I stated over a year ago at a managers' meeting the best light soprano of the day and the most likely to step in the Melba's shoes to who she is undoubtedly superior. In character she is capricious and wayward and if you wish to succeed in obtaining her you must pamper her like a spoiled child by sending her gifts, boxes for theatres, paying her compliments and little personal attentions; in a word you must appeal to the woman in her nature. She is extremely dissolute in her private life and much affected by flattery and champagne. She is besides a bright, clever woman and rather apt to treat everybody in an independent and off-hand fashion.[34]

Capricious and wayward, dissolute and clever at the same time, Tetrazzini embodies the stereotyped image of the bel canto diva; during her lifelong career, she was often able to draw the attention of the international press not only because of her unforgettable interpretations, but also on account of her extravagant personality and debauched behaviour. She often appeared in trials (more than once a lawsuit was brought against her), had controversial sentimental affairs with figures of public visibility (among them Julio Zeigner Uriburu, the son of a president of Argentina, who acted as her secretary and whom she sued for embezzling large sums of money while in her employ),[35] got married three times and died in poverty, having dissipated a fortune. Her disastrous third marriage to Pietro Vernati, an adventurer twenty-three years her junior, gave her the last and definitive blow. In her last years, Tetrazzini was surrounded by some good old friends, among them her protégée Lina Pagliughi, but also besieged by spiritualists and other charlatans who tricked her into unsuccessful real-estate investments and similarly disastrous financial enterprises. The lady who in 1910 was able to bring together and keep spellbound two-hundred thousand people in the streets of San Francisco for a memorable and unprecedented Christmas open-air concert, was lonely and almost destitute when she died on 28 April 1940.[36]

Before embarking upon the analysis of Tetrazzini's recordings, one last word needs to be said about bel canto, a term to which singers and music practitioners habitually refer in a broad sense, often signifying an uninterrupted operatic tradition where composers of different epochs may find their place upon condition that Italian be the common language. Lucie Manén writes that her teacher Anna Schoen-René, a former student of Mathilde Marchesi and Pauline Viardot—the second a daughter of Manuel García (1775–1832)—never mentioned bel canto, a term that, she says, has never been clearly defined.[37] Philip Duey agrees that bel canto is not so easily defined and suggests that it was not before Nicola Vaccai's *Dodici Ariette per Camera per l'Insegnamento del Bel-canto italiano*, published around 1838, that this term had been used in a more precise manner.[38] Although this expression appears in a collection of songs written by himself, Vaccai never used the term bel canto in his method entitled *Metodo Pratico di Canto Italiano per Camera in 15 Lezioni*, which he published in London in 1834. However, in the *Dodici Ariette* he seems to be concerned neither with the singing style of the past, nor with that of his contemporary colleagues. One might even doubt that referring to the teaching of Italian bel canto resulted from

---

34 Letter preserved at EMI Group Archive Trust, Hayes, partly reproduced by Gattey, *Luisa Tetrazzini*, p. 77.
35 John Pennino, 'Tetrazzini at the Tivoli: Success and Scandal in San Francisco', *The Opera Quarterly*, 8.2 (1991), 4–26.
36 Ample coverage was granted by *The San Francisco Chronicle* and *The San Francisco Call* to the unprecedented event which took place on 25 December 1910; reporters could not agree on the correct number of attendees: the estimates were between ninety and two hundred thousand persons.
37 Lucie Manén, *Bel Canto: The Teaching of the Classical Italian Song-Schools, Its Decline and Restoration* (Oxford: Oxford University Press, 1987), p. 3.
38 Philip Duey, *Bel Canto in Its Golden Age* (New York: King's Crown Press, 1951), p. 5. Duey refers to Nicola Vaccai, *12 Ariette per camera (in Ch. di Sol), per l'insegnamento del bel-canto italiano*, Ricordi [pre 1840], Catalogue number 12076–12087, https://www.digitalarchivioricordi.com/en/catalogo/12076. The second song, 'Il Cosacco della Volga' can be found at the Biblioteka Akademii Muzycznej, Katowice: https://www.sbc.org.pl/dlibra/publication/335300/edition/316819/content.

an editorial decision, and that marketing reasons had prevailed over musical ones. Still, the title suggests how the vocal culture that was associated with the concept of bel canto had assumed a more precise identity.

In the mid-nineteenth century, the notion of bel canto became increasingly associated with the idea of an old and unsurpassed school of singing which was all too often threatened by the composers of the new generations. It soon came to signify the growing concern of Italian authors over the aggressions of the German *stile parlante*, and the declamato style of Bellini and Verdi. This concern saw in Rossini the last champion of this glorious tradition and in Bellini the turning point towards its decline.[39] In touching upon the different aspects related to the bel canto tradition, Duey refers to a number of methods and treatises spanning the years from the early seventeenth to the mid-nineteenth century, also suggesting the idea of a long and uninterrupted tradition. In his comprehensive analysis James Stark also maintains that bel canto is a term still 'in search of a meaning, a label that is widely used but only vaguely understood'.[40] In his opinion, bel canto is a concept that takes into account two separate but related matters: a highly-refined method of singing in combination with any style of music that employs this kind of singing in a tasteful and expressive way.[41] He sets the foundation of this style at the beginning of the seventeenth century and elaborates on its main principles, referring to the method by Manuel García II (1840–1842); his analysis includes Giulio Caccini's *Le nuove musiche* (1602), Pier Francesco Tosi's *Opinioni de' cantori antichi e moderni* (1723), Giambattista Mancini's *Practical reflections* (1774) and Francesco Lamperti's *Guida teorica-pratica* (1864), among many others. What Manén, Duey and Stark have in common, is the idea that the scientific study of the voice has been a pivotal component in the bel canto tradition, that is to say the analysis of the physiological functions and the use of the mechanisms of voice production as investigated by Manuel García II thanks to the laryngoscope. Duey is mainly concerned with what he calls the physiological and hygienic factors in its development,[42] while Stark focuses on the mechanisms regarding voice production, registers, expression, and touches only *in passim* on the question of ornamentation and coloratura.

What appears to be problematic in this approach is the idea that the works of Caccini, Cimarosa, Rossini, and Verdi (at least in so far as his early operas are concerned) are to be associated with the same notion of bel canto, an approach that late nineteenth-century singers do not seem to have shared. Moreover, singers were trained in the bel canto tradition long after the mid-nineteenth century. If we look at the careers of Patti, Melba, Sembrich and Tetrazzini, their repertoires featured no composer earlier than Rossini, with the occasional exception of the worshipped Mozart; eighteenth-century operas were out of fashion and therefore no longer sung, while composers like Giulio Caccini and Claudio Monteverdi were virtually non-existent. Composers from the late nineteenth century were also out of the picture. In this regard Rodolfo Celletti argues that

> with Bellini and Donizetti (except for a few operas) the right of the opera historian to speak of bel canto, whether for or against, begins to decline, either positively, or in a polemical sense. When the hot-headed fan in the gallery, or the professional hagiographer, refers to a soprano who makes an impeccable job of the runs in *Traviata*, or a tenor who tosses off a top note in *Tosca*, as a bel canto singer, it is simply a misnomer. In fact, the moment opera begins to admit realism and to advocate it in place of abstraction, stylization, and ambivalence of timbre, bel canto is on the wane.[43]

In the turn towards the declamato style used in combination with more realistic plots and dramatic settings, what was lost was the aim of bel canto, or, as Celletti suggests, the capacity to evoke a sense of wonder through unusual quality of timbre, variety of colour and delicacy, virtuosic complexity of vocal display, and ecstatic lyrical abandon. In order for them to evoke the sense of wonder Celletti refers to, singers were not only entitled, but

---

39　Duey, pp. 8–10. See also Martha Elliott, *Singing in Style, A Guide to Vocal Performance Practices* (New Haven: Yale University Press, 2006), pp. 126–59. As we will see, Francesco Lamperti was among the first to point the finger at Vincenzo Bellini.
40　James Stark, *Bel Canto, A History of Vocal Pedagogy* (Toronto: University of Toronto Press, 2003), p. xvii.
41　Ibid., p. 189.
42　Duey, *Bel Canto in Its Golden Age*, p. 60.
43　Rodolfo Celletti, *A History of Bel Canto* (Oxford: Clarendon Press, 1996 (first Italian edition 1983)), pp. 12–13. Rossini himself seems to have declared that bel canto consisted of three elements: the instrument, that is the voice, the technique, and the style, this last involving taste and feeling. See Leonella Grasso Caprioli, 'Singing Rossini', in *The Cambridge Companion to Rossini*, ed. by Emanuele Senici (Cambridge: Cambridge University Press, 2004), p. 193.

encouraged, to make all those changes that were necessary to keep the audience spellbound, in accordance with the dramatic situation and the meaning of the lyrics. This idea informed bel canto singers' approach to music notation and guided their use of ornamentation, passages, runs, and roulades. This point has been emphasised by Robert Toft, who illustrates how central this practice was and provides modern singers with practical advice on how to approach the repertoire, taking reference from the relevant contemporary source documents.[44] The principles governing this performance practice are to be found in the most important voice tutors and singing methods of the time. Suffice here to say that, despite the continuous attacks coming from those contemporary critics and commentators who were concerned with the manner in which bel canto singers enslaved poets and composers to their vanity at the expense of dramatic consistency, singers were encouraged to work wonders by adorning melodies and making changes, on the condition that they did so with taste and consideration.

Hector Berlioz thus described Italian singing in 1832:

> No doubt beautiful voices—not only sonorous and clear, but agile and flexible—are more common in Italy than elsewhere. Such voices facilitate vocalisation, and, by pandering to that natural love of effect which I have already mentioned, must have given birth to the mania for *fioriture* which deforms the most beautiful melodies, and to those convenient formulas which give all Italian phrases so strong a family likeness. We may thank the same causes for those final cadences which the singer may embellish as he pleases, but which torture many a hearer by their insipid uniformity, as well as for that incessant tendency to buffoonery that obtrudes itself even in the most pathetic scenes; in fact, for all those abuses which have rendered melody, harmony, time, rhythm, instrumentation, modulation, the drama, the *mise-en-scène*, poetry, the poet, and the composer, all abject slaves to the singer.[45]

The idea that singers abused the scores and were not true to their intentions continued in the following decades. Traces of this concern can be found, among others, in Castil-Blaze, who wrote in 1856: 'The sopranists were at all times extremely insolent. They forced the greatest masters to conform to their caprices. They changed, transformed everything to suit their own vanity. They would insist on having an air or a duet placed in such a scene, written in such a style, with such an accompaniment'.[46]

On the other hand, García illustrates the application of this principle in his celebrated method:

> As the ornaments do not contain in themselves particular sentiments, the feeling they convey will depend of the way in which they are accented; their choice must, notwithstanding, be regulated by the meaning both of words and music, for instance, such ornaments as would be used to depict a *grandiose* sentiment, would be unsuitable to the air of Rosina in the *Barbiere*; the merest discrepancy between the character of the piece and its *fioritures* would constitute a striking fault.[47]

As an example, García offers two ornamented versions of the 'Cavatina' of the Conte in *Barbiere*, 'Ecco ridente il cielo' (Figure 8).

García considers the second version too languid for the character who sings it, a young and noble lover, while the first does not raise any question. Instead, to our eyes the first example is likely to appear overloaded with embellishments of different kinds, while the second might be understood as more discreet, hence more appropriate and tasteful. García then provides the reader with some more detailed instruction on how to add

---

44   Robert Toft, *Bel Canto, A Performer's Guide* (Oxford: Oxford University Press, 2013).
45   *Mémoires de Hector Berlioz: comprenant ses voyages en Italie, en Allemagne, en Russie et en Angleterre, 1803–1865*, English translation by Rachel (Scott Russell) Holmes, and Eleanor Holmes, *Autobiography of Hector Berlioz* (London: Macmillan and Co. 1884), p. 259.
46   Castel-Blaze, *L'Opéra-Italien de 1548 à 1856* (Paris: 1856) p. 317.
47   García, *Treatise on the Art of Singing,* ed. by Albert Garcia (London: Leonard, [1924]), p. 57. See also the Ricordi edition, 1842, p. 38. 'Siccome non é possibile di stabilire preventivamente delle categorie di fioriture adatte al bisogno dei diversi sentimenti, perciò l'allievo dovrà considerare gli abbellimenti, non in sé medesimi, ma relativamente al sentimento che esprimono. Questo sentimento dovrà il suo carattere, non solamente alia scelta delle note ed alla forma dei passi, ma forse più ancora all'espressione che loro comunica il cantante. Quello dunque che è mestieri consultare continuamente nella ricerca delle fioriture si è l'intenzione particolare delle parole e della musica. Quelle fioriture che dipingessero un sentimento grandioso non potrebbero convenire, per esempio, alla cavatina di Rosina, ecc. Il più píccolo disaccordo tra il carattere del pezzo e quello delle fioriture basterebbe per costituire un errore'. While the first volume of the French edition had appeared in 1840, the second volume appeared only in 1847, five years after the Italian translation (1842).

Figure 8 shows the two ornamented versions of 'Ecco ridente il cielo' in Rossini's *Barbiere* which García suggests in his *Scuola di Garcia*, Ricordi, pp. 38–39.

or substitute for an ornament. The general principle is, in short, that 'a musical idea, to be rendered interesting, should be varied, wholly or in part, every time it is repeated'. In the same chapter he discusses the use of appoggiaturas, turns, trills (or shakes) and cadenzas, whose importance should not be underrated.[48] In light of what he suggests, the example discussed above presents a richly embellished version that is consistent with the expression of the young Count's passion, where vigorous feelings equate to fast passages and brilliant runs. The cadenza in the penultimate measure invites a similar approach, in opposition to the second, which is more languid.

However, it is not easy for us today to understand what these authors meant when talking of good taste. Luigi Lablache thus defines it in his method.

> True taste consists in an exquisite judgment of what is appropriate; in an aptness to invest one's self with the character of the piece to be performed; in adding energy to it by analogous coloring, and in putting oneself into a state of feeling, so well in accordance with that of the author, that there results a oneness, perfect as if it were the product of a single thought. He who possesses this faculty, knows how to put grace and spirit into gay pieces; elegance into those which are only pleasing; sadness into pathetic songs; grandeur and mystery into religious music; warmth and transport into pieces where strong passions are in play. [...] There are two conditions dictated by good taste, and from which we should never swerve in adorning melody.—First, the adornment must never change or obscure the phrase. Second, the ornaments must always be of a character analogous to that of the piece. Thus it would be ridiculous to introduce light ornaments in grave and sustained pieces; it would be equally so to employ impassioned accents in songs of a merely pleasing and elegant character.[49]

He then provides a number of examples illustrating how a plain melodic phrase could be consistently adorned using divisions. These examples are of paramount importance for us to understand how different types of melodic modification were associated with different feelings. For instance, syncopated figures were related to the expression of an impassioned emotion, while a frequent use of appoggiaturas was typical of a mournful condition.

Other contemporary testimonies agree that the difference between a good and a bad singer lay in the taste and consideration with which they chose their ornaments with regard to the role and the aria they had to impersonate. Stendahl, for instance, lamented that bad singers started a new roulade in a light and brilliant way, to conclude it in a tragic and serious manner, or vice versa. A good singer, instead, would not make such a mistake for the sake of showing off the voice at the expense of both the music and the drama. A case in point was Giuditta Pasta.

> Extremely restrained in her use of *fioriture*, she resorts to them only when they have a direct contribution to make to the dramatic expressiveness of the music; and it is worth noting that none of her *fioriture* are retained for a single instant after they have ceased to be useful. I have never known her guilty of those interminable frescoes of ornamentation which seem to remind one of some irrepressible talker in a fit of absentmindedness, and during which one suspects that the singer's attention has wandered far out into vacancy, or else that he had started out with one intention, only to change his mind upon the subject half-way through.[50]

Of the same opinion was Henry F. Chorley, the music critic of *The Athenaeum*, who praised Pasta for her realism and for the careful attention with which she chose her *fioriture*, which she never changed. Chorley recalled her singing 'Il soave e bel content' from Giovanni Pacini's *Niobe* (1826) on two different occasions over two decades, with the same ornaments.[51] Fury, rage and revenge were associated with the use of brilliant divisions and rapid passages, frequent *appoggiaturas* convey a sense of gravity and dignity, small graces were synonyms for elegance

---

48 On the practical use of these devices see Toft, *A Performer's Guide*, pp. 106–63.
49 Luigi Lablache, *Method of Singing* (Philadelphia: Ditson, [n.d.]), p. 96. First edition: Luigi Lablache, *Metodo completo di canto* (Milan: G. Ricordi, 1842), p. 90, facsimile edition with an introduction by Rodolfo Celletti (Milan: Ricordi, 1997).
50 Stendhal, *The Life of Rossini* (*La vie de Rossini*, 1824), translated by Richard N. Coe (New York: Criterion Books, 1957), p. 368.
51 Henry F. Chorley, *Thirty Years' Musical Recollections* (London: Hurst and Blackett, 1862, two volumes), vol. I, p. 130.

and nobility.[52] As already mentioned, a completely different question would be whether and to what extent singers were really able to improvise these changes.[53]

Having been a long time dying, the age of bel canto expired with Giovanni Battista Rubini's last breath (1854), argues Henry Pleasants.[54] As early as the 1860s Francesco Lamperti was among the first to address the issue and lament the death of bel canto: 'It is a sad, but nevertheless undeniable truth, that the art of singing is in a terrible state of decadence', he laments in the opening chapter of his *The Art of Singing*.[55] If the repertoire associated with this tradition was such that a singer endowed with the necessary talent could find the best and surest master in the music itself, things changed dramatically with Bellini and Verdi. However, if it is not clear whether and to what extent operas later than Rossini's should still be considered as bel canto, it is safe to argue that singers continued to be trained in its principles well beyond the first decades of the nineteenth century. Tetrazzini's recorded interpretations, as well as those of many other contemporary divas, are testament to this tradition.

---

52 See also Henry Pleasants, *The Great Singers, from the Dawn of Opera to Our Own Time* (New York: Simon & Schuster, 1966), pp. 19–21.

53 Let us remind ourselves of the tirade against songstresses in Benedetto Marcello's *Teatro alla Moda*, or the concerns expressed by Maria Anfossi on whether singers were really able to improvise. Maria Anfossi, *Trattato teorico-pratico sull'arte del canto*, London, ca. 1840, p. 72, cited in Toft, p. 109. John Gothard also recommended that singers memorise their cadenzas in order to avoid useless risks: John Gothard, *Thoughts on Singing* (Chesterfield: Pike, 1848), p. 46. On this topic see also Damien Colas, 'Improvvisazione e ornamentazione nell'opera francese e italiana di primo Ottocento', in *Beyond Notes. Improvisation in Western Music of the Eighteenth and Nineteenth Centuries*, edited by Rudolf Rasch (Turnhout: Brepols, 2011), pp. 255–76.

54 Pleasants, *The Great Singers*, p. 134.

55 Francesco Lamperti, *The Art of Singing* (New York: Schirmer, 1890), p. 1. First edition Francesco Lamperti, *Guida teorico-pratica-elementare per lo studio del canto dettata dal Prof. Francesco Lamperti per le sue allieve del R. Conservatorio di musica di Milano* (Milan: Ricordi [1864]).

2. The Rossinian Repertoire

According to the chronology compiled by Charles Neilson Gattey and Thomas Kaufman, only one Rossinian opera features prominently in Tetrazzini's repertoire: *Il barbiere di Siviglia*.[1] The first record dates back to 6 March 1894, when she made her appearance as Rosina at the Teatro San Martin of Buenos Aires together with the baritone Pietro Cesari and C. Elias. On reporting how she triumphed in that role, the critic of *The Standard* wondered why she had insisted 'on gilding the purest musical gold extant. Was the marvellously florid score not florid enough for you, without taxing your grand voice by adding your *fioritura*?'[2] Tetrazzini adhered to a performance practice that was still shared among prima donnas, however strenuously music critics continued to disapprove of it. After 1894, Tetrazzini would be Rosina in sixty-one productions throughout her career, while her last public appearances in this role were in 1912, in Chicago, Boston and London.[3]

A second Rossini opera features in her chronology, although in a much more marginal position. On 7 June 1898 Tetrazzini made her appearance in Buenos Aires as Mathilde in *Guglielmo Tell* together with Francesco Tamagno, Eugenio Giraldoni and R. Ercolani; Leopoldo Mugnone conducted. She would assume this role again only on 2 February 1902, this time in St. Petersburg, with Michele Mariacher, Mattia Battistini and Vittorio Arimondi. The reason why she did not consider singing the role of Mathilde more often has been suggested by Tetrazzini herself, although in general terms. As we have already seen, in *How to Sing* she raises the question of stylistic appropriateness and suggests that every singer 'must be familiar also with the varying needs of the different schools of music, with the historical traditions associated with them'.[4] Since every repertoire has its own different requirements, in terms of both vocal technique and style, it is unlikely, if not impossible, for an artist to excel in all of them. The consequence is that every singer should confine herself to the class of work more particularly suited to her talent. Tetrazzini herself admitted that, at some point in her career, she had to make a choice and steer away from those works which did not fit her voice and personality.[5] If, on the one hand, flexibility was a quality that any singer should cultivate, it was not advisable to push oneself into foreign lands and embrace repertoires that did not fit one's voice. A case in point is represented by *Guglielmo Tell*, as the critic of *The Standard* remarked when reviewing her impersonation of Mathilde on 21 June 1898: 'Senorita Tetrazzini looked and sang charmingly and it is a pity that in this opera she has so little to show what an excellent soprano leggero she is'.[6] To put it bluntly, Mathilde did not offer sufficiently sparkling vocalisation to allow her to show off her voice and upstage the rest of the cast. Unfortunately, Tetrazzini has left no recordings from this opera.

Although no other title from the Rossinian repertoire can be found in the chronology of her live performances, *Semiramide*, a role she apparently never assumed on stage, appears in Tetrazzini's recordings. She recorded 'Bel raggio lusinghier', Semiramide's cavatina, on 2 November 1910 in London with Percy Pitt conducting the orchestra. A second recording for the Victor Talking Machine was realised on 11 May 1914 with Walter B. Rogers conducting the orchestra (matrix C14818-1); this has never been issued.

---

1 Gattey, *Luisa Tetrazzini*, p. 280.
2 Ibid., pp. 15–16.
3 This number represents an approximation, since each production of an opera could imply a different number of performances. For instance, we are informed of six performances of *Il Barbiere* when it was produced in London in 1908: 15 and 23 June, 4, 9, 17 and 22 July. See ibid., p. 102.
4 Luisa Tetrazzini, *How to Sing*, p. 95.
5 Ibid.
6 Gattey, *Luisa Tetrazzini*, p. 25.

Rosina, the Cunning Girl

It was typical of nineteenth-century Italian operas to give prima donnas and primi uomini a nice cavatina with which to make their entrance and present their character. In this case, Rosina introduces herself by singing an aria that is suggestive of the character's personality, dramatic role, and vocal quality. Although it is not my intention to elaborate on the extent to which Rosina simply embodies a stereotyped character within the stereotyped framework of a comedy of intrigue, in her cavatina she is showing the audience her double-faced quality. If, on the one hand, she is a sentimental, timid girl whose heart is now touched by the idea that Lindoro may have fallen in love with her, Rosina is also the kind of young woman who can show the determination and wit necessary to overcome any obstacle. This may easily result in designing a hundred tricks and deceiving people. One may even wonder which is her true nature, whether the timid or the cunning, and if she is not just putting on modesty like a social mask, as has been suggested by Janet Johnson.[7]

Andante

Italian	English		Structure
Una voce poco fa	A voice a moment ago		a $_{(2+2)}$
Qui nel cor mi risuonò,	Here in my heart resounded		
Il mio cor ferito è già	My heart has been wounded		a' $_{(2+2)}$
E Lindor fu che il piagò.	And it is Lindor who wounded it		
Sì, Lindoro mio sarà,	Yes, Lindoro will be mine,		b $_{(2+2)}$
Lo giurai, la vincerò.	I swore, I will win.		b' $_{(2+2)}$
Il tutor ricuserà,	The tutor will refuse,		c $_{(2+2)}$
Io l'ingegno aguzzerò,	I will sharpen my wits,		
Alla fin s'accheterà	In the end he will come to his senses		
E contenta io resterò.	And I shall remain content.		
Sì, Lindoro mio sarà,	Yes, Lindoro will be mine,		b $_{(2+2+1)}$
Lo giurai, la vincerò.	I swore, I will win		

Moderato

Italian	English			Structure
Io sono docile,	I am docile,	**A**		a $_{(2+2)}$
Son rispettosa,	I am respectful,			
Sono ubbidiente,	I am obedient,			a' $_{(2+2)}$
Dolce, amorosa,	sweet, loving,			
Mi lascio reggere,	I let myself be led,			b $_{(2+2)}$
Mi fo guidar.	I let myself be guided.			
Ma se mi toccano	But if they touch me	**B**		a $_{(2+2)}$
Qua nel mio debole,	Here in my weakness,			
Sarò una vipera,	I will be a viper,			a' $_{(2+2)}$
E cento trappole	And a hundred tricks			b $_{(2+2)}$
Prima di cedere	Before I give in			b $_{(2+3)}$
Farò giocar.	I will play.			coda

---

[7] See Janet Johnson, 'Il barbiere di Siviglia', in *The Cambridge Compaioni to Rossini*, ed. by Senici, pp. 170–74.

The lyrics consist of four six-verse stanzas of which the first two present eight-syllable truncated verses, while the second two change into five-syllable verses, thus leading to a clearly perceivable rhythmic acceleration. The music follows this segmentation: the first two stanzas, in which Rosina reflects on her new condition, are set to an Allegro moderato in ¾ time; Lindoro is in love with her and all the difficulties will be overcome. A Moderato in common time follows, which sets to music the second two stanzas; now Rosina moves to a more general description of her personality: respectful but determined, sweet and obedient but cunning and smart if necessary. The opening Allegro moderato consists of a sixteen-bar section followed by a twelve-bar section; it presents a more declamato-like style, with the orchestra supporting the voice mostly with isolated chords. The Moderato section features a more lyric style, and consists of three sections: ABB'. After the first, made up of three four-bar phrases, the aria continues with a livelier section which is repeated twice, to conclude with a short coda.

However used we are to recognising the sweet side of Rosina's personality in the first melodic idea of the Moderato, and her cunning in the second, more sparkling one, and however strongly we feel the connection between the lyrics and the music Rossini composed to set them to, the initial melodic motive is not original and involves some self-borrowing from previously written and already performed operas. More interestingly, each time it was used this melody was meant to express a different feeling, whether melancholy or joyful, depending on the situation and the dramatic persona. We find it in Arsace's rondo 'Non lasciarmi in tal momento' from *Aureliano in Palmira*, an opera seria in two acts set to a libretto by Gian Francesco Romanelli, which premiered at the Teatro alla Scala (Milan) on 26 December 1813, and also in Elisabetta's cavatina 'Quant'è grato all'alma mia' from *Elisabetta, regina d'Inghilterra*, a drama in two acts set to a libretto by Giovanni Federico Schmidt after a play by Carlo Federici based on Sophia Lee's *The Recess*. *Elisabetta* was premiered at the Teatro San Carlo (Naples), on 4 October 1815. In short, when *Il barbiere* was premiered in Rome on 20 February 1816, it was the third time that Rossini was using, at least in part, the same melodic material, each time for a different theatre and in a different city. The reason for this frequent self-borrowing was clarified by Rossini himself when Ricordi announced plans to publish vocal scores of all of his operas; in 1864 the composer thus expressed his preoccupation to Tito Ricordi: 'The edition you have undertaken will give rise, justifiably, to much criticism, since the same pieces of music will be found in various operas: the time and money accorded me to compose were so *homeopathic* that I barely had time to read the so-called poetry to set to music'.[8] The composer goes on reminding Ricordi that his only concern in those years was to support his parents and relatives financially. Although one may wonder whether these last apologetic remarks were entirely true, it is clear that the opera production system imposed a very tough working pace not only on composers, but also librettists and singers. Rossini seems to have expressed the same concern to Beethoven, when paying him a visit in Vienna in 1822. A detailed report of the conversation between Rossini and Beethoven has been left by Edmond Michotte, who took notes of the visit Richard Wagner paid to Rossini in Paris in 1860. On that occasion, Rossini told Wagner about his meeting with Beethoven, who had suggested that he confined himself to the composition of comic operas. Rossini told Wagner, as Michotte writes, that he had tried to explain to Beethoven how difficult it was for him to work on the composition of a new opera.[9] Librettos were imposed by impresarios, the scenarios were given to him one act at a time, and the composition of the music had to proceed without his even knowing how the story would end. On the other hand, not many operas survived for more than a few seasons and, since opera scores did not circulate in printed form, it was difficult, if not impossible, for critics and audiences to understand whether and to what extent self-borrowing was involved in the composition of a new opera.[10]

---

8   'L'edizione da voi intrapresa darà luogo (con fondamento) a molte critiche, poiché si troveranno in diverse opere gli stessi pezzi di musica: il tempo e il denaro che mi si accordava per comporre era sì *omeopatico* che appena avevo io il tempo di leggere la cosiddetta poesia da musicare'. *Lettere inedite e rare di Gioacchino Rossini*, ed. by Giuseppe Mazzatinti (Imola: Ignazio Galeati e figlio, 1892), pp. 174–75. The English translation can be found in *The Cambridge Companion to Rossini*, ed. by Senici, p. 81.

9   See Herbert Weinstock, *Rossini* (New York: Lilelight Editions, 1987), pp. 120–21. The full transcription by Michotte can be found reproduced in Luigi Rognoni, *Gioacchino Rossini* (Turin: Einaudi, 1977; first edition 1968), pp. 385–426.

10 See Philip Gossett, 'Compositional Methods', in *The Cambridge Companion to Rossini*, ed. by Senici, pp. 80–81.

'Una voce poco fa' and Nineteenth-Century Performance Practice

A number of reviews, accounts and recollections confirm that during the nineteenth century Rossini's *Barbiere* had become not only a favourite among international audiences but also a benchmark against which the value of any prima donna would be assessed. This implied that each emerging young soprano would undergo comparison with her colleagues and predecessors in terms of acting skills, vocal brilliancy, ornamentation and coloratura. Among others, this tradition involved the insertion of newly-designed ornaments, the substitution of new ornaments for those written by the composer, and even the insertion and substitution of entire arias. In particular, in the nineteenth-century *Il Barbiere* soon came to feature three major manipulations: the insertion of newly-written coloratura in Rosina's famous cavatina 'Una voce poco fa' in the first act, the addition of new ornaments to the soprano part in the duet 'Dunque io son', and the substitution of the aria 'Contro un cor che accende amore' in the so-called lesson scene in the second act. It is well-known that the insertion of new coloratura had been endorsed by Rossini himself, who wrote different ornamented versions for Rosina's cavatina: one was dedicated to Matilde Juva Branca in 1852 and is to be found in the Biblioteca Nazionale Braidense (Milan), while others are preserved in Brussels, at the Fonds Edmond Michotte, and in Munich, in the Franz Beyer Collection.[11] The intervention involving the addition of new ornaments to the soprano part of 'Dunque io son' is also well-documented and Rossini himself wrote an ornamented version for this duet, which he donated to the singer Eugénie Rouget.[12] The practice involving the substitution of the aria in the lesson scene arose as soon as Geltrude Righetti-Giorgi made her first appearance in this role in 1816 and continued uninterrupted until the beginning of the twentieth century, with Angiolina Bosio, Pauline Viardot García, and Adelina Patti among its worthiest representatives. Nineteenth-century commentators were not at all lenient towards those interpreters who endorsed these modifications; however, as we will see, they were willing to bestow signs of benevolence upon condition that the cantatrice of the night was of great repute and her talents extraordinary.

Evidence of this long-lasting tradition can be found in a number of contemporary reviews. When *Il Barbiere* was revived in London on 14 June 1858 at the Royal Italian Opera, the critic of *The Times* commented on Angiolina Bosio's delightful rendition of Rosina's cavatina but could not avoid observing that she would have been much better had she not taken so many liberties in the melody of 'Una voce poco fa'.

> Madame Bosio's Rosina would be still more delightful if she were to take fewer liberties with the music, and to preserve a little more of the original melody of 'Una voce poco fa', which is in itself so beautiful that we cannot help preferring it to all the delicate embroideries with which the most brilliant songstress may exhibit her skill in adorning it. Whatever Madame Bosio attempts she accomplishes to perfection, but she is apt to regard the music of Rosina, too, exceptionally from the ornamental point of view.[13]

Only a few days later, on 21 June, *The Times* reviewed another rendition of *Barbiere* at Drury Lane, this time with Madame Pauline Viardot García as Rosina.

> Judged from a musical point of view, Madame-Viardot's Rosina is a miracle of cleverness; but even more relentlessly than in the instances of some of her renowned predecessors and contemporaries is Rossini sacrificed on the altar of the singer's vanity. To 'ornament' and vary the cavatina 'Una voce poco fa' till scarcely a vestige of the original remains—to such excess, in short, that the composer might have spared himself the pains of doing anything more than note down a figured bass, is a privilege apparently claimed by every independent mistress of the florid style; and, however inclined to dispute the theory, it is impossible not to acknowledge the wonderful art with which Madame Viardot embellishes and disguises not only the plain melody, but even the 'bravura' of Rossini. With regard to the duet, 'Dunque io son', however, neither theory nor practice can be defended. If the lady has a right to embroider, so has her companion; and it would be simply poetical justice were some eager and adventurous Figaro, endowed with the ancient Tamburinian

---

11 These manuscripts have been transcribed and are reproduced in both the critical edition published by Ricordi in 2014 (edited by Alberto Zedda) and the one published by Bärenreiter in 2008 (edited by Patricia B. Brauner). See also Philip Gossett, *Divas and Scholars, Performing Italian Opera* (Chicago and London: University of Chicago Press, 2006), p. 315.
12 Again, see both the Ricordi 2014 and Bärenreiter 2008 critical editions.
13 *The Times*, 14 June 1858, p. 12.

fluency, unexpectedly to contend for vocal supremacy with Rosina herself, answering 'roulade' by 'roulade,' 'fioritura' by 'fioritura'. Our 'prima donna', thus caught in her own trap, the audience would laugh, the barber triumph, and Rossini be avenged. In the lesson scene, in lieu of Rode's variations, or some other conventional display, Madame Viardot introduced two Spanish airs, accompanying herself on the pianoforte. She sang them with inimitable spirit, and enraptured the audience beyond measure. But then her respectable guardian's protest against the music preferred by Rosina, and so different from that of his own early predilections,—

> 'Ma quest'aria, cospetto! È assai noiosa'
> 'la musica a miei tempi era altra cosa'—

lost its point—since in the first place there were two airs instead of one; and in the second, Dr. Bartolo would hardly have applied the epithet 'tedious' (nojosa) to the national melody of his own country. And now, having done with criticism, we need only add that the talent of Madame Viardot was never more brilliantly exhibited, and that her performance, from first to last, was received by the audience with unbounded tokens of satisfaction.[14]

The critic raised three issues of paramount importance. The first regards the cavatina and the way in which interpreters like Bosio and Viardot abused the composer, whose music was constantly sacrificed on the altar of the singer's vanity. Although no details are provided by the critic, it can be assumed that Viardot's ornamentation involved both the addition of new ornaments and the substitution of those written by Rossini, as suggested also by Manuel García in his *Scuola*.[15] The nineteenth-century history of the interpretation of this aria is accompanied by endless variants and cadenzas, of which numerous transcriptions exist that can be found reproduced in printed editions. Luigi Ricci's *Variazioni-Cadenze Tradizioni per Canto* (1937), Volume I, includes passages transcribed from Adelaide Borghi-Mamo (1829–1901), Maria Malibran García (1808–1836), Barbara Marchisio (1833–1919) and Adelina Patti (1843–1919).[16] In her *Méthode de chant composée pour ses classes du Conservatoire*, published in 1849, Laura Cinti-Damoreau includes, among others, a cadenza for this cavatina.[17] In 1900 Mathilde Marchesi wrote a collection of *Variantes et points d'orgue* dedicated to her students, which includes also a few variants and cadenzas for Rosina's cavatina.[18] The 1943 *Book of Coloratura [and] Cadenzas* edited by Estelle Liebling includes, among others, variants and cadenzas associated with Lily Pons and Luisa Tetrazzini.[19] More recently Austin B. Caswell has edited a volume of *Embellished Opera Arias* which offers, among others, both Marchisio's and Laure Cinti-Damoreau's cadenzas and variants.[20] Last but not least Karin and Eugen Ott have edited a volume entirely devoted to the ornamentation of nineteenth-century vocal music in which most of the variants from the operatic tradition have been accurately transcribed for the modern reader to learn and compare.[21] What these transcriptions have in common is the consistent choice of ornamentation figures and their position inside the aria; they all support the notion that, against many critics' better judgement, singers did not hesitate when it came to inserting new coloraturas and making substantial changes in the melodic line. The fact that these cadenzas and variants have come to form a body of published sources is a testament to the importance of this practice, at least in the eyes of the contemporary singers and possibly of the audience.

The second issue regards the duet 'Dunque io son' and the strikingly inconsistent use of the ornamentation between the two interpreters: while Pauline Viardot as Rosina deviated from the written text, Cesare Badiali, as Figaro, did not. The duet in question is divided into two sections, the first of which presents a characteristic voice setting where a first melodic idea is sung in turn by either character (Figure 9).

---

14 *The Times*, 21 June 1858, p. 12.
15 Talking of Viardot-García's Rosina in 1847, Robert Schumann wrote in his operatic notes from Dresden that 'Viardot makes a great variation of the opera: not one melody is left untouched'. Robert Schumann, *La Musica Romantica*, edited by Luigi Ronga (Turin: Einaudi, 1942), p. 231.
16 Luigi Ricci, *Variazioni-Cadenze Tradizioni* (Milan: Ricordi, 1937), vol. I.
17 Laura Cinti-Damoreau, *Méthode de chant composée pour ses classes du Conservatoire* (Paris: au Ménestrel, 1849), p. 93.
18 Mathilde Marchesi, *Variantes et points d'orgue* (Paris: Huguel, 1900).
19 Estelle Liebling, *The Estelle Liebling Book of Coloratura Cadenzas containing Traditional and New Cadenzas, Cuts, Technical Exercises, and Suggested Concert Programs* (New York: Schirmer, 1943).
20 *Embellished Opera Arias*, ed. by Austin Caswell (Madison, WI: A-R Editions, 1989), vols VII–VIII.
21 Karin und Eugen Ott, *Handbuch der Verzierungskunst in der Musik, Band 4, Die Vokalmusik im 19. Jahrhundert* (Munich: Ricordi, 1999).

Figure 9 shows the melodic material given to Rosina in the duet 'Dunque io son'.

In a typical love scene where the soprano and the tenor exchange their vows, the two voices eventually merge into a characteristic pattern of parallel-thirds or parallel-sixths.[22] Instead, in this duet, after briefly resuming the first melodic idea, the second part sees each voice assuming a different melodic-harmonic role, more like a concertato situation. The baritone does not take over the melody but supports it with a simple octave-note accompaniment figure (Figure 10).

Figure 10 shows the *concertato*-like setting in the duet 'Dunque io son'.

Despite the critic's perplexity, this modification had long established itself in the tradition. In fact, if we turn our attention to contemporary treatises, we see that this very situation is also contemplated. On addressing the issue of how to add ornaments when it comes to singing a duet, in his *Scuola* Manuel García suggests that 'in duets embellishments may be blended in both parts; but in trios, quartettes &c., no change is allowable';[23] the same concepts, although presented in the form of a Socratic dialogue, can be found in García's *Hints on Singing*, which were published in 1894, edited by Beata García: 'in duets singers combine their ornaments; but in concerted music where all parts are of equal importance, no change is ever admissible'.[24] At this point, it could be reasonably argued that, given the asymmetrical disposition of the roles, the second part of the duet 'Dunque io son' would not lend itself to any ornamentation. Instead, and to our surprise, García offers this very passage as an example to illustrate the way in which 'changes should correspond to the composer's idea and present the

---

22 Scott L. Balthazar, 'The Primo Ottocento Duet and the Transformation of the Rossinian Code', *Journal of Musicology*, 7.4 (1989), 471–97.
23 Manuel García, *The Art of Singing* (Boston: Ditson, [n.d.]), p. 59. This passage is to be found in the Italian translation by Alberto Mazzucato and published by Ricordi as early as 1842. 'Nei duetti, le due parti possono combinar le loro fioriture; ma nei pezzi concertati é proibito il più lieve cangiamento', p. 39.
24 Manuel García, *Hints on Singing by Manuel Garcia, Translated from the French by Beata Garcia* (New York: Ascherberg, 1894), p. 64.

same effect, but augmented'.[25] García offers more than one solution, suggesting that the ornamentation should augment the effect by increasing either the number of notes or their brilliance (Figure 11).

Figure 11 reproduces the variations to 'Dunque io son' from *Barbiere*, present in M. García's method (1842).

Interestingly, in his *Hints*, which were published in 1894 as a 'new and revised edition', García offers more solutions than in the previous one, making a distinction between a soprano and a mezzo, and offering ornamented variants that may fit either voice compass. As can be observed in Figure 12, the ornamented version for the mezzo soprano voice lies comfortably within the stave, reaching the upper A only twice.

Figure 12 reproduces the variations for mezzo soprano to 'Dunque io son' from *Barbiere*, present in M. García's *Hints* (1894).

---

25   García, *L'Arte del Canto* (Milan: Ricordi, 1842), p. 40.

Instead, the ornamented version for the soprano reaches the upper B and C (Figure 13).

Figure 13 reproduces the variations for soprano to 'Dunque io son' from *Barbiere*, present in M. García's *Hints* (1894).

The variants for mezzo soprano share a sixteen-note figure and are characterised by runs and arpeggios, while those for soprano reach the upper part of the voice compass using staccato octave figures. Interestingly, all the variants suggested by García belong to the second part of the piece.

Of course, it is all too easy to speculate on the position and type of ornaments Viardot may have added or substituted. What was her choice? Was she already enriching the first melodic idea while her colleague was adhering strictly to the text? Or should we assume, instead, that she was making changes similar to those we find described in Manuel García's method? The latter is entirely plausible, especially if we consider the close connection that existed between Pauline Viardot and her brother Manuel García and the fact that they belonged to the same vocal breed, so to speak.

The strength with which this tradition persisted into the twentieth century is testified to by singers belonging to the younger generations. A case in point is represented by Maria Callas's interpretation of this duet together with Tito Gobbi. Callas and Gobbi recorded this aria twice: a first live recording was made at La Scala Theatre in Milan in 1956,[26] with Carlo Maria Giulini conducting, while a second was realised in 1957,[27] this time together with Alceo Galliera. In either rendition, when returning to the second melodic figure Callas sings the variations transcribed in Figure 14 while her partner adheres to the written text. Her part already presents some melodic modifications at the beginning of the motive and the variants in the following bars are consistent with, if not similar to, those suggested by García for the soprano voice (Figure 14, second stave).[28]

---

26 https://www.youtube.com/watch?v=gGEsrluhuuY.
27 https://www.youtube.com/watch?v=8ExYq7iKT-o.
28 These examples can be found in García's *Hints on Singing* (London: Ascherbg, 1894), p. 65. See also Caswell, *Embellished Opera Arias*, p. 96.

Figure 14 presents the ornamented version sung by Maria Callas in 1956 and 1957.

Going back to Viardot-García's Rosina in 1858, the critic raised a third issue regarding the well-documented substitution in the so-called lesson scene in Act II. The critic makes two points; the first concerns the fact that, instead of Rode's variations, which were frequently chosen to replace the original aria, Viardot sang two Spanish songs; the second highlights the dramatic inconsistency that, in his opinion, this insertion generated. Bartolo should have liked those two songs, given that he is a Spaniard and the action takes place in Seville.

In this scene, Don Alonso, Count Almaviva in disguise, knocks at Bartolo's door and introduces himself as professor of music and student of Don Basilio. Since Don Basilio is sick, he will give Rosina her singing lesson. The lesson opens with Don Alonso asking her what she would like to sing, to which she answers 'Il rondo dell'*Inutil precauzione*', the newly-composed opera. The aria Rossini composed for this scene was 'Contro un cor che accende amore'. As has been already clarified by Hilary Poriss, the substitution of this aria with a virtuoso piece chosen to suit the prima donna's vocal qualities and musical taste (or lack thereof) dates back to Rossini's time: the first to make the change was Geltrude Righetti-Giorgi, the very first Rosina, who, already a few months after the 1816 premiere of *Barbiere* in Rome, performed a different aria in Bologna and yet another in Florence.[29] Eventually, not only did it become common practice to substitute this aria with others from either Rossini or any other later composer (including Verdi), but these had come to include mostly theme-and-variation arias, sometimes derived from instrumental pieces adapted for the voice. Among them, Pierre Rode's *Air Varié* Op. 10 for violin, which Henriette Sontag introduced in 1826, came to be a favourite.[30] Rossini himself wrote a second aria to substitute for the original, setting to music lyrics that reflected the trouble Rosina was in: 'La mia pace, la mia calma / vo' cercando e non ritrovo / ogni dì un tormento nuovo / per quel crudo ho da soffrir' (My peace, my tranquillity / I am in search of, but cannot find / every day I have to suffer / a new torment because of that cruel man). It soon became common practice to interpolate vocal pieces that had nothing to do with the original aria and its dramatic settings. As early as 1819 Giuseppina Ronzi de Begnis used to insert bravura variations to the barcarole 'La biondina in gondoleta' setting a precedent that would be followed by every interpreter of repute. Joséphine Fodor Mainvielle sang 'Di tanti palpiti' from *Tancredi*, Maria Malibran's choice was 'Yo soy contrabandera' by Cabella, while her sister Pauline Viardot preferred 'La fiancée du bandit' which she had composed.[31]

Of course, young singers of no great repute also endorsed this performance practice in the attempt to keep up with the expectations set by the international divas. This was the case with Russian-born contralto Anna De Belocca (née de Bellokh), who was twenty-one years old when she made her London début as Rosina at Her Majesty's Theatre in 1875. Her lesson scene included a Russian melody and an aria from Donizetti's *Lucrezia Borgia*.

> It was in the next act, however, that Mdlle. Belocca set all fears at rest and completed her success. 'The Lesson scene' won the sympathies of the whole assembly of connoisseurs. The first song was a Russian melody ('Solove') of plaintive character, which must have somewhat astonished Dr. Bartolo, being sung in the Russian language, but it was tuneful and expressive enough to enlist general and hearty sympathy. What followed was the *brindisi* 'Il segreto per esser

---

29 See Hilary Poriss, *Changing the Score: Arias, Prima Donnas, and the Authority of Performance* (Oxford: Oxford University Press, 2009), p. 135.
30 Ibid., p. 151.
31 *Tutti i libretti di Rossini*, ed. by Marco Beghelli and Nicola Gallino (Turin: UTET, 1995), p. 380.

felice' (*Lucrezia Borgia*), which, rendered in a characteristic and empathic way, roused general enthusiasm, and was loudly encored. By this time the general conviction was that a new 'star' had appeared in the operatic horizon. Such gifts as Mdlle. Belocca is endowed with, such rare personal attractions and such evident aptitude for the profession of her choice was well worth cultivating. The impression created on Saturday night will cause every amateur to watch with interest the future career of the interesting young Russian.[32]

Her London début was a success and in 1876 she would make her appearance, again as Rosina, at the Academy of Music in New York.[33]

Rosina was also one of the roles that best fitted Adelina Patti's voice and personality. According to an anecdote that has been told repeatedly, upon attending her first soirée at Rossini's place in Paris in 1862, the nineteen-year-old Patti sang 'Una voce poco fa' before the composer and the other guests. Camille Saint-Saëns recalled the episode:

Unhappily, I was not present at the soirée during which Patti was heard at Rossini's for the first time. It is known that when she had performed the aria from *Il barbiere*, he said to her, after many compliments: 'By whom is this aria that you just have let us hear?' I saw him a few days later: he still had not calmed down. 'I know perfectly well,' he told me, 'that my arias must be embroidered; they were made for that. But not to leave a note of what I composed, even in the recitatives—really, that is too much.'[34]

However, Rossini's opinion of Patti's vocal and musical talents would improve over time and the initial irritation was soon forgotten, as Saint-Saëns narrates.

In his irritation he complained that the sopranos persisted in singing this aria which was written for a contralto and did not sing what had been written for the sopranos at all. On the other hand the diva was irritated as well. She thought the matter over and realized that it would be serious to have Rossini for an enemy. So some days later she went to ask his advice. It was well for her that she took it, for her talent, though brilliant and fascinating, was not as yet fully formed. Two months after this incident, Patti sang the arias from *La Gazza ladra* and *Semiramide*, with the master as her accompanist. And she combined with her brilliancy the absolute correctness which she always showed afterwards.[35]

When in 1867 Eduard Hanslick paid a visit to the Pesarese he reported that at some point the name of Patti came up in a conversation: 'The Maestro', Hanslick wrote, 'speaks of the latter Patti with admiring esteem, and always singles her out as an exception when deploring the extinction of truly great singers'.[36] Unfortunately, no recording survives that may be a testament to her interpretation not only of this very piece, but also of any other aria from the Rossinian repertoire. However, many contemporary reviews survive that suggest how spirited her impersonation was. When she made her appearance in this role in London in 1863, the critic of *The Times* described her vocalisation in sparkling, vibrant colours.

Last, not least, the Rosina of Mademoiselle Adelina Patti—one of those impersonations which not merely exhibit to advantage her singular vocal facility, but show her to be a comic actress of the genuine stamp—lively, piquant, full of intelligence and sensibility, in every look, act and gesture *original* was quite worthy a match with the Almaviva [Mario] and Figaro [Ronconi] of the evening. The profuse embellishments with which she decks out the *cavatina* ('Una voce poco fa'), however the stickler for Rossini's text *quand même* may find objection (and we still declare ourselves of their party), are excused, if not rendered imperative, by the peculiar range and calibre of her voice. They are, moreover, in some measure, warranted by the precedents of Sontag, Persiani, Bosio, and other renowned singers—not excluding Malibran, who, like her sister, Madame Viardot—might easily have given the music without the alteration of a single note, a restriction to which, nevertheless, those celebrated artists rarely if ever condescended. Mademoiselle Patti's ornaments and *fioriture* have the merit of being entirely her own, and the unhesitating manner in which they are

---

32   'Her Majesty's Opera', *The Times*, 26 April 1875, p. 9.
33   On 13 April 1876 *The New York Times* remarked that she had completed her musical education with Maurice Strakosch, whose role, as we will see, was of pivotal importance in launching Adelina Patti's early career.
34   Herbert Weinstock, *Rossini* (New York: Limelight, 1987), p. 276 (first edition New York, Knopf, 1968, p. 66). Also cited in John Fr. Cone, *Adelina Patti Queen of Hearts* (Portland, Oregon: Amadeus Press, 1993), p. 56.
35   Camille Saint-Saëns, *Musical Memories*, translated by Edwin Gile Rich (Boston: Small, Maynard & Co. 1919), p. 207.
36   Weinstock, *Rossini*, p. 349.

delivered obtains acceptance and extorts applause. We are less inclined to submit without a word of protest to the alteration in the duet with Figaro ('Dunque io son'); nor can we believe they were either expedient or very effective—and this, in spite of the arch 'bye-play' and fluent vocalisation of this gifted little lady, which might almost reconcile the testiest amateur to any and every liberty she chose to take. In the lesson scene, Mademoiselle Patti introduced the very difficult *'valse,'* entitled *'Di Gioja,'* composed expressly for her by M. Strakosch, her brilliant execution of which elicited so general and spontaneous an encore that she was compelled to repeat it.[37]

Interestingly, the review touches upon the same issues we have discussed in the review of Viardot's rendition in 1858.[38] The rich and abundant fioritura added by the singer in the cavatina, a tolerated practice that found its justification in a number of worthy predecessors, the questionable alteration in the duet 'Dunque io son', and the insertion of a new piece in the lesson scene, this time a waltz composed by Maurice Strakosch, Adelina's brother-in-law and early manager. In 1895 the critic of *The Times* reviewed Patti in another performance of *Barbiere* and commented on the insertion of 'Bel raggio' from Rossini's *Semiramide* in the lesson scene, which an encore was likely to follow.

> Her delivery of 'Una voce' may have been a little mannered, but in the rest of the music, whether concerted or solo, she sang as brilliantly as of old. It is true that the quality of some of the higher notes in 'Bel raggio'—introduced into the 'lesson scene'—was a little less than beautiful, but the text of the opera was quite delightfully sung. As the aria from *Semiramide* was the only thing in which any fault was to be detected, it was most rapturously received, and Mme Patti kept to her old traditions of the part by singing 'Home Sweet Home' in her usual manner.[39]

Apparently, it was with Patti that the repertory of coloratura showpieces inserted into the lesson scene came to include Vincenzo Bellini, Giuseppe Verdi, Giacomo Meyerbeer, Charles Gounod, Heinrich Proch, Félicien David, Ambroise Thomas, and Leo Delibes, among others.[40] Afterwards, singers who took over this role followed in Patti's footsteps, as was the case with Tetrazzini: some of these showpieces can be found in her discs, for she recorded them in London in the early 1910s: the 'Bell Song' from Delibes' *Lakmé* (1907), Benedict's 'Carnevale di Venezia' (1909), the 'Polonaise' from Ambroise Thomas's *Mignon*, that is to say 'Io son Titania (1907 and 1911); 'Charmant oiseau' from David's *La Perle du Brésil* (1911), Proch's *Air and Variations* Op. 164 'Deh, torna mio bene' (1911), and Henry Bishop's 'Home, Sweet Home' (1912) are all included in Tetrazzini's London recordings which were reissued by EMI in digital format in 1992.

It is clear that towards the end of the nineteenth-century the character of Rosina came to feature the three major textual modifications discussed so far, and incorporate them as a stable, if not permanent, component of the opera; no singer would consider a different choice, no music critic would object to that tradition, no audience would give a wince. Quite the opposite; when in 1912 such an authoritative newspaper as *The Times* advertised the forthcoming opera season at Covent Garden and announced Tetrazzini's appearance as Rosina in *Il barbiere*, specific mention was made of the bravura piece that she would insert in the lesson scene: '*Il barbiere di Siviglia* (in Italian) Tonight, at 8.15—Mmes. Tetrazzini, Bérat; MM. McCormack, Marcoux, Malatesta, Zucchi, Sampieri and Sammarco. In the lesson scene Mme. Tetrazzini will sing "Polacca" (*Mignon*). Conductor, Signor Panizza'.[41] To announce the bravura piece chosen by the soprano singer would help market the production and appeal to the audience. At the same time, this confirms the status this interpolation had now achieved, thus suggesting that a body of changes, substitutions and interpolations had come to be part of the performative text.

Tetrazzini's international career is well documented and a number of reviews accompanied her appearances in this role over many decades, providing evidence of the way in which international audiences showed clear signs of appreciation while critics continued to express doubts about her real talents. In January 1905 Tetrazzini

---

37 *The Times*, 11 May 1863, p. 12.
38 In the 1850s and 1860s James William Davison was chief music critic of *The Times*. Although reviews were published anonymously at that time, it is possible to argue that the same person was behind the two reviews taken in consideration, possibly Davison himself.
39 *The Times*, 20 June 1895, p. 6. Interestingly, and to the critic's deepest disappointment, on the same occasion, a vocal waltz by Tito Mattei was inserted into the final scene of the opera.
40 Poriss, *Changing the Score*, pp. 160–61.
41 *The Times*, 1 June 1912, p. 8.

made her first appearance as Rosina in San Francisco where, despite a bad cold, she made a furore. Many a journal recorded the enthusiastic reception and described how the audience 'screamed, screamed, screamed until, cold or no cold, she had to cast the golden notes again at the end of the lesson scene'.[42] On 3 October 1905, when Tetrazzini sang Rosina again in San Francisco, Blanche Partington remarked how striking she had been not only as a songstress but also as an actress.

> Tetrazzini, if she lost her voice, could walk round to the Columbia any day right into comedy—if she does not prefer farce. Her Rosina was simply bubbling over with fun from beginning to end. She seemed glad, to get off the grand opera stilts—as glad as we were to have her. There was not the slightest hesitation in sacrificing the voice to the fun, yet she was in lovely voice, though tried a little in the 'music lesson' by the heat. But for the ungodly laughter that filled the haunts of grand opera last night Miss Tetrazzini was most largely responsible. Her 'music lesson' was encored as usual.[43]

In 1908 the critic of *The Musical Times* recorded the successful revival of her Rosina in London and addressed a question concerning the lack of evenness in her voice, a shortcoming that some critics noticed more than once during her career.

> A most successful revival of Rossini's *Barber of Seville* took place on June 15, Madame Tetrazzini being heard for the first time in England as Rosina. So brilliant was her singing in her first song, the familiar 'Una voce,' that the audience interrupted its continuance after the first verse, and from this point the evening was for her a series of triumphs. Madame Patti, who was present and was most generous in her applause, must have felt that her successor could not give the music in the medium part of the voice with the same beauty of tone as she had done, but the higher florid passages were delivered with exquisite finish and a volume of tone and vocal agility that frequently approached the phenomenal.[44]

Tetrazzini was Rosina again at the end of the year, on 14 November, at the Manhattan Opera in New York City. *The Times* correspondent in New York reviewed the opera season there and did not fail to mention how successful she had been.

> Mme. Tetrazzini's reappearance last night was the signal for another display of enthusiasm. The Italian singer has firmly established her position as a favourite here, and she essayed the part of Rosina with entire success. Slightly nervous at the outset, she was quite at her best in the 'Lesson' scene, in which she introduced Proch's famous 'variations,' with the Bell Song from *Lakmé* as an encore. She sang both pieces superbly.[45]

The following year the opera was repeated and the critic from *The Times* reported briefly on its popular success and how she had fulfilled the general expectations. This time, in the lesson scene Tetrazzini had inserted the Polonaise 'Io son Titania' from Ambroise Thomas's *Mignon*, followed by Benedict's *Variations de concert sur Le Carnaval de Venise*. Although a critical note was expressed with regard to her occasionally imprecise intonation and the signs of 'effort' in the polonaise, Tetrazzini's singing was almost perfect and the whole cast excelled in the vivacity of their acting.

> Those who care for *Il Barbiere* only as it serves to show off the agility of a favourite soprano were given all that they could want last night, for Mme. Tetrazzini was in excellent voice, and from 'Una voce' onwards, in the lively scene with Figaro in the second act, and in the famous lesson when she delighted her hearers by her singing of the polonaise from *Mignon*, followed by the 'Carnaval de Venise' variations, she sang everything with the ease and clearness which belongs to her work at its best. A note here and there not quite perfectly in tune could, indeed, be detected, and the trills at the climax of the polonaise showed slight signs of effort, but such things were only small flaws in singing which was nearly perfect of its kind. There are, however, quite other interests in the opera than the vocal skills of the

---

42 *San Francisco Bulletin*, cited by Charles Neilson Gattey, *Luisa Tetrazzini*, p. 46.
43 Blanche Partington, 'Throws Tivoli into Giggles', *The San Francisco Call*, 4 October 1905, p. 2.
44 'The Opera', *The Musical Times*, 1 July 1908, pp. 456–57.
45 'New York Opera Season', *The Times*, 17 November 1908, p. 7.

prima donna, and on the whole last night's company combined well to bring out all the humour of the thing by their acting and especially by their crisp and vivacious treatment of the *recitativo secco*.⁴⁶

As we can see, it had become customary for Tetrazzini to introduce a first bravura piece in the lesson scene and then to sing a second one as an encore. The same happened one year later, when she again was in London performing Rosina and other roles. *The Times* published a positive review suggesting again how the lesson scene had served as an opportunity to showcase the voice and ignite the now predictably enthusiastic response of the audience.

> *Il Barbiere*, with Mime. Tetrazzini as Rosina, has become a regular institution of the Opera season, and the audience, which was a large one, last night gave every sign of enjoying both the vocal gymnastics of the prima donna and the time-honoured jokes of the *buffa* parts. With Signor Sammarco, as Figaro, Signor Marcoux as Basilio, and Signor Malatesta as Bartolo there was no fear that the fun would flag, and these three carried on the dialogue with all the air of enjoying it themselves, which is the essence of success. Signor Armanini was a moderately successful Almaviva, though at the climaxes his voice was rather forced and thin in quality. In the Lesson Scene Mme. Tetrazzini sang the Polonaise from *Mignon*, and here, as elsewhere in the opera, she gave us a series of surprises by the beauty of certain notes and phrases contrasting with the hard metallic quality of others. The polonaise brought warm applause, supplemented by a loud 'Bravissimo' fired off when the applause had subsided by an enthusiast in the gallery, and when the singer had recovered from the embarrassment caused by this exhibition she responded by singing 'The Last Rose of Summer' in a way which showed the best qualities of her voice.⁴⁷

This time, in addition to the polonaise Tetrazzini sang 'The Last Rose of Summer' a traditional Irish song set to lyrics by Thomas More. Very much loved by Adelina Patti, who has left two recordings of the piece,⁴⁸ this is a very simple song, with a nice melancholy melody which shares nothing with a typical bravura piece.

As this survey suggests, Tetrazzini shows how she had embraced a long and uninterrupted set of conventions and brought it to its zenith. It is possible that her personal acquaintance with Adelina Patti might have offered her the opportunity to come into contact with a tradition going back to Rossini himself. Furthermore, she might have found the role of Rosina particularly suited to her sparkling personality and dramatic skills, especially in moments like the lesson scene, where she could break the fourth wall with the audience and show off herself, not only her voice.

Rosina in Tetrazzini's Recordings

The reviews published year after year during Tetrazzini's career do not tell us much more of the way in which she may have interpreted this opera, nor do they reveal the extent to which she may have adhered to the tradition of which Patti still was the most authoritative living representative. With the exception of the accounts discussed so far, not much can be gleaned from the reviews on how she approached this opera. Instead, if we turn our attention to Tetrazzini's discography and listen to the recordings she realised in the early 1910s, we can form an opinion on how she sang the famous cavatina.

Tetrazzini recorded 'Una voce poco fa' three times in total. The first recording was realised on 8 September 1904 (matrix number 3513, Zonophone catalogue number 2501). It lasts 2'20'', includes the first part only (Allegro moderato) and the first measures in the introduction have been cut, possibly owing to time constraints. A digital version was issued by Nimbus Records in 1998: *Tetrazzini*, 'Prima Voce', Volume 2 (NI 7891).

The second recording, with Percy Pitt conducting the orchestra, was realised in London in December 1907 by the Gramophone Company of London (matrix 2178f, Gramophone 053146; Victor 92020). This recording has been included in the three-CD box-set issued by EMI Classics in 1992 (CDH 7 63803 2). Although technological developments in 1911 allowed for longer recording time, two small cuts are still present in the orchestra (the

---

46 'Royal Opera', *The Times*, 14 May 1910, p. 12.
47 'Royal Opera', *The Times*, Thursday, 1 June 1911, p. 10.
48 See Cone, *Adelina Patti*, p. 315.

first in the introduction and the second in the final coda) and the B section is not present at all; Tetrazzini moves directly from section A to section B', where she performs her repertoire of variants.

The third recording was realised on 17 March 1911 by the Victor Talking Machine Company of Camden, New Jersey (US). The original audio (matrix C10071-1, Victor 88301, 6337; HMV 2-053046, DB 690) was transferred and reissued by Nimbus Records in 1990 (*Tetrazzini*, 'Prima Voce', NI 7808). In 1911 Walter Rogers, who was then music director of the Victor Company in Camden and took it upon himself to prepare the necessary orchestral adaptations, conducted the orchestra. This last recording presents cuts similar to those made in the 1907 recording, with a few more interventions made in order to shorten the orchestral introductions, both in the Andante and the Moderato (Figure 15).

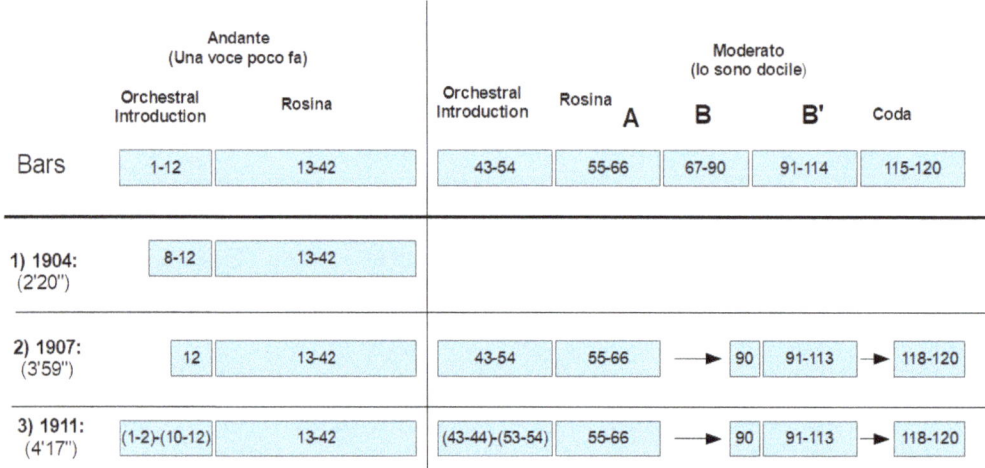

Figure 15. The chart shows the cuts in Tetrazzini's recordings of Rosina's cavatina.

As we have seen, after the difficult reception of its 1816 première in Rome, *Il barbiere di Siviglia* soon entered the international operatic repertoire and continued to score one success after the other, thus becoming a must in the playbills of opera theatres all over the world. As a consequence, and contrary to most of Rossini's other operas that were long neglected or completely forgotten, a richly-documented history of the performance practice of this opera survives, to which Tetrazzini's phonographic evidence makes an important contribution.[49]

Tetrazzini is consistent with the tradition of which she was said to be a worthy representative, and if we take a look at her ornamentation and cadenzas, we can see how old and new are often blended together in making the final result. The first visible addition in the Andante occurs at bar 28, where a sparkling cadenza concludes the first section (Figure 16).

---

49   The so-called Rossini Renaissance dates back to the late 1960s when an increasingly larger number of operas was staged and performed. See Charles S. Brauner, 'The Rossini Renaissance', in *The Cambridge Companion to Rossini*, ed. by Senici, pp. 37–38.

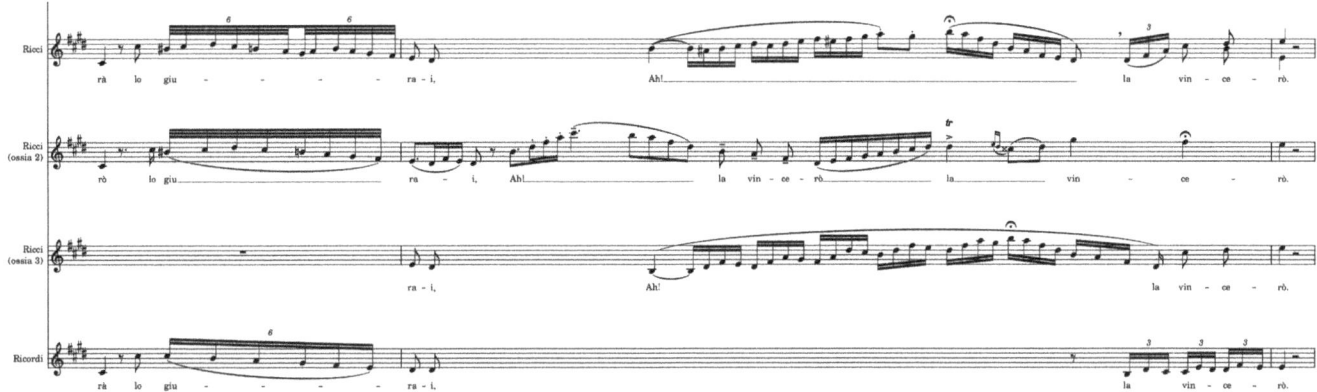

Figure 16 shows the cadenza at bar 28 of the Andante.

This cadenza can be found in Ricci's *Variazioni-Cadenze*, which collects a number of variants belonging to Borghi-Mamo, Malibran and Patti.[50] The same can be said of the cadenza with which the Allegro moderato concludes; this can be found in both Ricci's *Variazioni*[51] and Mathilde Marchesi's *Variantes et points d'orgue*[52] (Figure 17).

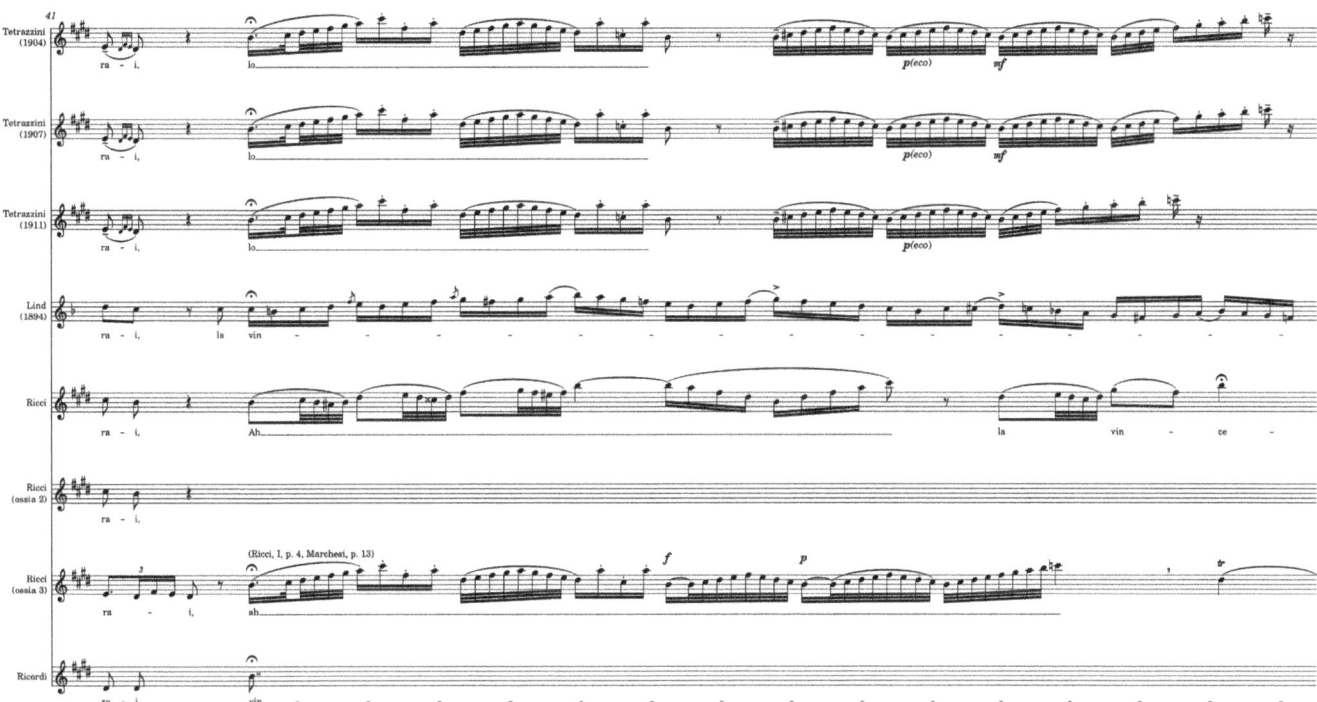

---

50 See Luigi Ricci, *Variazioni-cadenze tradizioni* (Milan: Ricordi, 1937), I, pp. 3–9. For an in-depth analysis of the intepretative tradition of Rossini's repertoire see Michael Aspinall, 'Il cantante nelle interpretazioni delle opere rossiniane', *Bollettino del centro rossiniano di studi*, 1 (1970), 11–21, and, more recently, *Rosina e la 'phonographic evidence': analisi di alcune variazioni vocali presenti nelle registrazioni storiche*, 'Opera Click', http://www.operaclick.com/print/speciali/rosina-e-la-%E2%80%9Cphonographic-evidence%E2%80%9D-analisi-di-alcune-variazioni-vocali-presenti-nelle-regi#_ftn13.

51 Ricci, *Variazioni-Cadenze*, p. 4.

52 Marchesi, *Variantes et points d'orgue*, p. 13.

Figure 17. The closing cadenza of the Andante.

At this point a doubt arises concerning the reliability of these sources. Considering that Ricci's first volume of collected cadenzas was published in 1937, when both Marchesi's *Variants* and Tetrazzini's recordings had long ago made their appearance, why did he fail to mention either singer? Should we doubt Ricci's sincerity when he attributes to Borghi-Mamo, Malibran and Patti a number of ornamentations that Tetrazzini had sung on a regular basis and that Marchesi had already published in 1900?[53] Or is Marchesi lying when she entitles her volume *Variants et points d'orgue composés pour les principaux airs du repertoire par Mathilde Marchesi pour les élèves de ses classes de chant*? Was she pretending she had composed these variants and cadenzas for her pupils, while instead she had taken them from her predecessors, be it Borghi-Mamo, Malibran or even Patti?[54] Going back to Tetrazzini, it is at least possible to argue that in her 1904 recording she had incorporated in her cadenza a passage that was already to be found in Marchesi's 1900 published volume. Whether this passage came from one of the predecessors Ricci mentions in his later collection, or from Marchesi, is another question. A plausible answer to these questions could be that Tetrazzini may have incorporated some coloratura passages among those Marchesi had written down in her volume, while Ricci's transcriptions, published in 1937 with Tetrazzini still alive, hide the name of the diva in order to avoid legal or copyright issues. In any case, one may still wonder whether Ricci had a reason for omitting either singer's name.

If we now turn our attention to those variants from Cinti-Damoreau and Marchisio that can be found collected in Caswell's volume, the difference between them and Tetrazzini is striking. When compared to the richly flourished, dashing cadenzas these two champions used to sing, Tetrazzini's coloraturas look discreet and hesitant, if not cautious. Much more noteworthy is the fact that only a few minor changes are present in Tetrazzini's recorded renditions, which, as we will see, is the case in all her recordings.[55] This seems to support the notion that, once she had learned a role, she was unlikely to go back to the relevant coloratura, add or modify the embellishments, and memorise and rehearse them anew. This theory finds confirmation in Tetrazzini's own words in 1908, when interviewed by *The Sun*.

---

53 Ricci reports also some variants for contralto and indicates Marchisio's name (p. 5).

54 It is my personal opinion that Ricci is not entirely trustworthy. Many of Tetrazzini's cadenzas can be found reproduced in his volumes although he does not mention her name. On the other hand, Tetrazzini, whose recording had been long available on disc, was still alive (she passed away in 1940) when Ricci's collections were published. Michael Aspinall reports that Ricci's students confirmed that Ricci transcribed many variations from discs that were commercially available, and among them those left by Tetrazzini, which remained in the catalogue of His Master's Voice until 1956.

55 The same can be said of other singers whose repeated recordings of the same arias show evidence of the consistency of their interpretative choices over time. Marcella Sembrich and Nellie Melba are two cases in point.

I do not practice at all during the season, except, of course, when I am going over a new role. When I go on the stage, the orchestra says 'la-la' and I respond 'la-la,' and the conductor nods that it is all right and I sing away. That is all the rehearsing I have.[56]

Consistently, a memory slip may explain why the passages B-F# and A#-C# appear to have been shortened in the second and third recording (Figure 17).

Moving to the Moderato, the cut of the B section involves a dramatic loss of information for, as a consequence of that cut, no evidence survives of the cadenza that was traditionally associated with the suspension leading to the repeat (B'). We do not have information on whether, and which, new melodic material may have been sung by Tetrazzini in a live performance (Figure 18).[57]

Figure 18 shows the cadenza traditionally sung before the repeat (B') in the Moderato section.

There seems to be sufficient evidence to suggest that not only the repeat (B'), but also the B section, was varied. This is clear from the sources that have been reproduced by Caswell[58] (Barbara Marchisio), and Ricci.[59] Something similar happens in the rest of the aria; Tetrazzini's ornamentation bears more than a resemblance to some of the variants reproduced by Ricci, regardless of the singer who originally sang them. Instead, strong differences can be observed when her ornaments are compared to those reproduced by Caswell, especially the versions transposed into F major, sung by Jenny Lind and Josefa Gassier (1821–1866). Lind's and Gassier's renditions are much more flourished; their interventions in the written music are much more conspicuous, if not invasive.

In the final measures Tetrazzini sings the variants Rossini himself wrote for Matilde Juva Branca but, in the 1911 recording, she concludes with the top E, a feat that kept the international audience breathless, before they erupted in frantic applause (Figure 19).[60]

---

56   'Making of a Great Singer', *The Sun*, 8 March 1908, p. 6.
57   Of course, Tetrazzini was adhering to a tradition that involved a number of cuts, and it is only by examining further evidence from the music scores used by her and her conductors that we can shed further light on this question.
58   Caswell, *Embellished Opera Arias*, p. 113.
59   Ricci, *Variazioni-Cadenze*, p. 6
60   See Appendice I, 'Varianti vocali autografe' of the new critical edition of Rossini's *Il barbiere di Siviglia*, edited by Alberto Zedda (Milan: Ricordi, 2014), p. 570. See also Philip Gossett, *Divas and Scholars, Performing Italian Opera* (Chicago: The University of Chicago Press, 2006), p. 329.

Figure 19 shows the final measures of the aria, where Tetrazzini sings the variants Rossini wrote for Matilde Juva; in the 1911 recording she concludes with an accented trill leading to the top E. Her cadenza was transcribed by Ricci in his *Variazioni-Cadenze*.

This last example draws attention to the trill and the different ways in which it could be executed. The accents on the trill at the final B, which can be clearly heard in Tetrazzini's recording, seem to be consistent with what has been suggested by García in reference to this embellishment. Commenting on how new habits have widened the palette of possible solutions, García also includes a trill with a number of inflections and an ascending tremolo (Figure 20).[61]

Figure 20 illustrates how a trill could be executed according to the new, modern habits discussed in García's *Scuola*.

As can be seen, Tetrazzini's recordings confirm how strongly her interpretations were rooted in a tradition in which some of the most widely shared interpretative devices of the nineteenth century can be recognised together with the influence that such preeminent personalities as Patti exerted on her.

The Lesson Scene

As already discussed, it was typical of Tetrazzini to substitute a showpiece for Rossini's aria 'Contro un cor che accende amore' in what is generally known as the lesson scene in Act II. This was consistent with a long-lasting performance tradition that dates back to 1816, and had in Adelina Patti a turning point; in fact, it was her who turned the lesson scene into a miniature concert involving a first interpolated coloratura showpiece followed by an 'encore'.

---

61   García, *Trattato di canto*, Part II, p. 46.

'Io son Titania'

The evidence presented so far suggests that Tetrazzini often substituted the 'Polonaise' from Ambroise Thomas' *Mignon* for the original aria. We are talking of the *Récit et Polonaise* 'Je suis Titania la blonde' ('Io son Titania' as the Italian translation sung by Tetrazzini reads) which Philine sings towards the end of Act II in Ambroise Thomas's *Mignon* (1866), an opéra comique based on Goethe's novel *Wilhelm Meisters Lehrjahre* and set to a French libretto written by Michel Carré and Jules Barbier. This is the moment in which Philine, an actress (the role was created by the Belgian coloratura soprano Marie Cabel) portrays the light-hearted Titania, from Shakespeare's *A Midsummer Night's Dream*. During her career Tetrazzini made her appearance in Thomas's *Mignon* on many an occasion, although this opera did not feature prominently in her repertoire. The first time was in Buenos Aires, at the Teatro San Martin, in 1895, then on 23 February 1899 and on 1 January 1900 in St. Petersburg, when Tetrazzini sang Philine with Sigrid Arnoldson as Mignon. She performed it yet again in 1902 (Tbilisi), 1903 (St. Petersburg, with Arnoldson), 1904 (Mexico City, with Livia Berlendi) 1905 (Guadalajara, Mexico), 1911 (Boston, USA for the first time, with Fely Dereyne as Mignon), and 1913 (Chicago, with Mabel Riegelman).[62]

Tetrazzini left four recordings of the aria: December 1907 (Matrix 2171f, Gramophone 053142; Victor 92015, 15-1001), August 1908 (Gramophone Matrix 2574f, unpublished), 17 March 1911 (Matrix C19973-1, Victor 88296, 6342), 14 July 1911 (Matrix ai5181f, HMV 2-053058, DB 540).

Tetrazzini sings the Italian translation prepared by Giuseppe Zaffira and published by Heugel in Paris shortly after the publication of the original score:[63]

Io son Titania la bionda	I'm now Titania, fair, entrancing,
Son Titania figlia del sol	Airy daughter of the morning light,
Vo' pel mondo ognor balda e gioconda,	Through the world I go, e'er gaily dancing,
Più lieve dell'angel che l'aer fende a vol.	More swiftly than the bird that upward takes his flight
Io son Titania la bionda,	I'am now Titania, fair, entrancing,
Ah! Corro ognor gioconda etc.	Ever gaily dancing,
Mille folletti intorno a me si,	A thousand fairies, gay and light,
danzando van con agil pie'	Night and day take round my car their bright flight!
E notte e dì, di mia corte ognor	Behind me all my courtiers move,
Va cantando i fasti dell'amor.	Rove and sing of pleasure and love.
Mille folletti intorno a me si,	A thousand fairies, gay and light,
danzando van con agil pie'	Nightly take round my car their bright flight,
Ma fuggon di Cinzia all'apparir!	Until the dawn breaks on their sight.
Per entro i fior che l'aurora	Among the flowers then unclosing,
Fa sbocciare	Safe reposing,
Per declivi adorni ognor	And 'mid grasses of the field,
d'erbe e fior, ...	Lie concealed. ...
E dell'onde sulle spume	On the waves so whitely foaming,

---

62 See Charles N. Gattey and Thomas G. Kaufman, 'A Chronology of Tetrazzini's Appearances', in Gattey, *Luisa Tetrazzini*, pp. 280–326.
63 Ambroise Thomas, *Mignon, Opéra in Trois Actes, Paroles de MM. Michel Carré et Jules Barbier, Traduzione di Giuseppe Zaffira* (Paris: Heugel). The Italian translation of the libretto was published separately in 1912 by Casa Editrice Madella in Sesto San Giovanni (Milan) and presents an almost identical reading of this aria (p. 24).

Fra le brume,	In the gloaming,
Godo ognor con agil pie'	You may see me turning round,
Saltellar!...	Lightly bound...
Con agil pie', fra l'erbette ed i fior	With footsteps light, thro' the forests at night,
E nelle brume, godo ognor saltellar,	'Mid shades profound my little footsteps are found,
Godo ognor saltellar	Where I trip over the ground.
Io son Titania la bionda	Behold, Fairy queen am I
Son Titania figlia del sol	I am now Titania, fairy child of the air
Etc.	Etc.

It is clear that the connection between the original lyrics and the newly-inserted aria is non-existent and all the concerns for the plot and its dramatic consistency were simply put aside.[64] While in the original text Rosina reflects on her condition and the boundless power of true love, thus anticipating the happy ending of the opera, the words uttered by Titania, the fairy queen, depict the character's flirtatious, light-hearted nature, surrounded as she is by fairies and birds. The music follows an A-B-A' form, with the first section, in B flat major, sparkling and vivacious, and the second, in B major, sweet and melodic. After the reprise the piece concludes with a cadenza that stretches up to a top E flat before concluding with a long trill on the leading tone.

In terms of musical contents and interpretative choices the three recordings are identical; Tetrazzini sings this bravura piece as written. The small modifications present in her renditions fall into the space we now understand as rightfully belonging to the interpreter: here and there she changes the articulation (staccato instead of legato), and gives special emphasis to specific passages by adding fermatas and indulging in a sustained note in the high register. A few bars are cut in the short staccato passage that leads to the central section, possibly because of the limited capacity of the disc. In all the recordings she makes a small modification to the final cadenza, perhaps to emphasise the moment where the climax is reached: she approaches the top E flat through a small grace then descends chromatically to the low F. The published score presents a simplified variant, with the C substituting for the top E, should the singer not possess it, and suggests also that the most challenging measures could be left out (Figure 21). The brilliance of the aria, with its sparkling melodic figures and vivacious polonaise rhythm, offered Tetrazzini a wonderful opportunity for vocal display.

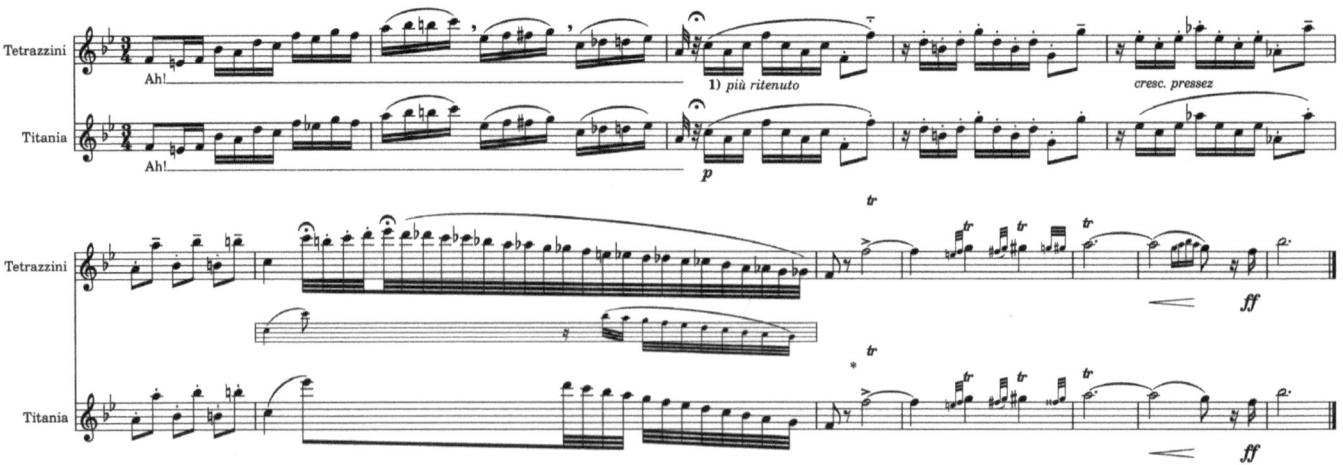

1) These five measures may be left out, and go on at the sign *

Figure 21. The cadenza concluding 'Io son Tatiana', which Tetrazzini recorded in 1907.

---

64   See Poriss, *Changing the Score*, pp. 156–65.

In sum, the recordings are identical, were it not for their different length: the third (4'24") is significantly longer than both the first (4'00") and the second (4'06"). This suggests a relatively fast pace in the earlier recording, which eases up in the second and the third, thus approximating the average length of later discs.

Proch's *Variations*

On other occasions, Tetrazzini inserted the *Air and Variations* Op. 164 by Heinrich Proch, which she recorded twice: on 18 March 1911 with Clement Barone playing the flute (Matrix C10077-1, Victor 88307, 6336; HMV 2-053045, DB 523) and on 14 July 1911 (Matrix ai5182f, HMV 2-053065).[65] Again, we have a showpiece that offers itself as a splendid opportunity for the singer to show off their voice and win the applause of the audience, no matter how inconsistent it is with the dramatic situation and the scene. The lyrics, in Italian, were published in English translation by White, Smith & Co. in their *Artists' Vocal Album* of 1887.[66]

Deh, torna mio bene,	Ah whence comes this longing
mio tenero amor,	My heart why so sad
dà tregua alle pene	Why come tear-drops thronging
del povero cor.	That pain and make glad.
Per te questo sen	Tis love that alone
più pace non ha,	Such joy can impart
sol teco mio ben	Tis love that alone
beato sarà	Makes bright my heart.

As can be observed, the text would lend itself to any dramatic situation, upon condition that a couple of young lovers be involved and their love hindered by the intervention of a greedy father or a heartless suitor. The melodic material of this *aria di baule* (*trunk aria*) consists of a simple theme in D flat major that unfolds through a double eight-bar structure, to which three variations follow: the first and the third are more brilliant while the second is slower and characterised by long trills and small grace notes.

Tetrazzini sings a shortened version of this piece: the first eight bars of the orchestral introduction to the theme are cut, the whole second variation is skipped and a few bars are cut from the third. Of special interest is this last variation, in which Tetrazzini modifies some passages in order to reach the high D and E flat on concluding a repeated and brilliantly sung arpeggio figure.

Figure 22. Tetrazzini adds some modifications to Proch's third variation.

---

65 A third recording was realised on 11 July 1911 (Matrix ac5162f) but never issued.
66 *Artists' Vocal Album* (Boston: White, Smith & Co., 1887), p. 70.

The aria concludes with a short cadenza with the flute, as we can see from the piano reduction published in the *Artists' Vocal Album* in 1887 (Figure 23).[67]

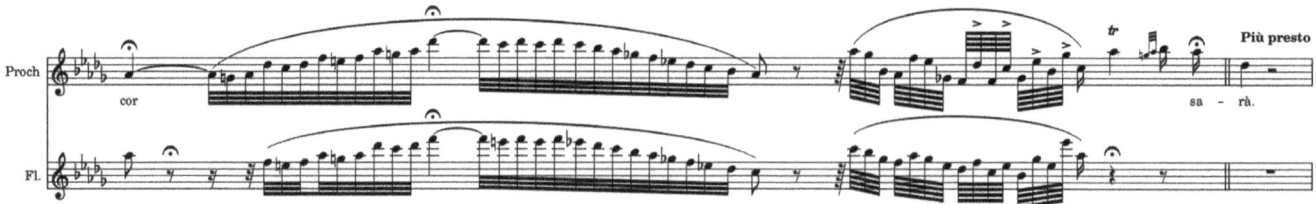

Figure 23. The cadenza with which Proch's *Variations* conclude.

In Tetrazzini's recording the cadenza, aside from some differences in the use of staccato, is enriched by the interpolation of an extra passage before the close, which, of course, allows her to indulge once again in the top E flat before resting on the high D flat (Figure 24).

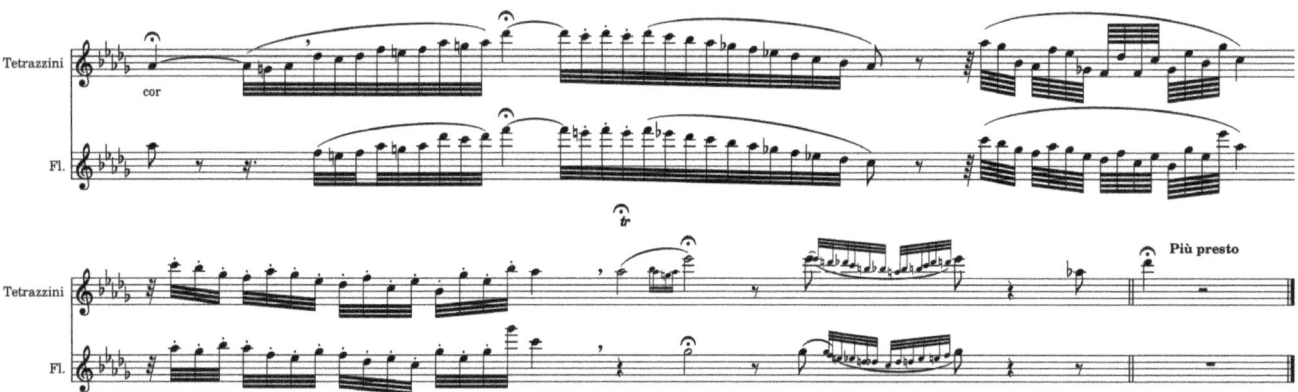

Figure 24. Tetrazzini's cadenza to Proch's *Variations*.

Tetrazzini was not alone in the habit of inserting additional passages into the written cadenza; at the beginning of the century other performers used to do the same and took a further opportunity to show off the voice in a longer vocal-instrumental arabesque. This is the case with Regina Pacini, who in 1905 recorded a version of this piece (Milan, Società Italiana di Fonotipia, matrix XPh 297, catalogue N° 39232), which includes the theme and the third variation only (3'15'' ca); although she is accompanied by the piano, the flute intervenes in the cadenza, which is slightly longer and more elaborate than the original. In November 1907 Maria Galvany recorded the Proch *Variations* (theme, first and third variation) with Carlo Sabajno conducting the orchestra for the Gramophone Company (Matrix 10894b, Gramophone 53526, DA 494, VA 46, Victor 87058); the recording does not include the flute, although the singer enriches the cadenza by adding new and original passages. Nor can the flute be heard in the recording realised by Frieda Hempel in 1908 with Friedrich Kark conducting the orchestra (Matrix xB 4330/xB 4331, Odeon 99217/99218, O-5532).[68] Tetrazzini recorded the *Variations* together with Clement Barone playing the flute on 18 March 1911 (Camden, matrix C10077-1, Victor 88307, 6336; HMV 2-053045, DB 523) and later at Hayes with an unnamed flautist on 14 July 1911 (matrix ai5182f, HMV 2-053065), and a few years later it was Amelita Galli-Curci's turn to commit them to disc. Again, Clement Barone played the flute in a new and slightly more elaborate cadenza (Matrix C20663-2, Victor 74557, 6134; HMV 2-053133, DB 265). In 1940 Estelle

---

67 In this collection, the aria is in B flat major.
68 Again, the second variation is missing, but the aria is split into the two sides of the disc and is ca. 4'38'' long. https://archive.org/details/1HempelProchVariationen/2+Hempel+Proch+Variationen.wav.

Liebling published a piano reduction of these *Variations*,[69] and included a first optional cadenza with the flute together with the transcription of what Tetrazzini and Galli-Curci used to sing, thus marking the end of a long period of performance practice and leading to its final canonisation in the form of a written, teachable, text-based document.

Encores

As we have observed, the showpiece that was generally used to substitute for the original aria in the lesson scene triggered the enthusiastic reactions of the audience, a circumstance that more often than not led to the diva singing a second aria as an encore. At least three pieces appear among those Tetrazzini chose in order to thank her devotees: 'The Bell Song' from Léo Delibes's *Lakmé* (recorded in 1907 and 1911), Julius Benedict's *Variations de concert sur Le Carnaval de Venise* (recorded in 1909 and 1911), and 'The Last Rose of Summer' (recorded in 1911). Tetrazzini made her appearance in Delibes's *Lakmé* six times in total over her entire career, starting in 1904 (Mexico City), then in 1910 (New York City, Philadelphia, London), and finally in 1911 (London, Chicago). The so-called 'Bell Song' is in reality the last section of the 'Scène et Légende de la Fille du Paria: "Où va la jeune Hindoue?"' sung by Lakmé, the title role, in Act II.[70] The role was created by Marie Van Zandt in 1883 and, in spite of many extremely difficult passages of staccato notes in the high register, this aria seems to defy our common understanding of showpieces, in that it does not offer so many opportunities for vocal display. The 'Légende' is mostly in a recitative style and only the Allegro moderato lends itself to a more brilliant vocalisation, with the characteristic octave-note figures imitating the bells (*imitant la clochette*) and leading to the final trill and top E to gain the final applause (the aria is in three sections, A-B-A', but the recordings are cut). The same can be said of 'The Last Rose of Summer', a traditional Irish song set to lyrics by Thomas Moore and characterised by a nice, melancholy melody far from typical bravura pieces. Tetrazzini, who sang this song on a number of occasions, recorded it on 15 March 1911 (Victor 88308, 6343 HMV 03241, DB 527). Instead, Benedict's *Variations de concert sur Le Carnaval de Venise* set to music a simple text that deals with a young lady waiting for her beloved one, whom she will be able to meet again after crossing the Laguna in a gondola. Here again, the variations offer a nice opportunity for vocal display and in fact Tetrazzini's recording features an elaborate cadenza as early as at the end of the first part, Andante con moto, which the well-known theme and variations follow.

As already suggested, Luisa Tetrazzini was following in Patti's footsteps: once the first substitution aria triggered the enthusiastic response of the audience, she indulged them and sang a second piece of a different character, maybe in a different language. The same had been done by Melba, Sembrich and Galli-Curci, the same would be done by other divas until the decline of this performance tradition between the 1920s and 1950s. By the time Tetrazzini sang and recorded them, both the showpiece and the encore had come to form a set of fixed and predictable components of this scene; each individual singer had a select repertoire of substitution arias to be used depending on the situation.

Semiramide, Queen of Babylon

Semiramide, a 'melodramma tragico' in two acts set to a libretto by Gaetano Rossi, was premiered at La Fenice theatre in Venice on 3 February 1823 and its length and musical style must have perplexed most members of the audience. The story of the Queen of Babylon was not new to nineteenth-century opera composers, and its first adaptation for the operatic stage dates back to the seventeenth century, with *La Semiramide in India*, performed in Venice in 1648. Of particular importance for the definition of the main character was Voltaire's *Sémiramis*, first shown at the Comédie Française in Paris in 1748, which at the end of the century inspired a number of operatic libretti. Rossi also drew on Voltaire and, having made the necessary adaptations, turned his drama into

---

69   Estelle Liebling, *Arrangements and Editings for Coloratura Voice*, Series I (New York: G. Schirmer, 1940), pp. 3–14.
70   Lèo Delibes, *Lakmé, Opéra en Trois Actes, Poème de MM. Edmond Gondinet et Philippe Gille* (Paris: Heugel, [between 1883 and 1889]).

a new libretto. The plot revolves around Semiramide, Queen of Babylon, who becomes a powerful and licentious monarch upon her husband's death. Many versions of this legend survive and in Rossi's libretto Semiramide poisons her husband, the legendary Assyrian King Nino, helped by Assur, Prince of the Blood of Baal. Semiramide now chooses Arsace as the new king and her husband. But, Arsace turns out to be her own son Ninia, who, long thought dead, upon learning of his real identity and the reasons behind his father's death, is now ready to take revenge. It is Nino's ghost who announces that Arsace will become king only when his death will have been vindicated.[71] In the final scene Arsace tries to stab Assur to death but accidentally kills his mother instead. Since the three main characters, Semiramide, Arsace and Assur are a soprano, a mezzosoprano *en travesti*, and a bass, Rossi had to introduce the character of Idreno, a tenor, to complete the typical operatic vocal cast.[72]

Rossini was undoubtedly familiar with this subject and must have had in mind the adaptation of Voltaire's text that Simeone Antonio Sografi prepared for a *Semiramide* set to music by Sebastiano Nasolini, which was first performed in Padua in 1790. In fact, Isabella Colbran, Rossini's wife and first Semiramide in 1823 Venice, had appeared in the title role of Nasolini's opera when it was produced in Naples in 1815 as *La morte di Semiramide*.[73] As had not been possible with most of his earlier operas, Rossini took his time to discuss the subject with the librettist and worked in a leisurely manner on the composition of the music. We can assume that he shaped the vocal part of the title role around Colbran's talent, although in 1823 her voice was not what it once had been. The fact that, when reviewing the opera in Venice on 6 February 1823 the critic of the *Gazzetta privilegiata di Venezia* failed to mention her cavatina may be read as a form of politeness towards a singer who could no longer keep up with her reputation. In his *Musical Reminiscences*, Richard Mount-Edgcumbe devotes a long section to Madame Colbran, suggesting how disappointing her performances had been when visiting London in 1824: 'She is entirely *passée*, and her powers are so diminished that she is unable to produce any effect on the stage, where she gave little satisfaction: but her taste was acknowledged to be excellent, and she was much admired in private concerts'.[74] Despite a difficult début, in Venice the opera was a success and would be performed twenty-eight times at La Fenice by 10 March.[75] In the course of the century *Semiramide* gradually disappeared from theatres, with occasional reprises here and there. Rarely staged at the beginning of the last century, the modern revival of *Semiramide* dates back to 1940 when it was staged in Florence, and then in 1962 at La Scala. The limited interest in this opera should not come as a surprise, since at the beginning of the twentieth century Rossini's comic works were more popular than his serious or tragic ones, and only a few remained in the regular repertoire.

Semiramide's cavatina 'Bel raggio lusinghier' adheres to the same two-part structure we have seen in *Barbiere*, with a first Andante grazioso (6/8) in A major followed by an Allegretto in common time (4/4).[76] The scene opens with a female chorus, with young citarists and damsels in various groups trying to cheer her up: Arsace is back and love is in the air. Semiramide's words echo the chorus and express her sense of relief: having trembled and sobbed for so long, Arsace's return gives her new hope.

		Andante grazioso	
Bel raggio lusinghier,	Beautiful flattering ray	A major	a $_{(2+2+2)}$
Di speme e di piacer	Of hope and of pleasure		
Alfin per me brillò:	finally shone for me:		
Arsace ritornò,—Sì, a me verrà.	Arsace returned,—Yes, he will come to me.		a^1 $_{(2+2)}$

---

71 Heather Hadlock, 'Tancredi and Semiramide', in *The Cambridge Companion to Rossini*, ed. by Senici, p. 142.
72 See *Tutti i libretti di Rossini*, ed. by Marco Beghelli and Nicola Gallino (Turin: UTET, 1995), pp. 735–56.
73 See the preface to Gioacchino Rossini, *Semiramide*, critical edition edited by Philip Gossett and Alberto Zedda (Milan: Ricordi, 2015), p. xxxiii.
74 Richard Mount-Edgcumbe, *Musical Reminiscences, Containing an Account of the Italian Opera in England from 1773* (London: J. Andrews, 1834), p. 153.
75 Weinstock, *Rossini*, p. 129.
76 The critical edition includes a first draft of the cavatina, which Rossini abandoned before orchestrating it, where the aria follows a single-section structure. See Appendix II in Rossini, *Semiramide*, Critical Edition (Milan: Ricordi, 2015).

2. The Rossinian Repertoire

Italian	English	Key	Phrase
Quest'alma che sinor	This soul that until now		b (2+3)
Gemè, tremò, languì...	Moaned, trembled, languished...		
Oh! come respirò!—	Oh, how it breathed!—		
Ogni mio duol sparì,	all my grief disappeared,		c (2+2+2)
Dal cor, dal mio pensier,	from my heart, from my thoughts,		
Si dileguò il terror... Si,	The terror vanished... Yes,		
Bel raggio lusinghier,	Beautiful flattering ray,	A major	d (2+2+2)
Di speme e di piacer	Of hope and pleasure		
Alfin per me brillò:	Finally shone for me:		
la calma questo cor	Calm this heart		e (2+2+2+2)
Arsace renderà	Arsace will return		
Arsace ritornò,—Sì, a me verrà.	Arsace returned,—Yes, it will come to me.		

The chorus intervenes again shortly in a *pertichini*[77] section, to proceed to the Allegretto, which makes up what is soon to become known as a typical cabaletta in A-A' form, with one more choral intervention before the reprise. The sweet thought of Arsace's love prevails, grief and sadness fade away, and the sparkling music conveys Semiramide's sense of cheerful anticipation.

Italian	English	Section	Key	Phrase
		Allegretto		
Dolce pensiero,	Sweet thought,	A		a (2+2)
Di quell'istante,	Of that moment,			
A te sorride	On you it smiles,			
L'amante cor.	The loving heart.			
Come più caro,	How much dearer,			b (2+2)
Dopo il tormento,	After the sorrow,			
È il bel momento	Is the beautiful moment			
Di pace, e amor.	Of peace and love.			c (4+4+1) fermata
		Pertichini		
Dolce pensiero, ...		A'		

The Andante grazioso section features a typical declamato-like vocal style, with a first six-bar (2+2+2) richly flourished phrase resting briefly on a dominant chord. The next four bars develop into a more assertive chordal figure that sets to music the words 'Arsace ritornò, sì a me verrà' (Arsace is back, yes, he will come to me), to which a more doleful phrase follows in the relative minor key of F# minor, to express the past trembling and sobbing. Having resumed the original key, the melody moves towards a more lyrical concluding motif. The Allegretto is characterised by an anacrusis figure that develops into a number of florid passages, which, according to the practice, singers used to change, as soon as they would present themselves for a second time.

---

77 The expression *con pertichini* (with *pertichini*) was used to indicate the intervention of secondary characters or the chorus, whose comments were interpolated in the main aria or in the recitativo.

'Bel raggio lusinghier' and Nineteenth-Century Performance Practice

When *Semiramide* was first performed in London in 1824, Rossini himself held the baton. The critic of *The Times* expressed profound scepticism and thought that the opera would never be popular.

> The plot possesses more interest than is usually found in the subject dramatized by the modern Italian poets, who seem to think that if they produce a given number of verses, no matter how trite and trifling, their work is done; the rest is left to the ingenuity of the composer, whose pleasant duty it becomes to clothe these poetical abortions in the rich robes of tasteful harmony. [...] The music of this opera is of an elevated and heroic character. Rossini felt that the personages introduced were 'the honourable of the earth'—princesses, princes, and warriors; and he has endeavoured very successfully to give them strains befitting their proud and lofty fortunes. We think, however, that the opera never will be popular. It is from beginning to end too abstrusely and elaborately scientific to please the million. To those who are well acquainted with the science of harmony, many of the marches and choruses will afford great delight; but there is little in the opera that can give pleasure to the lover of pure melody.[78]

About Giuditta Pasta, who made her appearance in the title role, the critic had little to say: 'Madame Pasta represented Semiramide with admirable effect. She wore her royal robes with dignity and looked "every inch a queen"'. Remorini, who sustained the character of Assur, was a worthy partner: 'We have rarely heard a singer with a voice of equal depth, who could introduce, with so much success, so many ornaments as this gentleman does'.[79] Interestingly, the critic refers to the bass role introducing new ornaments but fails to consider the soprano and the tenor; García's impersonation was said not to have been striking, although both arias for Idreno were maintained.[80]

Similar remarks were made by the critic of *The Harmonicon* who accused Rossini of blatantly borrowing from himself as well as many other composers, and to such an extent that his last opera may easily have been called a *pasticcio*.[81] To start with, for the opening symphony Rossini was 'indebted to the *Pastoral Symphony* of Beethoven, and the first subject of the last movement is very like a popular melody of Mozart'. The second part of the aria given to Idreno, 'Ah dov'è il cimento?' was said to be an inversion of Michele Carafa's favourite aria 'Fra tante angoscie': the cavatina for Semiramide had not the slightest pretence of quality; as for the ghost scene, the part was an imitation of 'the last incomparable scene in *Don Giovanni*' with passages copied from Mozart's music; the 'Preghiera', although 'its great beauty and pathos are undeniable, and the sentiment is most judiciously expressed', draws on 'E amore un ladroncello' from *Così fan tutte*, and on a cavatina in Winter's *Proserpina*.[82] The opera lacked originality, was far too long and showed clearly that the composer had out-Germanised the Germans. In *Semiramide* the orchestra was louder and heavier than any other predictably heavy German operatic work.[83] Not much was said of the singers and their interpretation.

> Having in another department of this work spoken at large of the musical merits of this opera, we have nothing to add upon that subject here. Madame Pasta is the main support of the piece, and is ably seconded by Madame Vestris. Signor García has little that is worthy of him to do, and Signor Remorini, who sustains his part well, gains no attention.[84]

Nor do we learn much from the review that *The Times* published in 1828, when Pasta was Semiramide again at the King's Theatre: 'Madame Pasta, as the Babylonian Queen, was on Saturday as powerfully effective as on all former occasions. Such is the peculiar influence exercised by her intense conception of great characters, that her latest efforts always increase the previous impression made on her audience'.[85]

---

78 *The Times*, 19 July 1824, p. 2.
79 Ibid.
80 See Rossini, *Semiramide*, Critical Edition, p. xxxix.
81 *The Harmonicon*, XX, August 1824, pp. 162–64.
82 Ibid. We can fairly assume that the author refers to *Il ratto di Proserpina*, a serious opera in two acts by Peter von Winter, set to a libretto by Lorenzo Da Ponte.
83 *The Harmonicon*, XX, August 1824, pp. 162–64 (p. 164).
84 Ibid., p. 167.
85 *The Times*, 21 April 1828, p. 2.

In 1829 it was Maria Malibran's turn to sustain the role of Semiramide and it was inevitable for the critics to draw a comparison between her and her predecessor.

> The vocal part of the character was given by Madame Malibran with great accuracy and effect. We might have said as much of her acting, had it not frequently forced comparison with the ablest personation of the character which has ever been witnessed on any stage,—a personation, no doubt, as fresh in the recollection of every opera frequenter who has seen it within the last five years at this theatre, as it is in our own. [...] Madame Malibran gave much dramatic force to the address in the 12th scene, wherein the nation is convoked to swear obedience to the new King about to be proclaimed; but it wanted the majestic dignity and the gracefulness of deportment which made it so impressive and interesting a scene in the hands of Pasta; and her slender and juvenile appearance was completely destructive of the required illusion.[86]

In the following years, more comparisons would be drawn between Pasta and Malibran, and the very fact that a comparison was possible meant paying the latter a great compliment. We have to wait until Giulia Grisi's impersonation in 1843 to have a first hint at those moments in the opera where the singer's interpretative decisions involving changes and substitutions may have made a difference.

> Grisi's Semiramide may stand by her Norma; it is one of those grand representations which this artist can give, seeming as if she merely obeyed the impulses of her own nature. A splendid performance was her *scena* 'Bel raggio lusinghier', with its nice expression, its brilliant embellishments, its delicate shading. Really tragic was 'La forza primiera'. It won a burst of energy directed against Assur,—we felt that it should have withered him; and yet how admirably did the vocal artist remain in spite of the impassioned actress. Seemingly hurried on by the rage of the moment, Grisi varied her embellishments when the air was repeated, and the effect was immense.[87]

Although it is not clear whether the critic, when talking of the cavatina, refers to the embellishments originally written by Rossini or those added by Grisi, in his review he draws attention to the cabaletta in the duet between Semiramide and Assur in Act II, 'La forza primiera'. When in 1843 this duet had to be repeated, the changes and new embellishments belonged to the interpreters. Similar comments accompanied Grisi's impersonation of Semiramide in 1846, when she was made the object of enthusiastic comments regarding her voice and dramatic impersonation: 'there is no other that can bring that weight of tragedy, that grandeur of emotion, that irresistible torrent of passion, which Grisi can throw into her characters of the highest walk'.[88] Grisi excelled in the brilliant 'Bel raggio' with the sparkling 'Dolce pensiero', and the conclusion of the duet with Assur, 'La forza primiera', was one of her most magnificent displays; however, no mention was made of the passages she may have inserted. Again, in 1847 *The Times* paid Grisi the usual compliments with regard to both the cavatina and the duet but no information can be gleaned from the review as to the addition of further embellishments.[89] In the following decade Grisi would be Semiramide in London almost every year, and only in 1851 *The Times* made short mention of the cavatina: 'The difficult cavatina "Bel raggio" was executed with remarkable fluency and one or two hardly perceptible waverings in the ornamental fioritura of the cabaletta, or quick movement, were overlooked in the fervour and animation of the whole'.[90] Again, from these words it is not possible to ascertain whether the ornamental fioritura the critic was referring to are those written by Rossini. We can only assume that, according to the performance practice of the time, the most proficient interpreters were both able and willing to interpolate new passages and add new embellishments.

After Grisi retired it was Thérèse Tietjens who had to take over the difficult responsibility of being as credible a Semiramide as Grisi had been. Still, no reference can be found in the columns of *The Times* to any possible modification in the cavatina when in 1871 Tietjens and Zelia Trebelli-Bettini were pronounced the worthy

---

86 *The Times*, 3 June 1829, p. 3.
87 *The Times*, 21 April 1843, p. 4.
88 *The Times*, 3 July 1846,
89 *The Times*, 7 July 1847.
90 *The Times*, 4 April 1851.

successors of Grisi and Alboni in the roles of Semiramide and Arsace respectively.[91] We have to wait for Adelina Patti to find some more explicit reference to the addition of embellishments and interpolation of passages in the cavatina, this time thanks to the intervention of the composer himself. According to Hermann Klein, when Adelina Patti decided to add *Semiramide* to her repertoire and sing it at the Kursaal Theatre in Bad Homburg on 22 August 1866, she managed to have Rossini himself write a new set of coloraturas and cadenzas.

> It is worthy of mention, if only for the fact that during this Homburg visit she made her first essay in the part of Semiramide. It was more or less of an experiment, but Rossini wished her to try it, and provided her with three entirely new cadenzas written expressly for the occasion. Despite her success in this role, she did not sing it in London until ten years later. It had long been associated there with the names of two glorious tragic artists, Grisi and Tietjens (the latter now at her best), and the public naturally regarded it as belonging exclusively to the repertory of a dramatic soprano. Rossini thought otherwise.[92]

This information finds confirmation in other contemporary sources, also suggesting that Rossini himself had written some new coloraturas for Patti. In 1868 the *Gazzetta musicale di Milano* reported briefly on Patti's appearance in Bad Homburg and mentioned the composer's intervention with regard to the cavatina and the duets between Semiramide and Arsace.

> Hombourg. Adelina Patti sang *Semiramide* for the first time and with brilliant success. It is well known that Rossini has adapted this cavatina expressly for her, together with the duets with the contralto. We can guarantee that the music of this opera fits wonderfully the voice of the famous songstress.[93]

When in 1878 Adelina Patti was Semiramide in London for the first time, singing at the Royal Italian Opera, she was said to excel in both dramatic skills and vocal style.[94] Again, *The Times* made explicit mention of Rossini's newly-written coloratura in the by-now celebrated cavatina:

> That Madame Patti, in adding this essentially Rossinian opera to her already varied and extensive repertory, has earned fresh laurels cannot admit of a doubt. [...] The great vocal triumphs of the evening were the *cavatina*, 'Bel raggio lusinghier', and the two duets with Arsace—'Serbami ognor sì fido' and 'Ebbene a te ferisci'. The first is profusely embellished by Madame Patti with extraneous passages and cadenzas; but as all the changes and *fioriture* were composed expressly for her by the master himself, the use of them cannot be regarded as otherwise than legitimate.[95]

This information is reported also in Hermann Klein's account of Patti's career:

> I remember the night well, more especially for two things—Patti's magnificent singing of 'Bel raggio' with the new Rossini changes and cadenzas; and the extraordinary effect that she created with Scalchi in the famous duet, 'Giorno d'orrore'. I thought the audience would bring the roof down.[96]

The evidence discussed so far is strongly suggestive of Patti's intention not only to follow in Grisi's and Tietjens' footsteps but to surpass them all, although it is not clear how and when she may have asked Rossini to write those new embellishments.[97] After her appearances in this role in 1866 and 1868 at Bad Homburg, in Germany, she sang Semiramide on many an occasion in the next decades, especially from 1880 to 1890. After London (Covent Garden), she would be Semiramide in New York (Academy of Music), Philadelphia, Chicago, St. Louis, Cincinnati, Boston etc.[98] Unfortunately, Patti never recorded the cavatina, nor do these variants appear in the

---

91 *The Times*, 6 November 1871.
92 Herman Klein, *The Reign of Patti* (London: T. Fisher Unwin, 1920), p. 173.
93 'Hombourg. Adelina Patti cantò per la prima volta, e con brillante successo, la *Semiramide*. È noto che Rossini ha espressamente ridotto per lei la cavatina e i due duetti col contralto. Assicurasi che la musica di quest'opera convenga mirabilmente alla voce della rinomata cantante'. *Gazzetta musicale di Milano*, 6 September 1868, p. 295.
94 *The Times*, 12 July 1878.
95 *The Times*, 23 July 1878.
96 Klein, *The Reign of Patti*, p. 194.
97 See also Henry Sutherland Edwards, *The Prima Donna: Her History and Surroundings from the Seventeenth to the Nineteenth Century* (London: Remington and Co., 1888), p. 123. See https://archive.org/details/primadonnaherhis02edwa?q=adelina+patti.
98 See John Frederick Cone, *Adelina Patti: Queen of Hearts* (Portland, OR: Amadeus Press, 1993), pp. 305–83.

critical edition of Rossini's *Semiramide* (Ricordi 2001). Instead, Patti seems to have taught Marcella Sembrich her Rossinian fioriture, and we should be able to find them incorporated, at least in part, in the recording the latter realised in 1908.[99]

Among Tetrazzini's immediate predecessors we find also Nellie Melba. She was Semiramide on 12 January 1894 and again in 1895 at the Metropolitan Opera House in New York but never recorded the cavatina.[100] Mathilde Marchesi includes this aria in her *Variantes et points d'orgue* (pp. 71–75) and offers a number of solutions. The same can be said of Ricci, whose transcriptions of embellishments from different singers include both the cavatina and the duets; unfortunately, it is not possible to ascertain to whom these variants belonged, since Ricci is not specific. Estelle Liebling also offers a few solutions in her *Coloratura Cadenzas* (1943), but, once again, she does not indicate whom these ornaments and variants come from.

'Bel raggio lusinghier' in Tetrazzini's Recording

As already mentioned, Tetrazzini never performed *Semiramide* on stage during her career, even though she twice recorded the cavatina. The first recording was made in London on 2 November 1910 with Percy Pitt conducting the orchestra (matrix 4578f, Gramophone 2-053034, HMV DB 537, VB 15); the second, which has never been issued, was made on 11 May 1914, this time in Camden with W. Rogers conducting the orchestra (matrix C14818-1). Tetrazzini's only available recording of 'Bel raggio lusinghier' is 4'18" long and presents a few substantial cuts (Figure 25).

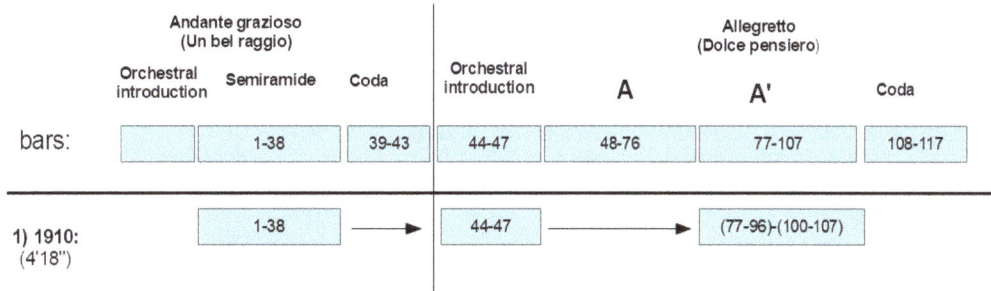

Figure 25 shows the cuts present in Tetrazzini's 1910 recording of 'Bel raggio lusinghier'.

The recording opens with the orchestra playing the final introductory chords before Semiramide's first entrance when the Andante grazioso is almost complete, at least as far as the vocal part is concerned. Only the final choral pertichini and orchestral coda are cut, to move immediately to the Allegretto. The fermata on the final orchestral chord represents a clear invitation for the interpreter to insert a cadenza, an instance of which, likely to have belonged to Marchisio, can be found in Ricci's volume (Figure 26).[101]

Unfortunately, no trace of this cadenza can be found in Tetrazzini's recording. The Allegretto is literally cut by half, and only the second part, A', is present, a circumstance that deprives us of the cadenza with which the A section concludes. For this cadenza many solutions can be found in the sources we have taken into consideration so far, that is to say Ricci, Marchesi, etc. In the second part of the cabaletta three bars are also cut when the vocal line approaches its close, and the recording ends on the chord that supports the singer's last note.

A closer look at Tetrazzini's and Sembrich's recordings (2 November 1908, matrix C6573-1, Victor 88141, 6356; Gramophone 053217, HMV DB 433) should allow us to check whether and to what extent any relationship

---

99   See Giancarlo Landini, 'Patti, Adela Juana Maria', *Dizionario Biografico degli Italiani*—Volume 81, Treccani (2014) http://www.treccani.it/enciclopedia/patti-adela-juana-maria-detta-adelina_(Dizionario-Biografico)/. See also Michael Aspinall, 'Rossini, il bel canto e Adelina Patti', *Musica*, 119 (2000), 58–61.
100   Thérèse Radic, *Melba the Voice of Australia* (St. Louis, MO: Magnum Music-Baton, 1986), pp. 189–98.
101   Ricci, *Variazioni*, vol. I, p. 72.

Figure 26 presents the cadenza reproduced by Ricci that concludes the Andante grazioso.

between the two divas exists and, if so, whether it is correct to assume that what Rossini wrote for Patti in the late 1860s and Patti handed over to Sembrich ever reached Tetrazzini. Again, the results show a mixture of old and new, with Tetrazzini featuring a number of passages that seem to have originated from personal choice rather than the model offered by Sembrich.

As can be observed in the opening bars, Tetrazzini's newly-inserted passages follow Sembrich's only to a limited extent; while the initial triplets at bar 3 are the same, the next long passage is clearly different from the one sung by the Polish soprano (Figure 27). Moreover, were the triplets at bar 3 from Rossini? It is impossible to say.

Figure 27 shows Sembrich's and Tetrazzini's recorded renditions of the initial measures of 'Bel raggio lusinghier'.

Similar solutions are present in the following bars, tentatively suggesting a line of continuity between the two interpreters (Figure 28).

Figure 28 shows Sembrich's and Tetrazzini's recorded renditions of 'Bel raggio lusinghier' (measures 4 to 9).

However, this line of continuity is blurred by a number of differences, as is strongly suggested by the close at bar 13 (Figure 29). Here, not only do Tetrazzini and Sembrich differ from each other, but their recordings also bear evidence of a marked individuality when compared to what both Ricci[102] and Marchesi[103] report.

Figure 29 shows Sembrich's and Tetrazzini's recorded renditions of 'Bel raggio lusinghier' (measures 11–15).

The closing phrase leads to a cadenza-like suspension, where all sources seem to converge into a similar solution, despite a few minor differences (Figure 30).

As already observed, both Tetrazzini's and Sembrich's recordings are cut, and no trace of the long final cadenza reported by Ricci can be found in either interpretation. A second cut concerning the Allegretto is present in each recording: section A is not present and the cadenza that bridges it with the reprise is also missing. Of this cadenza a number of examples can be found reproduced in both Ricci[104] and Marchesi[105] (Figure 31). Similarly, small differences appear in the Allegretto, which seem to suggest only a faint line of continuity between the two interpreters.

Tetrazzini's rendition includes a distinctive element in the final bars, when she inserts a diatonic descending-ascending passage to prepare the trill and lead to the final high A. This is not present in Sembrich's recording (Figure 32).

102　Ibid.
103　Marchesi, *Variantes et points d'orgue*, p. 71.
104　Ricci, *Variazioni*, p. 72
105　Marchesi, *Variantes et points d'orgue*, p. 73.

Figure 30 shows Sembrich's and Tetrazzini's recorded renditions of 'Bel raggio lusinghier'.

Figure 31 shows the traditional cadenzas before the reprise of 'Dolce pensiero'.

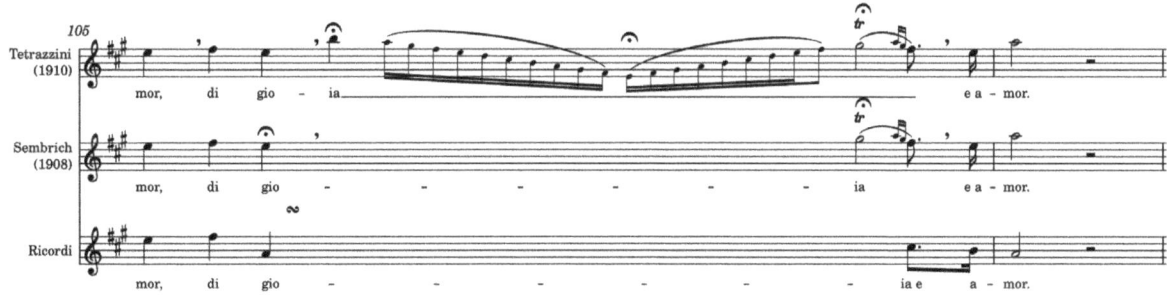

Figure 32 shows Sembrich's and Tetrazzini's recorded renditions of the final cadenza of 'Dolce pensiero'.

In conclusion, the idea that by drawing a comparison between Tetrazzini and Sembrich it would be possible to measure the distance between the former and a tradition that dated back to Rossini himself is only in part supported by the phonographic evidence discussed so far. While a few similarities may suggest a connection between the two divas and their renditions, many discrepancies indicate the opposite, and suggest that Tetrazzini may have followed a different, more personal path. Nor is it possible to ascertain whether and to what extent Sembrich's 1908 recording may have incorporated the Rossinian variants Patti may have passed over to her. Furthermore, many similarities in the choice of coloraturas, passages and cadenzas may easily stem from a consistent reading of the score, and a similar understanding of the harmonic language and the melodic contour among different musicians trained in the same tradition.

As already seen, more substitutions came to be part of *Semiramide*'s performance practice during the second half of the century; these can be found also in later sources; for instance, passages for the duet in the second act 'Se la vita ancor t'è cara... La forza primiera', can be found in Ricci,[106] who reproduces a number of variants belonging to the Marchisio sisters and to Bottesini. Unfortunately, no trace of these can be found in Tetrazzini's recordings.

The material discussed so far suggests how strong the connection between Tetrazzini and the nineteenth-century tradition was and, at the same time, how difficult it is to trace and identify the models that may lie behind her own interpretative choices. *Barbiere* must have offered Tetrazzini a wonderful opportunity not only for vocal display, but also to show off her skills as a delightful comedian. Her Rosina was said to be 'bubbling over with fun from beginning to end' and she showed no hesitation in sacrificing the beauty of her voice to the fun.[107] On the other hand, the cavatina of Semiramide, which she never sang on stage, should be considered as one of those many operatic old time favourites which found in the newly-born recording studio the springboard for reviving their success, despite the fact that the opera had virtually disappeared from the repertoire until the end of the nineteenth century.

---

106 Ricci, *Variazioni*, vol. I, pp. 73–77.
107 'Throws Tivoli into Giggles', *The San Francisco Call*, 4 October 1905, p. 2.

3. Donizetti's Operas

Tetrazzini made her first appearance in Donizetti's *Lucia di Lammermoor* on 21 November 1892 in Buenos Aires (Teatro San Martin), and *Lucia* is the opera that scores highest in her chronology; she sang this role in 113 productions over twenty years between 1892 and 1913. Verdi's *Rigoletto* follows at some distance with sixty-seven productions, while Rossini's *Barbiere* holds the third position with only sixty-one productions. If the bel canto repertoire was the one she felt most comfortable with, *Lucia* is probably the opera that gave her the best opportunity to exhibit her talents and show off her voice. Years after her début in this role, Tetrazzini noted that 'no opera could have been selected which gave me a greater opportunity, for Lucia's arias have more possibilities for the prima donna than any of the other operas'.[1] Three more works bearing the name of Donizetti appear in her chronology, although in a much less prominent position. Tetrazzini made her appearance in *La figlia del reggimento* (in Italian) twelve times between 1892 and 1910, ten times in *Linda di Chamounix* until 1902, twice in *L'elisir d'amore*, once in 1897 and yet again in 1907.[2] *Lucia*, *La figlia del reggimento* and *Linda di Chamounix* were instrumental in Tetrazzini's initial success; having made a few appearances in Italy in 1891, one year later she joined Raffaele Tomba's company together with Pietro Cesari and started gaining plaudits in Argentina. In addition to Donizetti, her repertoire then featured a few light comic operas, like *Crispino e la comare,* by the Ricci brothers, and Emilio Usiglio's *Le donne curiose* (set to a libretto by Angelo Zanardini drawn on Carlo Goldoni), beside Bellini's *La sonnambula*, Bizet's *Carmen*, and Verdi's *La traviata*. It is fair to assume that this repertoire was chosen to respond to the orientations of the conservative audience Raffaele Tomba was catering for in Buenos Aires and the Argentinian provinces. As already mentioned, Tetrazzini held Donizetti in very high esteem and cherished his coloratura music. In *My Life of Song*, she went so far as to suggest that 'the day will come, however, when there will be born another Donizetti. Then coloratura music will take a new lease of life. It may be that one or two great coloratura singers may first arise so as to inspire the new Donizetti. Yet he will come, and the world will assuredly welcome his advent'.[3] Great composers needed great interpreters. However, of the four Donizetti operas appearing in the diva's repertoire, only two are to be found also among her recordings, perhaps for reasons that have less to do with her personal inclinations than the rising discographic market: *Lucia di Lammermoor* and *Linda di Chamounix*. Tetrazzini recorded 'Splendon le sacre faci' from *Lucia* (Act II, Scene 2) in December 1907 with Percy Pitt conducting the orchestra and Albert Fransella playing the flute (matrix 2176f, Gramophone 053144, Victor 92018). Two years later, on 25 May 1909, she recorded 'Regnava nel silenzio' and 'Quando rapito in estasi' (scena, cavatina and cabaletta), in two different tracks (matrix 3077f, Gramophone 053223, HMV DB 528, Victor 92067/88303, 6396, & matrix 3078f, Gramophone 053224, HMV DB 528), again with Percy Pitt conducting. On 2 November 1910 it was the turn of 'O luce di quest'anima', from *Linda di Chamounix* (Act I, Scene 3), with Percy Pitt (matrix 4576f, Gramophone 2-053035), then again *Lucia* with 'Splendon le sacre faci' on 16 March 1911, this time together with Walter Rogers conducting the orchestra and Walter Oesterreicher playing the flute (C10068-1, Victor 88299, 6337; HMV 2-053047, DB 535). Later the same year, on 14 July 1911, she recorded 'O luce di quest'anima' (matrix 5179f, HMV 2-053061), to which she returned on 13 May 1914, with Walter Rogers ('Ah! Tardai troppo... O luce di quest'anima', matrix C14817-2, Victor 88506; HMV 2-053115, DB 543). As we will see, Tetrazzini's successful career is strongly associated with this composer, even though his

---

1   Luisa Tetrazzini, *My Life of Song* (London: Cassell, 1921), p. 74.
2   Again, these figures represent an estimate, for each production may have involved more performances.
3   Tetrazzini, *My Life of Song*, p. 313.

operas were often considered the emblem of an old and surpassed tradition, often referred to by London music critics as the 'palmy days of the opera':

> The 'palmy days' of the opera have faded away with the popularity of the works themselves. That is not a fact to be regretted, for, indeed, what was the opera house in its 'palmy' days, but a social institution, where members of society could outglitter each other in jewels, and where innumerable flirtations progressed with alarming rapidity beneath the combined influences of sentimental songs and dazzling chandeliers? A work of art cannot live in such an atmosphere, and opera was not a work of art, but a peg on which conversation and social intercourse could hang; at best, but a string of lyrical gems, oftener than of paste and glass, strung upon a thread of recitative—in short it was not organic drama, nor did it really aim at anything higher than to give the singers an opportunity of showing off their vocalization. It served its purpose and it has had its day; therefore *requiescat in pace*.[4]

Although not every critic shared with this author the same strong aversion to a tradition that many considered outmoded, a tension emerges from the folds of the contemporary critical discussion not only between old and new, but also between what was to be understood as a genuine form of art and what, instead, was musical entertainment devoid of any artistic value. In the background lay the figure of Richard Wagner and the recent achievements of a new generation of operatic composers. The discussion involved many issues, among them the quality of the libretto—which was often a pretext in the palmy days—the dramatic plot, and the role of the interpreters, especially the prima donnas. In this regard, fioriture were often seen as a pointless embellishment used by singers to show off the voice in a context in which the dramatic situation and the entire libretto counted for little or nothing.

The Performance Practice of *Lucia di Lammermoor*

As was typical of the Italian operatic culture in the first half of the century, the performance history of *Lucia di Lammermoor* is also accompanied by a number of substitutions and interpolations. Not only did Donizetti endorse a compositional routine that, in response to the fast production pace, forced composers to reuse musical material belonging to earlier, and possibly unsuccessful and forgotten works, but he also had to accept that singers would make changes and adapt his music in order to meet with their vocal characteristics, and their personal likes and dislikes. However exasperating he may have found singers' requests, and however strong his opposition may have been to those alterations (all the more so if another composer's music was involved), the performance history of *Lucia* features a number of such changes.

No matter how surprising it may sound to today's opera addicts and interpreters, evidence suggests that early nineteenth-century singers used to replace those very arias in *Lucia* that we now cherish the most and which, to a large extent, have led to its worldwide success in the twentieth century. It is well-known that Fanny Tacchinardi-Persiani, the first Lucia in 1835 Naples, chose Rosmonda's entrance scene (*aria di sortita*) and cabaletta from Donizetti's *Rosmonda d'Inghilterra* (1834) in place of 'Regnava nel silenzio' and 'Quando rapito in estasi', which together form Lucia's 'Scena e Cavatina'. Persiani maintained this substitution when she introduced *Lucia* at the Théâtre Italien in 1837, and Donizetti endorsed her choice when he decided to include this change in the printed score of the French edition of *Lucie de Lammermoor*.[5] Other changes are documented, such as the substitution of a different aria for the cabaletta in the fountain scene: in Pavia in 1837 Adelaide Mazza sang 'Nell'ebbrezza dell'amore' from *Ines de Castro* by Giuseppe Persiani; in 1838 Emilia Kallez made the same change in Novara; in 1837 in Florence Eugenia Tadolini replaced the original music with a double aria from Donizetti's *Sancia di Castiglia*; Eugenia García and Benedetta Coleoni Cori substituted 'Regnava nel silenzio' with 'Al pensier m'appare

---

4 'Why Mascagni is Successful', *The Musical Standard*, 9 November 1892, p. 405. See also Massimo Zicari, *Verdi in Victorian London*, p. 281, https://doi.org/10.11647/OBP.0090.

5 William Ashbrook, *Donizetti and His Operas* (Cambridge: Cambridge University Press, 1982), p. 210. Hilary Poriss has identified four productions including the same substitution; see Hilary Poriss 'A Madwoman's Choice: Aria Substitution in "Lucia Di Lammermoor"', *Cambridge University Press*, 13.1 (2001), 1–28.

ognora', from Donizetti's *Marino Faliero*; during the 1837–1838 opera season in Turin Mathilde Palazzesi sang 'Al sol pensiero del mio contento' from Vaccai's *Il precipizio*.[6] Palazzesi was instrumental in another important change when performing Lucia at the Teatro Ducale in Parma during the 1836–1837 season; this time, in the mad scene, she decided to sing Fausta's Rondo, from Donizetti's earlier opera *Fausta*. The choice resulted in a successful and well-reviewed performance, after which two more interpreters went for the same substitution in at least two productions: Giuseppina Strepponi (Bologna, 1837) and Eugenia Tadolini (Florence, 1837). As has been already suggested by Hilary Poriss, 'it is possible that not only did Lucia's final scene fail to make an impression on early audiences, but it was also outshone by Edgardo's finale'.[7] Palazzesi's decision is consistent with Fanny Tacchiardi-Persiani's; both must have felt uncomfortable with the idea that the opera should come to its close without a final grand aria for the protagonist. In fact, early reviews of the opera tend to pay little or no attention to the mad scene and prefer Edgardo's finale, a circumstance that may have led sopranos to consider a change in the score. A Grand Rondo for the soprano may have been thought more convincing, without altering the dramatic situation too much.[8] The early aversion to the mad scene is further attested by a number of instrumental transcriptions and pot-pourris that neglect the mad scene and include other vocal pieces in its place.[9]

Gradually, after its Naples premiere, *Lucia di Lammermoor* came to gain a permanent place in the operatic repertoire and, at the same time, the habit of substituting the Rondo for the mad scene was abandoned, with Donizetti's original music definitively restored. Once the original aria had resumed its position, it is not certain when the well-known flute cadenza made its appearance, and eventually became the most celebrated passage of the entire opera. Donizetti's manuscript indicates a dominant-seventh arpeggio for the interpreter to develop into a proper cadenza, as was customary at the time. In the printed score the passage leading up to the cadenza features the flute (originally a glass harmonica) proceeding in thirds and sixths with the voice, thus serving as an invitation to continue with the same figure in an instrumental-vocal arabesque. According to a prevailing tradition, the famous cadenza with the flute originated from Teresa Brambilla in the 1850s.[10] However, the first incontrovertible evidence suggesting its existence dates back to 1889, when *Lucie de Lammermoor* was produced in Paris, at the Opéra Garnier with Nellie Melba in the title role. On that occasion the critic of *Le Ménestrel* observed that 'After her mad aria, [...] [Melba] received ovations from all corners of the house. Here she had a vertiginous cadenza, in which she followed the acrobatics of Paul Taffanel's flute with incomparable mastery'.[11] A few leaves of white paper with the annotated cadenza that were added to the score and orchestra material belonging to the Opéra since 1847 confirm that the insertion was made in 1889 and later reviews of Melba's impersonations of the same role suggest that she went on singing 'the famous cadenza with flute'. This was the case when she made her appearance as Lucia at La Scala in Milan in 1893, on which occasion the critic of the *Gazzetta Musicale di Milano* had words of praise. Melba's voice was an exquisite example of beauty, evenness and width of compass; she sang the music as written by the composer, without all those baroque arabesques and fermatas, and with only a few traditional embellishments in the reprises; her technical virtuosity emerged only in the 'famous cadenza with the flute' where her performance reached perfection. Her triumph in Milan was such that the flute cadenza in the mad scene had to be repeated, on both the first and the second night.[12]

---

6   Ibid., p. 3.
7   Ibid., p. 13.
8   See also Romana Margherita Pugliese, 'The Origins of Lucia di Lammermoor's Cadenza', *Cambridge Opera Journal*, 16.1 (2004), 23–42.
9   See again ibid., p. 28.
10 See Guglielmo Barblan, *L'opera di Donizetti nell'età romantica* (Bergamo: Ed. del centenario, 1948), p. 125.
11 *Le Ménestrel*, 15 December 1889, p. 395, cited in Pugliese, 'The Origins', p. 31.
12 *Gazzetta Musicale di Milano*, 19 March 1893, n. 12, pp. 192–94. 'E il trionfale successo è pienamente giustificato: voce pura come il diamante; timbro dolce, insinuante eppure vigoroso; uguaglianza perfetta dei suoni in tutta l'ampia scala che da do basso ascende al mi sopracuto senz'alcun sforzo; agilità perfetta, nitida, perlata; buona pronuncia... Ma il pregio maggiore per me sta in questo: che non abusando della straordinaria facilità della voce, la Melba canta la musica *come fu scritta!*... non ghirigori barocchi, non rallentandi, non corone, ma la frase giusta, semplice, quadrata: poche e di buon gusto le tradizionali fioriture nelle riprese: nella *Lucia* il virtuosismo fa capolino soltanto alla famosa cadenza col flauto, nella quale l'esecuzione della Melba raggiunge una perfezione unica... La seconda rappresentazione della *Lucia*, ch'ebbe luogo ieri sera, confermò il successo: fu un nuovo trionfo per la signora Melba la quale, come nella prima sera, dovette ripetere la cadenza della scena della follia'.

When Mathilde Marchesi, who was Nellie Melba's teacher in Paris, published her *Variantes et points d'orgue* in 1900, she included three cadenzas for the mad scene. The first one carries Marchesi's dedication to Melba and coincides with the 1889 Paris manuscript, the third is a variation of the first, while the second includes a quotation of the reminiscence motif 'Verranno a te sull'aure' from the duet between Edgardo and Lucia in Act I, Scene 5.[13]

When first sung by Lucia in the duet, the motif presents itself as shown in Figure 33.

Figure 33 shows the motif as Lucia sings it the first time.

This motif is heard again in the mad scene: having murdered her husband, Lucia is in a delirious state and while uttering the words 'presso la fonte meco t'assidi alquanto', her thoughts go back to her meeting with Edgardo near the fountain in Act I, Scene 5. This time the motif is played by the flute and the clarinet (originally the glass harmonica), and works as a distant reminiscence of that moment (Figure 34).

Figure 34 shows the flute passage inserted in the mad scene as a reminiscence of the meeting between Lucia and Edgardo.

As mentioned before, we find the same motif again in the second cadenza that Marchesi included in her volume, this time with the voice singing a light arpeggio figure in counterpoint to the melody played by the flute (Figure 35).

Figure 35 shows the reminiscence motif from 'Verranno a te sull'aure' in Marchesi's second cadenza for Lucia's mad scene.

As has been suggested by Naomi Matsumoto, three more singers seem to have sung their own flute-cadenzas before Melba.[14] According to the *Pall Mall Gazette* when in 1868 Christine Nilsson (1843–1921) was Lucia at Her Majesty's Theatre in London, the orchestra conductor Luigi Arditi had provided her with a flute cadenza:

> Mdlle Nilsson's vocalization is always perfect and was never more so than in an elaborate cadenza written to the melody in question by Signor Arditi, with an obbligato accompaniment in which the notes of a fine toned flute serve to set off the superior beauty of Mdlle Nilsson's voice, and the skill of the player, her superior skill.[15]

---

13 Pugliese, 'The Origins', p. 35.
14 See Naomi Matsumoto, 'Manacled Freedom: 19th-Century Vocal Improvisation and the Flute-Accompanied Cadenza in Donizetti's Lucia di Lammermoor', in *Beyond Notes: Improvisation in Western Music of the Eighteenth and Nineteenth Centuries*, ed. by Rudolf Rasch (Turnhout: Brepols, 2011), pp. 295–316.
15 'Mdlle Nilsson as Lucia', *The Pall Mall Gazette*, 6 June 1868, cited in Matsumoto, 'Manacled Freedom', p. 299.

In the 1860s and 1870s Ilma de Murska (1834–1889) and Emma Albani (1847–1930) seem to have sung their own flute-accompanied cadenzas. In 1875 the latter was extremely successful when interpreting a very well-received cadenza together with John R. Radcliff (1843–1917), the flutist who invented the 'Radcliff system' flute in 1870.

> In the scene of the madness Mdlle. Albani, now a perfect mistress of her resources, gives fuller play to the emotions she wishes to portray than she ever did before, and the effect is all the greater. Her vocalisation here was always not merely distinguished by executive facility, but by varied and appropriate sentiment; and to this she now imparts dramatic as well as vocal expression, the interest of the scene being enhanced in proportion. The assistance she receives here from the flute (Mr. Radcliff) in the 'cadenza a due', where the instrument echoes the voice, phrase by phrase, cannot be overestimated. The whole display, however, ending with the melodious peroration, 'Spargi di qualche pianto', is admirable. The impression produced in the house was so vivid that at the end the singer was honoured with a triple 'recall', as unanimous as it had been well earned.[16]

Although it is not possible to determine its musical contents, it may be argued that the cadenza had little or nothing to do with the one Melba would sing a few decades later in Paris. In fact, no trace of the instrument echoing the voice phrase by phrase can be found in the manuscript preserved at the Bibliothèque de l'Opéra (MS A.549), where instead the parallel thirds and sixths continue until the closing trill. On the same occasion *The Daily News* commented on the flute cadenza and noted that 'the climax of [this performance] was attained in the great scena of delirium, commencing "il dolce suono" and comprising frenzied reminiscences of previously heard phrases'.[17] This strongly suggests that Albani's flute-cadenza included musical material heard earlier in the opera, as well as in Melba's second version published in 1900. Nevertheless, none of the cadenzas included in Marchesi's volume presents the echo effect described by the critic in 1875: with the exception of two trills in the first and second variants and a couple of ascending chromatic scales in the third, where the flute is echoed by the voice and not vice versa, the cadenzas proceed mostly in parallel thirds and sixths. Ricci's *Variazioni* also include a cadenza purportedly sung by Albani but, again, only a couple of passages present an echo effect, with no evidence of any previously-heard phrases.[18]

Further reference to the manner in which the mad scene was instrumental in the successful reception of the opera appears here and there in the press, and now and again explicit mention of a flute-cadenza is made by the music critic. Thus was the case when Marcella Sembrich was Lucia in London on 23 April 1881; on that occasion *The Musical Times* commented on her wonderful interpretation and the enthusiastic response of the audience.

> The first appearance this season of Madame Sembrich attracted a large audience on the 23rd ult. The Opera was *Lucia di Lammermoor*, the heroine of which is so well suited to exhibit the exceptionally fine qualities of Madame Sembrich's voice that her entire performance was a series of triumphs. Her singing in the mad scene was so admirable as to elicit an enthusiastic encore for the scena, with flute obbligato (excellently played by Mr. Radcliff), and the sestet in the second act gained so much in effect by her exquisite vocalisation that the latter portion had to be repeated.[19]

On reading that John Radcliff played the flute with Sembrich six years after Albani, one may only speculate that they may have performed the same cadenza.

If it is fair to assume that by the 1880s a flute-cadenza had come to be part of a performance practice shared among the interpreters of the earlier generations, as Christine Nilsson, Ilma de Murska, Emma Albani and Marcella Sembrich suggest, it seems also clear that Marchesi-Melba's 1900 printed cadenzas represent a turning point in the twentieth-century performance practice of Lucia's mad scene; as early recordings suggest, Marchesi served as a prototype for many singers of later generations.[20] What remains to be verified is whether, and to what extent, Marchesi's cadenzas incorporate, maybe in part, melodic material or performance models from the earlier generations. In this regard Ricci's volumes are of little help, since not all the examples he provides are

---

16 'Royal Italian Opera', *The Times*, 26 April, 1875, p. 9.
17 'Royal Italian Opera', *The Daily News*, 26 April 1875, also cited in Matsumoto, 'Manacled Freedom', p. 300.
18 Ricci, *Variazioni*, vol. I, p. 55.
19 'Royal Italian Opera', *The Musical Times*, 1 May 1881, p. 241.
20 See Matsumoto, 'Manacled Freedom', pp. 304–12.

accompanied by the name of the interpreter who may have originally sung them. Moreover, Patti and Sembrich appear with different cadenzas in the first volume and again in the *Appendice per voci miste*, thus making it difficult to identify which cadenzas each artist may have sung, and when.

Tetrazzini's Lucia in the Contemporary Press

As regards Tetrazzini, we do not know whether she inserted a flute-cadenza into the mad scene when first singing it in 1892; nor is it clear what she sang when she was Lucia in St. Petersburg on 22 February 1899, for the first time with Enrico Caruso in the role of Edgardo. Although the critic of the *Petersburgskie Vedomosti* suggested the role of the flute in the mad scene, his account is not sufficiently detailed to help us understand whether he was referring to the aria, where the flute plays a prominent role, or to the final cadenza:

> Already in the first aria one could not have asked for anything better than her coloratura which was shown off with full brilliance in the very difficult Mad Scene (the echoes with the flute demonstrated the singer's amazingly pure intonation). In the aria accompanying the scene everything was irreproachable—the scales and trills, and all those kinds of vocal tricks which Italian composers often try to substitute for lack of melody and dramatic effect.[21]

The only hint about the flute-cadenza is offered by the reference to the echoes; while the aria does not feature any of them, the cadenza Tetrazzini would record a few years later certainly does. Based on these considerations, one may speculate that as early as 1899, one year before Marchesi's *Variants* were published, Tetrazzini was singing a flute-cadenza that included the echo effect we find described in the columns of the *Petersburgskie Vedomosti*.

In January 1905 Tetrazzini was singing at the Tivoli in San Francisco, where she was immediately compared to Melba and Sembrich. When she appeared in *Lucia* on 17 January, *The Argonaut* reviewed her successful performance and emphasised the quality of her vocal technique and the easy manner in which she sang Donizetti's coloratura passages.

> Tetrazzini, the big little soprano, seems to fix her preference on the operas of the older school... Only a high pure soprano like her can scale such airy ladders of sound sending from each silver rung a spray of liquid pearls. Her voice is almost altogether made up of white notes and in effect her singing is as effortless as the flow of a running brook. It is odd to see how little she opens her mouth. Yet the tones come forth pure sterling silver, unalloyed by a single vocal blur resulting from misplaced effort. The real climax comes in the flute solo, which displayed not only the purity of Tetrazzini's voice, but the ease and brilliancy with which she duplicated all the chromatic flights of the flute.[22]

The last passage, although alluding to the presence and the importance of the flute cadenza, does not help us to reconstruct its musical content; the reference to the chromatic flights sung alongside the flute does not reveal much, although one may still wonder whether what she was singing in San Francisco was the same as what she would eventually record in 1907 and 1911. Instead, the review highlights a second issue of great import: the use of voce bianca, the 'white voice' which, as Tetrazzini would explain a few years later, consisted of a special use of head resonance for expressive purposes.[23]

In February 1905, Blanche Partington, music critic of *The San Francisco Call*, was also among the audience of the Tivoli where Tetrazzini was singing *Lucia*. The same night she attended a concert recital given by Nellie Melba at the Alhambra: both artists were in San Francisco for the season. Melba made her appearance surrounded by a small orchestra and a group of soloists, which included 'Gilibert, who develops as a thoroughly delightful concert singer; Sassoli, a young girl harpist who is a phenomenal sort of person; Ellison Van Hoose, an effective tenor, and Mr. North, a flutist worthy of his duties as obbligato maker to her majesty, Melba'.[24] The critic did not

---

21 Gattey, *Luisa Tetrazzini*, p. 26.
22 *The Argonaut*, 30 January, 1905, p. 72, also cited in Gattey, *Luisa Tetrazzini*, p. 46.
23 See Chapter One.
24 Blanche Partington, 'Melba Bewitches at the Alhambra. Queen of Song Charms Thousands in World's Greatest Music, Is not Tetrazzini's Equal in Tone', *The San Francisco Call*, 8 February 1905, p. 16.

miss the opportunity to draw a comparison between the two divas and highlight a few differences in the quality of their voices. While Melba, who was well past her prime, skipped a few notes in the high register, and even a 'cadenza or two' in the mad scene, Tetrazzini was in very good shape and could sing them all, including the by now 'immortal duel of sweets' with the flute.

> It is four years since Melba was here, singing the 'Mad Scene' from *Lucia* as she sang it last night. Of it and her I wrote then—in my young and enthusiastic days—'Her voice suggests as no other voice the word "perfect". It is the voice of which one has dreamed, dropping the "silver chain of sound without a break." It is as the lark's that at heaven's gate sings, crystal clear, each note pure as a pearl, from the merest silken thread of a sound to a round, full, victorious note of an infinite deliciousness of satisfaction. The suggestion of technique in the connection seems a fallacy and a superstition, yet it must be remembered that here to nature has been added perfect art, that highest art that conceals art. She has a wonderful staccato, drip—dripping its light and liquid note into the harmonious chalice of the orchestra below, or flying sheerly heavenward—where the angels probably make it over for home consumption.'
>
> I could not quite set my name to all of that now, that is as to last night's concert. There is still the same marvellous, absolute ease of method; still the wonderful liquid, fluty quality of voice, yet the voice had not last night the brilliant, sheer purity it had then. One got husky threads now and again, particularly in the upper range, which is possibly why the singer saved herself more than one top note—not to mention a cadenza or two—in the 'mad scene.' But it is a glorious voice, natheless [sic], so round and rich. Tetrazzini? Of course. Well, I dropped in for half of the 'mad scene' at the Tivoli last night—wading through six deep standing to get near to it. Little Tetrazzini and the flute were engaged in their immortal duel of sweets, and I had just heard the other. One may still be very glad of Tetrazzini. Of course, Melba's voice is larger, as I have before said, and it is sweeter, richer—richer now than when she was here before to my ear—yet the Tivoli prima donna distinctly has it in purity and freshness. And you got all the cadenzas. The curtain, too, fell on a clean, dazzling high note that Melba herself might have owned. We may be very glad of Tetrazzini.[25]

Unfortunately, Blanche Partington offers no detailed description of the cadenza. Two years later Tetrazzini would make her first appearance in London for the Covent Garden autumn season. She was Violetta in *La traviata* on 2 November, Lucia in *Lucia di Lammermoor* on 15 November, and Gilda in *Rigoletto* on 23 November, singing with Fernando Carpi, Giuseppe Mario Sammarco, Giuseppe De Luca, Edoardo Thos and Oreste Luppi; Ettore Panizza was the conductor. *The Musical Times* had words of praise and the critic emphasised that Tetrazzini's singing was testament to a long and still vibrant tradition in which, the critic reminded his readers, fioriture were not a pointless embellishment used by singers to show off the voice; instead, coloratura played a pivotal role in the dramatic scheme.

> The striking success of Madame Tetrazzini in *La Traviata* and *Lucia* at Covent Garden is a reminder that *il bel canto* is not as dead as many of the younger generation of opera-goers had supposed. Nothing in art that has ever been really alive—alive, that is, with true human feeling—can die; and the application of this truism to the present case is that the old and honourable art of *il bel canto* has been, and to all appearances will be again, the vitalising factor in opera. It has been charged with being a weakness and a snare; performances of the old Italian masterpieces have been sneered at as 'concerts in costume', and such mistresses of *agilità* as Jenny Lind and Patti have been disparaged as mere vocal gymnasts; but their triumphs have demonstrated, as Madame Tetrazzini's are doing, that even *fioriture* are more than decorative—that they have an essential place in the dramatic scheme of which they are part.[26]

After Tetrazzini's appearance as Lucia at Covent Garden, *The Times* commented on her interpretation and again a comparison was drawn between her and Melba.

> Her execution of scales and ornaments is almost comparable to that of Mme. Melba, and she has the power of putting a great deal of warmth into her voice. She has all the advantages of long stage experience, and is a very capable actress. Only in one respect is there a conspicuous defect in her singing, and that is that she does not hesitate to break any phrase in order to breathe quite comfortably. Of course this cannot make it very easy to accompany her, but Signor Panizza anticipated her every wish, and the music and action of the piece were kept waiting frequently while the new *diva* inhaled. Such a peculiarity is, of course, nothing very unusual with singers of all classes, and it would

---

25 Ibid.
26 'Occasional Notes', *The Musical Times*, vol. 48, no. 778, 1 December 1907, p. 787.

> pass without remarks if foolish *comparisons* had not been made with such artists as Patti and Melba, so that none but the highest standard can justly be used. Mme. Tetrazzini's singing is a true example of the *bel canto*, and it is most gratifying that the traditions of that art will be handed on for a few years longer. It is also probable that when the singer has recovered from a cold which affected the top note of one of her runs, she may prove to deserve to the full the triumph she has won. It is greatly to her credit that, in spite of her indisposition, she did not even have her music transposed. The 'Mad song' was admirably sung and the end had to be repeated.[27]

Not much can be gleaned from these notes about the manner in which Tetrazzini may have sung the cadenza, nor do we learn much about the presence of a flute. Instead, the critic found fault with Tetrazzini's way of breathing which, in his opinion, was at odds with the musical phrasing. Tetrazzini also gave four gala concerts on 3, 7, 10 and 12 December. Initially only two concerts had been planned, but the audience thronged the theatre to such an extent that it was impossible not to add two more nights.

In 1908 Tetrazzini was in New York, singing *La traviata* (on 15 January) and *Lucia di Lammermoor* (on 20 January); again she made a *furore*, again opera-goers thronged the Manhattan Opera House in their thousands. *The San Francisco Call* had the event fully covered by Reginald De Koven, its music critic.

> Never was verdict of an audience more spontaneous or unanimous, never was artistic success more complete and unqualified. Had Tetrazzini elected to appear first as Lucia I imagine that critical opinion might have been less varied and various, for there is no doubt that the role from every point of view suits her better than Violetta.[28]

De Koven argued that Tetrazzini was more remarkable as a coloratura singer than as a purely lyric artist, and Donizetti's music and vocal acrobatics offered her wider oppotunities to exhibit her talent than Verdi's dramatic style.[29] Even Lucia's cavatina was said to be problematic: 'the opening air "Regnava nel silenzio" was indifferently, even carelessly sung, with several lapses from pitch and a striking lack of color and resonance in the medium register, the music lying in the worst part of the voice'.[30] What De Koven was describing is consistent with what had been noted in 1905 about Tetrazzini's use of the white voice; the critic's remark about a surprising lack of colour and resonance in the medium register may be explained as a consequence of her using the 'voce bianca'. For the second time, doubtless, her expressive intentions had been misunderstood.

Things changed for the better with the cabaletta 'Quando rapito' when 'enthusiasm began and grew apace for in the singing of this number the great artist stood revealed'. The wonderful, birdlike facility with which Tetrazzini could sing trills and roulades was striking, and so were her intonation and evenness of sound. The cabaletta ended with 'another of those marvellous high notes, a D this time, whose effect was electrical in its intensity and power and the astonishing facility of it'.[31]

The D in the high register the critic referred to can also be found in Tetrazzini's 1909 recording, where in fact she sings her own variants and concludes with an ascending scale that rests on a fermata on the top D (Figure 36). Not one mention was made of the mad scene and the flute-cadenza.

In May of the same year Tetrazzini was Lucia in London, and the critic of *The Times* had to acknowledge her popular success; her feats of vocalisation were such that she was certain to be applauded. However, the critic was more hesitant when it came to drawing a line between popularity and refined artistry: while Tetrazzini's brilliant technique brought her popular success, one could search in vain for those details that would qualify her as a real artist.

> For the sake of hearing her reiterate a high note or execute a brilliant shake at the top of her register, all the various details in which refinement is vainly sought for are forgotten by most of her hearers, and the 'mad scene' was heartily applauded on Saturday as though it had never been sung so finely before.[32]

---

27 'Lucia di Lammermoor' (Royal Opera), *The Times*, 16 November 1907, p. 6
28 'Tetrazzini Is Triumphant in Score of Lucia', *The San Francisco Call*, 21 January 1908, front page.
29 Not every critic agreed with De Koven on this point; on the contrary, some of them pronounced Tetrazzini's Violetta one of her best achievements.
30 Ibid.
31 Ibid.
32 'Royal Opera', *The Times*, 4 May 1908, p. 14

Figure 36 shows the last bars of 'Quando rapito', where Tetrazzini reaches the high D, as also noted by De Koven in 1908.

One year later Tetrazzini sang Lucia again in London, together with Sammarco as Enrico and John McCormack as Edgardo. *The Times* reviewed her performance suggesting only a moderate success and presenting the same line of argument. Again, from Tetrazzini and this class of operatic works one could expect nothing more than a few coloratura passages nicely sung.

> Those who go to the opera in order to rejoice in the vocalization of the *prima donna*—and it is hard to imagine any other reason for going to *Lucia*—must surely have been satisfied last night, for Mme. Tetrazzini was in excellent voice and throughout nearly the whole opera gave her best singing, and its beauty was irresistible. But there was no crowd, and, at first, comparatively little enthusiasm. Even her prolonged high D at the end of 'Quando rapita' in her first scene (one of the few notes which were not absolutely pure in tone) only produced a moderate round of applause, and her delicately finished cadences, which a year ago were listened to with bated breath, seemed to cause very little sensation. Her admirers, who filled the upper parts of the house, waited for the celebrated cadenza in the mad scene, and contented themselves with calling for a repetition of this and cheering her heartily at the end of the scene. Mr. John McCormack and Signor Sammarco were as usual thoroughly efficient. Mr. McCormack's voice blended delightfully with Mme. Tetrazzini's in the first act, and he mourned her loss afterwards among the tombstones with proper intensity of feeling.[33]

It is fair to assume that Tetrazzini was singing the same coloratura and cadenzas she had sung a year before, as the reference to the top D suggests, even though this time her vocal technique did not appear to be entirely irreproachable.

Not much can be gleaned from later reviews, possibly also because *Lucia* had definitively established itself as a classic in the twentieth-century operatic firmament, and the flute cadenza in the mad scene had been firmly incorporated into the performing version, if not into its notated score. Instead, here and there music critics observed an improvement in the manner in which she now blended the different voice registers; Tetrazzini's use of the voce bianca may have undergone a development resulting not only in a smoother transition from one register to the other but also in a more uniform and even voice quality. In this regard, when she made her appearance as Lucia in New York on 27 December 1911, music critics expressed different opinions. The *Musical Courier* of 3 January 1912 approved of the diva's performance of *Lucia*:

> Mme Tetrazzini comes back to us in the full height of her powers, and while her marvellous facility in runs, passages, trills and all the other dazzling requisites of coloratura singing are undiminished in the slightest degree. Lovers of pure bel canto were delighted to find that she had added to her equipment a smoother joining of registers and a more liquid flow of tone production in sustained cantilena than she exhibited at the time she was one of the stars of the Manhattan Opera House.[34]

Again, we can argue that, over the years, Tetrazzini had come to gain better control of her voice, thus mastering a smoother transition from one register to the other.

---

33 'Royal Opera', *The Times*, 4 May 1909, p. 12.
34 Gattey, *Luisa Tetrazzini*, p. 168.

In general, by reading the reviews that accompanied her appearances as Lucia, we understand not only how contemporary music critics reviewed and often appreciated the manner in which Tetrazzini sang, but also how bel canto was conceptualised in a moment in which Italian verismo seemed to prevail over the traditional repertoire and Wagner's works had pushed music drama in a completely new and different direction. If, on the one hand, many commentators still considered bel canto a vibrant tradition that continued into the twentieth century thanks to a group of highly-talented interpreters, on the other hand some critics tended to understand it as an anachronistic form of musical entertainment of limited artistic value. While the first cherished the coloratura tradition and understood it as an important expressive device at the service of the dramatic situation, the second insisted that it was instrumental in showing off the voice at the expense of dramatic consistency.

Lucia's 'Scena e Cavatina'

Much scholarly attention has been paid to *Lucia di Lammermoor* and to those moments in the opera where the drama reaches its climax wonderfully supported by the music composed by Donizetti: Lucia's cavatina and cabaletta and the mad scene. Many an interpretation of their dramatic and musical contents has been offered, including discussions of gender issues prompted by the association of madness with women in the nineteenth century. In our case, suffice it to say that the lyrics of the 'Scena e Cavatina' 'Regnava nel silenzio' are set in two stanzas alternating description and action. The first quatrain sets the scene and describes the gloomy atmosphere at the fountain; then the ghost appears, communicating with Lucia by moving its lips (second quatrain); finally, on its disappearance, the water becomes red with blood, thus casting a bad omen on Lucia's destiny.[35] After an orchestral introduction (Maestoso) a first recitativo features the exchange between Lucia and Alisa that leads to the Larghetto 'Regnava nel silenzio'; a second short intervention of Alisa in the following Allegro serves as a preparation for the concluding Moderato. This four-section segmentation adheres to the conventions of the period, where typically a tempo d'attacco precedes a central cantabile and a tempo di mezzo leads to the final cabaletta.[36]

The Larghetto features the conventional structure of the Italian lyric form and presents a first pair of four-bar phrases in D minor (a_{2+2} - a^1_{2+2}) followed by a contrasting medial four-bar phrase (b_{2+2}) that hesitates on the dominant chord, to shift unexpectedly to F major.[37] This leads to a new four-bar phrase (c_4) featuring an ornamented cadential figure that rests on a typical subdominant-dominant chordal structure in F major. The second stanza presents different melodic material, mostly in F major, a key that seems to defy the sense of gloominess suggested by the lyrics.

Recitativo

LUCIA	LUCIA		
Ancor non giunse!...	Has not yet come!...		
...	...		
LUCIA	LUCIA		
Ascolta.	Listen.		
Regnava nel silenzio	It reigned in the silence	D minor	$a_{(2+2)}$
Alta la notte e bruna...	High the night and brown...		
Colpia la fonte un pallido	The fountain was struck by a pale	D minor - F major	$a^1_{(2+2)}$
Raggio di tetra luna...	Dark moonbeam...		

---

35 Mary Ann Smart, 'The Silencing of Lucia', *Cambridge Opera Journal*, 4.2 (1992), 119–41 (p. 133).
36 See Philip Gossett, 'Verdi, Ghislanzoni, and *Aida*: The Uses of Convention', *Critical Inquiry*, 1.2 (1974), 291–334, and Harold S. Powers, '"La solita forma" and "The Uses of Convention"', *Acta Musicologica*, 59 (1987), 65–90.
37 In the original manuscript, the aria is in E flat. See Ashbrook, *Donizetti*, pp. 146–47.

Quando sommesso un gemito	When softly a groaning		
Fra l'aure udir si fe',	Among the airs was heard,	D minor/F major	b$_{(2+2)}$
Ed ecco su quel margine	And behold, on that edge		
L'ombra mostrarsi a me!	The shadow showed itself to me!	F major	c$_{(2+2)}$ *(cadenza)*
		Larghetto	
Qual di chi parla muoversi	Moving like one who speaks	F major	
Il labbro suo vedea,	I saw his lips		d$_{(2+2)}$
E con la mano esanime	And with his lifeless hand		
Chiamarmi a sé parea.	He seemed to call me to himself.		e$_{(2+2)}$
Stette un momento immobile	It stood still for a moment		
Poi rapida sgombrò,	Then swiftly it cleared away,	dominant pedal	f$_{(2+2)}$ *cadenza*
E l'onda pria sì limpida,	And the wave so clear before,	D major	a$_{(3+4)\,cadenza}$
Di sangue rosseggiò!	With blood reddened!		

In the following Allegro Alisa comments on Lucia's words and on how they bode ill for her future. The final Moderato is a cabaletta and follows the nineteenth-century operatic conventions, with the first section repeated a second time, thus offering the singer the opportunity to add her coloratura and make her substitutions. The music is in G major, moving shortly to B flat major, expressing the feeling of blissful happiness in which Lucia is momentarily indulging.

ALISA	ALISA		
Chiari, oh ciel! ben chiari e tristi	Clear, oh heaven, clear and sad		
Nel tuo dir presagi intendo!	In your words I mean omens!		
Ah! Lucia, Lucia desisti	Ah! Lucia, Lucia desist		
...	...		
LUCIA	LUCIA	**Allegro**	G major
Quando rapito in estasi	When enraptured in ecstasy	a$_{(2+2+2+2)}$	
Del più cocente amore,	Of the most burning love,		
Col favellar del core	With the speaking of the heart	a$_{(2+2+2+2)}$	
Mi giura eterna fé;	He swears to me eternal faith;		
Gli affanni miei dimentico,	I forget my worries,	b$_{(2+2)}$	B flat major
Gioia diviene il pianto...	Joy becomes the weeping...		
Parmi che a lui d'accanto	It seems to me that next to him	c$_{(2+2+3+3)}$	G major
Si schiuda il ciel per me!	Heaven opens up for me!		
		Moderato	
Quando rapito in estasi	When enraptured in ecstasy	a$_{(2+2+2+2)}$	G major
Del più cocente amore,	Of the most burning love,		
Col favellar del core	With the speaking of the heart		
Mi giura eterna fé;	He swears to me eternal faith;		
Gli affanni miei dimentico,	I forget my worries,	b$_{(2+2)}$	B flat major
Gioia diviene il pianto...	Joy becomes the weeping...		
Parmi che a lui d'accanto	It seems to me that next to him	c$_{(2+2+3+3)}$	G major
Si schiuda il ciel per me!	Heaven opens up for me!		
		coda	

Tetrazzini's Recording

Tetrazzini recorded the 'Scena e Cavatina' only once, on 25 May 1909, but two takes were necessary to have the entire aria recorded.[38] The first take (matrix 3077f), corresponding to the Larghetto, lasts 3'18" ca. while the second (matrix 3078f) is 4'02" long. The Larghetto opens with the orchestral introduction (in 6/8) and closes with the chord on which the vocal cadenza rests. The first eight measures from Alice's short pertichini intervention in the tempo di mezzo have been cut and the second take starts five bars before Lucia sings 'Egli è luce'. The coda of 'Quando rapito in estasi' is also cut. Interestingly, the third bar of the orchestral introduction to the cantabile features a change in the articulation: although the score indicates pizzicato, the strings play legato and add a first, remarkably audible, ascending portamento between A and E and a second, descending portamento between C and B (Figure 37).

Figure 37 shows the change from pizzicato to legato with portamento in the strings at bar 3 in the Larghetto.

The legato in the strings anticipates the one in the voice and the portamento is strongly suggestive of the extent to which this expressive device was used not only by singers and soloists, but also by nineteenth-century orchestras. Evidence suggests that when playing in the orchestra, string instruments were expected to make portamento shifts audible as a means of tender expression, and not to hide them.[39] Tetrazzini's interpretation features some small rhythmic modifications and the addition of a number of portamentos, either to connect two distant notes or to emphasise the pathetic quality of a given melodic passage; she achieves this by taking the written note from below, even in a descending melodic contour, as is the case at bar 11 (Figure 38).

The first textual manipulation occurs at bar 15, where Tetrazzini seems to follow, at least in part, what Marchesi suggests in her *Variantes et points d'orgue*.[40] Her passages can be found reproduced also in Ricci's volume, along with two more solutions, all leading up to the top B flat.[41] On the other hand, in the following measures Tetrazzini does not include the short closing passages that can be found suggested in Marchesi[42] and Ricci.[43] Even the final cadenza is less conspicuous in Tetrazzini (Figure 39) than in both Ricci[44] and Marchesi.[45]

Something similar can be observed in the last measures before the Moderato, where Marchesi's four suggestions[46] seem to be more audacious than Tetrazzini's interpretative solution (Figure 40).

---

38 In 1992 EMI Classics published these two takes merged into one single audio track (7'22"), included in the CD-box *Luisa Tetrazzini: The London Recordings*.
39 See Raymond Monelle, 'The Orchestral String Portamento as Expressive Topic', *Journal of Musicological Research*, 31.2–3 (2012), 138–46. For the use of *portamento* in nineteenth-century vocal music see Deborah Kauffman, 'Portamento in Romantic Opera', *Performance Practice Review*, 5.2 (1992), 139–58.
40 Marchesi, *Variantes et points d'orgue*, p. 45.
41 Ricci, *Variazioni*, vol. I, p. 42.
42 Ibid.
43 Ibid.
44 Ibid., p. 43
45 Marchesi, *Variantes et points d'orgue*, p. 46.
46 Ibid.

Figure 38 shows Tetrazzini's small rhythmic modifications and portamentos in 'Regnava nel silenzio'.

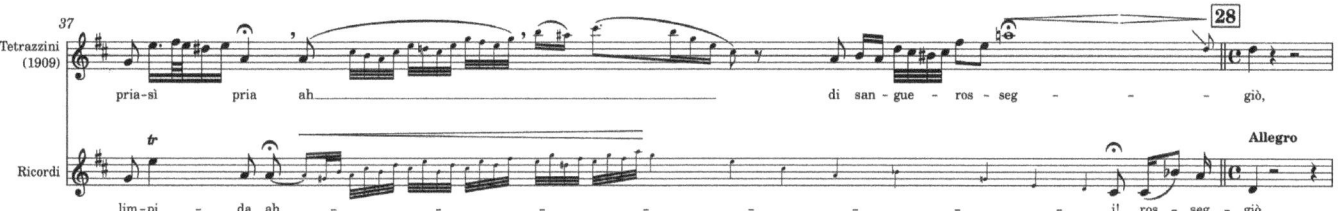

Figure 39 shows Tetrazzini's rendition of the cadenza that concludes the Larghetto of 'Regnava nel silenzio'.

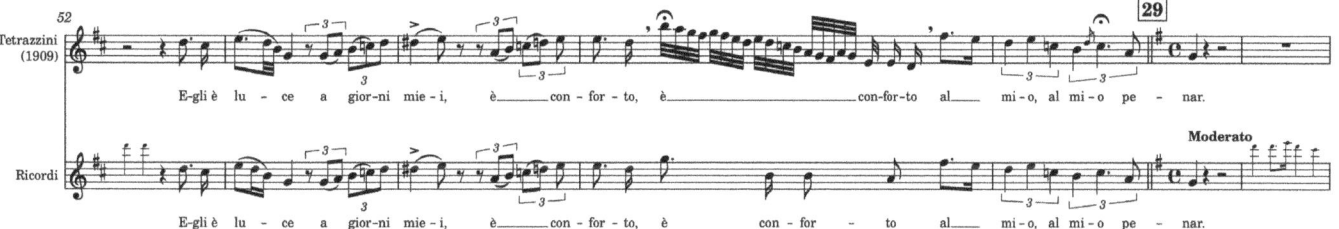

Figure 40 shows Tetrazzini's changes in the Moderato.

Tetrazzini sings the first part of the cabaletta as written, while some modifications are present in the reprise; these are similar to what is suggested by both Ricci[47] and Marchesi.[48] Instead, Tetrazzini's variants to the concluding virtuoso passages are slightly different from either written source and are instrumental in showing off her voice by means of brilliant staccato figures in the upper register (Figure 41).

---

47   Ricci, *Variazioni*, p. 43.
48   Marchesi, *Variantes et points d'orgue*, p. 47.

Figure 41 shows Tetrazzini's coloratura in the closing measures of 'Regnava nel silenzio'.

As already anticipated, Tetrazzini concludes the scene with a sustained top D, which some critics had already found worthy of notice in their reviews a few years before. This is consistent with what we have seen apropos Rossini's operas: once she had learned a role, which may have included a body of coloraturas, ornaments and passages, it was unlikely that a singer like Tetrazzini considered further extempore modifications. Unfortunately, Tetrazzini recorded this aria only once while neither Melba nor Sembrich ever recorded it, a circumstance that deprives us of a means of comparison.

The Mad Scene

As all opera lovers know well, in Part II–Act II the mad scene sees Lucia entering the stage dressed in a bloodstained, white night-gown after stabbing Arturo to death. Having murdered her husband, she is in a delirious state and while uttering the words 'presso la fonte meco t'assidi alquanto' her thoughts go back to her meeting with Edgardo near the fountain in Act I. Donizetti uses some previously heard melodic material, and while the motifs from 'Regnava nel silenzio' and from Lucia's wedding are barely recognisable in the orchestra, a clear citation from her love duet with Edgardo is to be found in the flute part, as already discussed.[49]

The aria follows the so-called customary form and the initial dramatic kinetic section is characterised by a frequent change of meter and by the indication recitativo in the score, which is used twice.

Coro:	Chorus:
(Oh giusto cielo!	(Oh, fair heavens,
Par dalla tomba uscita!)	she seems to have come out of the grave)

---

[49] See again Mary Ann Smart, 'The Silencing of Lucia', *Cambridge Opera Journal*, 4.2 (1992), 137–38.

Lucia:
Il dolce suono
mi colpì di sua voce!... Ah! quella voce
m'è qui nel cor discesa!...
Edgardo! Io ti son resa:
fuggita io son da' tuoi nemici... Un gelo
mi serpeggia nel sen!... trema ogni fibra!...
vacilla il piè!... Presso la fonte, meco
t'assidi alquanto... Ahimè!... sorge il tremendo
fantasma e ne separa!...
Qui ricovriamo, Edgardo, a piè dell'ara...
sparsa è di rose!... un'armonia celeste
di', non ascolti? Ah, l'inno
suona di nozze!... il rito
per noi, per noi s'appresta!... Oh me felice!
Oh gioia che si sente, e non si dice!

Lucia:
The sweet sound
Of his voice struck me!... Ah that voice
Has descended upon my heart!
Edgardo! I surrender myself to you:
I have fled from your enemies... A chill
Creeps into my heart!... every fibre trembles!
My feet falter! Near the fountain, with me
You sit... Alas, the dreadful ghost rises!
and separates us!
Let us take refuge here, Edgardo, at the foot of the altar...
scattered with roses!... a celestial harmony
say, do you not hear?... Ah, the hymn
sounds of a wedding!... the rite
is preparing for us, for us!... Oh happy me!
Oh joy that one feels, and does not say!

After the initial dialogic moment, the lyric session starts with the Larghetto 'Ardon gl'incensi'; an eight-bar melody is first heard in the orchestra (and the voice responds in declamato style) then is sung by Lucia ('Al fin son tua'), this time enriched by the insertion of short vocal passaggi with the chorus and the voices of Normanno and Raimondo in the background. Then the same melody is presented again in a varied form ('Del ciel clemente') to unfold into a vocal-instrumental arabesque with the flute. As already mentioned, a dominant-seventh arpeggio before the fermata serves as an invitation to introduce the cadenza.

Lucia:	Lucia:		
Ardon gl'incensi... splendono	The incense burns... around	$a_{(4+4)}$ (E flat major)	
le sacre faci intorno!...	the sacred torches shine		
Ecco il ministro! Porgimi	Here is the minister! Give me		
la destra... Oh lieto giorno!	your right hand... Oh, happy day!	*fermata*	
Alfin son tua, sei mio!	At last I am yours, you are mine!	$a_{(4)}$	Larghetto (Cantabile)
A me ti dona un dio...	A god gives you to me...	$b_{(4)}$	
ogni piacer più grato	every most grateful pleasure	$c_{(4)}$ (B flat major)	
mi fia con te diviso	will be shared with you	$c_{(4)\ fermata}$	
del ciel clemente un riso	from the merciful heavens a smile	$a_{(4+4+4+4)}$ (E flat major)	
la vita a noi sarà!	life will be for us!	cadenza	

A tempo di mezzo follows ('S'avanza Enrico'—Allegro, Allegro mosso) that leads up to the customary cabaletta 'Spargi d'amaro pianto' (Moderato); after Enrico and Raimondo's pertichini, together with the intervention of the chorus, the same motivic material (which adheres to the lyric form) is repeated a second time, to give the singer the opportunity to make her changes and add new passages. These two sections are not present in Tetrazzini's recordings.

Tetrazzini's Recordings of the Mad Scene

Tetrazzini recorded 'Ardon gl'incensi' twice. The first recording was made in London, in December 1907: Percy Pitt conducted the orchestra and the Dutch-born English flutist Albert Fransella, a prominent figure in the London scene of woodwind instruments, played the flute[50] (matrix no. 2176f, Gramophone 053144, Victor 92018). The recording is not complete, possibly because of the constraints imposed by the recording technologies: the opening phrase 'Ardon gli'incensi' is skipped and the orchestra starts with the Larghetto (6/8); the theme sung by Lucia ('Alfin son tua') is cut and Tetrazzini moves immediately to the following embellished phrase ('Del ciel clemente'). The take is 3'15'' long. Interestingly, a letter written on 22 April 1908 by Calvin G. Child from the Victor Talking Machine to Sydney W. Dixon[51] of the Gramophone Company makes reference to some of the difficulties incurred when working with Tetrazzini and suggests how hard it must have been to level the flute with the voice in the mad scene.

> April 22, 1908. Camden, NJ, USA
> However, I am indeed glad to know that you are going to make over some of the Tetrazzini numbers, as the records show plainly that she did not take quite all the care in singing some of the numbers that she should have, and may I suggest, if you do the Lucia Aria again, that the flute obligato should be suppressed just a little. In spots it is so loud as to interfere with the voice quite unpleasantly. Not with a view of praising our own work, but merely as an indication of the quality that appeals to me for a flute obligato, I wish you would try to hear our Gounod's Serenade by Calvé.[52]

Interistingly, the problem highlighted by Child can still be heard in the recording realised in 1907. In a previous letter Child had expressed himself in similar terms and had drawn a comparison with Melba. Even though Tetrazzini excelled in the higher compass of the voice, she could never cast a shadow on Melba's wonderful singing.

> March 9, 1908
> The records themselves are a great disappointment to me. While some of them show most marvellous technique in execution, great vocal agility and extreme ease in the very high notes, the voice seems to me lacking in sympathetic quality, and I believe that Melba's Lucia Mad Scene, even though she did not sing the 'D' or is it 'E' that Tetrazzini sings at the end, will be sought for and requested long after Tetrazzini's record is forgotten. With the possible exception of the last note, there is no comparison in my humble opinion in the two records, Melba's trill being far superior to that of Tetrazzini. Tetrazzini's 'Caro nome' I cannot understand ever having created a furore.
> I am not making these comparisons from a recording standpoint at all, but simply from the voice impressions, and I do not think that Tetrazzini's 'Caro nome' can be mentioned with Melba's, or even with that of Bessie Abott. The 'Voi che sapere' is not in the same class for a single moment with Madame Melba's. My admiration for Madame Melba is so very great that I must own up to a little personal satisfaction that the actual vocal comparison is decidedly in Melba's favour, at least so it seems to me, and I believe that it will not be long before the comparative sale of the records substantiates this.[53]

Child was not very appreciative towards Tetrazzini and in drawing a comparison with the American soprano Bessie Abott,[54] who enjoyed a moderately successful career at the Metropolitan, he did not intend to pay her a compliment.

Tetrazzini recorded the Larghetto again on 16 March 1911, this time at Camden (in New Jersey, US) with Walter Rogers conducting the Victor Orchestra and Walter Oesterreicher playing the flute (matrix C10068-1, Victor 88299, 6337; HMV 2-053047, DB 535). The Larghetto is complete and this time the take is 4'50'' long. Tetrazzini makes small changes in the rhythm and, contrary to the conventions of the time and to Donizetti's compositional idea, she also introduces some important changes into the initial melody, as can be seen in Figure 42.

---

50 See Robert Bigio, 'Albert Fransella: The Paganini of the Flute', *Pan*, 12 (1994), 19–25, and Jessica Ann Raposo, *Defining the British Flute School: A Study of the British Flute Performance Practice, 1890–1940*, unpublished doctoral thesis, University of Columbia, July 2007.
51 Calvin Child was Victor Recording Manager, while Sydney Wentworth Dixon (1868–1921) who had joined the Gramophone Company in 1902 as Assistant Manager and Company Secretary, between 1904 and 1909 was British Branch Manager of the company. From 1909 to 1912 he was joint Managing Director, with a seat on the board; in 1912, he became Sales Director. See Peter Martland, *Recording History: The British Record Industry, 1888–1931* (Lanham: The Scarecrow Press, 2013).
52 Document preserved in the EMI archive at Dawley Road, Hayes, Middlesex UB3 1HH (UK).
53 Ibid.
54 The American soprano Bessie Abott (1878–1919) was a pupil of Mathilde Marchesi and made a moderately successful career at the Metropolitan. See J. B. Steane, 'Abott [née Pickens], Bessie', *Grove Music Online*, 2002, https://www.oxfordmusiconline.com/grovemusic/view/10.1093/gmo/9781561592630.001.0001/omo-9781561592630-e-5000900277.

Figure 42 shows the changes made by Tetrazzini in the initial measures of 'Ardon gl'incensi'.

Her interventions are typical of the time: the elongation of the final syllable at bar 15, the addition of some small graces at bars 12, 14, and 16, and the substitution of the written passages in bar 18. The same happens when the main motif presents itself again: despite the additional passages written by Donizetti, Tetrazzini makes her own changes, as can be observed in bars 29–35 in Figure 43. Some of the small graces and passaggi sung by Tetrazzini can also be found in both Marchesi[55] and Ricci,[56] who says that they had belonged to Albani, Melba and Patti.

Figure 43 shows Tetrazzini's own changes in 'Ardon gl'incensi'.

As for the famous cadenza, Tetrazzini opens it with an arpeggio and a four-note figure echoed by the flute (Figure 44) that are not to be found in Marchesi's *Variantes et points d'orgue*.[57]

---

55 Marchesi, *Variantes et points d'orgue*, p. 50.
56 Ricci, *Variazioni*, vol. 1, p. 47
57 Marchesi, *Variantes et points d'orgue*, pp. 51–53.

Figure 44 shows the arpeggio and the four-note figure echoed by the flute with which Tetrazzini opens the cadenza.

Instead, the following passages, where the voice and the flute proceed together in thirds, are in Marchesi's volume;[58] the cadenza concludes with a long trill in the voice supported by an arpeggio in the flute part. The versions played by Fransella and Oesterreicher differ slightly in the concluding passage, with the latter repeating the arpeggio three times before joining the voice in the final trill (Figure 45).

Figure 45 shows the closing cadenza sung by Tetrazzini: in 1911 Walter Osterreicher plays a longer arpeggio.

A similar cadenza can be found in Ricci but the anonymous transcription he includes in his 1937 volume also features the so-called 'fountain' reminiscence motif alongside an additional passage; these are not to be heard in Tetrazzini's recorded interpretations.[59] Again, although it is clear that Tetrazzini was drawing from Marchesi's 1900 *Variantes et points d'orgue*, Ricci's volumes do not help us to understand to whom his transcriptions really belonged. In this case, one may wonder whether the extended cadenza transcribed by Ricci should be understood as the full version of what Tetrazzini used to sing on stage, and that had to be cut in order to fit into a studio

---

58   Ibid., p. 53.
59   Ricci, *Variazioni*, vol. 1, pp. 50–51.

recording. One may also wonder whether both Tetrazzini's and Marchesi's variants belong to a larger body of traditional modifications that, as we have seen, were shared by singers from earlier generations.

Linda di Chamounix, 'O luce di quest'anima'

When *Linda* was premiered in Vienna on 19 May 1842 with Eugenia Tadolini in the title role, it did not include the *cavatina di Linda* 'O luce di quest'anima'. Donizetti inserted the well-known bravura piece (without the customary cantabile) expressly for Fanny Tacchinardi-Persiani when she premiered it in Paris the same year.[60] In the recitativo (Moderato) Linda expresses her disappointment at not having met with her beloved Carlo but rejoices in the bouquet of flowers that he has left for her as a token of love. They are both poor but will marry as soon as he becomes a famous artist. The recitativo closes with a fermata where the composer writes two graces, thus suggesting that the singer could do the rest (Figure 47). This leads to a two-part cavatina (Allegretto), whose lyrics express Linda's happiness at the cheerful idea that they will soon be happy together. These consist of two stanzas,[61] with the first one repeated at the end of the second to accommodate the verses to the music. The cabaletta follows the typical two-part structure and consists of a main section which is repeated twice; the reprise is followed by a 22-bar coda. Both sections conclude with a short, written cadenza: at the end of the first section (A) Donizetti writes a simple arpeggio on the dominant chord, thus offering the singer the opportunity to consider inserting some additional passages; at the end of the repeat (A_1), before the coda, the composer writes a proper short cadenza. As we have seen with *Lucia*, Donizetti's written arpeggios are to be understood as a starting point, a springboard for further and possibly more adventurous additions. A third opportunity for vocal display is to be found in the last three bars of the coda, where two fermatas are strongly suggestive of a third opportunity for the singer to insert a vocal arabesque.

Lyrics		**Moderato**	
Ah! tardai troppo, e al nostro favorito convegno io non trovai il mio diletto Carlo; e chi sa mai quanto egli avrà sofferto! Ma non al par di me! Pegno d'amore questi fior mi lasciò! tenero core! E per quel core io l'amo, unico di lui bene. Poveri entrambi siamo, viviam d'amor, di speme; pittore ignoto ancora egli s'innalzerà coi suoi talenti! Sarà mio sposo allora. Oh noi contenti!	Ah! too long I have delayed, and yet I have not found my dear Carlo at our favorite place; and who knows how much he must have suffered! But not as much as I have! Token of love he left me these posies! tender heart! And for that heart I do love him, his only treasure. We are both but poor, living only on of love, of hope; Yet unknown painter, he will rise with his talents! He shall be my husband then. Oh, how happy we will be!!		
		Allegretto (A-A_1)	
O luce di quest'anima,	O light of this soul,	A (C major)	a_4
delizia, amore e vita, la nostra sorte unita, in terra, in ciel sarà.	delight, love and life, our fate united, on earth, in heaven shall be.		b_4
Deh, vieni a me, riposati	Come unto me, rest	B (progression on a dominant pedal)	$c_{(2+2+2+2)}$

---

60 Ashbrook, *Donizetti, Le opere*, p. 227.
61 See *Tutti i libretti di Donizetti*, ed. by Egidio Saracino (Turin: UTET, 1996), p. 1217.

su questo cor che t'ama,	on this heart that loves thee,	
che te sospira e brama,	that sighs and longs for you,	
che per te sol vivrà.	that for you alone will live.	A_1 (C major)
O luce di quest'anima,	O light of this soul,	a_4
delizia, amore e vita,	delight, love and life,	
la nostra sorte unita,	our fate united,	d_6
in terra, in ciel sarà.	on earth, in heaven shall be	

Tetrazzini sang Linda mostly in her early years. In 1893 she scored a tremendous success in this role during the winter-spring season in São Paolo and the summer season in Rio de Janeiro (Brazil); some critics wrote that her singing of 'O luce di quest'anima' was reminiscent of Patti's and her style was pronounced 'most persuasive'.[62] In 1894 she was Linda at the Teatro San Martin in Buenos Aires (Argentina) and at the Politeama in Montevideo (Uruguay). After a few more performances in South America in 1894 and 1895 she would appear as Linda on stage only twice, once in 1898 in Bologna (Italy) and once again in 1902 in Tbilisi (Georgia). On occasion, Tetrazzini continued to include 'O luce di quest'anima' in concert programs: for instance, on 26 March 1924 *The Times* published a short review of a concert recital she gave at the Albert Hall, where she sang Linda's cavatina alongside some other favourites from the old repertoire. The critic simply noted that these pieces 'were treated merely as a vehicle for her vocalization, and for that, one was as good as another'.[63]

Given the marginal role this opera played in her repertoire, and due to the lack of contemporary reviews describing the manner in which she may have interpreted the cavatina on stage, the analysis of her interpretative decisions has to rely uniquely on her recordings. She recorded Linda's cavatina three times, the first on 2 November 1910 with Percy Pitt conducting the orchestra (matrix 4576f, HMV 2-053035), the second on 14 July 1911 (matrix ai5179f, HMV 2-053061), the third on 13 May 1914 (matrix 14817-2, Victor 88506; HMV 2-053115, DB 543). While the earlier ones include only the aria (each ca. 2'54" long), the last one is complete and features both the recitativo and the aria (4'30" long). As already mentioned, little or no information can be gleaned from Tetrazzini's colleagues and predecessors with regard to the past performance practice of this aria, but a few comparisons can be drawn between her recordings, Marchesi's 1900 volume and the transcriptions collected by Karin and Eugen Ott.[64]

The recitativo is sung as written, with the customary appoggiaturas whenever the accented syllable falls on the downbeat (Figure 46).

Figure 46 shows Tetrazzini's use of appoggiaturas in the opening recitativo 'Ah! Tardai troppo'.

On concluding the recitativo Tetrazzini sings a long passage that closes with two more graces. Marchesi provides three cadenzas, which differ only slightly in the final passage: the first concludes ascending to the top C, the second presents an arpeggio between the two Cs, the third concludes descending from the top C (Figure 47).

---

62 Gattey, *Luisa Tetrazzini*, p. 15.
63 'Albert Hall Concert', *The Times*, 26 March 1925, p. 14.
64 Ott, *Handbuch*, pp. 338–46.

Figure 47 shows the fermata with which the *recitativo* closes, as sung by Tetrazzini and her senior colleagues.

Interestingly, Ricci offers solutions similar to those we find in Marchesi, but he refers to Patti in one specific case and more generally to Boccabadati, Brambilla and Tadolini in another.[65] Should we understand that Eugenia Tadolini, at some point, considered singing the passage we find transcribed by Ricci? And whose cadenza was the one he attributes to Brambilla? Marietta (1807–1875), Giuseppina (1819–1903) or, more likely, Teresa (1845–1921)? One may ask the same question when exploring the reference to Boccabadati, since Luigia (1800–1850) and her two daughters, Augusta (1821?–75) and Virginia (1828–1922), were all well-known sopranos. The aria presents a limited number of modifications, mostly in the use of articulation, tempo flexibility and small graces. Tetrazzini does not seem to take advantage of the opportunities offered by Donizetti himself as much as other singers have done. For instance, she does not insert a cadenza at the end of the first section when the fermatas written by the composer are to be understood as an invitation to insert a passage or two. Cadenzas for this bar can be found in Marchesi[66] and Ricci[67] (Figure 48).

Nor does she add a cadenza where the chord written by the composer before the reprise could be understood as a similar invitation (rehearsal mark number 58 in the score). Smaller interventions can be found in the reprise, where she modifies the melodic contour, although many more modifications and additions that can be found in other sources are not to be found in any of Tetrazzini's recordings. These sources include Marchesi, Patti, Boccabadati, Brambilla, Tadolini, Etelka Gerster, Marcella Sembrich and Amelita Galli-Curci. One can only speculate on why she decided not to adhere more strictly to an interpretative tradition that could count on many exemplary models; suffice it to say that this work did not remain among her favourites (see Figure 49).

As can be seen, the difference between how Tetrazzini approached Lucia and Linda is remarkable. In Linda she adheres more strictly to the text and even when the tradition offers a few models for inspiration, she does not seem to take them into consideration. Instead, in Lucia she takes all those liberties that the tradition had already incorporated into the performing tradition, and especially in the cadenza of the mad scene, her strong personality emerges clearly. This is audible in the overall interpretation and not only in the coloratura and the cadenza; in

---

65   Ricci, *Variazioni*, vol. I, p. 40.
66   Marchesi, *Variantes et points d'orgue*, p. 40.
67   Ricci, *Variazioni*, vol. I, p. 40.

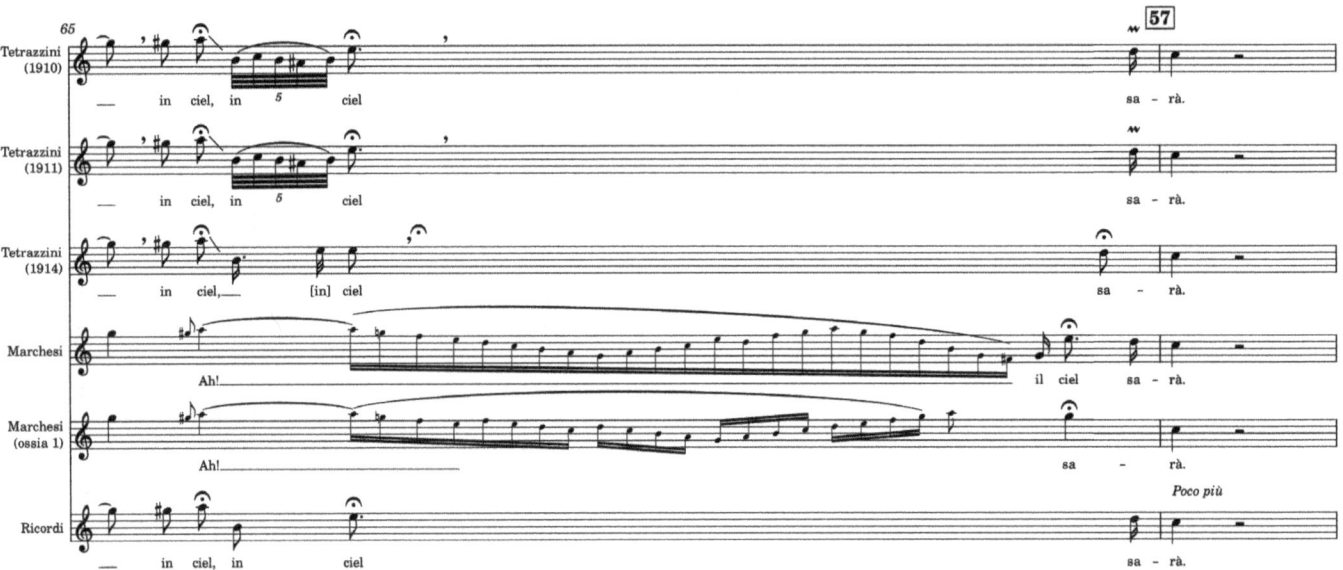

Figure 48 shows the fermata that concludes the first section: while Marchesi suggests two possible cadenzas, Tetrazzini does not sing any.

Figure 49 shows Tetrazzini's small modifications in the reprise of the aria.

this regard the difference between her and Melba's rendition is also worth noting. Melba's proverbial aplomb can be easily recognised in the homogeneous quality of the voice throughout the different registers and in the lack of large tempo modifications. Instead, Tetrazzini's means of expression translates into a number of inflections that affect every interpretative parameter. Tempo modifications and suspensions are comparatively large, the lower notes in the chest register are sometimes guttural—as opposed to the pearly quality she exhibits in the higher compass—and the use of portamento is more markedly audible. By comparing Melba and Tetrazzini it is possible to understand how differently such personalities as they, each with a different background and music training, could understand and embody the same tradition.

4. Bellini and the New Declamatory Style

In the course of her career Tetrazzini sang Bellini's operas on many an occasion, but only two titles feature in her repertoire: *La sonnambula* (1831) and *I puritani* (1835). However, before considering her recorded interpretations, it is imperative to remind ourselves of the role Bellini is assumed to have played in pushing the so-called bel canto style towards a more dramatic type of singing, in what was often described as the constant decline of Italian opera. As has been suggested, the collection of songs by Nicola Vaccai entitled *Dodici ariette per camera per l'insegnamento del bel-canto italiano*, which was published around 1838, may have been the first bearing the expression bel canto understood in this particular usage.[1] This expression came to be associated with the idea of a glorious past in which singers could keep their audience spellbound thanks to the beauty of their voices, as opposed to the much discussed dramatic style that prevailed among the younger generation. According to Rodolfo Celletti, terms like 'bel canto' and 'belcantismo' were unknown until the beginning of the nineteenth century. As he notes,

> they spread, in Italy and abroad, between 1820 and 1830, precisely at a time when bel canto opera was on the wane, giving way to other operatic trends and other styles more directly bound up with dramatic expression and at variance with the ancient concept of singing understood as beauty of sound and technical mastery.[2]

Celletti refers to those literary trends that accompanied the rise of Romantic opera and whose motto was the search for dramatic truth. Understood as the triumph of the free expression of feeling and passion over the canons of neo-classic tragedy, the idea of dramatic truth spread among authors like Victor Hugo and Alexandre Dumas père to exert a strong influence on both Italian Romantic composers and librettists. Among other things, Romantic opera was characterised by the portrayal of violent situations and the unrestrained expression of extreme feelings. This predilection for strong situations can be found also in Bellini, as testified by an undated letter to his librettist Carlo Pepoli: 'Carve in your head in adamantine letters: the "dramma per musica" [i.e., opera] must draw tears, terrify people, make them die, through song'.[3]

In composers like Bellini, Verdi, and to a limited extent Donizetti, this was accompanied by a gradually stronger preference for declamatory singing at the expense of florid vocalisation.[4] Many sources suggest how much concern Bellini's preference for declamatory singing generated among contemporary critics and commentators, some of whom mourned the passing of the bel canto. On 16 February 1829 the critic of the Milanese journal *L'eco* thus commented on the new turn taken by Bellini:

> He [Bellini] has taken up a method which we do not know whether it should be called sung declamation or declaimed singing. The goal of this method seems to be to combine the strength of declamation with the gentleness of singing; its danger could be that it confuses declamation and singing, and it causes monotony, slowness, interruptions and hesitation in the melody, and lack of motifs that please and stick to the ear.[5]

---

1   Philip Duey, *Bel Canto in Its Golden Age* (New York: King's Crown Press, 1951), p. 5. See also Martha Elliott, *Singing in Style: A Guide to Vocal Performance Practices* (New Haven, London: Yale University Press, 2006), p. 126.

2   Rodolfo Celletti, *A History of Bel Canto* (Oxford: Clarendon Press, 1996), p. 13.

3   Undated letter to Pepoli (but from May 1834); see Bellini, *Epistolario*, p. 400, cited in Pierluigi Petrobelli and Roger Parker, 'Notes on Bellini's Poetics', in *Music in the Theater, Essays on Verdi and Other Composers* (Princeton: Princeton University Press, 1994), pp. 162–75.

4   Celletti, *A History of Bel Canto*, pp. 188–92.

5   'Egli ha preso un metodo, che non ben sappiamo se debba dirsi declamazione cantata o canto declamato. Lo scopo di questo metodo sembra essere di riunire la forza della declamazione alla gentilezza del canto; il suo pericolo potrebbe essere quello di confondere

However, not every critic was against canto declamato and some even lauded it as a kind of antidote to Rossini's over-flourished vocalisation. Thanks to Bellini's new style, operatic music was given the opportunity to become more philosophical, that is to say more rationally connected to the dramatic text.[6]

In a letter that appeared in the *Gazzetta Musicale di Milano* on 6 February 1842 (one month before *Nabucco* was premiered) François-Joseph Fétis described the reasons why Italian opera lay in such a state of decadence: 'The exaggeration of declamatory style, the screams of the actors (for I do not dare to call them singers) and the din of the instrumentation have become a true necessity for the Italians; they do not understand dramatic music but under these forms'.[7] Twenty years later, when writing the entry on Bellini in his *Biographie universelle des musiciens et bibliographie générale de la musique*, Fétis confirmed his opinion, and condemned Bellini and his operas as the beginning of the fall of Italian dramatic music from the position it had gloriously held until the start of the century. This fall led to the deplorable situation in which musical Italy still remained, also owing to the manner in which Giuseppe Verdi had taken up Bellini's bad example.

> If one examines with attention the transformation of Italian dramatic music operated by Bellini's style, a transformation continued by Donizetti with less originality but with a much superior talent, one should not underestimate the tendencies which, while manifesting themselves more and more, have destroyed the beautiful art of Italian singing and replaced them with the production of forced voices thus leading fatally to the deplorable system of Verdi and his imitators.[8]

Back in 1842—only a couple of months after the appearance of Fétis' letter—Alberto Mazzucato reviewed Manuel García's *Method*, which he had translated into Italian, in the columns of the *Gazzetta Musicale di Milano*.[9] In commenting on the change that occurred between 1820 and 1840 in the Italian singing style he suggested that this was well illustrated by two star singers, Domenico Donzelli (1790–1873) who represented 'the school of twenty years ago' and Napoleone Moriani (1808–1878), who embodied the 'modern singer'. Among others, Donzelli's vocal style was characterised by the use of the so-called *voix sombrée*, a technique traditionally associated with the French tenor Gilbert-Louis Duprez (1806–1896), who is assumed to have been the first to use the chest register to reach the high C when singing the role of Arnold in Rossini's *Guillaume Tell* in 1837.[10] According to Mazzucato, Donzelli also used the *voix sombre* in 1839, when singing the *aria di sortita* in Saverio Mercadante's *Il bravo*. A second component of the so-called old style as represented by Donzelli was the constant use he made of

---

declamazione e canto, e produrre monotonia, lentezza, spezzatura, e titubanza nella cantilena, e mancanza di motivi che allettino, e rimangano nell'orecchio.' *L'eco*, 16 February 1829, n. 20, cited in Maria Rosaria Adamo and Friederich Lippmann, *Vincenzo Bellini* (Turin: ERI, 1981), p. 466.

6 Melina Esse, 'Speaking and Sighing: Bellini's *canto declamato* and the Poetics of Restraint', *Current Musicology*, 87 (2009), 7–45, https://openmusiclibrary.org/article/49112/.

7 'L'esagerazione dello stile declamatorio, i gridi degli attori, (chè non oso chiamarli cantanti) e lo strepito dell'istromentazione sono diventate vere necessità per gli Italiani; essi più non comprendono la musica drammatica se non se sotto queste forme'. François-Joseph Fétis, 'Discussioni Musicali, Seconda lettera del signor Fétis, intorno allo stato presente delle arti musicali in Italia', *Gazzetta Musicale di Milano*, 6 February 1842, p. 22. It is worth noting that the same complaints had accompanied the rise of Rossini about thirty years earlier.

8 'Si l'on examine avec attention la transformation opérée dans la musique dramatique de l'Italie par le style de Bellini, transformation continue par Donizetti avec moins d'originalité, mais avec un talent de facture très-supérieur, on ne peut méconnaître les tendances qui, se prononçant de plus en plus, ont anéanti le bel art du chant italien, lui ont substitué les émissions de voix forcées, et ont conduit fatalement au déplorable système de Verdi et de ses imitateurs' [my translation]. François-Joseph Fétis, 'Bellini, Vincent', in *Biographie universelle des musiciens et bibliographie générale de la musique* (Paris: Didot, 1860–1865), vol. I, p. 328, cited in Jean Littlejohn, 'France Meets Bellini, the Critical Reaction of François-Joseph Fétis', in *Vincenzo Bellini et la France: Histoire, création et réception de l'œuvre*, ed. by Maria Rosa De Luca, Salvatore Enrico Failla, Giuseppe Montenagno (Lucca: Libreria Musicale Italiana, 2007), p. 744.

9 Alberto Mazzucato, 'Il vecchio ed il moderno metodo di canto. Preliminari ad un esame critico sul *Metodo di Canto* di Garcia', *Gazzetta Musicale di Milano*, 3 April 1842, p. 55. The first volume of García's method had appeared in January that year: *Scuola di Garcia. Trattato completo dell'arte del canto, di Emanuele Garcia figlio, tradotto dal francese da Alberto Mazzucato* (Milan: R. Stabilimento Musicale Tito di Gio. Ricordi, 1842). The year of publication can be derived from the catalogue of publications of Casa Ricordi: http://www.archivioricordi.com/assets/img/clippy.svg.

10 Mazzucato, 'Il vecchio ed il moderno', p. 56. On concluding his article, however, Mazzucato, who was then only twenty-nine, confessed to be too young to have been able to witness this change. Manuel García also claims to have been the father of the *voix sombre*. See James Stark, *Bel Canto: A History of Vocal Pedagogy* (Toronto: University of Toronto Press, 1999), p. 41.

portamentos, which often covered large intervals, up to ten or even twelve notes.[11] One last feature was the fancy combination of a portamento and a gruppetto, with which Donzelli used to enrich the execution of recitatives, especially at the end of a plain verse.[12] All this, in addition to the customary repertoire of ornaments, passages, roulades, trills, and arpeggios, whether written by the composer or substituted by the interpreter. Unfortunately, the article concerning the characteristics of the modern voice published in the *Gazzetta di Milano* in the years 1842 and 1843 cannot be found. Nevertheless, it is clear that Mazzucato shared with Fétis the opinion that a dramatic change had occurred in the recent development of the so-called bel canto. What is not as clear is whether he considered this change an improvement or, like Fétis, a drawback. Most importantly, Mazzucato describes the use of expressive devices that, even though they were associated with the past tradition, were still used by singers of the younger generations, as was the case with portamento.

In the 1860s Francesco Lamperti opened his singing method with an introductory chapter entitled 'On the Decadence of the Art of Singing', where he reviewed the reasons why this ancient and illustrious art lay in such a deplorable state of decadence. One of them was the declamatory character which now prevailed over florid singing:

> Vocal music, in order to assume a more dramatic character, is almost entirely despoiled of agility of every kind; this is carried to such an extent that by degrees it will become little else than musical declamation, to the total exclusion of melody. Without entering here into the question whether or not any advantage may accrue to musical science through these innovations, I shall only briefly observe that as the singing of melodies, though not absolutely true to nature, is yet productive of much pleasure to the audience; it seems to me a pity that the melodramatic system should be exchanged for one perhaps more realistic, but which tends to the exclusion of melody, and is hence detrimental to the art of singing.[13]

Lamperti longed for that long-gone epoch in which castratos still dominated the operatic firmament, and regretted that a gradual shift in the use of the voice had accompanied the recent development of vocal composition: 'To these reasons may be added what I shall term the *spostamento della voce,* by which I mean the present habit of considering as mezzo-soprano the dramatic soprano of the past, and of making mezzo-sopranos sing also the parts written for contraltos, hence the almost total disappearance of music written for the true contralto voice in the modern repertoire'.[14] All in all, it was Bellini who had initiated this regrettable change.

> Bellini was the first to write parts of an exceptional range, and what was more, he introduced the system of putting a syllable to every note, thus rendering his music more fatiguing to the voice. His successors exaggerated his mannerism, as much in respect to range as in the arrangement of the words. Much of this displacement may be attributed to these reasons, coupled with the fact that syllabication in this music had in a great part to be executed by the head notes, which in men's voices, on account of their limited compass, was impracticable, and in women's, productive of much harm.[15]

A case in point in this regard was Sophie Löwe, whom Lamperti took as a perfect example of the dramatic consequences caused by such a change: having embraced the modern repertoire, at some point she was no longer able to replicate the wonders with which she had made her initial appearance in Donizetti's *Maria Padilla* in 1841.[16] Lamperti went as far as to recommend young singers to stay away from Donizetti and Bellini; their works, he claimed, were harmful to the female voice, and for this reason songstresses should confine themselves to Rossini's masterpieces.[17]

---

11   In the same article Mazzucato describes these *portamentos* as 'certe solenni stiracchiature o portamenti di voce ascendenti adoperati all'attacco delle note, i quali senza esagerazione, avevano l'estensione ascendente della decima, e spesso anche della duodecima, e talora anche molto più', ibid.
12   Ibid.
13   Francesco Lamperti, *The Art of Singing* (New York: Schirmer, 1890), p. 2, originally published in Italian as *Guida Teorico-Pratica-Elementare per lo studio del canto dettata dal Prof. Francesco Lamperti per le sue Allieve del R. Conservatorio di musica di Milano* (Milan: Ricordi [1864]), p. vi.
14   Ibid., p. 3.
15   Ibid., pp. 3–4.
16   Lamperti, *Guida Teorico-Pratica-Elementare*, p. vii.
17   Ibid., p. 49. Surprisingly, Lamperti does not mention the name of Verdi, whose operas had long been considered by contemporary critics as harmful to both male and female singers.

In spite of Lamperti's recommendations, by the 1860s the works of Bellini and Verdi had come to hold a prominent position alongside the traditional bel canto repertoire represented by Rossini and, to some extent, Donizetti; singers from the younger generations were now expected to excel in works belonging to either repertoire. Adelina Patti (1843–1919) is a case in point: during a life-long career she won the admiration of the most severe international critics and was soon recognised as an interpreter endowed with the intelligence necessary to extend her repertoire, assume new dramatic roles and still make a clear distinction between different compositional styles. In 1863 she proved that a properly trained and highly-talented singer could master Mozart's *Don Giovanni*, a model of classical composure, Rossini's *Barbiere*, a benchmark for the florid bel canto style, and Verdi's new dramatised style with equal success.[18] On reviewing her Rosina in 1884 at Covent Garden, the critic of *The Times* commented on how, thanks to her enormous talent and 'by dint of study and perseverance', she had been able to excel in this role as well as in *Aida* and *Semiramide*.

> Rosina belongs to a class of parts to which the famous *prima donna* owes her earliest successes among us, and in which she still is most at home. By dint of study and perseverance she has in the course of years acquired a touch of the majestic qualities which go to the making of Nubian princesses and Assyrian queens, and her Aida and Semiramide are in their way triumphs of art over natural bias. Where, however, as in the lighter characters above referred to, art and nature can go hand in hand, the result is, of course, still more harmonious, and in the case we are speaking of is not likely to be surpassed by any artist now on the lyrical stage.[19]

Contrary to what Lamperti claimed when talking of Sophie Löwe, it was possible to embrace both the modern and the old repertoire without harming one's voice on condition that the singer in question be endowed not only with a wonderful voice, but also with great intelligence and strong determination. Furthermore, exceptionally talented singers continued to represent an incredibly rich source of inspiration for those accomplished composers who, like Bellini, Donizetti and Verdi after Rossini and Mozart, often moulded their melodies with a specific voice in mind. It is well-known that Bellini wrote the roles of Norma and Amina for Giuditta Pasta, whose wonderful vocal and dramatic skills Stendhal praised in his monograph on Rossini's life and career. Stendhal described how she enchanted the audiences and held them spellbound thanks to 'a voice whose compelling inflections can subdue the most recalcitrant and obdurate of hearts, and oblige them to share in the emotions which radiate from some great aria'.[20] As Pleasants argues, 'here [in Bellini's *Norma* and *La sonnambula*] was vocal writing that provided the long, plastic line required for the ultimate unfolding of Pasta's interpretative genius, the sustained cantilena that she could mould and bend and embellish to her high artistic purpose'.[21] Or, as Susan Rutherford suggests, it was on Pasta's vocal qualities and dramatic skills that Bellini and Romani shaped their musical drama, not only in the spinning melody we find in the main arias, but also in the dramatic recitatives.[22] Considering the manner in which Bellini and, as we will see, Verdi entertained close relations with their interpreters and chose to work with those individual singers whose voice and talent they treasured, it is difficult to think of these composers as a threat to singers. Furthermore, whether singers accommodated themselves to composers' new demands or vice versa, the change towards a more dramatic vocal style about which many complained did not prevent prima donnas from persisting in the much-contested practice of modifying the melodic line and adding or substituting coloraturas and ornaments whenever the occasion presented itself. In fact, most of the interpretative features that were typically associated with the so-called bel canto are to be found also in the works of Bellini.

Evidence of the extent of this practice is provided, again, by Manuel García, whose method includes a number of examples taken from *La sonnambula* and *Norma*, together with lesser-known works like *Beatrice di Tenda* and

---

18   Massimo Zicari, 'Expressive Tempo Modifications in Adelina Patti's Recordings: An Integrated Approach', *Empirical Musicology Review*, 12.1–2 (2017), 42–56.
19   *The Times*, 25 June 1884, p. 12.
20   See Henry Pleasants, *The Great Singers from the Dawn of Opera to Our Own Time* (New York: Simon & Schuster, 1966), p. 141.
21   Ibid.
22   One has been detected in Act II, Scene 1, bars 83–87 where Norma is determined to put an end to her children's life. Susan Rutherford, '"La Cantante Delle Passioni": Giuditta Pasta and the Idea of Operatic Performance', *Cambridge Opera Journal*, 19.2 (2007), 107–38, https://doi.org/10.1017/S0954586707002303.

Il pirata; these examples can be found also in sections where the author does not deal with the use of textual modifications and vocal ornamentation. For instance, in the chapter entitled 'Dell'articolazione nel canto' where García focuses on the accentuation and distribution of the words, he suggests that in specific situations it is possible to add further syllables into the lyrics, or substitute for the written ones, if their meaning allows it. Two examples are then discussed, the first taken from Rossini's *Tancredi*, and the second from Amina's cavatina 'Come per me sereno' in Bellini's *La sonnambula*.[23] Interestingly, García does not draw attention to the modifications present in the melody, which, one may speculate, are to be taken for granted, but to the exclamation 'ah' added twice in order to adapt the lyrics to the predictably modified melodic line. The passage, reproduced in Figure 50, shows how the insertion of the first 'ah', should help the singer to attack the top A with a more sonorous voice before the modified descending passage. The second insertion shows how the same simple stratagem can be used to vocalise a newly-inserted cadential passage; similar, although less demanding, solutions to the cadenza are suggested in Marchesi's *Variantes et points d'orgue*.[24] None of the solutions suggested by García and Marchesi can be found in Tetrazzini's 1912 recording, which, instead, features a sustained accented trill (Figure 50).

Figure 50 shows an example from García, Volume II, p. 16, regarding 'Come per me sereno' from Bellini's *La sonnambula*.

A second example taken from the same aria, this time the Moderato section, shows a similar situation, with García using an ornamented passage to illustrate how to commence a melody after a pause or a suspension. The author indicates the position in which the breath should be placed after a fermata or a pause and suggests that, when approaching the reprise, the interpreter should resume the same sound, intensity, tempo and expressive quality as before the interruption. García offers three examples, the first comes from Rossini's *Tancredi*, the second from Meyerbeer's *Il crociato*, the third from Bellini's *La sonnambula*. On discussing this last example, it seems to be unnecessary for García to highlight that the passage in the cadenza differs from the original. Instead, he indicates where an almost inaudible *mezza respirazione* (half-breath) should be taken after the descending scale that leads to the reprise in pianissimo.[25]

---

23   García, vol. II, p. 16. The same example can be found in the English translation edited by Albert Garcia in 1924, *Treatise on the Art of Singing* (London: Leonard, 1924), p. 47.
24   Marchesi, *Variantes et points d'orgue*, p. 77
25   García, *Scuola di Garcia*, p. 36. The 1926 English edition does not include the examples we can find in the Ricordi edition from 1842.

Figure 51 shows an example from García, vol. II, p. 36, regarding the use of a half-breath before the reprise in *La sonnambula*.

García uses the same passage again when elucidating the manner in which a fermata should be dealt with, this time in the chapter dedicated to the changes a singer can introduce to make the music more expressive. In García's opinion, and consistently with Pier Francesco Tosi as well as other authors from the eighteenth century, the ornamented figure inserted into a fermata should be sung in one single breath. If the change involves more words or the repetition of the same word, García continues, it is permitted to take one or two extra breaths.[26] This is the case with the passage discussed above, which is now presented in a slightly different form (Figure 52). A gruppetto is now inserted immediately after the fermata, above the C, and the repetition of 'ah' justifies the breaths we now find introduced. Despite the negligible differences, García seems to be informing us that it was common practice to insert a passage in fermatas of this kind.

Figure 52 shows the same example as that in Figure 51 from García (p. 36). Now the half-breath can be found placed on the 'ah' (penultimate measure).

It is also worth noting that the passage in the example appears transposed to F major while the key signature we find in the Ricordi printed edition is A flat major. One may speculate that García was referring to the version sung by his sister Maria Malibran at the Theatre Royal Drury Lane,[27] a supposition that finds further confirmation in another example, this time transposed to B flat major, from 'Ah! Non credea mirarti', where García writes

---

26 Ibid., p. 50.
27 See Philip Gossett, *Divas and Scholars*, p. 355.

'variante della Malibran' and concludes the passage with an incredibly challenging two-octave descending leap to the lower B (Figure 53).²⁸

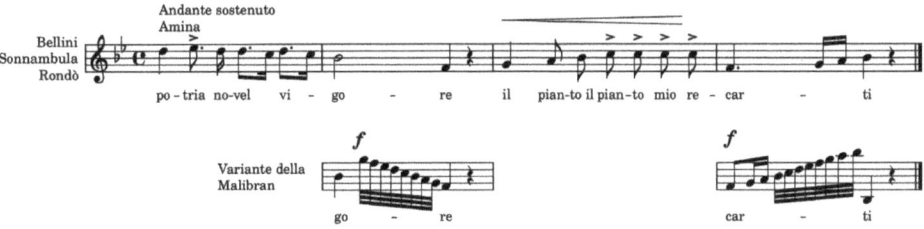

Figure 53 shows an example from 'Ah! Non credea mirarti' on which García writes 'variante della Malibran' (vol. II, p. 39).

Transpositions were common among singers whenever the melody did not fit their voice compass and may have become more frequent, one may argue, as a consequence of what Lamperti called the *spostamento della voce*. Less frequently singers transposed their favourite bravura piece higher than they had been originally notated, to show off the upper register of their voice.²⁹ However, as has been suggested by Gossett, 'the problem of transpositions in the opera of Bellini becomes intense whenever *La sonnambula* is mentioned'.³⁰ The Royal Drury Lane and Covent Garden transposed version sung by Malibran should be attributed to Henry Bishop, while other changes to the score were made by Giovanni Battista Rubini, because Bellini's music was too high for voice.

One last example, again taken from Amina's cavatina 'Come per me sereno', is discussed by García to show how it is possible to prevent an excess of ornament in a cadenza: in fact, he writes, by dropping the fermata between the two dominant chords, one could also suppress the relevant passage.³¹ The first part of the example shows how the music is written (the example differs slightly from the Ricordi edition), while the second offers an instance of how it could be modified, with the two chords now following each other and a long cadenza 'con brio' following the seventh dominant chord (Figure 54).

---

28 García, *Scuola di Garcia*, p. 39. On this topic see also Emanuele Senici, 'Per una biografia musicale di Amina', in *Vincenzo Bellini: verso l'edizione critica. Atti del convegno internazionale, Siena, 1–3 giugno 2000*, ed. by Fabrizio Della Seta and Simonetta Ricciardi (Florence: Olschki, 2004), pp. 297–314.
29 Philip Gossett, *Divas and Scholars*, p. 332.
30 Ibid., p. 352.
31 'Spesso, onde evitare una soverchia lunghezza di abbellimenti, si riuniscono i due accordi, di quarta e sesta, e di settima. Così si ottiene di sopprimere il punto coronato che apparterrebbe al primo accordo', García, p. 51. The English translation reads as follows: 'To prevent excess of ornament, the two chords of 6/4 and seventh are sometimes united, and the passage which corresponds with the first chord is suppressed'. García, *Treatise on the Art of Singing* [1924], p. 63. The same cadenza can be found reproduced in Ricci, but without the necessary piano accompaniment. Ricci, vol. I, p. 78. See also Ott, *Handbuch*, pp. 368–85.

Figure 54 shows García's suggestion as to how to prevent excess of ornament in a cadenza by dropping the fermata between the two dominant chords (vol. II, p. 51).

According to García, one may assume, the original notation would have led to a first arguably too long passage starting from the top B, in addition to the second one from the F (third bar in Figure 54), thus making an overflourished cadenza. If García considered a cadenza that is likely to appear excessively long to many of us today entirely appropriate, how much more complex would the solution he did not consider have been?

Other sources concerning the contemporary performance practice of *La sonnambula* date back to Maria Malibran, whose successful appearance in the title role in 1835 in Venice received generous coverage in the local press. References to her changes in the cavatina 'Come per me sereno' can be found in the 'Gazzetta privilegiata' of the 9 April:

> She repeated the cavatina ['Come per me sereno'] and in the repeat she varied, and almost always with advantage and style, the most difficult and graceful passages, to which she added new difficulty and grace. She replicated and after the encore she repeated again for the third time the aria at the end of the opera ['Ah! non credea mirarti'] in which she also changed many phrases in the music [...].[32]

We can glean only a rough idea of these changes from the *Memoirs of Maria Malibran*, published in 1840 by her friend Maria Merlin.[33] Here, as Merlin suggests, Malibran transposed the original key to G major, and descended with her voice down to the tenor register to leap up to the high G (Figure 55). The rapid transition produced a sensation or, to use her own words, an 'electrifying effect'.[34]

Figure 55 presents the variants sung by Maria Malibran as reported by Maria Merlin in 1840.

---

32 'Ella replicò la cavatina ['Come per me sereno'] e nella replica variò e quasi sempre con convenienza di stile i passi più leggiadri e difficili, a cui ella aggiunse nuove difficoltà e leggiadria. Ella replicò e dopo la replica ripeté ancora per la terza volta l'aria alla fine dell'opera [«Ah! non credea mirarti»] in cui pure mutò molte frasi della musica [...].' *La gazzetta privilegiata*, 9 April 1835, reported in Michele Girardi, '"Il mio soggiorno a Venezia forma per me un'epoca faustissima di mia vita": Maria Malibran a Venezia nel 1835', in *La sonnambula* (La Fenice avanti l'opera), 2012, n. 2, p. 40.

33 Maria de las Mercedes Merlin, *Memoirs of Madame Malibran* (Philadelphia: Carey and Hart, 1840, 2 vols), vol. I, p. 180. Vincenzo Bellini, *La sonnambula. Melodramma in due atti di Felice Romani*, ed. by Alessandro Roccatagliati e Luca Zoppelli (Milan: Ricordi, 2009), pp. 448–49 (*Edizione critica delle opere di Vincenzo Bellini*, 7).

34 Merlin, *Memoirs of Madame Malibran*, vol. I, p. 179.

However strenuously one may argue that composers like Bellini were not happy with the idea that divas intervened in their compositions with changes and substitutions, a letter written by the composer from London to his friend Francesco Florimo in 1833 suggests how much he appreciated Malibran's rendition of Amina in London, and how enthusiastic he was about her vocal and interpretative qualities. Malibran was singing *La sonnambula* at Drury Lane, in the English translation, and Bellini even promised her that he would write an opera on a subject of her choice.[35] Other variants from the nineteenth century belong to Cinti-Damoreau and Barbara Marchisio and can be found reported in Caswell's *Embellished Arias*[36] and in Karin and Eugen Ott's *Handbuch*,[37] in addition to the well-known volume by Ricci.[38] All these examples indicate the extent to which nineteenth-century singers approached this opera in a manner that was consistent with the bel canto tradition, no matter how strenuously music critics opposed the new declamatory style of which Bellini was said to have been the initiator.

Unfortunately, evidence of how contemporary singers approached *I puritani* is scarce.[39] Although pieces like Elvira's polacca 'Son vergin vezzosa' and the cabaletta to the Scena N. 7, 'Vien, diletto, è in ciel la luna' soon became the object of textual manipulations that were typical of this epoch, we do not know much about the extent of these changes, unless we move forwards to the second half of the century. One instance can be found in Jenny Lind (182087):

> Bellini's *I Puritani* Act II. Scena N. 7. Andante: Elvira, 'Qui In voce'.
>
> Madame Goldschmidt, more particularly in later years, when singing the Andante only—without the Allegro which follows—repeated the 17 bars at the end of this movement, substituting the second time instead of Bellini's bars 15 and 16 (in the voice part) the following two.[40]

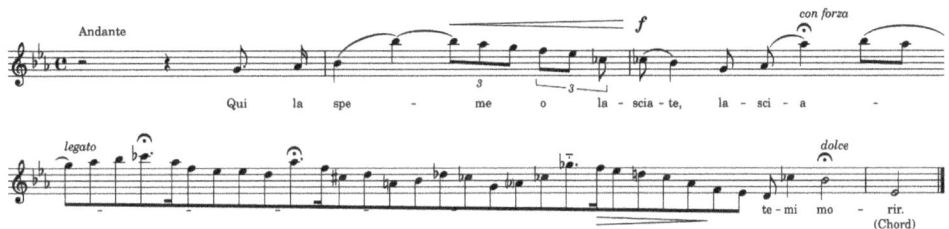

Figure 56 shows the modifications sung by Jenny Lind in Bellini's 'Vien diletto'

This single instance is interesting for the number of C flat and A flat that give the passage a particularly sad and doleful connotation, which was typically associated, as this case illustrates, with feelings of despair. Further evidence concerning singers from the younger generations can be found in Ricci, who reproduced some passages belonging to Regina Pacini[41] (1871–1965), a pupil of Mathilde Marchesi, while Karin and Eugen Ott include the ornamentation sung by the Austrian soprano Selma Kurz[42] (1874–1933). Mathilde Marchesi herself includes a few passages in her 1900 volume.[43]

All in all, even though many contemporary commentators lamented that Bellini had pushed singers towards a declamato style which was even harmful to the voice, the evidence considered so far suggests that divas like Malibran and Lind approached *La sonnambula* in a manner that was not different from any other 'bel canto'

---

35 Luisa Cambi, *Vincenzo Bellini. Epistolario* (Milan: Mondadori, 1943), pp. 363–66, cited in Adamo and Lippmann, *Vincenzo Bellini*, pp. 225–26.
36 Caswell, *Embellished Arias*, pp. 15–29.
37 Karin and Eugen Ott, *Handbuch*, pp. 368–85.
38 Ricci, *Variazioni*, vol. I, pp. 78–82.
39 Mention of this is made also in the critical edition of the opera. See Vincenzo Bellini, *I puritani*, edizione critica a cura di Fabrizio Della Seta (Milan: Ricordi, 2013), p. XL.
40 William Smyth Rockstro, *Jenny Lind: A Record and Analysis of the 'Method' of the Late Madame Jenny Lind-Goldschmidt*, ed. by Otto Goldschmidt (London: Novello 1894), p. IV.
41 Ricci, *Variazioni*, vol. I, pp. 63–68.
42 Ott, *Handbuch*, pp. 422–26.
43 Marchesi, *Variantes et points d'orgue*, pp. 68–71.

work. As has been suggested by Melina Esse, in this very opera the composer shows himself to have 'abandoned his resolutely sparse melodies of the late 1820s to embrace a more florid Rossinian idiom',[44] a circumstance that might account for the interpretative approach we have seen also in García's *Scuola*. Instead, with 'Vien diletto' we are confronted with showpieces whose popularity had little or nothing to do with the limited success of the operas to which they originally belonged, whether or not they fell into the new or the old singing style.

Bellini in Tetrazzini's Recorded Interpretations

In the course of her career Tetrazzini sang Bellini's operas on many an occasion. She made her first appearance as Amina on 8 February 1893 at the Teatro San Martin, Buenos Aires, and was Elvira for the first time in 1894 at Buenos Aires again, in the same theatre. As we have seen, in those years, Tetrazzini was regularly touring South America together with Pietro Cesari in the troupe Raffaele Tomba had recruited in 1891.[45] She continued to sing both operas regularly, scoring success after success. When she sang Amina at the Tivoli in 1905 in San Francisco, the critic of *The San Francisco Call* wrote that the diva and her colleagues, the tenor Giorgio Bazelli and the bass Giovanni Gravina, had worked wonders.

> The soprano was Tetrazzini, scintillating staccato upper notes ad lib.; making long skips with dazzling ease and certainty; warbling like a robin at sunrise on an old apple tree, whenever there was a warbling mood in the score—which was often; hitting so far up among the ledger line notes that the admirers of sheer vocalism went daft over what she did with so little show of exertion. There was Bazelli, for tenor, whose voice was in the best shape that it has been since the season opened; who made musical sounds about all the time with his vocal apparatus and whose supply of sentiment met all demands, so that he was a success. For basso Gravina figured, and he was amply able to do all that was needed without imparting any thrills, but careful and conscientious.[46]

The critic referred also to the condition in which this repertoire lay; however, he did not address the triteness of the old repertoire, especially when compared to the modern works by the younger generations of composers, but rather the poor quality of the past interpreters.

> The end of the second act, with the triply sweet languishing duet between Tetrazzini and Bazelli, naturally made the most impression upon an audience that quickly came into sympathy with the music that our grandmothers and grandfathers loved. From this time on the standing of the old opera, so often abused by incompetent conductors and slurred by indifferent singers, gained steadily in current estimation.[47]

Similar comments appeared in the columns of *The Times* in 1909, when Tetrazzini was Amina at Covent Garden, with John McCormack as Elvino and Ettore Panizza conducted the orchestra. As the critic observed, *La sonnambula* had not been mounted for nearly thirty years at Covent Garden—except for the single appearance of Etelka Gerster in 1890—and the part admirably suited Tetrazzini's voice, which reached the highest notes so easily: 'There are such a multitude of high E flat in the music of Amina that the success of Mme. Tetrazzini in the part is a foregone conclusion and in fact she did better in it than in any part she has sung this year'.[48] In 1910 the same journal reviewed Tetrazzini's rendition of Amina, again with McCormack in the role of Elvino, this time with Cleofonte Campanini holding the baton. The trope of observing the triteness of bel canto operas was revived but, the critic commented ironically, the pleasure of hearing some high E flats beautifully sung could make up for the lack of dramatic strength. An improvement in Tetrazzini's vocal technique was also noticeable.

> The days are long past when the saccharine allurements of works like *La sonnambula* were supposed to endanger the success of works of greater dramatic force; and there is no longer any conceivable reason why they should not be

---

44 Melina Esse, 'Speaking and Sighing: Bellini's Canto Declamato and the Poetics of Restraint', *Current Musicology*, 87 (2009), 7–45 (p. 9).
45 Gattey, *Luisa Tetrazzini*, pp. 11–18.
46 '*Sonnambula* Moves Crowd to Cry "Brava"', *The San Francisco Call*, 12 October 1905, p. 7
47 Ibid.
48 'Royal Opera', *The Times*, 31 May 1909, p. 9.

given as long as there are sopranos with high E flats available and opera-goers who like to renew the pleasures of their youth, or to realize what it was that charmed their grandparents. Mme. Tetrazzini is heard perhaps to greater advantage in the part of Annina [sic] than in any other; she now phrases more carefully than when she first sang here, and gives us fewer than formerly of those strangely-produced middle notes which lessened the environment of what she sang. 'Ah, non credea' was given with genuine expression.[49]

In raising the question of the distance between the so-called palmy days of operas and modern drama, the critic was drawing attention not only to the dramatic and musical quality of these different repertoires, but also to the vocal skills and talent necessary to interpret them.

More detailed descriptions of her interpretations of Bellini's operas are difficult to find in the reviews that accompanied her appearances; often, critical remarks concerning the distance between the modern repertoire and those old operas that were so dear to the earlier generations seem to have impinged on the value judgement expressed by some contemporary commentators.

In Tetrazzini's interpretations of Bellini's operas, all recorded with orchestra, *La sonnambula*[50] holds a prominent position, with four discs realised between 1909 and 1912; *I puritani*[51] is present with one recording only, made in 1912. A first recording of 'Ah, non credea mirarti' was realised in London on 2 June 1909, with Percy Pitt conducting the orchestra (matrix 3101f, Gramophone 053227; Victor 92069); 'Ah, non credea mirarti' and 'Ah, non giunge' were recorded on 16 and 18 March 1911, conducted by Walter B. Rogers (the former matrix C10064-1, Victor 88305, 6396; HMV 2-053049, DB 533; the latter, with flute obbligato by Clement Barone, matrix C10076-1, Victor 88313, 6345; HMV2-053041, DB 533). 'Come per me sereno... Sovra il sen' (Act I n. 2) were recorded on 9 July 1912 at Hayes, Middlesex (matrix HO188ac, HMV 2-053070), while the following day, 10 July 1912, it was the turn of 'Vien diletto' from *I puritani* (Atto II, n. 7), which was recorded also with orchestra (matrix HO193ac, HMV 2-053072). As we will see, with these arias the recording studio was transformed into an experimental lab, in which new and unprecedented cadenzas with obligato instruments were developed.

La sonnambula

'Ah! Non credea mirarti... Ah non giunge'

We are now in the final scene of the opera, 'Scena ed Aria Finale [di] Amina', where the mystery that surrounds the woman is clarified and the happy ending is approaching. The scene follows the *solita forma* conventional structure and Elvino's recitativo opens the scene in which we see Amina sleepwalking on a high, dangerously unstable mill bridge; all the peasants can see that she has not betrayed her fiancé. In the Andante cantabile Amina mourns her lost love, but her tears cannot revive it. A kinetic section follows, in which the chorus rejoices at the unexpected turn of events; As soon as Amina wakes up she realises that her destiny has changed for the better, at which point she sings the cabaletta 'Ah! Non giunge' (Allegretto moderato).

Elvino, Rodolfo et al.		**Recitativo**
Si Signor?... che creder deggio?	Yes Sir? What should I believe?	(tempo d'attacco)
...		
Amina		**Andante cantabile**
Ah! Non credea mirarti	Ah! I did not think to see thee	

---

49 'Royal Opera', *The Times*, 27 May 1910, p. 12.
50 Vincenzo Bellini, *La sonnambula*, Melodramma in due atti di Felice Romani, Riduzione per canto e pianoforte condotta sull'edizione critica della partitura a cura di Alessandro Roccatagliati e Luca Zoppelli (Milan: Ricordi, 2010).
51 Vincenzo Bellini, *I puritani*, Opera seria in tre atti di Carlo Pepoli. Riduzione per canto e pianoforte condotta sull'edizione critica della partitura a cura di Fabrizio Della Seta (Milan: Ricordi, 2015).

Sì preso estinto, o fiore.	So soon extinct, O flower.	
Passato al par d'amore,	Passed in the manner of love,	
che un giorno sol durò.	Which one day only lasted.	
Potria novel vigore	Could my tears	
Il pianto mio donarti…	Give you new strength	
Ma ravvivar l'amore	But to revive love	
Il pianto mio non può.	My tears cannot	
Elvino et al.		**Recitativo**
No, più non reggo.	No, I no longer bear.	(tempo di mezzo)
Amina		**Allegretto moderato**
Ah! Non giunge uman pensiero	Ah! No human thought understands	(cabaletta)
Al contento ond'io son piena:	The happiness with which I am full:	
a'miei sensi io credo appena;	I hardly believe my senses;	
tu mi affida, o mio tesor.	entrust me to you, my treasure.	
Ah! Mi abbraccia, e sempre insieme,	Ah, he embraces me, and always together,	
Sempre uniti in una speme,	Always united in one hope,	
della terra in cui viviamo	of the earth in which we live	
ci formiamo—un ciel d'amor.	we form—a heaven of love.	
Tutti		Pertichini
Innocente, e a noi più cara,	Innocent, and dearest to us,	
bella più del tuo soffrir.	More beautiful than your suffering.	
Vieni al tempio, e a piè dell'ara	Come to the temple, and at the altar	
Incominci il tuo gioïr.	Begin your joy.	
Amina		
Ah! Non giunge uman pensiero	Ah! No human thought understands	Reprise

The cantabile defies the conventional structure of the Italian lyric form, where a first pair of four-bar phrases (a_4 a_4^1) is followed by a contrasting medial four-bar phrase (b_4), which either leads back to the initial melodic material (a_4) or to a new, closing four-bar phrase (c_4).[52] Instead, Amina's aria combines phrases of different lengths that move from A minor to C Major.[53] The first stanza is set to a four-bar phrase followed by a five-bar phrase that is prolonged by two more bars. In the second stanza a four-bar phrase in C Major is followed by a contracted three-bar phrase leading to the final cadenza through six more bars, which set to music the opening lines ('Ah, non credea'). In the bridge section a shift from A minor to C Major occurs which, according to contemporary conventions, should find its justification in a distinct change in the emotional content of the text, for example from sadness to joyfulness. But Amina is not any happier; rather, she expresses resignation, since her sorrowful tears (at least apparently) can do nothing to change her destiny. However, while she expresses her grief in a state of unconsciousness, all the villagers are watching her. Amina's sleepwalking in front of the passers-by proves her innocence, and her words testify to her immaculate love. Therefore, the key change in the music may find its justification in the external conditions of the scene. Since the nature of Amina's disease is now made known to everybody and her virginal virtue is no longer in question, Elvino will marry her.

---

52 See Steven Huebner, 'Lyric Form in Ottocento Opera', *Journal of the Royal Musical Association*, 117.1 (1992), 123–47. Adamo and Lippmann, *Vincenzo Bellini*, pp. 428–29.
53 Luca Zoppelli, 'L'Idillio Borghese', in *La Sonnambula*, ed. by C. Chiarot (Venice: Teatro La Fenice, 1996), pp. 49–62; Adamo and Lippmann, *Vincenzo Bellini*, 1981, p. 484.

Tetrazzini recorded 'Ah! Non credea mirarti' in 1909 and 1911 and her interpretations bear a resemblance to that of her senior colleague, Adelina Patti.[54] This continuity between the two divas is suggested by some small details in the ornamentation like, for instance, the small grace at bar 119 (p. 314 in the new critical edition), which seems to be reminiscent of the version sung by Jenny Lind published in 1894 (Figure 57).[55]

Figure 57 shows Tetrazzini's modifications in *La sonnambula*, 'Ah! non credea mirarti' (measures 119–20, p. 314, Ricordi, 2010) compared to Patti and Lind.

Another similarity between Patti and Tetrazzini can be noted in the chromatic ascending passage in coincidence with the word 'recarti' at measure 133 (Figure 58) which, apparently, neither Maria Malibran nor Jenny Lind used to sing. It is also worth noting how differently the four repeated notes pronouncing 'pianto mio' are treated by Tetrazzini. These choked sobs for which Bellini adopts a syllabic figure become an opportunity for Tetrazzini to insert an appoggiatura and a small grace, which seem to defy the dramatic, almost mimetic quality of this passage, in favour of a more Rossinian, flourished singing.

Despite these similarities, the idea of a direct connection between Tetrazzini, Patti and Lind remains confined to the realm of speculation. Tetrazzini could not possibly have met Jenny Lind in person—she died in 1887—and her method, 'together with a selection of cadence, solfeggio, abellimenti [sic] &c. in illustration of her vocal art', was published posthumously in 1891 and 1894. On the other hand, Adelina was present when Luisa sang Violetta at Covent Garden in April 1908, one year after her London triumph in 1907. The two women became close friends, as some letters suggest,[56] and it is entirely possible that they may have exchanged opinions about how to interpret the bel canto arias they both sang. But, if we remember that Tetrazzini's first appearance in this role dates back to 1893, we realise how unlikely it must have been for her to have taken reference from either colleague when first developing her interpretation of this role. Furthermore, it is unlikely that a star like Tetrazzini would refer to other artists, given the strenuous routine that characterised her professional life and the difficulty of hearing other singers, at least until the gramophone was invented. An indication on the matter is provided by Tetrazzini herself who, one month before what we assume may have been her first meeting with Patti in 1908, was interviewed by *The Sun*.

---

54 For an anlysis of Patti's rendition of this aria see Massimo Zicari, 'Expressive Tempo Modifications in Adelina Patti's Recordings: An Integrated Approach', *Empirical Musicology Review*, 12.1–2 (2017), 42–56.

55 William Smyth Rockstro, *Jenny Lind: A Record and Analysis of the 'Method' of the Late Madame Jenny Lind-Goldschmidt*, ed. by Otto Goldschmidt (London: Novello 1894), p. xiv.

56 Gattey, *Luisa Tetrazzini*, pp. 100–01.

86   The Voice of the Century

Figure 58 *La sonnambula*, 'Ah! non credea mirarti' (Ricordi, 2010, bb. 132–33, p. 315).

Have I ever heard Patti? Melba? Not until quite recently except through a gramophone, which I listen to frequently. Curiously enough, when I sang for the first time in America, at the Tivoli in San Francisco, Melba was singing then at the Alhambra. I was crazy to hear her, but how could I when we sang the same nights? It has often been so in my travels about the world. That is why I so often go to the Manhattan, the evenings I am not singing; for the delight of hearing my musical friends.[57]

While Melba was still an active performer in the first decade of the century—between December 1908 and January 1909 she was in New York, singing *La Bohème*, *Rigoletto*, and *Otello* at the Manhattan Opera[58]—Patti was well past her prime and even her recordings were realised in a moment when her voice no longer was what it once had been. Since 1902 contemporary critics, although showing much delicacy and consideration, could not avoid touching on Patti's flaws: 'an extra breath here and there; a transposition of a semitone down or maybe two, fewer excursions—and those very "carefully" managed—above the top line of the treble stave'.[59]

It is fair to assume that Tetrazzini may have heard Patti's recordings not long before she could meet her in person, and we can also reasonably argue that, among them, 'Ah! Non credea mirarti', which Patti realised in 1906, held a prominent position on Tetrazzini's disc shelf. But, at the time when she met Patti, Tetrazzini had long developed a strong musical personality, and her interpretative choices are likely to have stemmed from the same vibrant tradition of which Adelina had been a major representative, rather than from Adelina's discs. In the rest of the aria Tetrazzini seems to have made her own interpretative decisions, as is suggested by the trill on 'amore' at measure 135 which, according to Blanche Roosevelt, Erminia Frezzolini's parrot used to sing.[60] Her suspension on the top B is rather distant from the vocal arabesque Jenny Lind seems to have sung, as well as from what we find in Patti's recording (Figure 59).

Of extreme interest is, instead, the cadenza with the cello that we find in Tetrazzini's recordings (Figure 60), which was first transcribed by Ricci in 1939 and more recently by Emanuele Senici.[61]

---

57 'Making of a Great Singer', *The Sun*, 8 March 1908, p. 6.
58 See Radic, *Melba*, p. 191.
59 See Herman Klein, *The Reign of Patti* (New York: The Century, 1920), pp. 354–55.
60 Emanuele Senici, 'Per una biografia musicale di Amina', in *Vincenzo Bellini: verso l'edizione critica. Atti del convegno internazionale, Siena, 1–3 giugno 2000* (Florence: Olschki, 2004), pp. 297–314.
61 Ricci, *Appendice*, 1939, p. 55. Senici, 'Per una biografia', pp. 297–314.

Figure 59 *La sonnambula*, 'Ah! non credea mirarti' (Ricordi, 2010, measures 134–135, pp. 315–16).

Figure 60 shows Tetrazzini's rendition of the closing cadenza with cello obbligato in *La sonnambula*, 'Ah! non credea mirarti' (measures 144–145, p. 316 in Ricordi, 2010).

We do not know where this cadenza comes from, nor do we have any information regarding the cadenza with the flute that Tetrazzini sings in the following cabaletta. The habit of inserting an obbligato instrument in a cadenza, which we will pursue in the next section, was not widespread among contemporary singers.

Tetrazzini's rendition of the cabaletta 'Ah non giunge' does not diverge significantly from the picture presented so far. If, on the one hand, we can observe some analogies with Marchesi and Ricci, on the other she presents some more original interpretative choices. As previously mentioned, much more fascinating is the flute cadenza, which, although echoing that of *Lucia di Lammermoor,* seems to be unprecedented in this aria.

We know that the first incontrovertible evidence of the origins of the famous apocryphal cadenza for Lucia's mad scene dates back to 1889, when *Lucie de Lammermoor* was produced in French at the Opera Garnier after an absence of twenty years, with Nellie Melba in the title role.[62] As already discussed, the cadenza was written by her teacher Mathilde Marchesi who included it in the variants she published in 1900. Ten years later, we find Luisa Tetrazzini recording Marchesi's flute cadenza, the cello cadenza discussed apropos 'Ah! non credea mirarti', and one more flute cadenza for the cabaletta 'Ah! non giunge'. Tetrazzini recorded this last piece twice, once in 1904 and again in 1911. In 1904 she recorded a final passage that is close to what we find written by Bellini, while in 1911 we find a flute playing along in a cadenza that reminds us of the one Marchesi wrote for Melba, with its nice passages in sixths and thirds. Ricci transcribed this cadenza (Figure 61) in the appendix for mixed voice published in 1939[63] but, as in other cases, did not mention Tetrazzini's name.[64]

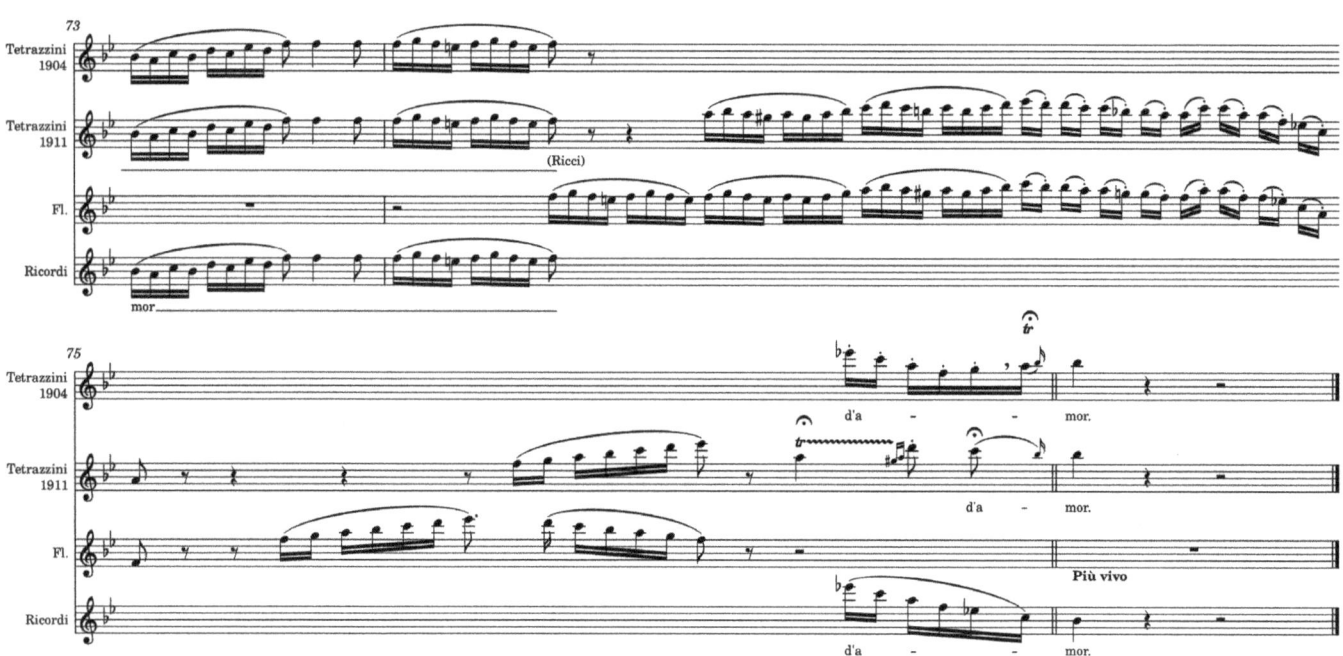

Figure 61 *La sonnambula,* 'Ah non giunge', Ricordi, 2010, b. 272, p. 334.

A glance at the recording sessions which took place between 15 and 18 March 1911 may help us understand the reason behind the addition of an obbligato flute cadenza to 'Ah! non giunge'. During a three-day recording session in Camden in March 1911, Tetrazzini recorded sixteen arias, with Walter Rogers conducting; among them we find:

---

62   Romana Margherita Pugliese, 'The Origins of "Lucia di Lammermoor"'s Cadenza', *Cambridge Opera Journal,* 16.1 (2004), 23–42.
63   Ricci, *Appendice,* 1939, p. 55.
64   To my knowledge, there are no similar flute cadenzas in other contemporary recordings, such as the one Marcella Sembrich realised in 1904.

- 16 March,
  - *La sonnambula*: 'Ah, non credea' with an unprecedented cello cadenza (unknown cellist)
  - *Lucia di Lammermoor*: 'Splendon le sacre faci' with the flute cadenza played by Walter Oesterreicher (from Marchesi)
- 17 March,
  - *La Perle du Brésil*: 'Charmant oiseau' with the 'Nevada' flute cadenza played by Walter Oesterreicher
- 18 March
  - *La sonnambula*: 'Ah, non giunge' with flute cadenza played by Clement Barone
  - Proch: *Variations* with an extended flute cadenza played by Clement Barone

What these recordings have in common is the presence of an obbligato instrument to play either a newly-written or an extended cadenza, should the composer have provided one already. We do not know who played the cello on 16 March 1911, but we see that Walter Oesterreicher played the flute when recording 'Splendon le sacre faci' and 'Charmant oiseau' from Félicien David's *La Perle du Brésil* while Clement Barone recorded 'Ah, non giunge' and Proch's *Variations* 'Deh! Torna mio bene'.

The score of Proch's *Air and Variation 'Ah Whence Comes this Longing'* published in Boston by White, Smith & Co. in 1887 presents, in the piano reduction, a short cadenza with the flute, which eventually became the incipit of other artists' more flourished vocal-instrumental arabesques (Figure 62).[65]

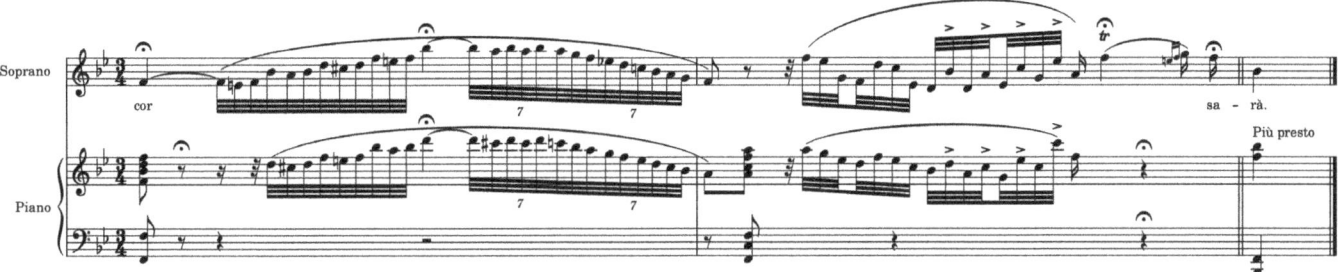

Figure 62 shows the closing measure of Heinrich Proch's *Variations* 'Deh torna mio bene'.

In 1940 Estelle Liebling edited the vocal score of the *Variations* published by Schirmer, which included some traditional flute cadenzas and, among them, those recorded by Tetrazzini and Galli-Curci.[66]

Something similar can be said of 'Charmant oiseau' from Félicien David's *La Perle du Brésil, opéra comique en trois actes* first performed in 1851, and set to a libretto by Gabriel de Lurieu and Sylvain Saint-Étienne. In Act III Zora sings the 'Couplets du Mysoli' with obbligato flute that presents a cadenza where the voice responds to the short arpeggio figure 'in echo' played by the flute, which is repeated, unchanged, for a second time upon conclusion of the piece (Figure 63).[67]

---

65 Heinrich Proch, 'Air and Variations', in *Artists' Vocal Album* (Boston: White, Smith & Co., 1887), pp. 70–79. In Europe these variations must have been published much earlier than this. This version is in B flat, but this is transposed down from the key of D flat, which Tetrazzini, Pacini, Galli-Curci etc. all use (see Chapter Two).
66 Heinrich Proch, *Theme and Variations*, op. 164, ed. by Estelle Liebling (New York: Schirmer, 1940), p. 14.
67 Félicien David, *La Perle du Brésil, opéra comique en trois actes* (Paris: Launer, [n.d.]), p. 263.

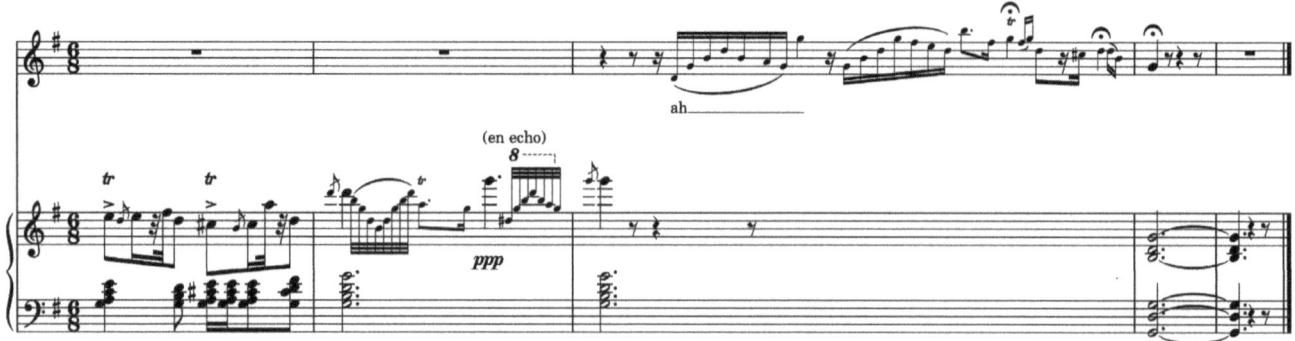

Figure 63 shows the final cadenza of 'Charmant Oiseau' from David's *La perle du Brésil* (Paris: Launer, [n.d.]), p. 263.

In 1883 Emma Nevada made her Paris début at the Opéra-Comique singing Zora in David's *La Perle du Brésil* of which in 1885 Henry Heugel published a *nouvelle édition*; this new edition features the 'Variante de M.lle Nevada' possibly the variant Emma Nevada introduced on the occasion of her Paris début.[68]

This time we observe two different cadenzas: the first is more closely based on the original arpeggio figure (Figure 64) while the second expands on the same melodic material, thus leading to a more elaborate vocal arabesque (Figure 65).

Figure 64 shows the first variant sung by Emma Nevada in Paris, as was published by Heugel in 1885 (p. 311).

---

68   Félicien David, *La perle du Brésil, opera en trois actes, paroles de J. Gabriel et Sylvain Sant-Étienne, partition piano et chant complète* (Paris: Heugel, 1885), p. 311.

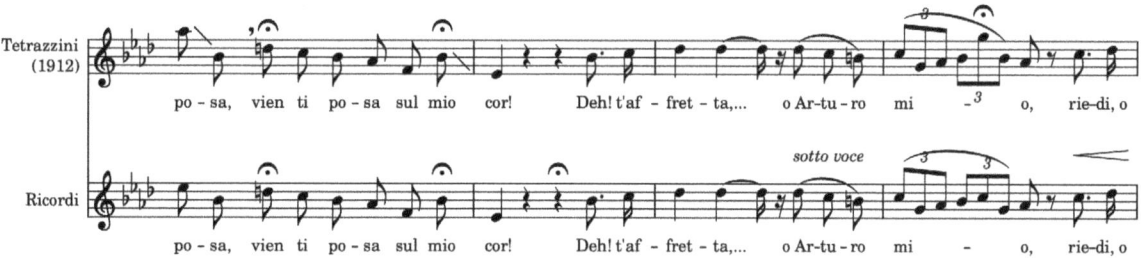

Figure 65 shows the second variant sung by Emma Nevada in Paris, as was published by Heugel in 1885 (p. 313–14).

Tetrazzini recorded the aria twice in 1911: at the Victor Studios in Camden on the 17 March (matrix C10072-1, 88318, 6343) and for His Master's Voice on the 11 July (matrix ac5161f, HMV 2-033027).

Tetrazzini's recordings feature Nevada's variant, where the voice chases the flute and responds in echo to its chirping calls, to proceed in thirds and sixths in the following passages and conclude with a final series of trills. We find the Nevada version in many other early discs. Clement Barone would record the aria with Amelita Galli-Curci on 14 September 1917 in Camden, with the same final cadenza (matrix C20664-4, Victor 74552, 6124; HMV 2-033062, DB 255). The same cadenza had already been recorded in 1902 by Maria Michailova (1866–1943) in St. Petersburg, with A. N. Semenov playing the flute (matrix 313z, G&T 23170);[69] Emma Calvé recorded it with the flautist Darius Lyons in 1907 (matrix C-4425, Victor 88087; G&T 033060) and in 1908 (matrix C-6024, Victor 88087, 6054; Gramophone 033056, DB 161).[70] In 1917 Maria Barrientos would record the cadenza with Marshall P. Lufsky playing the flute, in Italian as 'Gentil augel' (Columbia, matrix 49112).[71]

Given the evidence I have collected, it could be fairly argued that the reasons that lie behind the recording of a new flute cadenza to 'Ah! non giunge' may have been entirely circumstantial. I suspect that during the recording session that took place on 18 March 1911 the conversation between Luisa Tetrazzini, Walter Rogers and Clement Barone may have led to the idea of putting together a new version of the cadenza for the Proch *Variations* and a completely new and unprecedented cadenza for Amina's cabaletta to be recorded alongside those songs that already included a similar cadenza, and in addition to a cello cadenza for the cantabile 'Ah! Non credea mirarti', first recorded in 1909. This decision could be understood as a response to the habit, emerging at the end of the century, of having an additional obbligato instrument playing along with the voice in the cadenza, as many other contemporary discs show. In this regard, the recording studio might have been turned into a creative lab where the prima donna, together with the conductor and the other instrumentalists involved, may have explored new interpretative possibilities, well beyond the constraints imposed by the tradition.

'Come per me sereno'

If we turn our attention to Tetrazzini's recorded interpretation of 'Come per me sereno' we see that some of the changes resulted from the limitations imposed by early recording technologies. This is particularly so for the cuts, which were most probably made due to the limited length of early discs. The curtain has just risen on the opening scene which sees the Swiss peasants gathering in the main piazza of the village, to celebrate Amina's wedding to Elvino. Amina expresses her gratitude to her mother and her boundless happiness to her friends: the day could not be brighter.

---

69 'Gramophone matrix 313L. Charmant oiseau / M. A. Michailova', *Discography of American Historical Recordings*, https://adp.library.ucsb.edu/index.php/matrix/detail/1000003468/313L-Charmant_oiseau.

70 'Victor matrix C-4425. Charmant oiseau / Emma Calvé.' *Discography of American Historical Recordings*. UC Santa Barbara Library, 2021, https://adp.library.ucsb.edu/index.php/matrix/detail/200006151/C-4425-Charmant_oiseau.

71 *Discography of American Historical Recordings*, s.v., 'Columbia matrix 49112. Gentil augel / Maria Barrientos; Marshall P. Lufsky', https://adp.library.ucsb.edu/index.php/matrix/detail/2000143465/49112-Gentil_augel.

The Recitativo [e] Cavatina d'Amina 'Come per me sereno' (Atto I, Scena 3) is set in four main sections, and adheres to the compositional convention that contemporary musicians and commentators refer to as the *solita forma*, the usual form.[72] The first and the third sections are dialogic, are set in recitativo style and frame the melodic section, the central cantabile, to conclude with the customary cabaletta. This last involves two sections (A-A¹) with a choral pertichini concluding with a cadenza before approaching the reprise.

		Recitativo
Amina, Teresa e detti		
Care compagne, e voi...	Dear comrades, and you...	
		Cantabile sost. assai
Amina	**Amina**	
Come per me sereno	How serene for me	$a_{(2+2)}$
Oggi rinacque il dì!	Today the day was reborn!	
Come il terren fiorì	How the land flourished	$a^1_{(2+2)}$
Più bello e ameno!	More beautiful and pleasant!	
Mai di più lieto aspetto	Never of a happier aspect	$b_{(2+2)}$
Natura non brillò:	Nature ever shone:	
Amor la colorò	Love coloured her	$c_{(4+4)}$
Del mio diletto	Of my beloved	
		All.o brillante
Tutti	**Tutti**	
Sempre, o felice Amina,	Always, O happy Amina,	
Sempre per te così	Always for you so	
Infiori il Cielo i dì	Heaven blooms the days	
Che ti destina...	Which has destined for you...	
		Moderato
Amina	**Amina**	**A**
Sovra il sen la man mi posa,	Over my breast the hand rests,	$a_{(2+2)}$
Palpitar, balzar lo senti:	Feel it throb and leap:	
Egli è il cor che i suoi contenti	It is the heart that has no strength	$a^1_{(2+2)}$
Non ha forza a sostener.	No strength to sustain the bliss.	$b_{(2+2)}$
		$c_{(6+2)}$
Sovra il sen la man mi posa...	Over my breast the hand rests...	$a_{(2+2)}$
Tutti	**Tutti**	
Di tua sorte avventurosa	Of your adventurous fate	
Teco esulta il cor materno...	My mother's heart rejoices...	**Amina's cadenza**
Amina	**Amina**	**A¹**
Sovra il sen la man mi posa...[73]	Over my breast the hand rests...	$a(2+2)$

The recording Tetrazzini made in 1912 is 3'57" long, the recitativo is not present and the disc opens with the orchestral introduction of the cantabile, which is complete. The Allegro brillante is missing and the recording continues with the orchestra playing the four measures that introduce the vocal part in the Moderato (cabaletta).

---

72 We do not know which edition Tetrazzini used of the many which circulated at the time. Ricci's volume refers to the Ricordi printed edition, plate number 41686 [1869], reprinted in 1971.

73 *Tutti i libretti di Bellini*, ed. by Olimpio Cescatti (Turin: UTET, 1995), p. 173.

This last section is not complete: the central cadenza and the reprise are missing; with the vocal part moving immediately to the coda: 'balzar, balzar lo sento' (Figure 66).

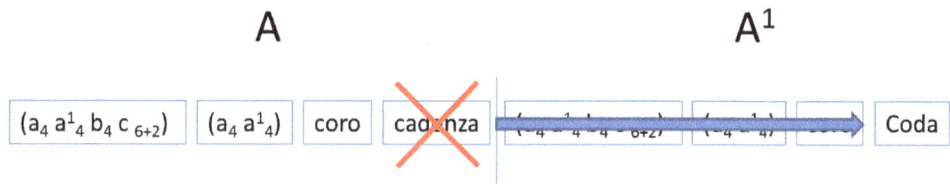

Figure 66 shows the cuts present in Tetrazzini's 1912 recording of 'Sovra il sen'.

It is clear that the recitativo-like sections could be sacrificed in order to make room for the sections of greater musical interest; it should also be remembered that the reasons as to why the cabaletta was cut are not exclusively owing to the rudimental recording technologies of the time, since the habit of cutting the repeat in the cabaletta, or even dropping it, became increasingly common towards the end of nineteenth century.[74] Tetrazzini's ornamentation and cadenzas do not seem to follow on from or adhere to any of those we find in Marchesi's 1900 volume.[75] For instance, in the fermata that precedes the cadenza of the cantabile, Tetrazzini concludes the trill with a descending arpeggio figure, while Marchesi suggests a richer solution (Figure 67) and the passages by Manuel García and Laure Cinti-Damoreau are far more flourished.[76]

---

[74] A glance at more recent recordings shows that the same cut can be found, among others, in the disc recorded by Anna Moffo and Bruno Bartoletti with the Orchestra di Milano della Rai in 1956 and in that of Maria Callas with the La Scala Orchestra in 1955.
[75] Marchesi, *Variantes et points d'orgue*, pp. 76–91.
[76] See Caswell, *Embellished Arias*, pp. 15–29, and Ott, *Handbuch*, pp. 370–71.

Figure 67 shows the fermata of 'Come per me sereno' as was sung by Tetrazzini, compared to those of García and Marchesi.

The same can be said of the cadenza that closes the cantabile, which does not bear a resemblance to any of those belonging to her predecessors, Marchesi[77] and Cinti-Damoreau,[78] or any other diva from the past, whose passages have been transcribed by Ricci: Albani, Pasta, Patti, Regina Pinkert, Malibran, Mancinelli and Regina Pacini.[79]

Figure 68 shows Tetrazzini's rendition of the cadenza preceding the Allegretto brillante in *La sonnambula*, 'Come per me sereno', Ricordi, [1869], reprint 1971, p. 24, measure 11 after rehearsal mark number 21. For this example, the earlier edition was preferable, since the critical edition includes a different passage for the cadenza (Ricordi, 2010, b. 58, p. 29).

Since the reprise in the Moderato is missing, we do not know how Tetrazzini intervened in the central cadential suspension written by Bellini, for which Marchesi (Figure 69), Ricci and Cinti-Damoreau (as reported by Ott) offer a number of possibilities.[80]

---

77   Marchesi, *Variantes et points d'orgue*, p. 77.
78   Ott, *Handbuch*, pp. 372–73.
79   Ricci, *Variazioni*, vol. I, p. 78.
80   Marchesi, *Variantes et points d'orgue*, p. 79, Ricci, vol. I, p. 79. Ott, *Handbuch*, p. 377.

Figure 69 shows the different rendition of the central cadenza in *La sonnambula*, 'Sovra il sen la man si posa' (measures 119–20, pp. 35–36 in the Ricordi 2010 edition).

The distance between Tetrazzini's recorded interpretation and the variants sung by Laure Cinti-Damoreau and Barbara Marchisio, which we find collected in the volume edited by Austin B. Caswell in 1989, could not be more striking.[81] When compared to the richness that characterises Cinti-Damoreau, Tetrazzini's approach to this aria seems very discreet, if not inconspicuous.

In the cabaletta (Moderato) we see a first group of variants to the original melodic figure, which Tetrazzini sings as soon as this presents itself a second time already in the first section (Figure 70).

---

81 Caswell, *Embellished Arias*, pp. 15–29.

Figure 70 shows the modifications sung by Tetrazzini in *La sonnambula*, 'Sovra il sen la man mi posa', Ricordi, [1869], reprint 1971, p. 27, measure nine before rehearsal mark number 25. The critical edition differs from the one then published by Ricordi (Ricordi, 2010, bb. 98–106, pp. 33–34).

As we have seen in García's method, this kind of manipulation was desirable whenever the change would make the repeated melody more interesting. Altough the distance between Tetrazzini and her forerunners is remarkable, it is difficult to understand from these examples whether, in consideration of his declamato style, she was approaching Bellini in a new manner, or whether her personal sense of Amina's drama prevailed over questions of vocal and compositional style.

I puritani

'Vien diletto'

With 'Vien diletto' from the second act of *I puritani*, which she recorded in 1912, Tetrazzini is consistent with what we have observed when talking of *La sonnambula*.[82] It is the cabaletta which concludes the 'Scena d'Elvira' for which Marchesi wrote some variants and cadenzas.[83] Tetrazzini does not seem to take Marchesi's suggestions into consideration; instead, she develops her own variants to the final cadenza (Figures 71 and 72), and makes her own melodic changes in the repeat (Figure 73).

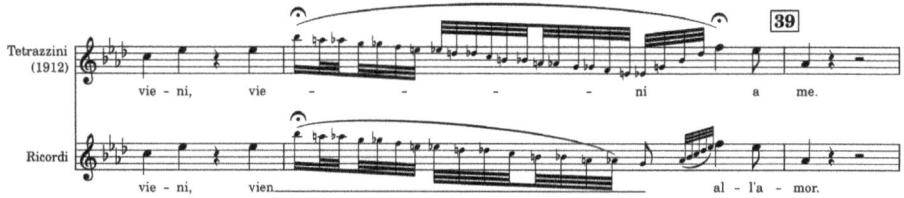

Figure 71 shows Tetrazzini's variant in *I puritani*, 'Vien diletto' (Ricordi, 2015, vol. I, measures 222–23, pp. 420–21).

---

82 The examples from *I puritani* refer to the Ricordi edition, plate number 41685 [1870].
83 Marchesi, *Variantes et points d'orgue*, pp. 65–68.

Figure 72 *I puritani*, 'Vien diletto', Ricordi, 2015, measures 276–77, p. 427.

Figure 73 shows Tetrazzini's variants in the reprise of *I puritani*, 'Vien diletto' (Ricordi, measures 252–65, pp. 425–26).

Some of the passages sung by Tetrazzini can be found, again, transcribed by Ricci,[84] but it is not clear where these come from, since Ricci mentions the names of Grisi, Patti and Regina Pinkert at the beginning of the entire section dedicated to *I puritani*.[85] Two hypotheses seem to be plausible at this point: the first is that Tetrazzini derived her melodic material from the tradition of which Grisi, Patti and Pinkert had been among the most authoritative representatives; the second is that Ricci, as already suggested, transcribed Tetrazzini's coloraturas from her discs without making any explicit reference to them.

In spite of the discussion occasioned by Bellini's new declamatory style and the negative critical responses we find in the contemporary press, it can be reasonably argued that *La sonnambula* soon came to be associated with the so-called bel canto tradition. Thanks to its saccharine allurements, it entered the same repertoire of stock operas to which *Lucia* and *Barbiere* belonged, which appealed to large audiences and were regularly mounted by touring companies and large theatres. Evidence from early discs suggests that divas like Tetrazzini approached *La sonnambula* in a manner that was not different from earlier works. Even the occasionally less flourished treatment of Bellini's beautiful melodies that can be observed in Tetrazzini's recorded interpretations does not necessarily suggest a substantially different understanding of the new compositional style. Furthermore, when Tetrazzini recorded these arias, the time was ripe to experiment with new and more courageous interpretative solutions which found an unprecedented opportunity in the new medium—the disc and the recording studio.

---

84 Ricci, *Variazioni*, vol. I, p. 67.
85 Although Ricci (p. 63) refes to Grisi, no variants to this cabaletta likely to have belonged to her have been included in the critical edition. See Vincenzo Bellini, *I puritani*, critical edition edited by Fabrizio Della Seta (Milan: Ricordi, 2013), Appendice 4, pp. 1303–305.

5. Verdi's Style: The End of Bel Canto?

If it was Bellini who pushed singers towards a more dramatic, declamato-like singing style, it was with Verdi that this transformation was carried to its completion. Although soon celebrated as the most talented Italian composer in a moment in which Italian opera was said, again and again, to lie in a sad state of decadence, Verdi became the object of harsh criticism and was especially condemned for the manner in which he abused the voice.

According to music critic and composer Alberto Mazzucato, in 1842 Verdi had put himself at the head of a group of composers who, regardless of the bad taste then prevailing, were committed to interpreting the dramatic content of the libretto and breaking away from the hackneyed operatic conventions consisting of the unavoidable cabalette, finali, strette and rondo.[1] In 1847, on reflecting on the change that occurred in the 1840s, Mazzucato went back to Eugenia Tadolini's creation of Odabella in Verdi's *Attila* in Milan. In his opinion, Verdi's new vocal style favoured energy and passion over virtuosity and the sheer beauty of vocal sounds. As suggested by Claudio Vellutini, these latter qualities, in which Tadolini excelled, were no longer sufficient: a passionate, vigorous and brilliant spirit was now required in what Mazzucato called the *cantante di slancio*.[2] By the 1850s the notion that Verdi pursued dramatic effect at the expense of proper singing had spread among a number of music critics and commentators all over Europe.[3] In 1854 Carlo Lorenzini referred to two claques then operating in Italy, Verdists and anti-Verdists, and suggested that, according to the second, Verdi had killed Italian singing, the most distinctive feature of Italian music ever.[4] Abramo Basevi, who wrote the first extensive critical account of Verdi's life and operas as early as 1859, also objected to the treatment Verdi reserved for the voice: 'Considering the human larynx as an instrument, for such it is, Bellini treated it like a wind instrument while Verdi, one may occasionally say, like percussion'.[5] Basevi was among those contemporary commentators who first detected an evolution in Verdi's compositional style, with *Luisa Miller* (1849) and *La traviata* (1853) representing two fundamental turning points in his compositional trajectory. However, the tropes concerning the composer's arguable preference for strong dramatic effect and the manner in which he sacrificed proper vocalisation to dramatic singing continued in the columns of many periodicals. Lung-power was said to be more essential than ever since Verdi's operas featured an exceedingly noisy orchestration. The accumulation of loud instrumental effects had become intolerably frequent, brass and percussion instruments were taken full advantage of and, as a consequence, the poor singers had to struggle to make themselves audible in the middle of the orchestral clamour. Some critics even sympathised with those unfortunate interpreters who had to bear with the composer and endure the repeated strains he put on their voice.

---

1   Alberto Mazzucato, 'I. R. Teatro alla Scala. *Nabucodonosor*, Dramma Lirico di T. Solera, Musica del Maestro Verdi', *Gazzetta Musicale di Milano*, 13 March 1842, p. 43. See also Massimo Zicari, *Verdi in Victorian London* (Cambridge: Open Book Publishers, 2016), p. 6, https://doi.org/10.11647/OBP.0090.

2   See Claudio Vellutini, 'Adina Par Excellence: Eugenia Tadolini and the Performing Tradition of Donizetti's *L'elisir d'amore* in Vienna', *19th Century Music*, 38.1 (2014), 3–29.

3   For a discussion on the reception of Verdi's operas in Victorian London see Zicari, *Verdi in Victorian London*, https://doi.org/10.11647/OBP.0090; for France see Hervé Gartioux, *La reception de Verdi en France* (Weinsberg: Musik-Edition Lucie Galland, 2001); for the Italian press see Marco Capra, *Verdi in prima pagina* (Lucca: Libreria Musicale Italiana, 2014); for Germany see Gundula Kreuzer, *Verdi and the Germans* (Cambridge: Cambridge University Press, 2010).

4   Carlo Lorenzini, 'I verdisti e gli antiverdisti', *Lo Scaramuccia*, I/14, 19 December 1854, pp. [2–3]. See Marco Capra, *Verdi in prima pagina* (Lucca: Libreria Musicale Italiana, 2014), p. 121. Although Lorenzini did not use the expression bel canto he seems to refer to that glorious tradition that was then generally defined in those terms.

5   Abramo Basevi, *Studio sulle opere di Giuseppe Verdi* (Florence: Tipografia Tofani, 1859), p. 162. See also Marco Capra, '"Effekt, nicht als Effekt". Aspekte der Rezeption der Opern Verdis in Italien des 19. Jahrhunderts', in *Giuseppe Verdi und seine Zeit*, ed. by Markus Engelhardt (Laaber: Laaber Verlag, 2001), pp. 117–42.

In France, after the generally favourable reception of *Nabucco* in 1845, with *Ernani*, which was premiered in Paris on 6 January 1846 at the Théâtre Italien as *Il proscritto*, music critics turned against the emerging Italian composer and, similarly to what had happened in Italy, warned him against the temptation of favouring dramatic effect at the expense of proper singing: by doing so he was turning singing into shouting. The repertoire of complaints in the contemporary French press includes the use of trivial rhythmic formulas in the accompaniment, a noisy orchestration, especially when the frequent use of unisons was given to the brass instruments, the lack of dramatic and melodic consistency.[6] The response of the Austro-German press was not that different: many critics hailed *Nabucco* as typical of the 'new Italian school' and 'rehearsed the latest clichés' on this new type of opera: the noisy and unrefined orchestration, the trivial rhythmical formulas, the much-too-frequent use of unisons, and so forth.[7] The same can be said of the reception of Verdi's operas in Victorian London. While the first reviews were hesitant, if not benevolent, with *Nabucco* critics like Henry F. Chorley and James W. Davison soon became Verdi's most acrimonious enemies. Chorley, a conservative critic, was willing to acknowledge in Verdi only an occasional burst of brilliance:

> Signor Verdi's *forte* is declamatory music of the highest passion. In this, never hesitating to force the effect, or to drive the singers to the 'most hazardous passes'—he is justified for some extravagance, by an occasional burst of brilliancy, surpassing that of most modern composers [...] But Signor Verdi 'is nothing if not noisy;' and, by perpetually putting forth his energies in one and the same direction, tempts us, out of contradiction, to long for the sweetest piece of sickliness which Paisiello put forth long ere the notion of an orchestra had reached Italy, or the singer's art was thought to mean a superhuman force of lungs.[8]

Likewise, when reviewing *Nabucco* in 1846, Davison was particularly aggressive: a complete lack of melody and rhythm, an exaggerated preference for choruses singing in unison and a deplorable use of wind and brass instruments in the orchestra were his main concerns.

> *Ernani* led us to suspect, and *Nabucco* has certified our suspicion, that of all the modern Italian composers Verdi is the most thoroughly insignificant. We listen, vainly, as the work proceeds, for the semblance of a melody. There is positively nothing, not even a feeling of rhythm—but rather indeed, a very unpleasant disregard for that important element of musical art. The choruses are nothing but the commonest tunes, arranged almost invariably in unison—perhaps because the composer knows not how to write in parts. The concerted music is patchy, rambling and unconnected. The cantabiles are always unrhythmical—and the absence of design is everywhere observable. The harmonies are either the tritest common-places, or something peculiarly odd and unpleasant. Nothing can possibly be more feeble than the orchestration. The employment of the wind instruments is remarkably infelicitous, and all the experiments are failures. The overture is the poorest stuff imaginable, and yet the only glimpses of tune in the opera are comprised within its limits—and these are subsequently employed throughout the work *ad nauseam*.[9]

What Chorley and Davison had in common with their Italian, French and German counterparts was that they conceptualised Verdi's first compositional and dramatic achievements having in mind the operas of Rossini and even Paisiello and Cimarosa, who were now considered as imperishable classics. They both expressed regret for the palmy days of Italian opera and reproached the manner in which modern composers were progressing. Even though it was consistent with the bloody plots so dear to romantic dramatists, librettists and composers, Victorian music critics showed aversion to the new declamato-like singing and longed for the beauty and freshness of genuine melody.[10] In the following years, when denying the increasing popularity of Verdi had become impossible, those critics who could not admit that the composer had some merits credited the singers with the popular success of his operas. It was thanks to interpreters like Pauline Viardot (the first Azucena in 1855 London), Marietta Piccolomini (the first Violetta in 1856 London) and Adelina Patti (the first Aida in

---

6   Hervé Gartioux, *La réception de Verdi en France, Anthologie de la presse 1845–1894* (Weinsberg: Galland, 2001), p. 16.
7   Kreuzer, *Verdi and the Germans*, pp. 31–32.
8   *The Athenaeum*, 7 March 1846, p. 250. See Zicari, *Verdi in Victorian London*, p. 46, https://doi.org/10.11647/OBP.0090.
9   *The Musical World*, 7 March 1846, p. 105.
10 See Zicari, *Verdi in Victorian London*, pp. 54–55, https://doi.org/10.11647/OBP.0090.

1870 London) that works like *Il trovatore*, *La traviata*, and *Aida*, Victorian critics argued, had won international audiences despite the limited talent of the composer. Even in the United States the reception of Verdi's operas was often accompanied by a sense of distress, with the more conservative critics grudgingly objecting to his poor melodic invention, his trivial choruses, his guitar-like orchestral accompaniments and the exaggerated use of wind and brass instruments.[11]

But if, as many contemporary critics argued, Verdi's compositions led to a new and more dramatic style, how did singers accommodate themselves to that change? Did bel canto soon turn into a different way of singing? As has been suggested by David Lawton, we should not forget that Verdi worked within a powerful operatic tradition and vocal performance practice changed more gradually than compositional conventions. For years to come, conventions of performance prevailed over those of composition and singers continued to enjoy a high degree of interpretative liberty, however strenuously composers like Verdi, and Donizetti and Bellini before him, defended their own sovereignty over their compositions.[12]

If, as noted before, vocal performance practice changed only gradually, how should we understand the relationship between a composer like Verdi and the performance conventions in which singers were still trained? Is it correct to assume that singers continued to refer to the style described in contemporary singing methods even when approaching Verdi's new operas? For obvious chronological reasons García's *Scuola* does not refer to Verdi's operas; still, how long did his precepts remain valid, and when did singers start modifying their singing style and vocal technique because of the new repertoire? Signs of the tension between the composer's demands and contemporary performance conventions—not to mention the talents and inclinations of individual interpreters—emerge occasionally from the folds of a scarcely documented discussion. As has been suggested by Claudio Vellutini, Eugenia Tadolini is, again, a case in point. When she interpreted the character of Elvira in *Ernani* at the Kärntnertortheater on 30 May 1844 in Vienna she replaced the original cabaletta 'Tutto sprezzo che d'Ernani' with Giselda's 'Non fu sogno' from *I Lombardi alla prima crociata*. On learning about this change Verdi expressed his frustration and his resentful words are preserved in a letter to Leo Herz, written on the 7 June 1844.[13] Tadolini is also remembered for Verdi's claim that her voice was 'far too good' to sing Lady Macbeth: as he wrote in a letter to librettist Salvatore Cammarano on 23 November 1848, 'Tadolini sings to perfection; and I would like the Lady not to sing. Tadolini has a stupendous voice, clear, limpid, powerful; and I would like the Lady to have a harsh, stifled, and hollow voice'.[14] While the letter to Leo Herz reflects the composer's aversion to those textual manipulations that were typical of contemporary performance practice, the opinion on Tadolini reflects the manner in which Verdi, although appreciative of her vocal skills, was pushing towards a new vocal aesthetic, one that valued energy and passion over virtuosity and the pure beauty of vocal sounds. In this regard Verdi shared with Bellini a preference for strong situations: if Verdi was criticised for pursuing the 'Effect, nothing but effect',[15] Bellini, as we have seen testified by an undated letter, insisted that the 'dramma per musica' [i.e., opera] must draw tears, terrify people, make them die, through song'.[16] However, and notwithstanding Verdi's protestations, episodes like that of Tadolini substituting a new piece for the written aria should not be taken at face value; Verdi himself regularly endorsed alterations of his scores, changed the music, or allowed it to be changed for the sake of the dramatic effect.[17] Such was the case when *Nabucco*, which was premiered in Milan on 9 March 1842 with Giovannina Bellinzaghi as Fenena, was put on again in Milan later that year with Amalia Zecchini in the role. Since Zecchini's voice compass was lower than Bellinzaghi's, Verdi revised the part in order to accommodate

---

11   See George W. Martin, *Verdi in America* (Rochester: University of Rochester Press, 2011).
12   David Lawton 'Ornamenting Verdi's Arias: The Continuity of a Tradition', in *Verdi in Performance*, edited by Alison Latham and Roger Parker (Oxford: Oxford University Press, 2001), pp. 49–78.
13   Claudio Vellutini, 'Adina Par Excellence', 3–29.
14   Ibid., p. 8.
15   Capra, 'Effekt, nicht als Effekt', pp. 117–42.
16   Undated letter to Pepoli (but from May 1834); see Bellini, *Epistolario*, p. 400, cited in Pierluigi Petrobelli and Roger Parker, 'Notes on Bellini's Poetics', in *Music in the Theater, Essays on Verdi and Other Composers* (Princeton: Princeton University Press, 1994), pp. 162–75.
17   Roger Freitas, 'Towards a Verdian Ideal of Singing: Emancipation from Modern Orthodoxy', *Journal of the Royal Musical Association*, 127.2 (2002), 226–57.

not only the different pitch range, but also a more delicate voice quality.[18] When the same opera was mounted in Venice in December 1842, this time with Almerinda Granchi as Fenena, Verdi composed a new version of the same aria, again adapting the music to the voice of the new singer.[19] Similar changes are documented for other operas, like, for instance, *I Lombardi alla prima crociata* and *Ernani* (Verdi composed an aria for the tenor Nicola Ivanoff to substitute for 'Odi il voto'). We can consider also the case of *I due Foscari*, which was premiered in Rome in 1844: for the Paris premiere in December 1846 Giovanni Matteo De Candia (also known as Mario) asked Verdi to prepare some puntature and compose a new cabaletta to conclude the 'Cavatina di Jacopo' in the first act.[20] When preparing *Il Trovatore* for the Théâtre Italien in Paris (1854 and 1855) Verdi made some modifications for Erminia Frezzolini, who would appear as Leonora; of the French version (1857) Verdi's fioriture for the 'Aria del Conte' have been preserved, together with four new versions (two of them are autographs) of the cadenza for the 'Cavatina di Leonora'. More changes were endorsed by Verdi when Pauline Viardot, who had to sing it in London, asked him.[21] Other examples reinforce the notion that Verdi was much more lenient towards his interpreters than we are sometimes inclined to think.[22] In this regard, the connection between Verdi and the tradition he was said to be threatening is very strong and changes of the kind Rossini, Donizetti and Bellini were forced to accept were not exceptional especially in Verdi's early career.

In spite of his reputation as the arch-enemy of bel canto, Verdi seems to have preferred singers trained in the traditional style: 'In the teaching of singing, I would like the old-fashioned studies, combined with modern declamation'.[23] Verdi praised unreservedly Adelina Patti, who was acknowledged as a bel canto diva throughout a lifelong career: 'but Patti is more complete: marvellous voice, purest style of singing, stupendous actress with a charm and naturalness that no one else has'.[24] Verdi's position with regard to ornamentation has been also the object of scholarly discussion and, again, the notion that he was 'content to hear simply and exactly what is written'[25] should not be taken at face value. Numerous signs indicate how open he was when it came to negotiating interpretative solutions, on condition that the interpreter understood his dramatic intentions.[26]

Sometimes, precise markings in Verdi's score help us to better understand the relationship between the performance conventions of the time and the composer's demands and expectations. For instance, the indication 'Questo Recitativo dovrà essere detto senza le solite appoggiature' (this recitativo must be said without the usual appoggiaturas) which appears at the beginning of the 'Scena, terzetto e tempesta' in Act III of *Rigoletto*, should be understood as an exception to an interpretative convention widely shared among contemporary interpreters and endorsed by Verdi himself. Likewise, Verdi prescribes 'senza appoggiatura' in the last act of *Otello*, when Emilia pronounces the words 'Stolto! E tu il credesti?' It is clear that the composer warned against its use in those specific passages where the tradition of the insertion of the appoggiatura would be incompatible with the desired dramatic expression. This tradition, we may presume, was otherwise considered by Verdi as a common trait of the Italian operatic tradition, the very same tradition to which he belonged.

Even with regard to tempo modifications, the old trope according to which the composer wanted singers to sing *a tempo* needs further consideration. On reviewing *Ernani* in 1850 London (its London premiere dates back to 1845) Henry Fothergill Chorley, the authoritative critic of *The Athenaeum*, referred to the tenor John Sims Reeves and commented that 'Verdi's music, in its solo passages and closes, gives him [Sims Reeves] scope for that

---

18 See Ott, *Handbuch*, pp. 456–59.
19 See ibid., pp. 459–63.
20 See ibid., p. 482.
21 Marco Beghelli, 'Per fedeltà a una nota', *Il Saggiatore Musicale*, 8.2 (2001), 295–316 (p. 298).
22 See again Ott, *Handbuch*, pp. 447–564.
23 From a letter of 20 February 1871 to Giuseppe Piroli; as translated in Osborne, *Letters*, p. 75. Quoted in Freitas, 'Towards a Verdian Ideal of Singing', p. 231.
24 From a letter to Count Opprandino Arrivabene, December 1877, as reproduced in Abbiati, *Giuseppe Verdi* (Milan: Ricordi, 1963), IV, p. 38, quoted in Freitas, 'Towards a Verdian Ideal of Singing', p. 231.
25 Letter to Giulio Ricordi of 11 April 1871: 'm'accontento che si eseguisca semplicemente ed esattamente quello che è scritto'. Gaetano Cesari, Alessandro Luzio and Michele Scherillo (eds.), *I copialettere di Giuseppe Verdi* (Milan: Commissione, 1913), p. 256, https://archive.org/details/icopialettere00verd.
26 Will Crutchfield, 'Vocal Ornamentation in Verdi: The Phonographic Evidence', *19th Century Music*, 7.1 (1983), 3–54.

slackening of tempo and elongation of favourite notes which are considered by 'Young Italy' as the style dramatic'.[27] When *Rigoletto* was premiered in London in 1853 Chorley made a similar comment, this time with regard to Angiolina Bosio: 'By him [Verdi] singers are invited, not forbidden, to slacken tempo'.[28] Although contemporary interpreters and commentators seem to have understood Verdi's dramatic style as an encouragement to tempo flexibility, it is not as clear whether the composer was in favour of such fluctuations. In December 1883, when *Don Carlos* was in rehearsal, Verdi wrote to Giulio Ricordi insisting that the conductor, Franco Faccio, should make sure that the singer pronounce the lyrics correctly and keep the tempo.[29] Ten years later, in February 1893, when *Falstaff* was in preparation in Milan, Giulio Ricordi published a special issue of *L'Illustrazione italiana* which included an article on 'how Verdi writes and rehearses' ('Come scrive e come prova Giuseppe Verdi'). According to this article, 'Verdi desires that no phrase or rhythm be changed by useless tenuti or rallentando'.[30] However, contemporary eyewitnesses sometimes testified to the opposite. For instance, according to Marianna Barberini Nini, when rehearsing *Macbeth* in 1847 in Florence, Verdi, unable to explain his musical intentions to the conductor Pietro Romani, helped himself with gestures, banging on the score, slackening or speeding up the tempo with his hand'.[31] Again, when Verdi conducted his *Messa* in Köln in 1877, music critic August Guckeisen noted how Verdi allowed himself some rubato.[32] During the preparation of his *Pezzi sacri* in Turin in 1898, Arturo Toscanini, still a young conductor, met the composer, who approved of his decision to insert an allargando which was not written in the score. Verdi seems to have confessed to Toscanini that he had decided not to write it to avoid the exaggerated expression of that effect.[33] Or again, when Toscanini conducted Verdi's *Falstaff* in 1899 Verdi declared his aversion to metronomes.[34] Although the composer started to regularly insert metronome marks in 1846, it seems that he did it especially for those orchestral passages where the voice was not involved.[35]

As already observed with regard to *Ernani* in 1844, Verdi was convinced that a singer would take the right tempo if he or she adhered to the dramatic situation and paid careful attention to the meaning of the words: 'Basta badare alla posizione drammatica ed alla parola difficilmente si può sbagliare un tempo' (it would suffice to observe the dramatic situation and the lyrics and it is unlikely that you choose the wrong tempo).[36] Further confirmation of this can be found in a letter Verdi wrote to Pietro Romani in 1845, where the composer gave him instructions on how to conduct his *Giovanna d'Arco*.[37]

> The Adagio from the Tenor's Aria as it suits the voice: the chorus in C minor very lively. The cabaletta slow and cantabile. I do not speak of Giovanna's cavatina, which goes without saying. [...] I recommend you the Duet between Tenor and Donna... Let the orchestral movements be lively, and the Cantabili be slow: the Adagio in G minor should be slow, and Giovanna should be very agitated, especially when she joins in at the words 'Son maledetto' (I am cursed). Let there be a great contrast between the two songs.[38]

---

27 *The Athenaeum*, 23 March 1850, p. 320.
28 *The Athenaeum*, 21 May 1853.
29 *Letters of Giuseppe Verdi*, ed. by Charles Osborne (New York: Gollancz, 1971), p. 221.
30 'Egli [Verdi] desidera che nessuna frase o ritmo vengano cambiati da inutili tenuti o rallentando.' See James Hepokoski, 'Under the Eye of the Verdian Bear: Notes on the Rehearsals and Première of Falstaff', *Musical Quarterly*, 71.2 (1985), 135–56.
31 '...si aiutava con gesti, con grandi percosse sul libro, rallentando con la mano o rafforzando i tempi.' Marcello Conati, *Interviste e incontri con Verdi* (Milan: Emme Edizioni, 1980), p. 24.
32 Ibid., p. 121.
33 Ibid., p. 292.
34 Rodolfo Celletti, *Il canto* ([Milan]: Vallardi, 1989), p. 160.
35 Roberta Montemorra Marvin, 'Verdi's Tempo Assignments in "I masnadieri"', *Revista de Musicología*, XV Congreso de la Sociedad Internacional de Musicología: culturas musicales del mediterráneo y sus ramificaciones, 16.6 (1993), 3179–195.
36 G. Morazzoni and G. M. Ciampelli, *Verdi: lettere inedite: le opere verdiane al Teatro alla Scala (1839–1929)* (Milan: Libreria editrice milanese, 1929), p. 26.
37 Martin Chusid, 'A Letter by the Composer about "Giovanna d'Arco" and Some Remarks on the Division of Musical Direction in Verdi's Day', *Performance Practice Review*, 3.1 (1990), 7–57, https://doi.org/10.5642/perfpr.199003.01.10.
38 Ibid., pp. 8–9. 'L'Adagio dell'Aria del Tenore come starà bene alla voce: il Coro in Do minore vivo assai. La cabaletta Larga e cantabile. Non ti parlo della cavatina di Giovanna che va da se. [...] Ti raccomando il Duetto fra tenore e Donna... Siano vivace i movimenti d'orchestra, larghi i Cantabili: l'Adagio in sol minore sia largo, agit[at]o assai da Giovanna specialmente quando s'unisce a due alle parole 'Son maledetto' siavi gran contrasto fra i due canti.' My translation.

Verdi made a clear distinction between those vocal sections where the voice should 'go by itself', and those orchestral passages where the tempo, whether slow or vivacious, should be decided by the conductor.

All in all, given the evidence discussed so far, it is fair to assume that Verdi was not against the use of tempo modifications, on condition that these found their justification in the meaning of the words and in the dramatic situation. Verdi endorsed those changes that were consistent with the expressive quality of the lyrics and the music and opposed those that originated from the whim of the singer.[39] The composer's authority should be reinscribed in the tradition and context in which he operated, along with its conventions and performative habits. Instead, it is not easy to reconstruct the manner in which coloraturas and ornaments were applied by late nineteenth-century singers in Verdi's operas and whether his compositional style soon prevented those modifications in the melodic line that traditionally involved small graces, ornaments and roulades. As has been suggested, at the simplest level, towards the end of the nineteenth century we observe a shift from a highly-nuanced style, with some remaining link to the age of florid vocalism, to a more straight-forward, louder one with only incidental interest in coloratura.[40] Hints of this change can be found also in sources like Mathilde Marchesi's *Variantes et Points d'orgue*, and Ricci's *Variazioni*, where the presence of Verdi is limited to five works, in which melodic modifications are confined to the final cadenzas of the main arias. Marchesi includes only short cadenzas for *Ernani*, *La traviata*, *Il trovatore* (she uses the French reading, *Le trouvère*), and *Les vêpres siciliennes*. In Ricci, the comparatively marginal position occupied by Verdi's operas is suggested by the few short cadential passages he reproduced, as opposed, for instance, to the more numerous, richly flourished cadenzas and passages that accompany the works of Rossini and Donizetti. There we find a single cadenza for Elvira in *Ernani*,[41] a small change in a single bar to Elvira in *La forza del destino*,[42] some suggestions for the cadenza of Gilda's aria, belonging to Virginia Boccabadati,[43] Nellie Melba and Fanny Toresella, a few passages belonging to Patti and Claudia Muzio for Violetta in *La traviata*, and some more for the character of Leonora in *Il trovatore*, this time belonging to Muzio and Marchisio.[44] The same can be said of the volume edited by Estelle Liebling, where we find reported a few cadential passages from *Il trovatore*, *La traviata*, *Un ballo in maschera* and *I vespri siciliani*. Of all Verdi's operas, only these four, together with *Ernani*, came to be associated with the tradition of bel canto; for them a body of textual modifications soon developed, to which singers of the younger generation continued to adhere: among them Luisa Tetrazzini. These modifications, unlike those in works of earlier composers, tended to remain confined to the final cadenza of the main aria, or, less often, to the central semicadenza. In documenting the vocal style connected with Verdi's late operas a pivotal role has been played by those male singers who were close to the composer and became involved in the burgeoning discographic industry at the beginning of the century. Among them, Victor Maurel and Francesco Tamagno occupy a prominent position, since they created the roles of Otello and Iago in Milan on 5 February 1887, and eventually recorded select sections of the opera.[45] A similar position is held by Antonio Pini-Corsi, Edoardo Garbin and Adelina Stehle who created the characters of Ford, Fenton and Nannetta in *Falstaff* in 1893 and left a few recordings which attest to their vocal style and technique.

On the value of early recordings as evidence of a tradition that lived on in the performance practice of the early twentieth century much has been said, and reference to the interpretation of Verdi's music as documented

---

39 See again Freitas, 'Towards a Verdian Ideal of Singing', pp. 226–57.
40 Will Crutchfield, 'Vocal Ornamentation in Verdi: The Phonographic Evidence', *19th-Century Music*, 7.1 (1983), 3–54.
41 Ricci, *Variazioni*, vol. I, p. 27
42 Ibid., p. 37.
43 Verdi mentions Virginia Boccabadati, Marietta Piccolomini and Maria Spezia in a letter to Vincenzo Torelli written in Paris on 11 November 1856. In the letter he is considering these three singers for the role of Cordelia in *King Lear*, an operatic project he was then planning. 'Per questa parte non conosco che tre artiste: Piccolomini, Spezia, e Virginia Boccabadati. Tutte tre hanno voce debole ma talento grande, anima e sentimento di scena. Eccellenti tutte nella Traviata'. Verdi, *I copialettere*, p. 197.
44 Ricci, *Variazioni*, vol. I, pp. 83–84.
45 A collection of historical recordings of these two roles, interpreted by singers like Victor Maurel, Titta Ruffo, Mario Sammarco, Enrcio Caruso, Aureliano Pertile, Francesco Tamagno and many others, was published in 2010 by the Istituzione Casa della Musica di Parma, under the supervision of Professor Marco Capra and is distributed by EMI. The recordings included in the CD-set chart the period from 1902 to 1951 and follow the evolution that the singing style underwent over the first half of the twentieth century.

in early recordings can be found both in scholarly writings and music methods and manuals.[46] Suffice it here to say that what early recordings show, at least as far as Verdi's operas are concerned, is a gradual shift towards a less flourished, more declamato-like interpretative approach. If a more nuanced style and a stronger presence of florid vocalisation can be observed in the earlier generations, younger singers were more inclined to a louder, straight-forward reading of the text with 'only incidental interest in coloratura'.[47] However, as recent scholarly investigation into early recordings suggests, individual differences often prevail over a more broadly shared interpretative style.[48] In the case of Tetrazzini, her proverbial vocal talent and dramatic skills, combined with a careful choice of repertoire, resulted in a well-defined musical personality. The distance between her distinctive interpretative style and that of other divas of the time is sometimes remarkable.

Verdi in Tetrazzini's Interpretations

Of all Verdi's operas only two hold a prominent position in Tetrazzini's repertoire, *Rigoletto* with sixty-seven productions and *La traviata*, with sixty, while *Un ballo in maschera*, which she sang in nine productions, occupies a more marginal position. Her first appearances in the roles of Gilda and Violetta date back to 1892 and 1893 but it was not until the first decade of the new century that Tetrazzini's popular success reached its apex thanks to her impersonation of Violetta in 1905 in San Francisco and then in 1907 in London.

As we have seen, at the beginning of the century the so-called bel canto repertoire was often described as trite and hackneyed, and those more progressive music critics who had come to appreciate the works of Wagner and Strauss looked down upon Italian composers. Moreover, operas like *La traviata* and *Il trovatore*, together with Donizetti's *Lucia di Lammermoor* and Rossini's *Barbiere di Siviglia* were often considered trifles and were tolerated for the sake of those ignorant opera-goers who rejoiced in a few old tunes sung in costume: popular success had nothing to do with musical quality, as the vast popularity of these operas demonstrated. These operatic trifles were also often criticised for the poor quality of the performances, which were entrusted to insufficiently experienced conductors and singers of little or no talent. To some extent, it was thanks to interpreters like Luisa Tetrazzini and conductors like Giorgio Polacco and Cleofonte Campanini that at the outset of the century this prejudice could be combatted. Contemporary critics credited these artists with the quality and the careful preparation that, after decades of poor productions, could revitalise a repertoire that had long been undervalued.

Such was the case of *La traviata* when it was given in 1905 at the Tivoli in San Francisco with Tetrazzini in the title role, which drew enthusiastic responses also among those music critics who considered the bel canto repertoire as trite and Verdi's *La traviata* hackneyed.

> *La Traviata*, that one has been accustomed to regard as a hackneyed, thin enough vehicle for the human lark, with Tetrazzini, crammed the theatre. Practically the season has divided itself into Tetrazzini nights and other nights. When Tetrazzini sings the people will go whether Mr. Verdi, Mr. Bizet or anyone else made the opera, and no matter how he made it. The attitude is not artistic but perfectly natural. One can very fully excuse it while Tetrazzini sings, for her every appearance only makes it more apparent that here indeed is an extraordinary singer, a rare vocal preciousness.[49]

It was thanks to the extraordinary talent of Tetrazzini and her colleagues—who all deserved the critic's appreciative words—if an inartistic opera like *La traviata* could score such an enthusiastic success. And it was thanks to the conductor, Giorgio Polacco, and his refined interpretation that 'the careless old "tum-tum" took on astonishing

---

46 See Crutchfield, 'Vocal Ornamentation in Verdi: The Phonographic Evidence', *19th Century Music*, 7.1 (1983), 3–54, Zicari 'Expressive Tempo Modifications in Early 20th-Century Recorded Performances of Operatic Arias', *Music&Practice*, 5 (2019), https://doi.org/10.32063/0507, Ott, *Handbuch*, pp. 447–564.
47 Crutchfield, 'Vocal Ornamentation in Verdi', p. 13.
48 Dorottya Fabian, 'Commercial Sound Recordings and Trends in Expressive Music Performance', in *Expressiveness in Music Performance*, ed. by Dorottya Fabian, Renee Timmers, and Emery Schubert (Oxford: Oxford University Press, 2014), pp. 58–79, https://doi.org/10.1093/acprof:oso/9780199659647.003.0004.
49 Blanche Partington, 'Traviata at the Tivoli a Great Hit', *The San Francisco Call*, 20 January 1905, p. 4

grace and distinction. It sparkled; it thrilled'.[50] The critic valued the manner in which the interpretation conveyed to the audience the sense of the drama.

> Every phrase, every note of the opera was charged with meaning, the whole thing gathering significance, picturesqueness, dramatic intensity, as with no other *Traviata* of my experience... Tetrazzini contributed tremendously to the dramatic illusion. The woes of Violetta became actually human in her interpretation. All the vocal embroidery was most deftly fitted to the dramatic need.[51]

Tetrazzini showed herself an admirable and accomplished resource, not just as a singer, however talented, but also as an exceptional actress. In September that year *La traviata* was produced again with Polacco conducting and Tetrazzini in the title role, and again Blanche Partington uttered words of appreciation: Polacco had the merit of ennobling the music of Verdi and lifting it up to the level of Mozart, after decades of poor conducting and inadequate interpretations:

> The trivial old tum-tum of the orchestra—in the careless readings to which one has been so haplessly accustomed, becomes a thing of infinite gayety and sparkle in Polacco's hands. Its every note glitters. Almost Mozartean in its freshness the opera becomes. One would give a good deal to hear a *Don Giovanni* from Signor Polacco[52]

The star of the evening was, of course, Luisa Tetrazzini, whose Violetta was a masterpiece of dramatic realism.

> To me Tetrazzini is a little at her best here. Her Lucia is a wonderful performance; and a pretty trick of comedy makes Tetrazzini's Rosina a thing wholly delightful. But as Violetta the little diva wheedles the quite unusual tear from the grand operatic eye. She brings a pathos as rare as it is effective to the acting of the role. *La Traviata* is conspicuously more human throughout as Polacco has set it before us; but as in the scene between Violetta and Armand's [sic] father one forgets that it is opera in the realism that both bring to the scene.[53]

Two years later Tetrazzini made her début in London as Violetta and the response of the critics was similar. When first mounted at Covent Garden on 2 November, *La traviata* did not draw a large audience, a circumstance that made the critic of *The Times* hope 'that not many evenings of the season will be wasted upon *La Traviata*, despite the presence of a young and talented interpreter'.[54] The interpretation of Madame Tetrazzini made the opera worth attending and changed the initial situation, attracting larger crowds of opera-goers. Her understanding of the part was simply complete:

> Not only has her voice the flexibility and clearness which enable her to make great effect with 'Sempre libera degg'io' and other airs of the kind, but she has a definite and consistent conception of the character, which gives it a genuine dramatic significance. It followed that her scene with Signor Sammarco in the second act was finely expressed, and the last difficult scene was a success, whether looked at from a dramatic point of view or as a piece of refined singing.[55]

If Mario Sammarco, in the role of Giorgio Germont, Alfredo's father, was a valid companion both in terms of singing and acting, the same could not be said of Fernando Carpi, whose rendition of Alfredo, the critic continued, was just conventional. A few days later, *The Times* reviewed Tetrazzini as Gilda in *Rigoletto*, with Sammarco in the title role and John McCormack as the Duke; Ettore Panizza conducted. Tetrazzini, who had caught a cold, had recovered completely and her success could not be greater.

> The highest expectations must have been gratified long before the opera was over, for it was quite clear from the opening phrases 'Oh quanto dolor' in the duet in the first act that she had thrown off all traces of her cold and was singing unhampered by any obstacles. The notes came pouring out with absolute certainty and ease, and, apart from a tendency to harden the very last note of a phrase when it was taken *forte*, her tone retained its beauty even in the most ornate passages. For Mme. Tetrazzini, in spite of her brilliant technique, is not one of those singers who sacrifice

---

50   Ibid.
51   Ibid.
52   Blanche Partington, 'Tetrazzini's Art Ascends', *The San Francisco Call*, 27 September 1905, p. 9
53   Ibid.
54   'La Traviata' (Royal Opera), *The Times*, 4 November 1907, p. 9.
55   Ibid.

beauty of tone to neatness of execution; she is an artist with the real singing traditions in the sense that she uses *coloratura* as a means of expression, and not simply as so much decoration. She showed herself an artist, too, in the duet and in the great quartet by the way she kept her place in the *ensemble,* and in the scene with Rigoletto in the third act she made the situation really poignant by the sincerity of her acting. She had the advantage of playing with that great artist Signor Sammarco, who seemed fired to surpass himself by the unusual event of finding himself the father of a Gilda who took her part seriously; at any rate, he has seldom acted with such conviction or sung the familiar airs so magnificently as he did on Saturday. The honours of the evening were not, however, confined to these two artists, for Mr. John McCormack took the part of the Duke and made quite a *furore* by his beautiful singing of 'La donna è mobile.' Throughout the evening he sang with ease and with something of the real Italian *abandon* in the lilt with which he took the lighter passages, although his voice still sounds a little cold in the more passionate moments. With Miss Maud Santley as Maddalena and Signor Luppi as Sparafucile, the last act lost none of its impressiveness through want of care in the smaller parts, and the great quartet has seldom been better sung. The whole performance, from the point of view of an already excited public, was in fact a *succèss fou*.[56]

The critic paid careful attention to the voice quality of Tetrazzini, and his remark on how she used coloratura as a means of expression rather than a form of decoration is of particular interest. The critic's value judgement was not biased by the notion that coloratura as such was wrong and tasteless; instead, he showed he was knowledgeable about a performance practice that had often been judged against criteria that were foreign to that tradition.

Of the same opinion was the critic of *The Musical Times*, who reported on the enormous success Tetrazzini scored as Violetta, Lucia and Gilda, and observed that it was thanks to Tetrazzini that a tradition long misunderstood and often ill-treated could be successfully revived and fully appreciated.

The striking success of Madame Tetrazzini in *La Traviata* and *Lucia* at Covent Garden is a reminder that *il bel canto* is not as dead as many of the younger generation of opera-goers had supposed. Nothing in art that has ever been really alive—alive, that is, with true human feeling—can die; and the application of this truism to the present case is that the old and honourable art of *il bel canto* has been, and to all appearances will be again, the vitalising factor in opera. It has been charged with being a weakness and a snare; performances of the old Italian masterpieces have been sneered at as 'concerts in costume,' and such mistresses of *agilità* as Jenny Lind and Patti have been disparaged as mere vocal gymnasts; but their triumphs have demonstrated, as Madame Tetrazzini's are doing, that even *foriture* are more than decorative—that they have an essential place in the dramatic scheme of which they are part.[57]

One month later, the same journal published a description of her vocal skills and a short summary of her career in South America.

Madame Tetrazzini, who made her first appearance in England at Covent Garden as Violetta in *Traviata*, on November 2, is one of those rarely-gifted artists who combine a soprano voice of rare quality and exceptional compass with a keen dramatic intuition and an artistic and sensitive temperament that endow her singing and gestures with fascinating significance. The gifted lady, who is a native of Florence, has had eleven years' operatic experience, the last four of which have been spent in the Argentine. She therefore came to us a matured artist, and her success was immediate and so great that the house was completely sold out for her second appearance in the same opera on November 7. A still greater success was achieved by her impersonation of the heroine of Donizetti's *Lucia di Lammermoor*, on November 15, her rendering of the 'mad scene' calling forth an extraordinary demonstration of enthusiastic appreciation. In both these operas it was her command of tone-colour quite as much as the perfection of her vocalization which so distinguished her performances, and one must go back to the time when Madame Adelina Patti was in her prime to find such perfect renderings of old Italian opera numbers.[58]

Besides the remarks on her rare vocal skills combined with a keen dramatic intuition, of special relevance are, for us, the comments on the line of continuity that connected Tetrazzini to Adelina Patti, the epitome of bel canto. Still, one may wonder whether the journalist ever had the chance to hear Patti singing in her prime.

Upon the conclusion of the Covent Garden autumn season in 1907, in which Luisa Tetrazzini made her appearance in *La traviata* (2 November), *Lucia di Lammermoor* (15 November) and *Rigoletto* (23 November), the

---

56 'Rigoletto' (Royal Opera), *The Times*, 25 November 1907, p. 7.
57 'Occasional Notes', *The Musical Times*, 1 December 1907, vol. 48, no. 778, p. 787.
58 'The Opera', *The Musical Times*, 1 December 1907, vol. 48, no. 778, pp. 807–08.

celebrated soprano gave four gala concerts on 3, 7, 10 and 12 December. Initially only two concerts had been scheduled, but the audience thronged the theatre to such an extent that it was impossible not to add two more performances. Tetrazzini made a *furore* but *The Times* could not spare its readers a negative comment on the arguable musical taste of the British public: thronging the theatre to listen to Tetrazzini singing an Italian bel canto aria was something the country should have been ashamed of.

> The concert given in Covent Garden Theatre last night [Dec. 3] reflected rather unfavourably upon the musical taste of the British public; for long before any detailed programme was published there was the certainty of a crowded audience, the truth being, of course, that the bulk of the nation is still ready to rush after special singers quite without regard to what they sing; and the mere announcement of Mme. Tetrazzini's appearance is just now enough to fill Covent Garden to the ceiling.[59]

Despite the concerns expressed by *The Times* the success was enormous, and the response of the public boundlessly enthusiastic. The journalist of the *New York Daily Tribune*, reporting on this almost unprecedented furore, defined 'Tet nights' as those nights when large crowds of enthusiasts rushed for seats at Covent Garden. This phenomenal response was not new to London, and similar reviews had appeared also when Jenny Lind and Marietta Piccolomini had made their appearances there, the former in Verdi's *I masnadieri* in 1847, and the latter in the London premiere of *La traviata* in 1856.[60]

> Mme. Tetrazzini is a soprano with remarkable purity of tone and refinement of method. Her voice is not powerful, and in the lower register may even be described as having ordinary quality; but her high notes are marvellously clear and sweet and her command of all the resources of vocalization is complete. She sings with simplicity and masterful facility, and the effort required for the highest passages is minimized by the art that conceals art. She has the birdlike purity of tone for which Mme. Melba was famous in her best days; and she has also an exquisite sensibility which reminds oldtime music lovers of the emotional thrills experienced when Mme. Christine Nilsson used to sing in *Faust*, *The Magic Flute*, *Martha* and *Mignon*. Without having beauty of feature or graceful figure, she has the charm of a gracious manner and unaffected simplicity in giving pleasure to audiences. The enthusiasm at her closing concerts this week has been intense and uncontrollable. She has been recalled a dozen times after each number and has been forced to respond to encores even when she had a slight cold and there was every reason for saving her voice. She seems destined to become the favorite interpreter of Verdi and the oldtime school of opera at Covent Garden, and to make the Italian nights, so far as wealth and fashion are concerned, as popular as the Wagner nights.[61]

The critic's words shed new light on three issues of paramount importance. First, in describing Tetrazzini's vocal technique he provides us with valuable information on the extent to which her live performances were consistent with what we hear in her recordings; second, he connects Tetrazzini to Nellie Melba and, more oddly, to Christine Nilsson, whom he recalls for a repertoire so different from that for which Tetrazzini came to be appreciated. Third, he refers to the different manner in which Verdi and the so-called 'oldtime school of opera' were understood in opposition to the popularity of Wagner. But while the comparison between Tetrazzini and her colleagues, as well as the reference to the old-timers, linger in the background of this analysis, the remarks on Tetrazzini's voice are of far greater interest: besides her proverbial agility in the high register the critic mentions the uneven quality of her voice in the passage register. This characteristic would draw the attention of other critics in the following years and is audible also in her recordings; as has already been suggested, this had to do with an expressive method called voce bianca, 'white voice' used by high sopranos.[62] The unevenness in the voice resulted in a particularly expressive contrast that, as Tetrazzini would reveal, she adopted in passages where the dramatic situation called for such a richness of shades.[63]

---

59 'Concerts', *The Times*, 4 December 1907, p. 12.
60 Marietta Piccolomini's *Traviata* was her London début, while Jenny Lind first appeared there in *Roberto il diavolo* in 1847.
61 '"Tet" Nights and other Social Recreations' (London Notes), *New York Daily Tribune*, 22 December 1907, p. 5.
62 Nicholas Limansky, 'Luisa Tetrazzini: Coloratura Secrets', *Opera Quarterly*, 20.4 (2004), 540–69. Marco Beghelli, 'A ritroso: indizi nella divulgazione extrateatrale per il recupero della prassi esecutiva verdiana', in *Fuori Dal Teatro. Modi e Percorsi Della Divulgazione Di Verdi*, ed. by Antonio Carlini (Venice: Marsilio, 2015), pp. 247–64.
63 Tetrazzini, *My Life of Song* (London, New York, Toronto and Melbourne: Cassell, 1921), p. 316. See Chapter One.

Reviews that were published in the more mature phase of Tetrazzini's career suggest that she had come to master a more even transition between low and high notes. Other critics drew attention to the fact that although Tetrazzini had been called the new Patti, not every commentator agreed on this comparison. For instance, on 11 January 1908, when Tetrazzini was expected to make her appearance as Violetta in New York, the critic of *The Evening World* stirred up the audience's expectation by presenting her as the singer of the century:

> Her phenomenal success, which has been heralded the world over, did not come to her, however, until the local autumn season of grand opera at Covent Garden, where she had never sung before. Her first audience went wild over her. She was cheered again and again and the critics exhausted their vocabulary in sounding her praises. She was Patti and Jenny Lind and Melba all in one, they declared. Hers was the voice of the century.[64]

On the other hand, one week later, Sylvester Rowling commented on the furore that had accompanied her brilliant début at the Manhattan Opera House as Violetta, and expressed his reservations on the possibility that a comparison could really be drawn between her and her illustrious predecessors. Even those who had had the privilege to hear Patti could hardly trust their memory.

> There are few people living who have an intelligent remembrance of the voice of the 'Swedish Nightingale.' Even of Patti, in her prime, there are not so many who can speak with authority as to how well she sang. Most of us were privileged to hear her when her warmest admirers admitted that some of the bloom of her voice had departed. Then Memory, at best—especially of sounds—is scarcely to be trusted, and most of us develop taste with years, and the judgment of youth is not always final.[65]

Tetrazzini's voice was of wondrous flexibility and great range but, Rowling continued, it presented a childlike quality in the lower register: 'her middle register is luscious. She takes her upper notes with bird-like sweetness. Her lower tones are clean cut even when she falls into an odd utterance that savors somewhat of a child's'.[66] This last reference is in line with the notion of white voice as we have seen described by the singer herself. However, Tetrazzini never showed a sign of effort: 'Her singing seems to be the easiest and most natural thing in the world. Whether it be to breathe or to whisper a sound, or to give it with all her might, makes no difference'.[67] More interestingly, the critic addresses a question that helps us to understand how bel canto came to be understood as a means for dramatic expression:

> Tetrazzini's voice is not only full of color—it is a marvel of dramatic expression. She is not content with giving an artistic rendition of the melodies. She makes the notes significant. They almost speak sentences. It this particular [sic] she is easily the superior of any coloratura soprano and has few equals among dramatic sopranos...[68]

Tetrazzini was well aware of this particular quality, as she would admit a few years later in her *How to Sing*:

> They were all more especially struck by the manner in which I managed, while singing Verdi's florid music brilliantly and effectively in the purely vocal sense, at the same time to make it expressive; and this I took as the greatest possible compliment which could be bestowed on me. For that I think is what coloratura properly sung should be. It should please the ear by its brilliance, but at the same time it should not, and need not, obscure the dramatic significance of what is sung.[69]

Finally, Sylvester Rowling provides us with some details on the changes he could notice in Verdi's music as the diva sang it: 'It may be recorded that in the "Ah, fors'è lui" Tetrazzini took a high C, and in the "Sempre libera" an E flat. Both were emitted with the easy grace that distinguishes all of this great artist's singing'.[70] Similar remarks

---

64 'New Patti Here, Ready for Debut at Hammerstein's', *The Evening World* (NY), 11 January 1908, front page.
65 Sylvester Rowling, 'Her Voice Has Wonderful Flexibility and Charm', *The Evening World* (NY), 16 January 1908, p. 3.
66 Ibid.
67 Ibid.
68 Ibid.
69 Tetrazzini, *How to Sing*, p. 78.
70 Sylvester Rowling, 'Her Voice Has Wonderful Flexibility and Charm', *The Evening World* (NY), 16 January 1908, p. 3.

appeared in the reviews published by *The New York Sun* and *The New York Times*, which we find reproduced at the end of Rowling's article. Similarly, *The New York Times* expressed words of appreciation and referred to the same changes in the score, this time adding a description of the remarkable messa di voce with which Tetrazzini embellished the high C at the end of 'Ah, fors'è lui'.

> Her voice is an exceptional one in the firmness and clearness and apparent ease with which she takes and prolongs these tones. Thus at the end of the air 'Ah, fors'è lui,' she took a high C and swelled and diminished it with evenness and precision, and at the end of the succeeding 'Sempre libera' she sustained a strong and clear E flat. Of course, whatever the artistic value of this may be, it is in the highest degree impressive and it set the audience in an uproar.— *New York Times*.[71]

As we will see, the reference to high C and E flat is consistent with what we hear in her recordings, and the description of the messa di voce fits perfectly her recorded renditions of the same aria, thus strongly suggesting that her interpretations did not follow the whim of the moment, nor did they change when it came to making a disc in a recording studio. On the same day, the *New York Daily Tribune* published a lengthy article on 'the advent of Tetrazzini' at the Manhattan Opera House:

> Signorina Tetrazzini appeared. A most disappointing figure with a most disappointing walk and a manner that savoured of everything but distinction. The opera was *La Traviata*, one long ago set aside for the barrel organ repertory. Grievously disappointing were, her voice and vocal manner. Connoisseurs looked into each other's faces with quizzical amazement. Then came the drinking song and expressions began to change. After the 'Ah fors'è lui' and its brilliant cabaletta the audience went wild with excitement. It seemed as if the glad shoutings would never cease. A dozen times the curtain went up to permit the lady to bow her thanks-alone, repeatedly with Bassi, the tenor, with Mr. Hammerstein, with Signor Campanini, whom an opening in the scenery had shown in the act of embracing and kissing his sister-in-law, and then again and still again.
>
> And what caused this extraordinary demonstration? Not the singer's voice. That has charms, but save in the volume and brilliancy of its upper renter, it is not especially noteworthy. Not the technical execution of the florid music alone, for the present generation, with memories of Patti, Nilsson, Gerster and Sembrich in the role, could recall many more finished performances. Not the person of the singer, for that was in crass contradiction of the ideal picture of the heroine. The secret lay in the combination of beautiful singing as such, and acting. Not acting in the sense of attitude, motion and facial expression, although these were all admirable, but in the dramatic feeling which imbued the singing—the dramatic color which shifted with kaleidoscopic swiftness from phrase to phrase, filling it with the blood of the play. The voice, weak and pallid in its lower register, had a dozen shades of meaning nevertheless, and as it soared upward it took on strength and glitter, though it lost in emotional force as it gained in sensual charm.
>
> Judged by such standards as this public is familiar with, Mme. Tetrazzini is neither a voice of consistent beauty throughout its several rather sharply marked registers, nor an organ consummately educated, in the strict sense. There were notes whose true pitch was reached only when the singer put added force into their utterance, and there was something left to be desired in her adjustment of vocal values when sustaining part of a dialogue or trio. But in spite of these obvious flaws in her art, the newcomer made a genuinely fine impression, and it is likely that her star will be in the ascendant for some time to come.[72]

In addition to some unkind remarks on Tetrazzini's unattractive figure, the critic reiterates the tropes we have already discussed: the reference to the barrel organ repertory to which operas like *La traviata* belonged, the necessary distinction between true artistic value and popularity, the connection, whether blurred or not, with her more illustrious predecessors, the uneven quality of her voice, the dramatic feeling which imbued her singing, which was the real strength of the young diva.

The critic of *The Sun* made similar remarks and, in a more nuanced language, started by uttering his doubts as to the figure of Tetrazzini and her credibility as a young lady dying of consumption.

> Like the traditional Violettas of old time Mme Tetrazzini does not appear to be in any immediate danger of wasting away with consumption. Her figure is well nourished and her face is as round as the silver moon. But she is a woman of pleasing appearance for all that, and her smile is both generous and frequent. Her countenance cannot fairly be

---

71 Ibid.
72 'Manhattan Opera House: The Advent of Tetrazzini' (Music), *New York Daily Tribune*, 16 January 1908, p. 7.

called mobile or sensitive, but for the workaday conventions of opera world it will suffice. And after all the singing is the thing.[73]

The description of Tetrazzini's voice quality is not dissimilar from what we have already seen, and the references to the high pitches are again consistent with the recordings she has left.

> Mme Tetrazzini has a fresh, clear voice of pure soprano quality and of sufficient range, though other roles must perhaps disclose its furthest flights above the staff. The perfectly unworn condition and youthful timbre of this voice are its largest charms, and to these must be added a splendid richness in the upper range. Indeed, the best part of the voice as heard last evening was from the G above the staff to the high C. The B flat in 'Sempre libera' was a tone of which any singer might have been proud. The high D in the same number was by no means so good, and the high E flat which the singer took in ending the scene was a head tone of thin quality and refused to stay on the pitch. In coloradure Mme Tetrazzini quite justified much that had been written about her. She sang staccato with consummate ease, though not with the approved method of breathing. Her method is merely to check the flow between notes instead of rightly attacking each note separately. But the effect which she produces, that of detached notes rather than of strict staccato, is charming. Of her shake less can be said in praise. It was neither clear in emission nor steady, and the interval was surely at least open to question. Descending scales she sang beautifully, with perfect smoothness and clean articulation. Her transformation of the plain scale in the opening cadenza of 'Sempre libera' into a chromatic scale, though a departure from the letter of the score, was not at all out of taste, and its execution fully obtained its right to existence.[74]

As we will see, the transformation of the scale in the opening cadenza of 'Sempre libera' can also be found in her recordings. Nevertheless, the critic showed himself particularly fastidious when it came to judging the quality of her voice and technique: in his opinion, the ascending scales were sung in a manner that would not be tolerated in a first year student: 'they began with a tremulous and throaty voce bianca and ended in a sweep into a full medium, with the chest resonance carried up to a preposterous height'.[75] The uneven quality of her lower medium notes was particularly noticeable, since 'these were all sung with a pinched glottis and with a colour so pallid and a tremolo so pronounced that they were often not a bad imitation of the wailing of a cross infant'.[76] The cantabile, the critic continued, was not only uneven in tone quality, with many breaks between her medium and her upper notes, but also replete with the breaths taken capriciously and without consideration of either text or music.

> For example, in beginning 'Ah, fors'è lui', she deliberately made a phrase after the U, and, taking a leisurely breath, introduced the I as if it belonged to the next word. The continued employment of cold colour in cantabile quite removed the possibility of pathos from 'Non sapete', while a pitiless description of her infantile delivery of 'Dite alla giovane' would read like cruelty. One of the neatest pieces of singing she did was her 'Ah, se ciò è ver', in which the staccato effect previously mentioned and some crisply executed diminutions in short phrases were excellent.[77]

Possibly in response to this criticism, a few days later Reginald De Koven published an article in the columns of *The San Francisco Call*, where he took it upon himself to defend Tetrazzini's lyric art against her few detractors.

> One fact must always be borne in mind to appreciate justly the finished art of this great singer, and that is she acts with her voice. Her phrasing of vocal passages which some—and I think wrongly—have called in question is governed and inspired by the dramatic meaning of the text rather than solely by the vocal aspect of the phrase. In this way she may at times violate the tradition, but is justified by the greater clarity of the expression of emotion and feeling gained thereby. Comparisons with other great singers of her class are valueless and misleading, for as an artist she is so distinctively individual and sui generis that she is practically in a class by herself.[78]

---

73 'Mme Tetrazzini Welcomed', *The Sun*, 16 January 1908, p. 7.
74 Ibid.
75 Ibid.
76 Ibid.
77 Ibid.
78 Reginald De Koven, 'Tetrazzini's Big Triumph is Repeated', *The San Francisco Call*, 19 January 1908, pp. 17–18.

In the same issue of the journal, Sylvester Rowling took up his pen to plead for her unique vocal skills and the effortless manner in which she could sing the most difficult and, for many, impossible passages in the highest register, even when bending over to pick up the train of her fancy costume.

> Tetrazzini's high E flat, taken nonchalantly while she stooped to pick up her skirts, is the talk of the town. Expectation is on tiptoe for her impersonation of Lucia at the Manhattan opera-house next Monday night. Meanwhile her debut as Violetta in *La Traviata* last Wednesday is eagerly discussed everywhere. Although there was some carping criticism of the new star's methods by one or two of the reviewers, none denied that her voice was of remarkable range and quality. In this particular, at least, the verdict of the great audience that acclaimed her was confirmed by the experts. Making allowances for the natural nervousness [with] which even a singer of experience such as Tetrazzini must have been affected in facing a new audience, known to be the most critical and exacting, the writer believes the new prima donna has qualities yet to be disclosed. The marvellous ease with which she sings—apparently with no effort—has not been adequately exploited. In the hurry of a first review, for instance, the manner in which she took that E flat in the 'Sempre libera' was overlooked. There was something of contemptuousness about it. She bent over, picked up her skirts and walked off most indifferently, carrying the note with the utmost ease. What other artist could have done it?[79]

In March the journalist of *The Sun* interviewed Tetrazzini, who confirmed how easy it was for her to sing even the most difficult passages; this was a characteristic she shared with the great Patti.

> The conversation, duly interpreted, begins with an interrogation in regard to the high note that Mme. Tetrazzini takes so nonchalantly in *La traviata*, the vocal height being emphasized, not as usual, by a step forward toward the orchestra, a raising of the head so as to give the throat full expansion and an uplift of the eyes to the fly gallery. When Mme. Tetrazzini accomplishes it she leans over and picks up her long train as coolly as if she were asking in an ordinary conversational tone what the weather was. 'It is no effort for me to take a note in any position', is the quick answer. 'I can sing lying down, walking about, sitting, leaning over, whatever pose suggests itself. The resonant cavities in the head of the born singer are so formed that she does not have to find out the best position of the mouth for every vowel tone and practice in that position until the movements become automatic. To an audience it is perhaps a wonderful thing to see this done, especially if they have been trained by singers who make considerable effort of it and emphasize the difficulty of the high note by giving the impression of a tremendous physical strain, but I do not think any more of taking that note leaning over than of those that precede it. Patti could sing in any position'.[80]

In the same interview Tetrazzini confessed also that her time for rehearsal was limited and her very demanding travelling schedule and performing routine did not allow for much practicing. 'I do not practice at all during the season, except, of course, when I am going over a new role. When I go on the stage, the orchestra says "la-la" and I respond "la-la", and the conductor nods that it is all right and I sing away. That is all the rehearsing I have'.[81] This, as we will see, is consistent with the idea that once she had developed her interpretation of a role, it was unlikely that she made changes, also for practical reasons.

Talking of *La traviata*, Tetrazzini made explicit reference to the manner in which she used coloratura to be more expressive and clarified how her interpretative intentions translated into specific expressive devices.

> I try to phrase my part according to the meaning of the words, not with the idea of musical display, the run expressive, the high note a natural dramatic climax. At the end of 'Ah! Fors'è lui' which is so much admired by the New York people, the upward trill I endeavour to make express the hysterical feeling of Violetta. My range? It is said to be extraordinarily elastic, going from B below the stave to E in alt.[82]

As already discussed, in the same interview Tetrazzini answered a question that illustrates, at least in part, her relationship with her senior colleagues and the limited extent of their influence. In May that year Tetrazzini was in London singing Violetta again and *The Times* reported how 'the audience made the most of her last night, especially when, in the coda to the air at the end of the first act, she soared up to a high E flat'.[83] A few days later,

---

79 Ibid.
80 'Making of a Great Singer', *The Sun*, 8 March 1908, p. 6.
81 Ibid.
82 Ibid.
83 'Royal Opera', *The Times*, 1 May 1908, p. 14.

the same journal commented on the inconsistency of the costumes she wore: 'Mme. Tetrazzini's admirers had another opportunity for observing the incongruity between her costume—which, like her handshake, is of the 20th century—and the quaint Victorian dresses of the rest of the performers, which afford a strong argument for a return to that style of dress'.[84]

Tetrazzini's rendition of Gilda drew much less interest. When she was Gilda in New York on 29 January 1908, the critic of the *New York Press* detailed her rendition of 'Caro nome':

> She produced a few beautiful *messa di voce* effects; she gave a scintillant chromatic scale; she seized with astonishing precision purity and clearness of tone two or three high notes in mezza voce; she obtained a pretty trill on middle D sharp and E; she sang what might be called a slow trill [...] on high B and C sharp.[85]

Both the messa di voce and the staccato passages in the upper register can be considered distinctive traits of her vocal style: the slow trill on high B and C sharp can be found in her recordings, in the final cadenza, which also features the descending chromatic scale described by the critic (see the section on Gilda in Tetrazzini's recordings).

On 5 December 1908 Tetrazzini sang Gilda again in New York; the critic of the *Global and Commercial Advertiser*, enchanted by her singing, remarked that 'she had an entire new set of vocal ornaments for the close',[86] probably referring to the cadenza. In London in May 1909 *The Times* recorded briefly her success and the flawless performance of Gilda's most famous aria: 'In the second act she sang with wonderful cleanness and perfection of tone, and "Caro nome" was received with such an uproar of enthusiasm from the upper parts of the house that it had to be repeated, thereby entirely spoiling the effect of the exit'.[87] Of the same opinion was *The Musical Times*, whose critic observed that the success of *Rigoletto* on 14 May was Tetrazzini's success: 'Great enthusiasm characterized the performance of Verdi's melodious opera *Rigoletto* on May 14, due in no small measure to the superb singing of Madame Tetrazzini, whose vocal achievements recalled the palmiest days of Italian opera. Signor Campanini conducted'.[88] One year later *Rigoletto* was performed again in London, this time framed by the performance of some sections of Wagner's *The Ring*: compared to Wagner, Verdi's work represented a moment of relaxation. Tetrazzini had not yet recovered from an indisposition and her notes, especially those in the high register, were hard and not all in tune; '[h]owever she delighted a large audience by her singing of "Caro nome" and answered expectations by going to the E in alt at the end of it'.[89]

Needless to say, Tetrazzini's Violetta and Gilda became regulars at Covent Garden and music critics continued to report on her successes, sometimes elaborating further on the value of the repertoire and the enthusiastic, and therefore tasteless, response of the public. Such was the case when *La traviata* and *Rigoletto* were staged in 1910.

> In succession to *La Traviata* the same composer's *Rigoletto* was mounted, when Madame Tetrazzini made her postponed appearance and soon showed that her E flat in alt was unaffected by her indisposition. A growing tendency to wait for Madame Tetrazzini's high notes is to be regretted, for there is much that is truly admirable in her interpretation of the old Italian music a little lower in the scale, as she clearly demonstrated in the *Barber of Seville* which followed.[90]

A few years later *The Musical Times* commented on the short bravura pieces that Tetrazzini had included in a recital at the Albert Hall. Similarly to what Melba and Patti had often done in the past decades, she sang a few songs in English, which were not, and could not, the critic said, be tolerated any more.

> At the Albert Hall, yesterday, Madame Tetrazzini gave a concert to a huge audience. She was in brilliant form, but is apparently unaware that a fine voice cannot transmute rubbish into good music [...] Madame Tetrazzini has kindly returned to England, after five years' absence. Since her last appearance here she has apparently learned nothing, and

---

84 'Royal Opera', *The Times*, 9 May 1908, p. 11.
85 *New York Press*, 30 January 1908, p. 5 (see Martin, *Verdi in America*, p. 212).
86 Martin, *Verdi in America*, pp. 211–12.
87 'Royal Opera', *The Times*, 15 May 1909, p. 10.
88 'Royal Opera', *The Musical Times*, 1 June 1909, vol. 50, no. 796, pp. 385–86.
89 'Royal Opera', *The Times*, 28 April, 1910.
90 *The Musical Times*, 1 June 1910, vol. 51, no. 808, pp. 377–78.

forgotten nothing. Either her own musical taste is deplorable or (what is worse still) she thinks ours is. On no other grounds can we account for her choice of songs, especially of such a thing as 'Somewhere a voice is calling'—an all-too-successful ballad that even our own tenth-rate singers dare no longer inflict on us. We must frankly express our resentment at a choice which is an insult to English music.[91]

Despite Tetrazzini's incontestable success, the bel canto repertoire continued to represent, at least in the eyes of some critics, a trifle and a nuisance, not only when compared to the Wagnerian repertoire, but also to the works of the younger generation of Italian composers: Giacomo Puccini, Pietro Mascagni, Ruggero Leoncavallo.[92]

Violetta: 'Ah! Fors'è lui'

'Ah! Fors'è lui' is the 'Scena ed Aria [di] Violetta—Finale Atto I' of Giuseppe Verdi's *La traviata*.[93] This is the moment in the first act when Violetta remains alone after the ball, and reflects on the unexpected turn her life has taken. Hesitant and, perhaps, confused as she is, Violetta wonders whether Alfredo, who has kindled in her the burning flame of love, is the man her heart has been longing for and dreaming of. Mysterious and unattainable, love is now the torment and delight of her heart. Francesco Maria Piave's lyrics revolve around the expression of three main emotions, Violetta's longing for a man to love (first stanza), the sense of unrest that follows Alfredo's words (second stanza), and the thrilling hesitation that accompanies what seems a turning point in her entire life.[94] These three emotional states are presented again in the second group of stanzas to form a large two-section structure (A-A'). In each section, we find two main melodic ideas, the first in F minor, the second in F major, each being segmented following the so-called lyric form: first stanza ($a_{4+4}\ a_{4+4'}$) in F minor; second stanza (b_{4+4}) featuring a modulation; third stanza (c_{4+4}) in F major.[95] While the first melodic idea in F minor presents a sobbing quality and features a minor sixth interval that provides a strong sense of melancholy, the second opens lyrically toward the high register to express Violetta's sudden, unrestrained abandon. A similar connection between the lyrics and the music characterises the repeat (A').

		Andantino	
Ah, fors'è lui che l'anima	Ah, perhaps it is he who the soul	a_{4+4}	A (F min.)
Solinga ne' tumulti	Lonely in tumults		
Godea sovente pingere	Often enjoyed painting	a_{4+4}	
De' suoi colori occulti!...	With his hidden colours!...		
Lui che modesto e vigile	He who modest and vigilant	b_{4+4}	modulation
All'egre soglie ascese,	Ascended to the high thresholds,		
E nuova febbre accese,	and ignited a new fever,		A
Destandomi all'amor.	Arousing me to love.		
A quell'amor ch'è palpito	To that love which is the throb	c_{4+4}	B (F maj.)
Dell'universo intero,	Of the whole universe,		
Misterioso, altero,	Mysterious, proud,	d_{4+4}	
Croce e delizia al cor.	Cross and delight to the heart.		

---

91 *The Musical Times*, 1 November 1919, vol. 60, no. 921, pp. 600–03.
92 See Massimo Zicari, *The Land of Song* (Bern: Peter Lang, 2008).
93 For the musical examples I refer to the edition originally published by G. Ricordi and republished by Dover: Giuseppe Verdi, *La traviata* (New York: Dover, 1990, M1500.V48T5, 89-755862) pp. 80–107. Of course, one can only speculate about the edition Sembrich, Melba and Tetrazzini may have used, given the number of reprints circulating at the end of the nineteenth century.
94 *Tutti i libretti di Verdi*, ed. by Luigi Baldacci (Turin: UTET, 1996), p. 276.
95 Steven Huebner, 'Lyric Form in "Ottocento" Opera', *Journal of the Royal Musical Association*, 117.1 (1992), 123–47.

A me fanciulla, un candido	To me maiden, a candid	a $_{4+4}$	**A (F min.)**
E trepido desire	And anxious desire		
Questi effigiò dolcissimo	He sweetest moulded	a $_{4+4}$	
Signor dell'avvenire,	Lord of the future,		
Quando nè cieli il raggio	When in the heavens the ray	b $_{4+4}$	modulation
Di sua beltà vedea,	Of his beauty I saw,		A^1
E tutta me pascea	And all of me fed		
Di quel divino error.	With that divine error.		
Sentìa che amore è palpito	I felt that love is the throb	c $_{4+4}$	**B (F maj.)**
Dell'universo intero,	Of the whole universe,		
Misterioso, altero,	Mysterious, proud,	d $_{4+4}$	
Croce e delizia al cor![96]	Cross and delight to the heart!		

Francesco Maria Piave's choice of wording offers a broad palette of emotions; a richly nuanced vocabulary leads up to the image of love seen as a mysterious combination of joyful bliss and sorrowful grief. Verdi's music underpins the expression of these feelings with skilled ability, and the different melodic ideas offer a large choice of interpretative solutions involving changes in vocal colour, tempo, and dynamics.

The Andantino ('Ah fors'è lui') is followed by a short kinetic section that leads to the final cabaletta, the Allegro brillante, 'Sempre libera'. Violetta does not want to renounce the pleasures she has been enjoying so far; every new day will offer her new delights. Here a sense of frenzied determination prevails over the dilemma. She has made up her mind, perhaps, and so be it. The text involves two stanzas, which are repeated after Alfredo's short intervention (pertichini), thus forming the two-section structure which was typical of a cabaletta.

		Allegro brillante	
Sempre libera degg'io	I must always be free	a_4	
Folleggiare di gioia in gioia,	To romp from joy to joy,		A flat Major
Vo' che scorra il viver mio	I want my life to flow	a_4	
Pei sentieri del piacer.	Along the paths of pleasure.		
			A
Nasca il giorno, o il giorno muoia,	Let the day dawn, or let the day die,	b $_{4+2}$	F min.
sempre lieta ne' ritrovi;	ever happy in hangouts;		(suspended)
a diletti sempre nuovi	To delights ever new	a_3	A flat Major
dee volare il mio pensier.	My thoughts must fly.	c $_{4+6}$	
		Andantino	
Alfredo: Amor, amor è palpito…	Alfredo: Love, love is throb	(Pertichini)	
Violetta: Follie, follie	Violetta: Madness, madness		
		Tempo I	
Sempre libera degg'io	I must always be free	a_4	A flat Major
Folleggiare di gioia in gioia,	To romp from joy to joy,		
Vo' che scorra il viver mio	I want my life to flow	a_4	
Pei sentieri del piacer.	Along the paths of pleasure.		
			A^1
Nasca il giorno, o il giorno muoia,	Let the day dawn, or let the day die,	b $_{4+2}$	F min.
sempre lieta ne' ritrovi;	ever happy in hangouts;		(suspended)
a diletti sempre nuovi	To delights ever new	a_3	A flat Major
dee volare il mio pensier.[97]	My thoughts must fly.	c $_{4+6}$	
		stretta with pertichin*i*	

---

96   *Tutti i libretti di Verdi*, ed. by Baldacci, p. 276.
97   Ibid.

If we now look at the overarching structure, we see that the scene adheres to the formal segmentation conventionally defined as solita forma (the usual form), as was described by Abramo Basevi in 1859 when talking of vocal duets in Verdi's works. This consists of an initial kinetic section followed by a cantabile, then a second kinetic section leading to the final cabaletta: tempo d'attacco, adagio, tempo di mezzo, cabaletta.[98] In Violetta's first aria, a cavatina, the tempo d'attacco is missing; instead, after a short recitativo 'È strano! È strano!... ' (Allegro), we have a cantabile 'Ah fors'è lui' (Andantino), a second recitativo 'Follie!... follie...' (Allegro), and the final cabaletta 'Sempre libera' (Allegro brillante).

Violetta in Tetrazzini's Recordings

Luisa Tetrazzini recorded the 'Scena ed Aria finale' from the first act of *La traviata* four times in the years between 1907 and 1911. A first partial recording was made in London in December 1907 for the Gramophone Company, on which occasion the tempo di mezzo and the cut version of the cabaletta 'Sempre libera' were recorded (matrix 2179f, Gramophone 053147). One year later Tetrazzini recorded the opening recitativo and the cut version of the Andantino ('Ah, fors'è lui') again for the Gramophone Company (matrix 2573f, Gramophone 053196). These two different takes are now to be found merged in one single track in the first CD of the set *Luisa Tetrazzini, the London Recordings*, which EMI Classics released in 1992. In the same set, again merged in a single track, we find two recordings made on the 11 July 1911: 'Ah! Fors'è lui' including 'Follie!...' (matrix ac5164f, HMV 2-053059, DB 531) and 'Sempre libera' (matrix ac5169f, HMV 2-053062, DB 531). These two takes together make an almost complete recording of the 'Scena e aria' despite some of the customary cuts.[99] On 16 March 1911, Tetrazzini recorded for Victor the complete 'Scena e aria' in a single take; the recording presents the usual cuts and includes neither recitativo (matrix C10065-1, Victor 88293, 6344)[100] (Table 1).

Table 1 shows the recordings of 'Ah! Fors'è lui' from 'Scena ed Aria [di] Violetta—Finale Atto I' of Giuseppe Verdi's *La traviata* that Tetrazzini realised in the years 1907–1911.

Title	Date	Matrix	Catalogue
'Sempre libera'	December 1907	2179f	Gramophone 053147
'È strano!... Ah, fors'è lui'	August 1908	2573f	Gramophone 053196
'Ah! Fors'è lui... Sempre libera'	16 March 1911	C10065-1	Victor 88293
'Ah, fors'è lui... Follie!...'	11 July 1911	ac 5164f/2	HMV 053059
'Sempre libera'	11 July 1911	ac 5169f/2	HMV 053062

The cuts present in the recordings cannot be ascribed uniquely to the constraints imposed by the still rudimentary audio technologies; in fact, a performance tradition lay in the background that already featured cuts of single sections, especially if a repeat presented itself. This seems to suggest that despite a long-lasting tradition, at the beginning of the twentieth century, repeats no longer presented an opportunity to add new coloratura and substitute them for the written bravura passages. Instead, they were generally avoided, perhaps because they were considered redundant and musically uninteresting.[101] In this regard Hermann Klein, comparing various recordings and commenting on Tetrazzini's disc DB 531, says:

> the Tetrazzini [record] is in two parts, on a double disc; but commits the error of omitting the preliminary recit. 'È strano' (for which there was plenty of room), and then on the other side, strangely enough, provides an entire

---

98 Abramo Basevi, *Studio sulle opere di Giuseppe Verdi* (Florence: Tofani, 1859) p. 191. For a discussion on the use of this conventional formal segmentation see also Harold S. Powers, 'La solita forma and the Uses of Conventions', *Acta Musicologica*, 59.1 (1987), 65–90.
99 *Luisa Tetrazzini, the London Recordings* (EMI Classics, CHS 7 63802 2, 1992).
100 *Tetrazzini* (Nimbus Records, NI 7808, 1990).
101 Massimo Zicari, 'Expressive Tempo Modifications in Early 20th-Century Recorded Performances of Operatic Arias', *Music&Practice*, 5 (2019), https://doi.org/10.32063/0507.

'repeat' of 'Sempre libera,' which I cannot remember to have heard done more than once or twice on the stage in all my experience.¹⁰²

If we now consider Tetrazzini's interpretation, we see that the opening section of the 'Scena e aria' shows small alterations, all suggesting a certain degree of dramatic freedom, but with no significant modifications of the melodic line. The elongation of the penultimate syllable is often present, although without the additional ornamental passages that were common, for instance, in Rossini's works. The small modifications of the written rhythm, sometimes involving over-dotting the dotted figures, emphasise the sense of agitation that pervades the entire section (Figure 74).

Figure 74 shows Tetrazzini's rendition of 'È strano...' compared to Regina Pacini's.

In the Andantino, Tetrazzini's interpretation is characterised by a conspicuous use of the portamento which, together with a number of expressive ritardandos, conveys a strong sense of languishing hesitation. While her use of portamentos is consistent with that of most of her contemporary colleagues, thus suggesting that this was still a commonly used expressive device, the small rhythmic modifications used to convey a stronger dramatic sense appear to be a more individual feature. For instance, the interpretation left by Marcella Sembrich conveys a strong sense of agitation by a clearly perceivable rhythmic displacement of the notes in the first eight bars, which sound 'molto rubato' and push the tempo towards an audible shortening of the figure in the passage 'solinga ne' tumulti' (lonely in the turmoil). Instead, Nellie Melba's recording shows her proverbial aplomb: she remains in tempo and even the rhythmic modification of the ascending sixth (C-A) remains unaltered (Figure 75).

In Tetrazzini's recordings the presence of melodic modifications involving the addition of or substitution for ornamentation figures is reduced to a minimum. Even when she adds her own melodic ornaments, these consist mainly of small graces that remain almost completely unaltered throughout the different recordings.

---

102 William R. Moran (ed.), *Herman Klein and The Gramophone* (Portland, Oregon: Amadeus Press, 1990). According to Michael Aspinall, since Klein had heard all the famous Violetta performers at Covent Garden from 1869 to 1901, we must assume that it was traditional among the divas to sing only one stanza of 'Sempre libera' (as in the case of 'Ah, fors è lui'). In 1901 Klein moved to New York where he lived until 1909. Actually, at the Metropolitan Marcella Sembrich sang both stanzas, as heard in a Mapleson Cylinder. 'In the 1960s, when I was living in London', Aspinall told me, 'I met the record collector Vivian Catchpole, who had been present at Tetrazzini's Covent Garden début in 1907, and he assured me that "Tet" had sung both stanzas not only of "Sempre libera" but also of "Addio del passato"'.

Figure 75 shows the first measures of 'Ah! Fors'è lui' in Tetrazzini's recordings compared to those of Melba, Sembrich and Pacini.

However, again with the only exception of Nellie Melba, interventions of the same kind can also be observed in the recordings of other interpreters (Figure 76).

The first important changes appear in the cadenza which, however elaborated, remains mostly unaltered in all the recordings (Figure 77). If we compare Tetrazzini's renditions to those of some of her contemporary colleagues, we see differences that are consistent with what we have observed so far. While Melba's cadenza looks (and sounds) inconspicuous, Sembrich and Pacini show a stronger personality with Tetrazzini being the only one featuring the top C and a magnificent messa di voce.

Most crucially, the textual modifications we observe in Tetrazzini's recordings are consistent with what was reported in some contemporary reviews of live performances of *La traviata*. As already illustrated, when Tetrazzini was Violetta in 1908 in New York, on 16 January *The Evening World* wrote that 'at the end of the air "Ah, fors'è lui", she took a high C and swelled and diminished it with evenness and precision'.[103] This very passage can be found in her recordings, as can be seen in Figure 77.

One last change can be observed in the last bar of the cantabile, where a descending chromatic passage substitutes in part for the written diatonic scale (Figure 78).

---

103 'Two critics and Tetrazzini's high E flat', *The Evening World*, 16 January 1908, p. 3.

Figure 76 shows the small interventions in Tetrazzini's rendition of 'Ah! Fors'è lui' compared to those of Melba, Pacini and Sembrich.

Figure 77 shows the different cadenzas sung by Tetrazzini, Melba, Sembrich and Pacini to 'Ah! Fors'è lui'.

Figure 78 shows the descending chromatic passage before the reprise, that Tetrazzini used to sing in 'Ah! Fors'è lui'.

A similar change can be found at the end of the first section, in the bar leading to the reprise. Here, Tetrazzini sings the same chromatic scale, but in the recording made in July 1911 she shows off her pearly staccato. Similar alterations of the same passage can also be found in other contemporary recordings (Figure 79).

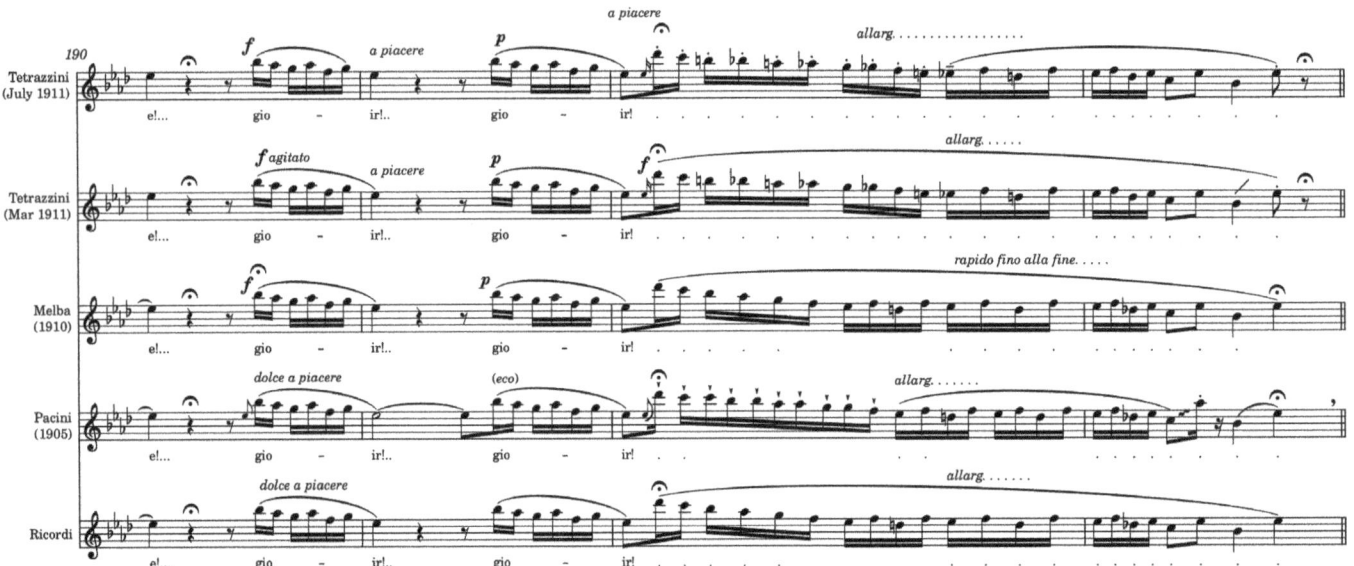

Figure 79 shows the second descending chromatic passage typical of Tetrazzini, compared to those of Melba and Pacini.

This change was noted by the critic of *The Sun* who, on 16 January 1908, wrote that 'her transformation of the plain scale in the opening cadenza of "Sempre libera" into a chromatic scale, though a departure from the letter of the score, was not at all out of taste and its execution fully obtained its right to existence'.[104] A similar solution can be heard in Regina Pacini's recording, where she sings a staccato passage consisting of double notes, and glides up to the A before concluding. Tetrazzini added another chromatic passage in the suspension before the last appearance of the main motif, this time in the form of a cadential close of the written fermata (Figure 80). Pacini did the same in 1905.

Towards the end of the cabaletta Tetrazzini indulges in a number of high Cs, clearly to show off her impressive facility in the highest register while emphasising Violetta's sense of hysteria (Figure 81).

As the critic of *The Evening World* noticed in his review of 16 January 1908, 'at the end of the succeeding "Sempre libera" she sustained a strong and clear E flat'.[105] Again, this passage can be found in her recordings, as shown in Figure 82.

---

[104] 'Mme. Tetrazzini welcomed', *The Sun*, 16 January 1908, p. 7.
[105] 'Two critics and Tetrazzini's high E flat', *The Evening World*, 16 January 1908, p. 3.

Figure 80 shows the last chromatic passage Tetrazzini used to sing in 'Ah! Fors'è lui'.

Figure 81 shows how Tetrazzini conveys Violetta's sense of hysteria thanks to the repeated high Cs.

Figure 82 shows the final measures of 'Ah! Fors'è lui' featuring Tetrazzini's top Es.

The comparison between Tetrazzini and her colleagues shows how each diva presents a different musical personality, combined with different vocal skills. These led to changes and the addition of embellishments that, although consistent with regard to position and harmonic-melodic function, changed depending on both the personality and the voice of each prima donna.

Looking at what can be found in Ricci and Marchesi, not much can be added to the discussion thus far. As mentioned before, Ricci reproduces four cadenzas for the cantabile and mentions the name of Claudia Muzio,[106] while Marchesi offers nine solutions for the same passage.[107] Two more cadenzas are to be found in Liebling,[108] while Karin and Eugen Ott report on what can be heard in the recordings of Tetrazzini, Gemma Bellincioni, Sembrich and Melba.

Gilda: 'Caro nome'

In 'Caro nome' from Act I, Scene 13 of Verdi's *Rigoletto*, Gilda, Rigoletto's daughter, sings her new-found love. The aria follows the long scene where she and the Duke, who have been seeing each other for a while in church, meet in Rigoletto's house and declare their mutual love in a typical cantabile-stretta form. Gilda, who has been made to believe that the person she is in love with is 'Gualtier Maldè', a poor student, remains alone in her rooms and indulges in the feelings the sweet name of her beloved rouses in her bosom. The text consists of two stanzas, each a quatrain of truncated octosyllables; the music follows the conventional structure of the Italian lyric form,

---
106 Ricci, *Variazioni*, vol. I, p. 83
107 Marchesi, *Variantes et points d'orgue*, p. 85.
108 Liebling, *Arrangements*, p. 62.

where a first pair of four-bar phrases (a_4 a_4^1) is followed by a contrasting medial four-bar phrase (b_4), which either leads back to the initial melodic material (a_4), as in this case, or to a new closing four-bar phrase (c_4).[109]

		All.o moderato
Caro nome che il mio cor	Dear name that my heart	a_4
Festi primo palpitar,	You first made throb,	
Le delizie dell'amor	The delights of love	a_4^1
Mi dêi sempre rammentar!	You must always remind me!	
Col pensier il mio desir	With my thought my desire	b_4
A te sempre volerà,	Will always fly to you,	
E fin l'ultimo sospir,	And until the last sigh,	a_4^1
Caro nome, tuo sarà.	Dear name, will be yours.	
Col pensier il mio desir	With my thought my desire	b_4^2 (varied)
A te sempre volerà,	Will always fly to you,	(short cadenza)
E fin l'ultimo sospir,	And until the last sigh,	a_4^2 (varied)
Caro nome, tuo sarà.	Dear name, will be yours.	
Col pensier il mio desir	With my thought my desire	b_4^3 (varied)
A te sempre volerà,	Will always fly to you,	(cadenza)
A te volerà,	To you it will fly,	$c_{(3+2)}$ (variations)
Fin l'ultimo sospir,	Until the last sigh,	d_4
Caro nome, tuo sarà.[110]	Dear name, yours it will be.	$e_{(3+3)}$
		(final cadenza)

The structure of the melody and that of the two stanzas match perfectly, with each four-bar phrase setting to music a new couple of verses. To this a second section follows where the verses of the second stanza are repeated, and the melodic material is presented in a varied form. The aria concludes with what could be understood as a new set of variations (c, d, e); although the original melodic material is presented in a more freely elaborated manner, we can still recognise the initial descending diatonic phrase in the new syncopated melodic figure. At bars 40–41 Verdi makes use of a descending chromaticism which, in setting to music the words 'fin l'ultimo sospir' (even my last sigh) assumes, although temporarily, a characteristically doleful connotation.[111] Gilda's indulging in the thought of his beloved name translates into a coda-like section leading to the final cadenza. Interestingly, the final cadenza arrives after a first short suspension at bar 28, and a longer internal cadenza at bar 36, a combination that increases the sense of hesitating cheerfulness that Gilda is expressing. This sense of hesitation is emphasised, in the music, by the melodic/harmonic diversion Verdi introduces at bars 46–49, where an abrupt shift to G major is introduced, soon to return to the home key of E major.

Gilda in Tetrazzini's Recordings

Tetrazzini recorded 'Caro nome' three times, first in New York for the Zonophone label on 8 September 1904 (matrix 3511, Zonophone 2502, 10001). Her London recording was conducted by Percy Pitt (matrix 2170f, Gramophone 053141; Victor 92014), and while in Camden on 18 March 1911 her recording was conducted by Walter B. Rogers (matrix C10074-1, Victor 88295, 6344; HMV 2-053050, DB 536). If we listen to Tetrazzini's rendition, we notice that, similarly to what we observed in 'Ah fors'è lui', she introduces a number of portamentos and small rhythmic

---

109 Steven Huebner, 'Lyric Form in Ottocento Opera', *Journal of the Royal Musical Association*, 117.1 (1992), 123–47. Adamo and Lippmann, *Vincenzo Bellini*, pp. 428–29.
110 *Tutti i libretti di Verdi*, ed. by Baldacci, p. 239.
111 Marco Beghelli, 'L'emblema melodrammatico del lamento: il semitono dolente', in Verdi 2001: atti del Convegno internazionale = proceedings of the international Conference, Parma, New York, New Haven, 24 gennaio–1 febbraio 2001. (Historiae musicae cultores; 96) (Florence: L. S. Olschki, 2003).

and melodic modifications, which, we may assume, are meant to convey the sense of amorous languor that the lyrics suggest. For instance, in the initial melodic figure, where each quaver is followed by a pause, Tetrazzini stretches the value of the first and the third note into a crotchet. At bar 17 she anticipates the Cs, creating a syncopated trilled figure, which can be understood as a means to convey a stronger sense of agitation, while at bar 20 she inserts a fermata on the final G (Figure 83).

Figure 83 shows Tetrazzini's modifications in the opening measures of 'Caro nome' in Verdi's *Rigoletto*.

The final cadenza is an extended version of the original one, with a staccato, virtuoso passage that reaches the high B with a long messa di voce to conclude on the final E. Although in the 1911 version the semiquaver passage is longer than in 1907, the two cadenzas are virtually the same (Figure 84).

The most recent version of the cadenza can be found transcribed in Ricci,[112] while Marchesi does not include this opera among her *Variantes et points d'orgue*. Karin and Eugen Ott transcribe what can be heard in the recordings of Tetrazzini, Sembrich and Maria Barrientos.[113]

Other Recordings of Verdi's Arias

Not much more can be said of the other arias from Verdi that Tetrazzini recorded during her career, at least not in so far as textual modifications are concerned. Among them we find the 'Canzone di Oscar' from *Un ballo in maschera*, which she recorded on 25 May 1909 (matrix 3076f, Gramophone 053222) with Percy Pitt and on 15 March 1911 with Walter Rogers (matrix C10059-1, Victor 88304, 6341; HMV 2-053048, DB 539). Being a short and vivacious piece where two stanzas are set to music in two main sections A-A^1 each featuring two melodic motives repeated more times, the 'Canzone' lends itself to some melodic variations.

Tetrazzini takes advantage of this possibility only to a limited extent and we do not find the same small variations in both her recordings. In fact, the later one presents some more graces, thus suggesting an evolution

---

112 Ricci, vol. I, p. 69.
113 Ott, *Handbuch*, p. 509.

Figure 84 shows Tetrazzini's cadenza to 'Caro nome' in Verdi's *Rigoletto*.

			Allegretto
Saper vorreste	You would like to know	a$_{(4+4+4)}$	
Di che si veste,	Of what he dresses,		
Quando l'è cosa	When it is a thing		
Ch'ei vuol nascosa.	That he wants hidden.		
Oscar lo sa,	Oscar knows it,		
Ma nol dirà,	But he will not say,		**A**
Là, là, là, là.	Là, là, là, là.	b$_{(2+2+2+2)}$	
Oscar lo sa,	Oscar knows it,	a$_{(4)}$	
Ma nol dirà,	But he will not say,		
Là, là, là, là.	Là, là, là, là.	b'$_{(4+4)}$	
Pieno d'amor	Full of love	a$_{(4+4+4)}$	
Mi balza il cor,	My heart leaps,		
Ma pur discreto	But still discreet		
Serba il secreto.	It keeps the secret.		
Nol rapirà	Neither grade nor beauty		
Grado o beltà,	Will steal it,		**A**^{1}
Tra là, là, là,	Tra là, là, là,	b$_{(2+2+2+2)}$	
Là, là, là, là.	Là, là, là, là.	Cadenza	
Oscar lo sa,	Oscar knows it,	a$_{(4)}$	
Ma nol dirà,	But he will not say,		
Là, là, là, là.[114]	Là, là, là, là.	b'$_{(4+4)}$	

in her interpretation of this aria or, one may assume, the intervention of the conductor. The first interventions consist in the addition of some portamentos and small triplets as substitutes for the octave notes (Figure 85).

---

114 *Tutti i libretti di Verdi*, ed. by Baldacci, p. 358.

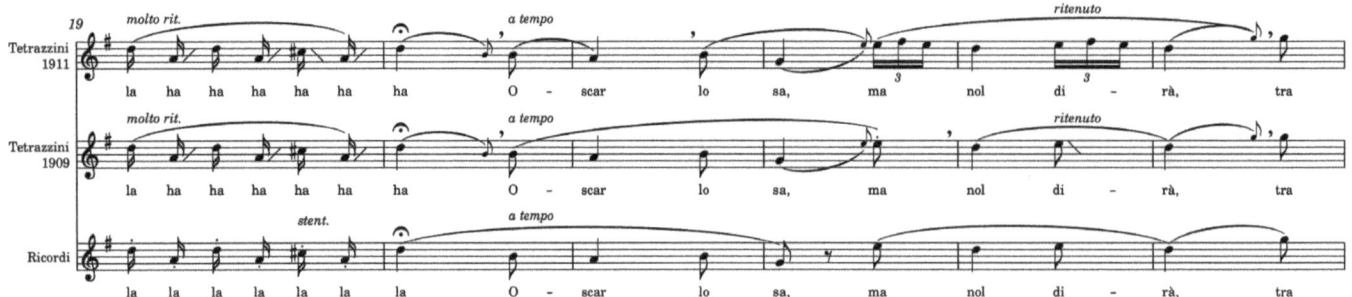

Figure 85 shows Tetrazzini's small modifications in the 'Canzone di Oscar' from Verdi's *Un ballo in maschera*.

Similarly, the beginning of the repeat appears to be characterised by a more conspicuous presence of portamentos and small graces (Figure 86).

Figure 86 shows modifications sung by Tetrazzini in the repeat of the 'Canzone di Oscar'.

Of greater interest is the final cadenza, which illustrates, once more, the very peculiar vocal qualities and sparkling personality of the diva; it is a combination of high staccato notes leading up to the top D, which then descend and conclude with a chromatic passage (Figure 87).

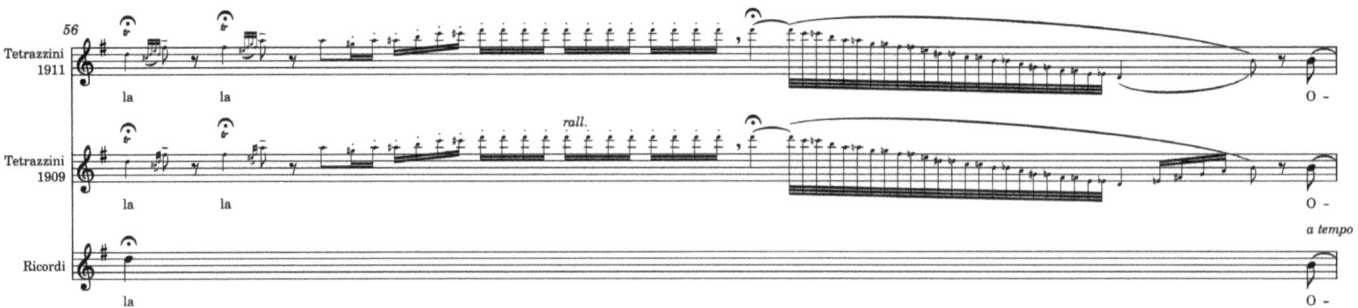

Figure 87 shows the cadenza sung by Tetrazzini in the 'Canzone di Oscar'.

The most striking quality of these interpretations lies in the agogic flexibility associated with the insertion of small nuances and a number of portamentos, which convey a sense of winking maliciousness. Of special interest, in this regard, is the peculiar timbre in the descending passage in measure 43 (G-D). The unevenness that was noted by some contemporary critics in the lower register, perhaps associated with the use of the voce bianca, is clearly audible in this very passage.

One single recording exists of 'Tacea la notte placida' from *Il trovatore*, which Tetrazzini recorded on 18 February 1913 with Walter Rogers (Matix C12918-1, Victor 88420, 6346; HMV 2-053084, DB 540). The 'Scena e Cavatina di Leonora' consists of the four main sections that were typical of the time and to which we commonly refer as solita forma. A first kinetic section 'Che più t'arresti' (Andante Mosso—Allegro) is followed by a lyric section, a so-called cantabile (Andante) whose structure is A-A¹; the first part is repeated to conclude with a short cadenza. This leads to a second kinetic dialogic section (Allegro Vivo) which leads to the final cabaletta (Allegro Giusto). The latter also consists of a main part followed by its repeat (A-A¹), thus inviting singers to show off the voice by adding new and more sparkling ornaments and roulades. In Tetrazzini's recording, not only are both kinetic sections (tempo d'attacco and tempo di mezzo) missing, but also the repeats of the main lyric moments, the Andante and the final cabaletta (Allegro Giusto). These cuts deprive us of what may have been the most interesting parts of her interpretation, that is to say those parts that were generally modified and embellished with ornaments. Tetrazzini adheres to the score and sings as written, the only exception being the final cadenza, where she shows off her voice by adding an ascending scale to reach the top E flat (Figure 88).

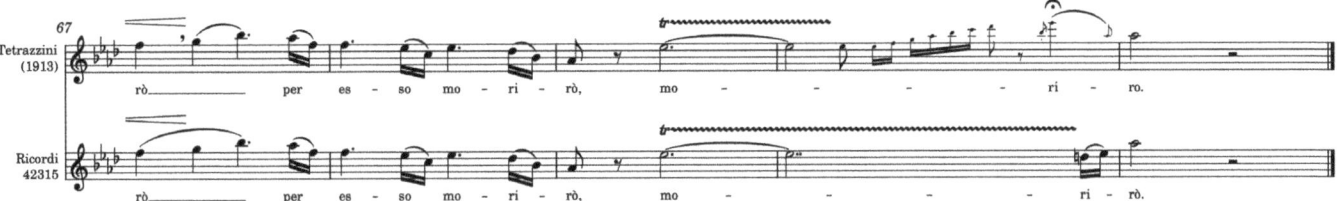

Figure 88 shows the ascending scale which concludes 'Tacea la notte placida' as sung by Tetrazzini.

Interpretative devices consisting of sparkling staccato passages in the high register, trills and messa di voce in the fermata were, we could say, idiomatic in Tetrazzini's style and typical of her very distinctive vocal technique.

One last recording comes from *I vespri siciliani*: Tetrazzini recorded 'Mercé dilette amiche' twice, on 2 November 1910 with Percy Pitt (Matrix 4577f, HMV 2-053033) and on 12 May 1914 with Walter Rogers (Matrix C14822-1, Victor 88504; HMV 2-053118, DB 529). Here Tetrazzini adheres to the text almost strictly and we find only two moments in which she allows herself some changes. The first is in the coda, where she inserts a puntatura in the descending passage from the C# to the A below the stave (beginning with 'D'ignoto amor mi balza'). The change, which allows her to avoid reaching the lowest and most uncomfortable register of the voice, can be heard also in Marcella Sembrich's and Giuseppina Huguet's discs. The second modification is the final candenza (Figure 89).

Figure 89 shows Tetrazzini's modifications in the closing measures of 'Mercé dilette amiche' from *I vespri siciliani*.

While in the 1910 rendition we recognise Tetrazzini's vocal hallmark, consisting in an ascending scale leading to the top E that ends with a portamento to the final note, in 1914 she sings the trill as written. In this case we see how much less courageous the later recording is when compared to the earlier one. This sort of regression towards a less acrobatic interpretative approach can be better understood once we consider that Tetrazzini was now past her prime. Signs of this change were noted by some contemporary critics who, while appreciating the evenness she had developed in the lower register, suggested that her voice had lost some of the original splendour in the high compass.

> Her voice retains its peculiar bird-like quality and pleases by the wealth of vocal splendour and elasticity of expression. It shows some slight changes from the voice of a year or more ago. Her lower tones, once childish and distressingly thin, she has developed to a considerable degree. Last night they were full, vibrant and of definite quality. This gain has been made at some sacrifice of the pure coloratura quality of the upper register but the net gain in her singing is indisputable.[115]

A more precise idea of this change is offered by the critic of the *Boston Evening Transcript*, who reviewed Tetrazzini's impersonation of Gilda in Boston in December 1913 and suggested that she was now avoiding some of the top Es that were typical of her past interpretations.

> It is customary to say nowadays that Tetrazzini's voice is not what it used to be. Such a remark is likely to be made on every occasion, whether at the time it happens to be true or not. Last night it was certain that Gilda did not take her high E in the *Caro nome*. It also seemed that she was not always on the pitch; some said that she was sharp and others that she was flat; perhaps both were right, certainly both were uncomfortable.[116]

In 1914 the forty-three-year-old diva decided to conclude her operatic career and confine herself to solo concert recitals, which she continued to give until the 1930s.

The manner in which Tetrazzini approached Verdi's operas, especially if we consider Violetta and Gilda, seems to confirm the picture drawn when discussing Bellini. Despite the fact that Verdi's new style was understood as a threat to bel canto, these two operas soon came to be associated with the tradition and singers like Tetrazzini included them in their repertoire. What can be observed in her recordings is a gradual shift towards a less flourished vocal technique, combined with a more richly nuanced interpretation. Tetrazzini shows a clear understanding of Verdi's strong sense of drama, which she conveys by means of tempo modifications and by resorting to frequent use of portamento, as can be observed in her interpretations of Violetta's cantabile (Andantino) and Gilda's aria. Even, in a cabaletta like 'Sempre libera degg'io', which offers her the opportunity to show off the voice, Tetrazzini expresses Violetta's inner conflict and the sense of hysteria it conveys. In this regard, the traditional notion of bel canto is forced to its utmost limit in consideration of the character and the drama without trespassing on a more forceful vocal approach. Here, the triumph of free expression of feeling and passion over the canon of bel canto does not defy its principles but, instead, bends them to the needs of a different form of expressiveness.

---

115 *The Daily Advertiser*, 13 December 1913, quoted in Gattey, *Luisa Tetrazzini*, p. 182.
116 *Boston Evening Transcript*, 30 December 1913, quoted in Gattey, *Luisa Tetrazzini*, p. 184.

Conclusions

To form an opinion about the vocal style of a performer like Luisa Tetrazzini through the analysis of her recorded interpretations is not an easy task. As anticipated at the outset of this volume, to embark on such a thankless task as the transcription of the operatic arias a singer may have recorded a century ago may result in a challenging exercise, all the more so if one considers how many details can get lost in the process.

Still, an incredible amount of information can be gleaned from the recordings left by Luisa Tetrazzini, especially if one takes into consideration the context in which she worked and the manner in which the operatic repertoire and its interpretative canons were evolving. One first indication emerges repeatedly from the folds of this discussion, regarding the anachronistic position occupied by Tetrazzini at the outset of the twentieth century. This condition assumes special value if we consider that her recorded interpretations are a testament to a tradition that, although considered as *passé*, was still vibrant. As we have seen, changing the score was a distinctive feature of this tradition and operas that were ascribed to the so-called bel canto repertoire were all subject to textual manipulations of some kind. In the case of *Barbiere*, Tetrazzini's interventions went beyond the music and followed a long-lasting tradition involving a metatheatrical dimension. With the lesson scene, divas took the opportunity to transform an aria into a miniature recital where they took over the entire stage, leaving aside the composer, the libretto, the plot and the notion itself of dramatic consistency; the character of Rosina abandoned the stage, to return only after a token of appreciation was paid to the singer, thus originating a mechanism of theatrical estrangement. For this mechanism to work smoothly the complicity of the public was an indispensable condition and, as we have seen, at some point announcing what encore the star of the evening would insert at the end of the lesson scene came to be part of a marketing strategy that was strongly embedded in the operatic production system. However unconceivable for us today, the habit of creating a miniature recital at the expense of the opera, the dramatic mimesis and the composer's intentions tells us a lot about the pivotal role the diva played when it came to promoting the work to be performed, and her status in relation to the composer.

To glean an idea of the charisma these stars exerted on the audience, and their ability to attract thousands of spectators, we should go back to the manner in which ample press coverage was granted to Tetrazzini's public appearances, with detailed accounts of her performances and private life occupying many columns of daily and weekly periodicals. When Tetrazzini arrived in New York in January 1908, the *Evening World* reproduced pictures of Oscar Hammerstein welcoming her upon disembarking from a French liner with two truckloads of trunks. The event was covered by the press, with the attention of the readers drawn to her difficult relationship with her sister Eva, whom she had not seen for years, the contract with the Manhattan Opera House, the quality of her voice, the phenomenal success she had scored at Covent Garden, her seasickness, and the new costumes she would wear on stage.[1] In 1910 *The San Francisco Call* granted ample coverage to an unprecedented Christmas open-air concert Tetrazzini gave in San Francisco on 24 December and described in great detail how the entire city had been kept spellbound by her voice.

> The opulent stream of golden voice stopped the city's traffic last night, stilled the din of cars, emptied stores of Christmas eve shoppers, drew families from thousands of homes, where waited the Christmas tree with its unlighted candles and its wrapped mysteries, and turned this town into a grand opera house, the like of which the world has not seen before, nor will again, I fear.[2]

---

[1] 'New Patti here, Ready for Debut at Hammerstein's', *The Evening World*, 11 January 1908, front page.
[2] Walter Anthony, 'Diva Sings Gloriously to Stilled Throngs', *The San Francisco Call*, 25 December 1910, front page.

At five o'clock in the afternoon people were already thronging the streets to hear Tetrazzini, and estimates ranged from 90'000 to 250'000 spectators attending the event.

> Mme. Tetrazzini, most popular singer of her generation, stood in the free, breezleless air and sang to nigh on 100,000 people. By her an orchestra whispered its accompaniment. Before her, in packed streets, the tens of thousands stood bareheaded, motionless, rapt. The only sound heard was the beautiful tone of the world's most popular coloratue soprano—her voice and the balanced undertone of the instruments.[3]

Similar pictures were not unusual in the nineteenth century and accounts of incidents in which opera-goers stormed into the theatre and rushed inside to secure the best places were not exceptional in many European cities; nor was the representation of a successful diva being celebrated to the verge of public hysteria, with members of the overexcited audience dragging her carriage home and serenading her until sunrise. Marietta Alboni, Jenny Lind, Marietta Piccolomini, like Giuditta Pasta, Maria Malibran, and many more, scored triumph after triumph and the excitement they could ignite among international audiences could easily be compared to today's pop and rock stars.[4] In this regard, the presence of Luisa Tetrazzini's public persona in the international press is consistent with a production system that was typical of Italian bel canto operas and would vanish after the World Wars, possibly with the exception of Maria Callas.

What were the reasons for Tetrazzini's phenomenal success? Of course, the quality of her voice and her extraordinary vocal technique were of pivotal importance; still, for a good songstress to rise to the status of a diva other talents were necessary: among them, a strong personality and an even stronger theatricality. Tetrazzini's impersonation of Rosina, as we have seen, was exceptionally successful because it combined an outstanding vocal talent with a sparkling personality and rare dramatic skills. Tetrazzini shared these qualities with, among others, Adelina Patti, whose Rosina was said to exhibit her singular vocal facility and 'to show her to be a comic actress of genuine stamp—lively, piquant, full of intelligence and sensibility'.[5] As Blanche Partington noted in 1905, Tetrazzini appeared to be as comfortable in the part of young Rosina as she was in Lucia and Violetta.

> To me Tetrazzini is a little at her best here. Her Lucia is a wonderful performance; and a pretty trick of comedy makes Tetrazzini's Rosina a thing wholly delightful. But as Violetta the little diva wheedles the quite unusual tear from the grand operatic eye. She brings a pathos as rare as it is effective to the acting of the role.[6]

Again, when she made her appearance as Rosina at Covent Garden in 1908 the *Evening Standard* wrote:

> The perfect command with which she blended and voiced both the declamatory and the vocal passages of the florid music, the intuitiveness of her gestures, the subtlety of her inflexions, and moreover the humour and reality with which she invested some very unreal situations was little short of amazing.[7]

What is even more remarkable is that Tetrazzini's figure was not particularly elegant, nor was she handsome or beautiful, like, for instance, Nellie Melba. Little Tetrazzini was short, plump, and her well-rounded face was anything but graceful. Her lack of distinction was noticed by the critic of the *New York Daily Tribune* who, when reviewing her Violetta on 7 January 1908, could not help but notice that 'the person of the singer was in crass contradiction of the ideal picture of the heroine'. Still, the critic remarked, the secret of her success lay 'in the combination of beautiful singing as such, and acting. Not acting in the sense of attitude motion and facial expression, although these were all admirable, but in the dramatic feeling which imbued the singing—the dramatic color which shifted with kaleidoscopic swiftness from phrase to phrase, filling it with the blood of the

---

3 Arthur L. Price, 'Treasures of Song Fills Ears of City', *The San Francisco Call*, 25 December 1910, front page.
4 Massimo Zicari, 'Cultural Stereotypes and the Reception of Verdi's Operas in Victorian London', *Journal of Modern Italian Studies*, 26.1 (2021), 27–40.
5 *The Times*, 11 May 1863, p. 12.
6 Blanche Partington, 'Traviata at the Tivoli a Great Hit', *The San Francisco Call*, 20 January 1905, p. 4.
7 Cited in Gattey, *Queens of Song*, p. 210.

play'.⁸ This quality was emphasised even more strongly by the critic of the *Daily Mail* when Tetrazzini made her appearance as Violetta at Covent Garden in 1907.

> She brings to the old Verdi opera a human tenderness and pathos which few of us realised that it possessed. She has the magic gift of 'tears in the voice' and is withal a consummate actress... There were actual tears among the audience, too, on Saturday night when she sang 'Dite alla giovine' lifted out of its customary vocal display into a song of renunciation, heart-rendering in its emotional intensity.⁹

Moreover, Tetrazzini was able to sing in whatever position, an ability she used to impress the audience, as was the case with 'Ah! Fors'è lui', even though this ostentation outraged the most conservative critics, who did not spare her some very harsh criticism. Tetrazzini became a diva, one may assume, because she was able to mesmerise the audience thanks to a combination of vocal and dramatic talents. Her strong personality and dissolute lifestyle added to the visibility of her public persona and made her a *prima donna assoluta*. Still, the image of a vain, affected and temperamental creature, a woman who constantly changes her mind and is dedicated to her talent as described by Susan Rutherford,¹⁰ does not fit Tetrazzini's profile in so far as her vocal style and her interpretative approach to the repertoire are concerned. As I have already suggested, once she had learned a role, Tetrazzini, like her colleagues, remained consistent over time and only small changes can be detected in her recorded interpretations. The claim that she followed the whim of the moment is not supported by the evidence I have amassed so far.

In terms of voice quality, style and technique, Tetrazzini helps us better understand how much of the tradition of which she was said to be one of the most valuable representatives still lived in the new century. In addition to the practice of textual manipulations, other interpretative devices are characteristic of this tradition: the use of voce bianca, vibrato, messa di voce, portamento and tempo modifications.

We have seen how often Tetrazzini was criticised for using the voce bianca, which consisted in a clearly audible gap between the very sweet quality of her high notes in the head register and the childlike sound of her lower notes in the chest register. These last were sung with a pinched glottis and their pallid colour and pronounced tremolo were often considered a bad imitation of the wailing of a cross infant. This gap, also described in terms of a yodel effect, was associated with the Rossinian contralto, a singer able to reach the extreme ends of the voice compass, from below the stave up to the top notes above it. This incredible extension, however, was possible only at the expense of a homogeneous timbre and a smooth transition between the lower and the higher register, which instead is typical of today's opera singers. Tetrazzini's strong connection with the past is even more clearly manifest in the frequent use of portamento, which was associated with the expression of sorrowful and pathetic affections. In this regard, the strong continuity between Patti and Tetrazzini is clearly audible in their recordings and is consistent with what nineteenth-century methods recommended. Other signs of this tradition can be recognised in the accented trill she uses, for instance, in 'Come per me sereno' from Bellini's *La sonnambula*, which we find described in García (see here Figure 20), and in the messa di voce, which Tetrazzini used in combination with the trill on a final note. To this can be added the use of tempo modifications, whose importance as an expressive device is strongly emphasised by García. Still, the extent of tempo modifications depended more on the individual taste rather than a widely shared notion of tempo variability. In 'Ah! Fors'è lui', for instance, Tetrazzini's recordings present a higher degree of agogic freedom than Nellie Melba's, while those left by Marcella Sembrich feature a much higher variability than both Melba and Tetrazzini. Although they were all said to be the best representatives of bel canto of their time, their approach to the same repertoire presented remarkable differences.¹¹

---

8 'Manhattan Opera House: The Advent of Tetrazzini' (Music), *New York Daily Tribune*, 7 January 1908, p. 7.
9 Cited in Gattey, *Queens of Song*, p. 206.
10 Susan Rutherford, *The Prima Donna and Opera, 1815–1930* (Cambridge: Cambridge University Press, 2006), p. 27.
11 See Massimo Zicari, 'Expressive Tempo Modifications in Early 20th-Century Recorded Performances of Operatic Arias', *Music&Practice*, 5 (2019), https://doi.org/10.32063/0507.

Similarly, to individuate specific differences between Tetrazzini and those interpreters who, although belonging to the same epoch, are said to have created (vocally at least) operatic verismo can be challenging, especially if we consider, again, how often individual differences prevail over more generally shared stylistic traits. For instance, the voice of Gemma Bellincioni (1864–1950), who created the role of Santuzza in Pietro Mascagni's *Cavalleria Rusticana* in Rome, was uneven, featuring a thick and sometimes throaty vibrato that would be deemed faulty today. On the other hand, Angelica Pandolfini (1836–1916), who studied in Paris and was one of the best Mimì in Puccini's *La bohème* in Bologna with Arturo Toscanini and in Milan with Leopoldo Mugnone, seems to have belonged to a completely different vocal breed. Her voice is clear and even, her vibrato light and regular, she rarely uses portamento but a gap in the lower register of her voice, similar to Tetrazzini's voce bianca, can be heard on occasion in her recordings. Even closer to our modern standards sounds the round, smooth voice of Cesira Ferrani (1863–1943) who created the roles of Mimì and Manon.[12]

What these recordings suggest is that a gradual shift towards a less flourished style and a more homogeneous, louder voice quality would become typical of the younger generations of singers; this change should be considered in relation to and possibly as a consequence of the compositional style typical of the so-called *giovane scuola*, that is to say the group of young composers more or less loosely connected with operatic verismo: Pietro Mascagni, Ruggiero Leoncavallo, Giacomo Puccini, Umberto Giordano. Singers involved in the interpretation of verismo operas came to abandon coloraturas and embellishments typical of bel canto, while the voice moved from the purity of tone that was so patiently cultivated by songstresses like Tetrazzini to the fuller sound we hear in more recent discs. At the same time the upper register was sacrificed to the middle range of the tessitura, which lends itself better to those sobbing, shouting, whispering utterances that are so dear to verismo characters.[13]

While the success of bel canto old-timers was strongly dependant on the talent of the interpreters, modern operas attracted the attention of audiences and critics alike by virtue of their compositional and dramatic qualities. After the success of Verdi's late operas *Otello* and *Falstaff*, the works of Puccini, Leoncavallo and Mascagni monopolised the attention of the international press because of the degree of novelty they presented; finally, the notions of compositional progress and dramatic consistency were emerging from the folds of the discussion and a genre traditionally considered as a form of entertainment was rising to the status of music drama. Hence, it is not surprising that many contemporary commentators drew attention to the triteness of the so-called bel canto repertoire and the countless incongruities that were attached to it. In the constant tension between old and new, music cognoscenti considered the tradition embodied by singers like Tetrazzini a nuisance, a distraction, a pastime between yesterday's Wagner and tomorrow's Puccini. Bel canto divas were often tolerated for the sake of those aficionados who still cherished a theatrical genre that consisted of set pieces to be sung in costume. On the other hand, younger composers rose to the status of international musical stars, drawing the attention of the international press to the new music drama.

What music critics could neither imagine nor foresee was that Tetrazzini, as well as her more advanced colleagues, worked in a moment where opera as a genre was approaching its conclusive phase. After three hundred years of glamour and fascination, opera was undergoing its final mutation and approaching its concluding phase, soon to become a thing of the past.[14] Although still a widely disseminated form of musical entertainment, in the 1930s opera seasons turned into a living museum or, as has been suggested, a mortuary full of wonderful performances. At the same time, not only did a select number of operatic works from the past find an ideal place in this portrait gallery, but so too did the interpreters whose unsurpassed artistry inspired their composers and kept audiences spellbound for centuries. Together with Mozart, Rossini, Donizetti, Bellini, Verdi

---

12 These recordings can be found reissued in a double CD recently produced by Michael Aspinall and Ward Martson: *The Creators of Verismo* (vol. I), Martson, 2010.

13 See Rodolfo Celletti, 'La vocalità mascagnana', in *Atti del primo convegno internazionale di studi su Pietro Mascagni*, edited by Fedele D'Amico (Milan: Casa Musicale Sonzogno, 1987), 39–48 (p. 41). A discussion on this shift can be found also in Barbara Gentili, 'The Changing Aesthetics of Vocal Registration in the Age of "Verismo"', *Music and Letters*, 102–01 (2021), 54–79, https://doi.org/10.1093/ml/gcaa029.

14 See Carolyn Abbate and Roger Parker, *A History of Opera* (New York: Norton, 2012), p. 519.

and many more, the divas who impersonated their heroines have also graduated into this gallery, thus becoming symbols of an iconic past to be revived season after season, with aficionados and cognoscenti continuing to cherish the old melodies of their fathers and grandfathers. Maria Malibran, Giuditta Pasta, Adelina Patti and, of course, Luisa Tetrazzini, to name a few, are part of this living museum.

As Anthony Tommasini suggested in 1998, we have to wait until Maria Callas and Joan Sutherland arrived on the scene in the 1950s and 60s to unlock the gates of this museum and revive bel canto. Despite some occasional productions now and then during the post-war period, the operatic world at large had forgotten this repertory. As Tommasini recalls, 'when Ms. Joan Sutherland, at 33, won international acclaim in Donizetti's *Lucia di Lammermoor* at Covent Garden in 1959, the opera had not been performed there in 34 years. When she sang her first Covent Garden Elvira in Bellini's *Puritani*, in 1964, the opera had not been heard in the house since 1887'.[15] Tommasini's advocacy of bel canto reminds us of those critics who felt like they had to plead for Tetrazzini's vocal talent against her detractors.

> But these great artists made the public realise that bel canto operas were not just dramatically preposterous showpieces for brainless, chirpy sopranos. When Callas sang Bellini's *Norma*, the opera emerged as a refined and emotionally shattering piece; to hear Ms. Joan Sutherland and Marilyn Horne in Rossini's heroic *Semiramide*, and Callas in that composer's madcap *Italiana in Algeri*, was to marvel at the range of Rossini's compositional ingenuity.[16]

How does Sutherland's approach to bel canto approximate the tradition embodied by Tetrazzini and Patti? What is the distance between Tetrazzini's generation and those singers who took it upon themselves to revive this illustrious tradition? Generally described as a dramatic coloratura soprano, Sutherland's voice went from G below the stave up to the F above it; it was big and powerful but could be bent to the needs of bel canto, thus allowing her to master long runs and pyrotechnic coloraturas. Her worldwide success depended on her contribution to the revival of long forgotten bel canto; still, her repertoire included not only Rossini's *Semiramide*, Donizetti's *Lucia di Lammermoor* and Bellini's *La sonnambula*, but also Francesco Cilea's *Adriana Lecouvreur*, Strauss's *Die Fledermaus*, Puccini's *Suor Angelica* and *Turandot*, Wagner's *Die Meistersinger*. It is even more difficult to draw a comparison with Maria Callas, whose very peculiar voice and personality bear no comparison with any other. Even though she was sometimes said to be the reincarnation of Giuditta Pasta and Maria Malibran because of her soprano sfogato texture, opinions on her vocal size, range and registers could not be more diverse. However, what the audience appreciated in Callas was her ability to breathe life into the characters she interpreted; this, together with the scandals that accompanied her life, made her a veritable diva.

The merit of these last interpreters lies in reviving a long-forgotten repertoire and drawing the attention of modern singers to its musical value. Still, the distance between Tetrazzini and singers like Maria Callas and Joan Sutherland could not be more striking. If, on the one hand, these last resumed a performance practice that involved coloratura passages, extended cadenzas and textual manipulations, the quality of their voice is noticeably different: while Tetrazzini's voice could be uneven, featuring frequent use of portamento and messa di voce, both Callas and Sutherland presented a more homogeneous voice, a thick vibrato, with sparing use of both portamento and messa di voce.

Possibly the most revealing sign of the interest modern singers take in their colleagues from the past is offered by Cecilia Bartoli's recent project on Maria Malibran. Bartoli's attempt to dig into Malibran's archival documents to reconstruct her spectacular vocal mastery and personality is emblematic of this interest. Still, as I have already suggested, one must feel on firmer footing when investigating and reviving the singing style of a diva who has left no recordings than when researching one whose voice can be found recorded on discs or wax cylinders. Would it be the same if Bartoli considered an artist whose musical taste and vocal technique, still audible from old discs, were now perceived as intolerably out-of-date? A survey I have conducted among a group of music professors

---

15 Anthony Tommasini, 'A New Generation Revels in Bel Canto', *The New York Times*, 8 November 1998, section 2, p. 41. https://www.nytimes.com/1998/11/08/arts/a-new-generation-revels-in-bel-canto.html. The music critic must have confused *L'Italiana in Algeri* with *Il turco in Italia*.
16 Ibid.

and students confirms the tension between the manner in which early recordings are valued by expert musicians and the extent to which they tend to cause a sense of strangeness. Music practitioners are constantly confronted with recorded interpretations, but the likelihood that one may consider reproducing the interpretative solutions offered by an old disc is remote. Reviving a style now considered outdated or, even worse, aping the voice of an old but unsurpassed master would jeopardise any artist's effort to gain credibility and climb the podium of international recognition. The imperative of originality dominates the arts and even when a performer decides to revive the style of our ancestors, the urge for novelty and originality prevails over the imitation of the past. Still, to be able to dig into the past and reconstruct its performance style (or styles) represents a wonderful opportunity for getting a stronger sense of historical perspective, questioning our current notion of romantic interpretation, and developing new, inspirational renditions of a much-cherished repertoire.

Transcriptions

The closing section of this volume includes the full transcription of all the arias I have discussed and analysed; this should be understood as a working tool for any practitioner, singer or conductor eager to get an insight into Luisa Tetrazzini's vocal style and willing to consider some of her interpretative solutions. For the sake of comparability, these transcriptions are accompanied by source materials belonging to other reference interpreters and teachers from the late nineteenth century. Some of them, like Cinti-Damoreau and Marchesi, are already available in printed editions, while others, like Patti, Melba and Sembrich, are not.

As for the transcription criteria, a number of decisions had to be taken, with regard to what should be notated and what could remain relegated uniquely to the aural experience. Features like the different use of vibrato and the changes in the voice registers were not considered. Instead, portamentos were notated as carefully as possible, together with every modification in the text, whether a grace note, an embellishment, a roulade or an entire cadenza. As can be observed from the transcriptions, Tetrazzini remained consistent with what may have been her first choice and only minor changes can be detected across the years.

Although a rich body of scholarly literature demonstrates how effectively audio recordings can be investigated with regard to tempo modifications and how precisely internal relative tempo modifications can be measured, I decided not to provide metronome marks or other similar indications. As we have seen, interpretative choices involving tempo modifications were dramatically affected by the rudimentary technologies available at the time. Thus, only those tempo changes which are clearly noticeable by ear can be found in these transcriptions. These are indicated by means of *accel., rall.* etc.

For similar reasons, limited attention has been paid to dynamics. In fact, due to technological constraints, it is not always easy to detect changes in dynamics that are musically relevant, even though the direction of a phrase approaching its climax is often perceivable thanks to the combination of different expressive parameters.

Bars are numbered with reference to the vocal part, regardless of the original numbering; when possible, rehearsal marks are also indicated as they appear in the relevant Ricordi printed edition.

Il barbiere di Siviglia (1816)
"Una voce poco fa"
Cavatina di Rosina

Cesare Sterbini Gioacchino Rossini

14
Tetrazzini (1904)
rà lo giu
Tetrazzini (1907)
rà lo giu
Tetrazzini (1911)
rà lo giu
Lind (1894)
rà, lo giu
Ricci
rà lo giu
Ricci (ossia 2)
rò lo giu
Ricordi
rà lo giu
15
Tetrazzini (1904)
ra - i, la vin - ce - rò la vin - ce -
Tetrazzini (1907)
ra - i, la vin - ce - rò la vin - ce -
Tetrazzini (1911)
ra - i, la vin - ce - rò la vin - ce -
Lind (1894)
legato
ra - i, la vin - ce -
Ricci
ra - i, Ah! la vin - ce -
Ricci (ossia 2)
ra - i, Ah! la vin - ce - rò la vin - ce -
Ricci (ossia 3)
ra - i, Ah! la vin - ce -
Ricordi
ra - i, la vin - ce -

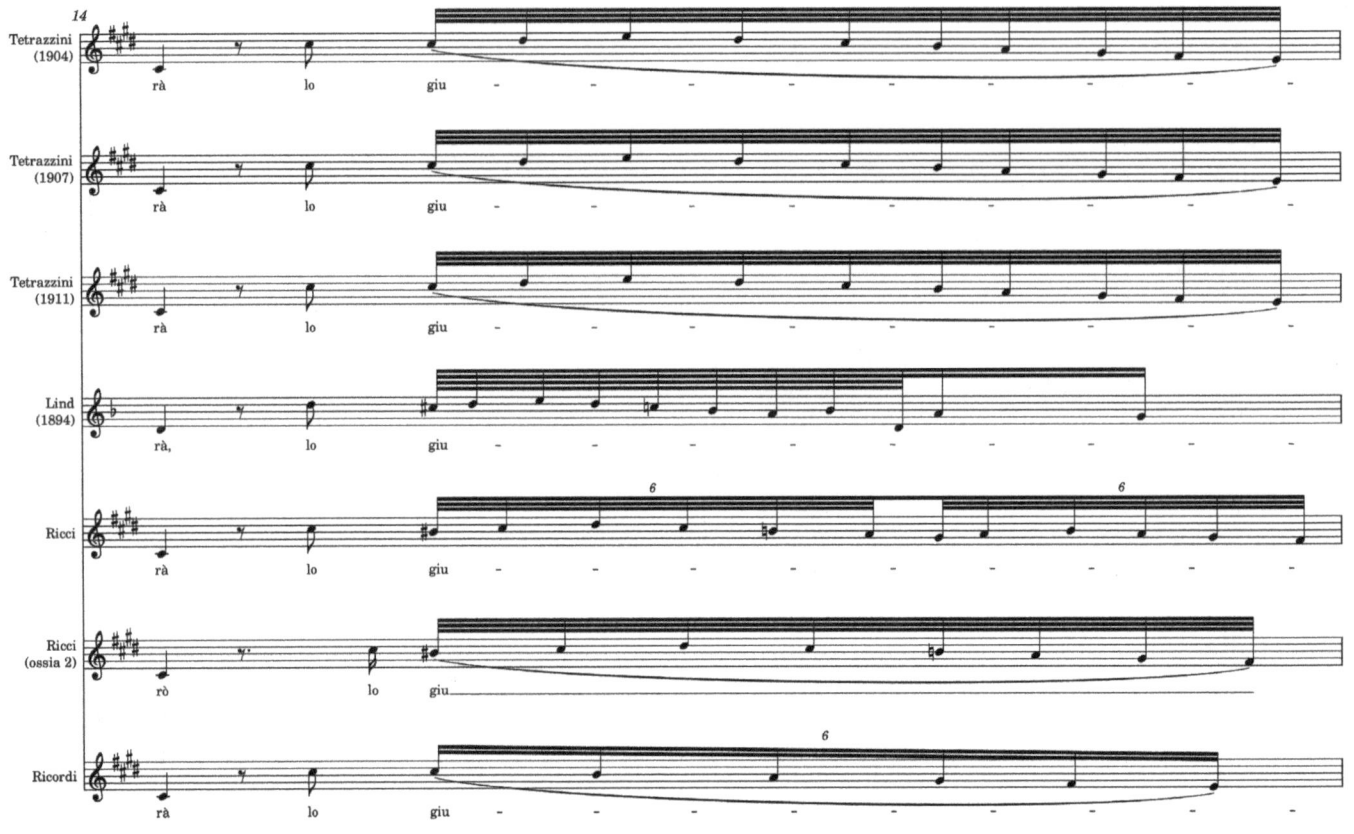

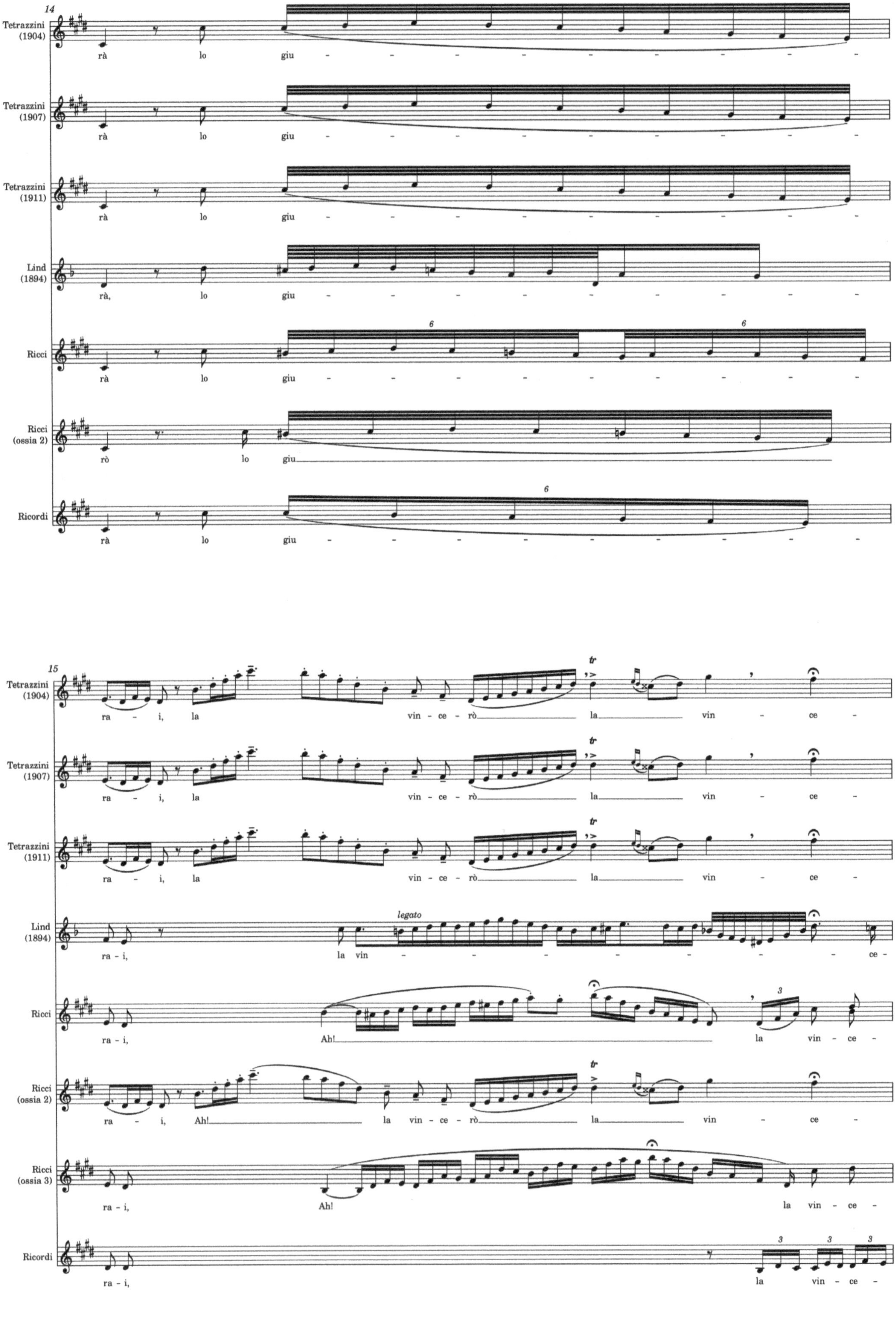

16
Tetrazzini (1904)
rò. Il tu-tor ri-cu-se-rò, io l'in-gegno_a-guz-ze-rò; al-la fin s'ac-che-te-rà, e con-tenta_io re-ste-rò... si Lin-
Tetrazzini (1907)
rò. Il tu-tor ri-cu-se-rò, io l'in-gegno_a-guz-ze-rò; al-la fin s'ac-che-te-rà, e con-tenta_io re-ste-rò... si Lin-
Tetrazzini (1911)
rò. Il tu-tor ri-cu-se-rò, io l'in-gegno_a-guz-ze-rò; al-la fin s'ac-che-te-rà, e con-tenta_io re-ste-rò... Lin-
parlando
f
Lind (1894)
rò. Il tu-tor ri-cu-se-rò, io l'in-gegno_a guz-ze-rò; al-la fin s'acche-te-rà, e conten ta_io re-ste-rò... si Lin-
Ricci
rò. Il tu-tor ri-cu-se-rò, io l'in-gegno_a-guz-ze-rò; al-la fin s'ac-che-te-rà, e con-tenta_io re-ste-rò... si Lin-
Ricci (ossia 2)
rò. rò... si Lin-
Ricci (ossia 3)
rò.
Ricordi
rò. Il tu-tor ri-cu-se-rò, io l'in-gegno_a guz-ze-rò; al-la fin s'ac-che-te-rà, e con-tenta_io re-ste-rò... si Lin-
22
Tetrazzini (1904)
do-ro mio rà, lo giù-
Tetrazzini (1907)
do-ro mio sa-rà, lo giu-
Tetrazzini (1911)
do-ro mio sa-rà, lo giu-
mf
Lind (1894)
do-ro mio sa-rà, lo giù-
Ricci
do-ro mio sa-rà, lo giu-
Ricci (ossia 2)
do-ro mi-o sa-rà, lo giu-
Ricci (ossia 3)
mi-o sa-rà, lo giu-
Ricordi
do-ro mio sa-rà, lo giù-

27
Tetrazzini (1904)
rà lo giu -
Tetrazzini (1907)
rà lo giu - - - - -
Tetrazzini (1911)
rà lo giu -
Lind (1894)
rà, lo giu - 3 -
Ricci
rà lo giu - - - - -
Ricci (ossia 2)
rà lo 3 giu -
Ricci (ossia 3)
rà lo giu -
Ricci (ossia 4)
rà
Ricci (ossia 5)
rà
Ricordi
6
rà lo giu - - - - - -
28
Tetrazzini (1904)
ra - i, lo p(eco) mf
Tetrazzini (1907)
ra - i, lo p(eco) mf
Tetrazzini (1911)
ra - i, lo p(eco)
Lind (1894)
ra - i, la vin - - - - - - - - - - - - - - - -
Ricci
ra - i, Ah la vin - ce -
Ricci (ossia 2)
ra - i,
(Ricci, I, p. 4, Marchesi, p. 13)
Ricci (ossia 3)
3 f p tr
ra - i, ah
Ricordi
ra - i, vin - - - - - - - - - - - - - - - - - -

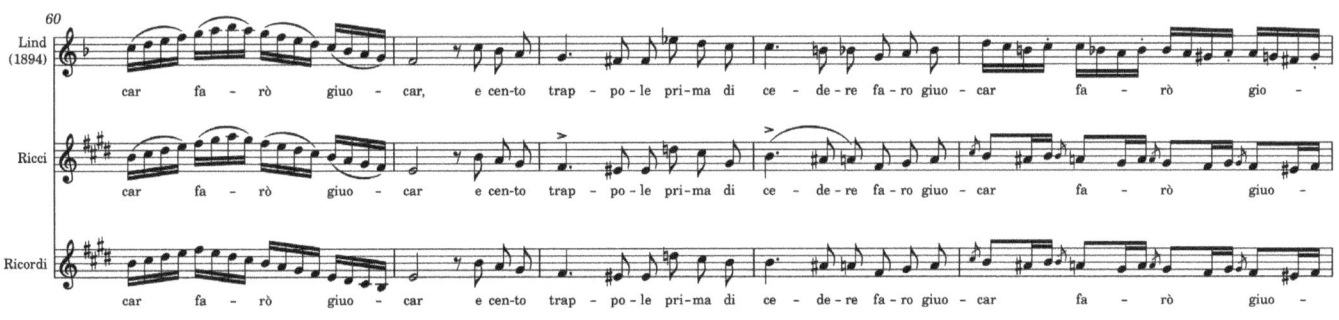
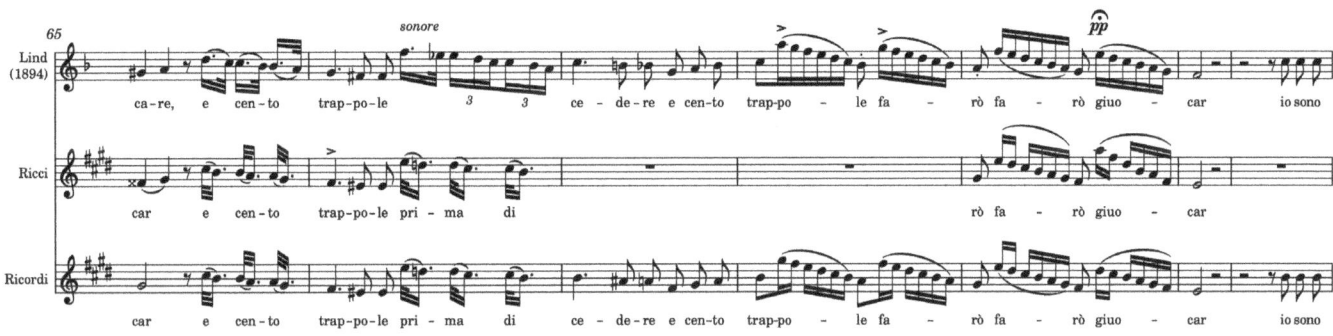

77
Tetrazzini (1907)
rall.....
Ma se mi toc-ca - no do-v'è_il mio de-bo - le sa-rò_u-na vi - pe - ra sa - rò e cen-to
Tetrazzini (1911)
Ma se mi toc-ca - no do-v'è_il mio de-bo - le sa-rò_u-na vi - pe - ra sa - rò e cen-to
Lind (1894)
a tempo
- Ma se mi toc-ca - no do-v'è_il mio de-bo - le sa-rò_u-na vi - pe-ra sa-rò, e cen-to
rall.....
Ricci
ten.
ma, Ma se mi toc-ca - no do-v'è_il mio de-bo - le sa-rò_u-na vi - pe - ra sa - rò e cen-to
Ricci (ossia 2)
ma, Ma se mi toc - ca-no do-v'è_il mio de - bo-le sa-rò_u-na vi - pe - ra, sa - rò e cen-to
Ricci (ossia 3)
ma, sa-rò u-na vi - pe - ra, sa - rò e cen-to
Ricci (ossia 4)
ma, Ma se mi toc-ca - no do-v'è_il mio de-bo - le sa rò u-na vi-pe-ra, sa-rò e cen-to
Ricordi
Ma se mi toc - ca-no do-v'è_il mio de - bo-le sa-rò_u-na vi - pe - ra sa - rò e cen-to

82
Tetrazzini (1907)
rall. . . .
meno
trap-po - le pri-ma di ce - de - re fa-rò giuo car re e cen-to
Tetrazzini (1911)
rall. . . .
meno
trap-po - le pri-ma di ce - de - re fa-rò giuo car re e cen-to
Lind (1894)
trap - po - le, pri-ma di ce - de - re, fa-rò gio - car - re e cen-to
Ricci
pri-ma di ce-de - re fa-rò giuo car, gio - car e cen-to
Ricci (ossia 2)
pri-ma di ce - de-re fa-rò giuo car, fa - rò gio - car
Ricci (ossia 3)
trap-po - le pri-ma di ce-de - re fa-rò giuo car, gio - car
Ricci (ossia 4)
trap-po - le pri-ma di ce-de - re fa - car, fa - rò gio - car
rò gio - car
Ricordi
trap - po-le pri-ma di ce - de-re fa-rò giuo-car fa - rò giuo - car e cen-to

86
Tetrazzini (1907)
trap - po - le pri - ma di ce - de - re fa - rò giuo - car fa - rò giuo - car e cen - to
200
Tetrazzini (1911)
trap - po - le pri - ma di ce - de - re fa - rò giuo - car fa - rò giuo - car e cen - to
con abandon
Lind (1894)
trap - po - le pri - ma di ce - de - re fa - rò giuo car, fa - rò gio - ca - re, e cen - to
Ricci
trap - po - le pri - ma di ce - de - re fa - rò giuo car fa - rò giuo - car e cen - to
Ricci (ossia 2)
car fa - rò
Ricci (ossia 3)
car fa - rò giuo - car e cen - to
Ricci (ossia 4)
car fa - rò gio - car e cen - to
209
Ricordi
trap - po - le pri - ma di ce - de - re fa - rò giuo car fa - rò giuo - car e cen - to

90
Tetrazzini (1907)
trap - po - le pri - ma di ce - de - re fa - rò-giuo-
Tetrazzini (1911)
trap - po - le pri - ma di ce - de - re fa - rò-giuo-
Lind (1894)
trap - po - le pri - ma di ce - de - re e cen - to-
Ricci
trap - po - le ah! pri - ma di ce - de - re e cen - to
Ricci (ossia 2)
trap - po - le pri - ma di ce - de - re e cen - to-
Ricci (ossia 3)
trap - po - le Ah! pri - ma di ce - de - re e cen - to-
Ricci (ossia 4)
trap - po - le pri - ma di ce - de - re e cen - to
Ricordi
trap - po - le pri - ma di ce - de - re e cen - to

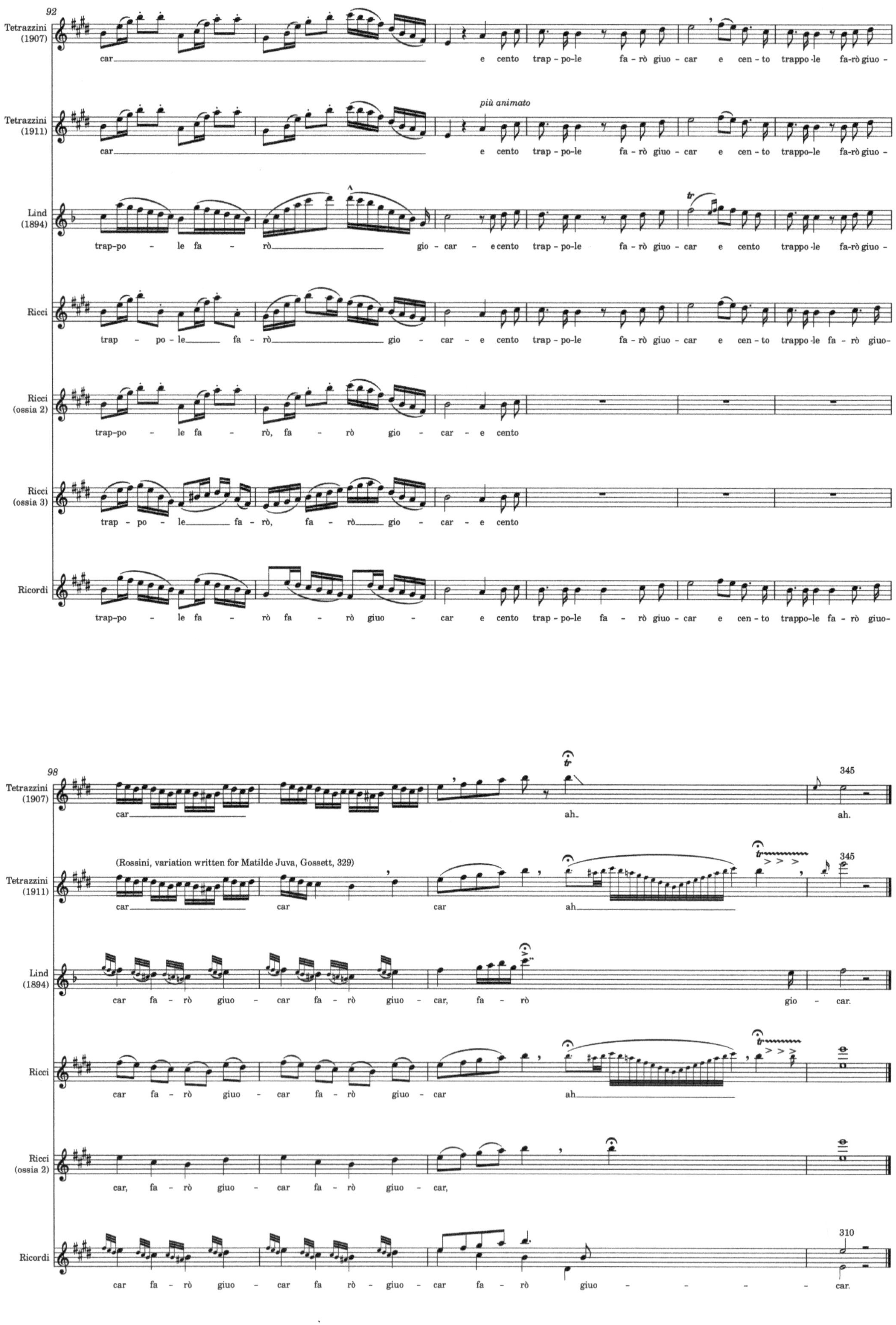

92
Tetrazzini (1907)
car e cento trap - po-le fa - rò giuo - car e cen - to trappo -le fa-rò giuo -
più animato
Tetrazzini (1911)
car e cento trap - po-le fa - rò giuo - car e cen - to trappo-le fa-rò giuo -
Lind (1894)
trap-po - le fa - rò gio - car - e cento trap - po-le fa - rò giuo - car e cento trappo -le fa-rò giuo -
Ricci
trap - po - le fa - rò gio - car - e cento trap - po-le fa - rò giuo - car e cen - to trappo-le fa - rò giuo-
Ricci (ossia 2)
trap-po - le fa - rò, fa - rò gio - car - e cento
Ricci (ossia 3)
trap - po - le fa - rò, fa - rò gio - car - e cento
Ricordi
trap-po - le fa - rò fa - rò giuo - car e cento trap - po-le fa - rò giuo - car e cen - to trappo-le fa - rò giuo-
98
Tetrazzini (1907)
car ah ah.
345
(Rossini, variation written for Matilde Juva, Gossett, 329)
Tetrazzini (1911)
car car car ah
345
Lind (1894)
car fa - rò giuo - car fa - rò giuo - car, fa - rò gio - car.
Ricci
car fa - rò giuo - car fa - rò giuo - car ah
Ricci (ossia 2)
car, fa - rò giuo - car fa - rò giuo - car,
Ricordi
car fa - rò giuo - car fa - rò - giuo - car fa - rò giuo - car.
310

Semiramide (1823)

"Bel raggio lusinghier"
Cavatina di Semiramide

Gaetano Rossi
Gioacchino Rossini

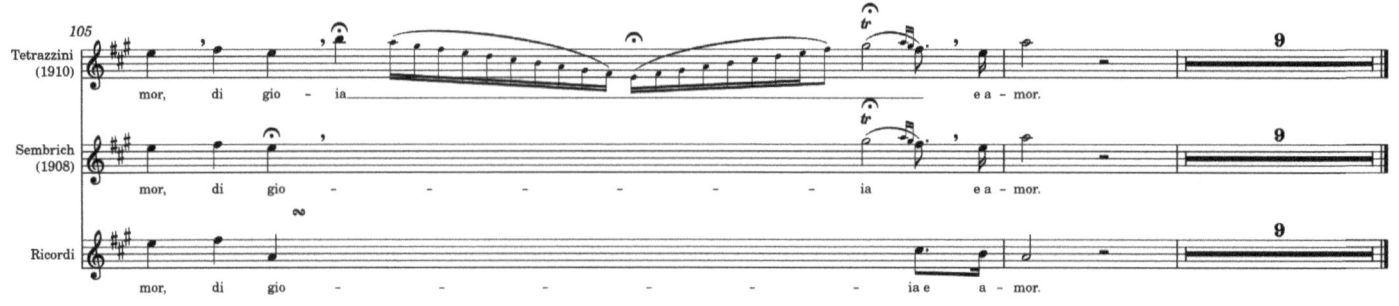

Lucia di Lammermoor (1835)
'Regnava nel silenzio'
Scena e cavatina

S. Cammarano
G. Donizetti

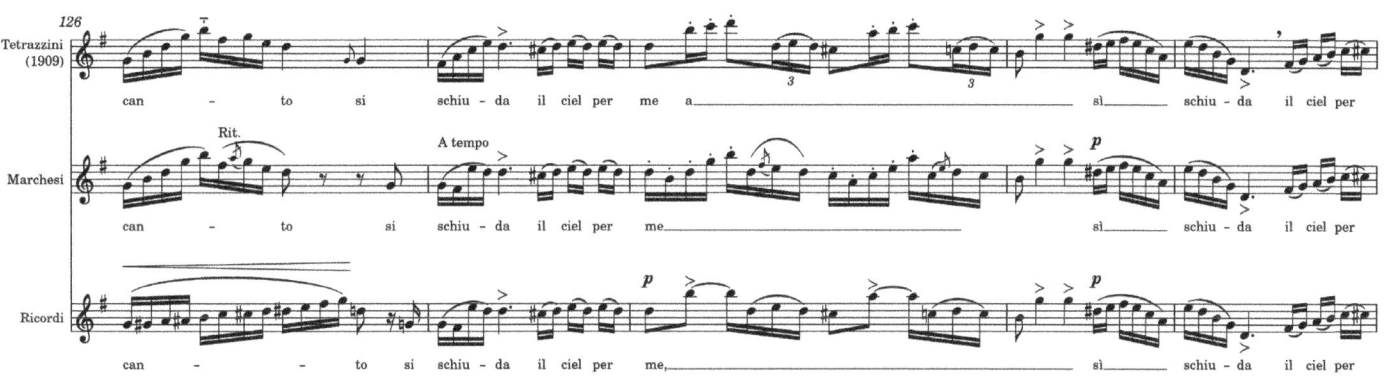
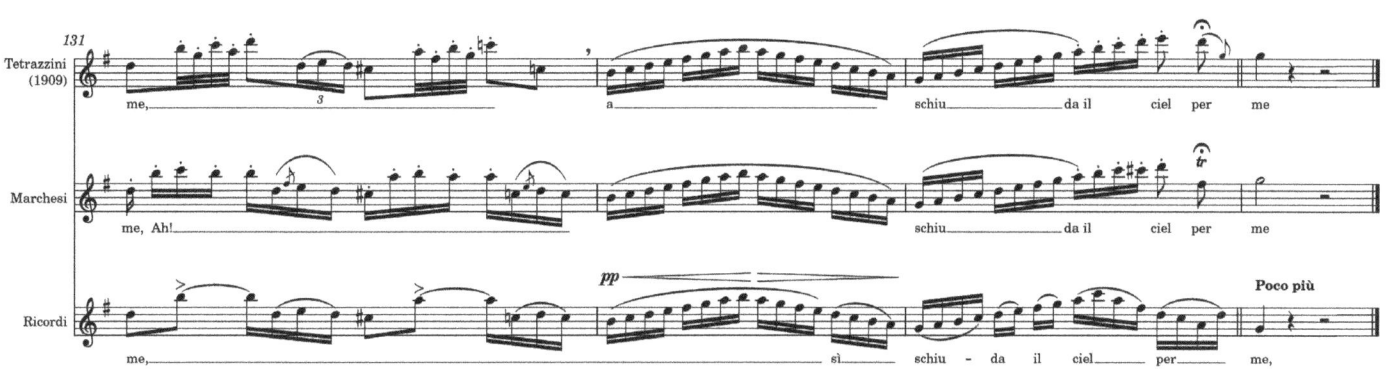

Lucia di Lammermoor
"Ardon gl'incensi"
(Parte II, Atto II, sc. 5)

Salvatore Cammarano
Gaetano Donizetti

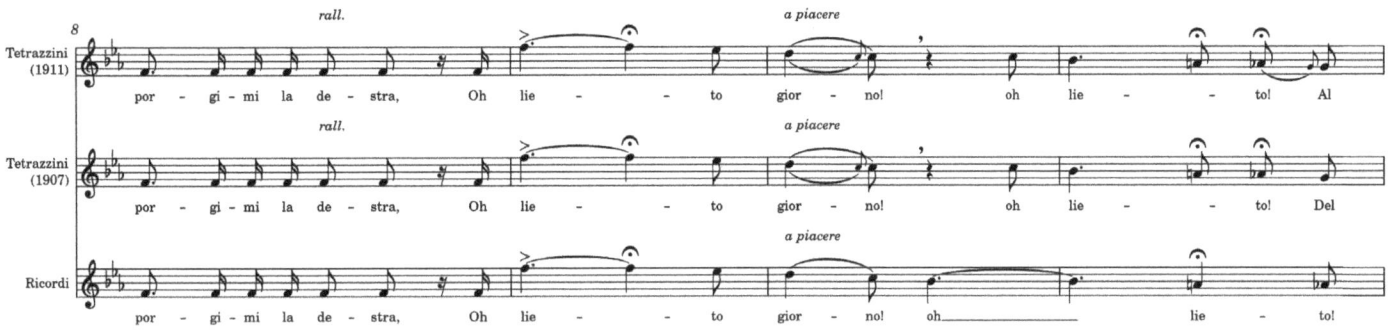

Tetrazzini (1911)
Tetrazzini (1907)
Flute (1907)
Flute (1911)
rall
rall
rall
tr
p
[sa - - - - - - - rà.]
Ricordi
sa - - - - - - - rà.

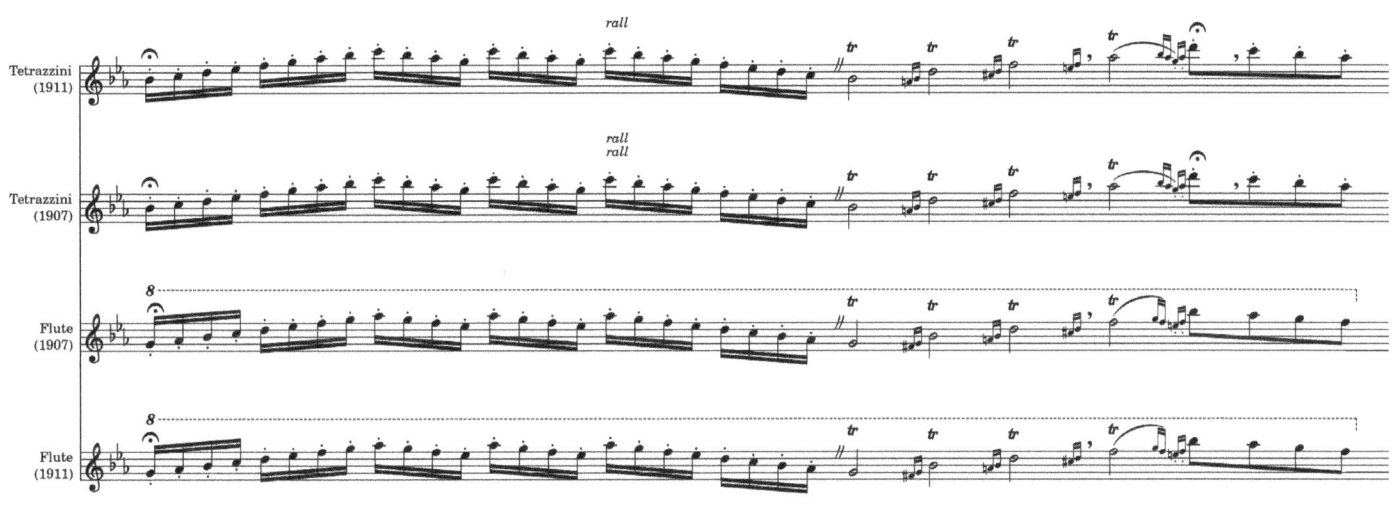

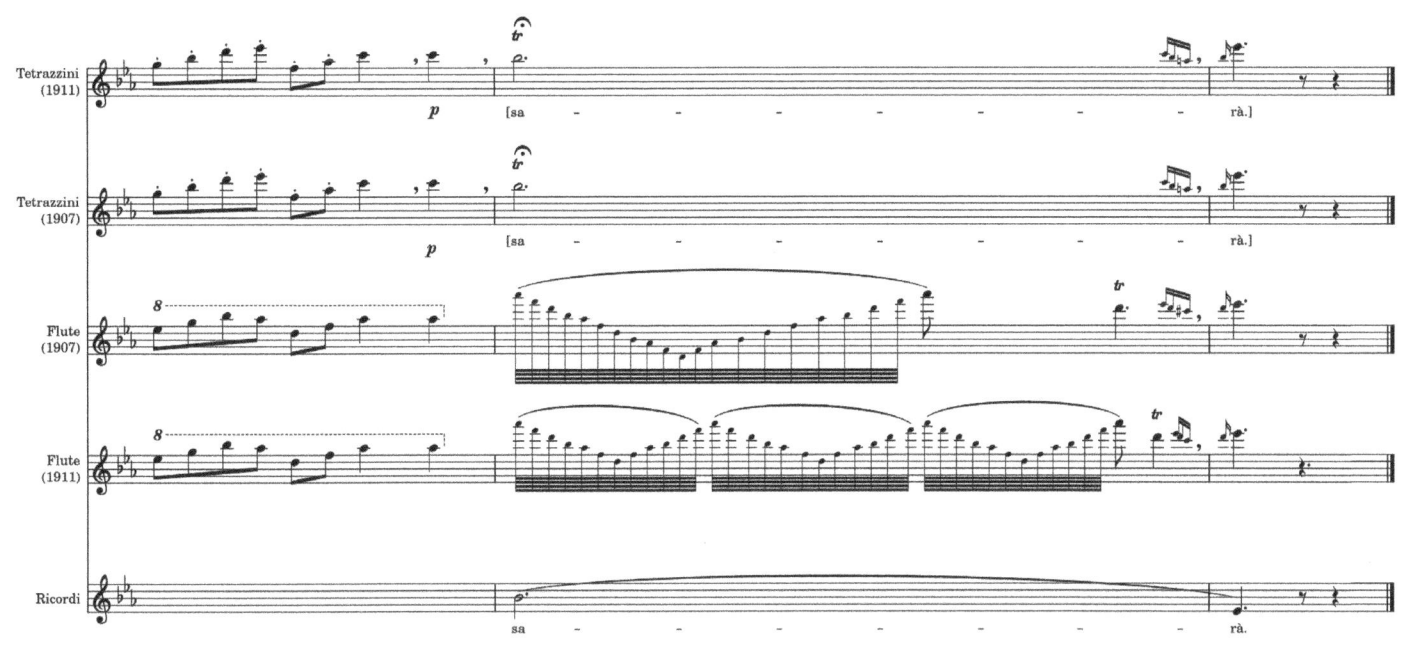

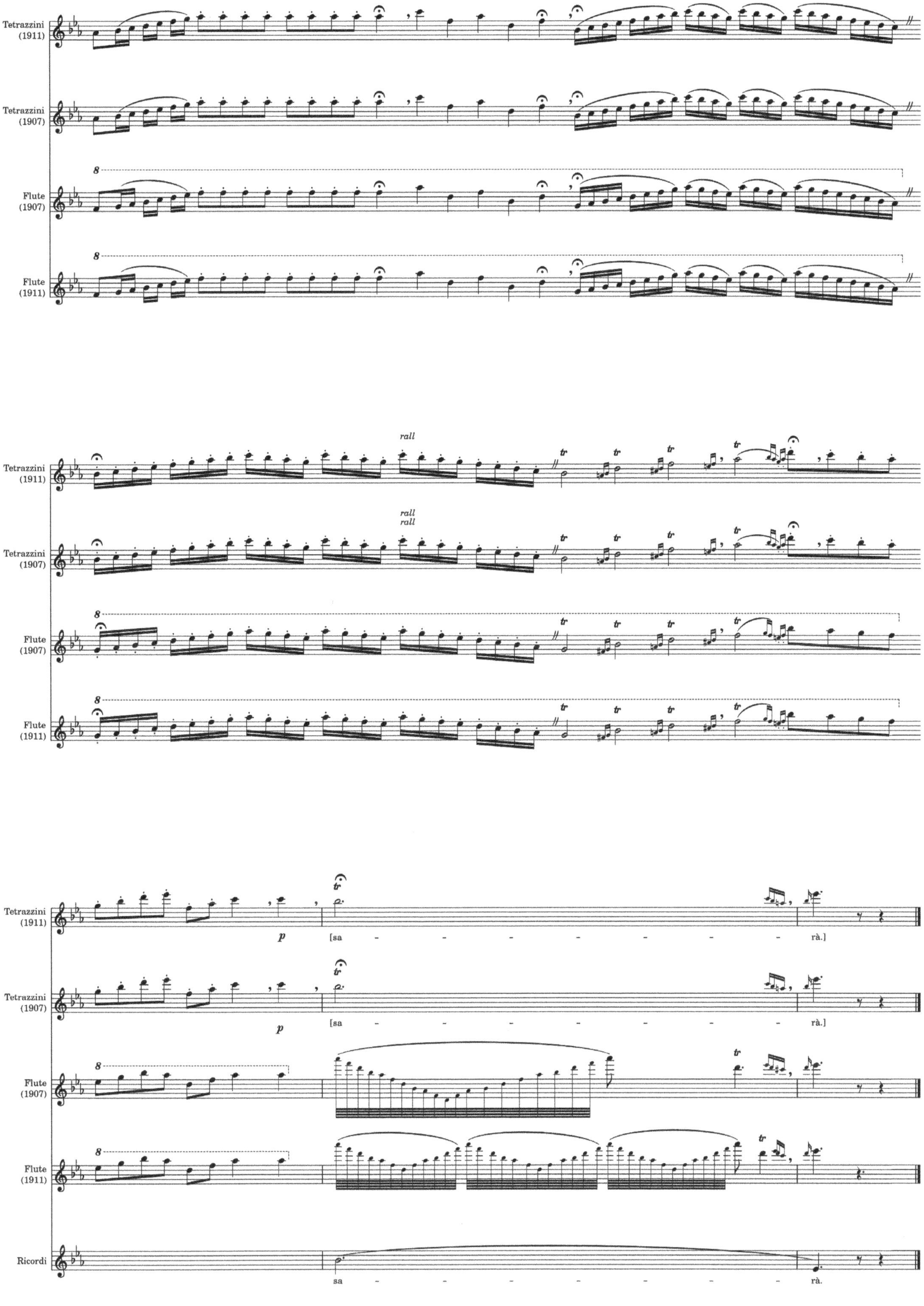

Linda di Chamounix

'O luce di quest'anima'
Recitativo e Cavatina

Gaetano Rossi / Gaetano Donizetti

La sonnambula (1831)
'Come per me sereno'
Recitativo e cavatina di'Amina

Felice Romani
Vincenzo Bellini

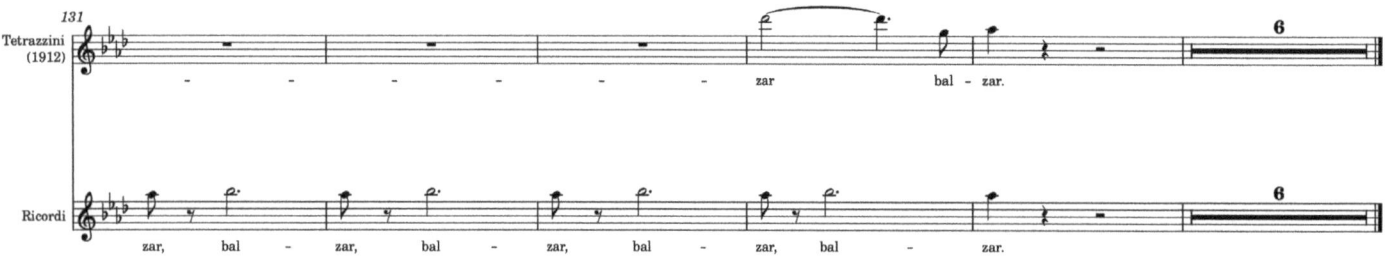

La Sonnambula (1831)
'Ah non credea mirarti'

Felice Romani
Vincenzo Bellini

La sonnambula
'Ah! non giunge'

Felice Romani V. Bellini

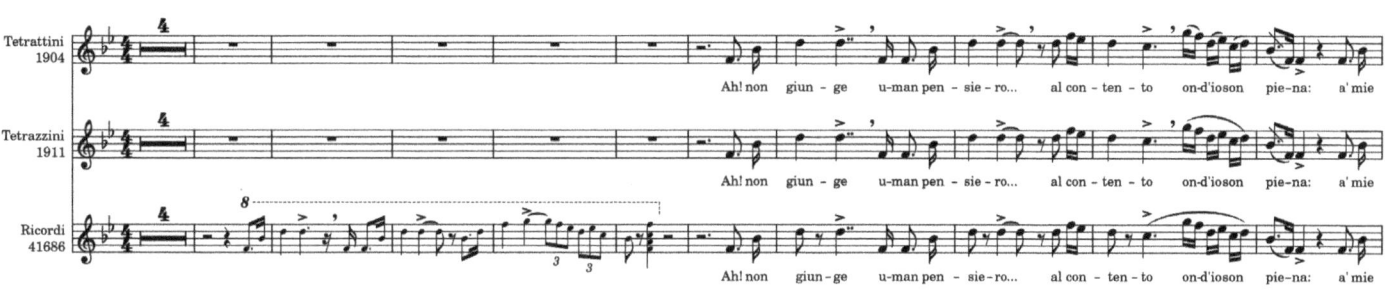

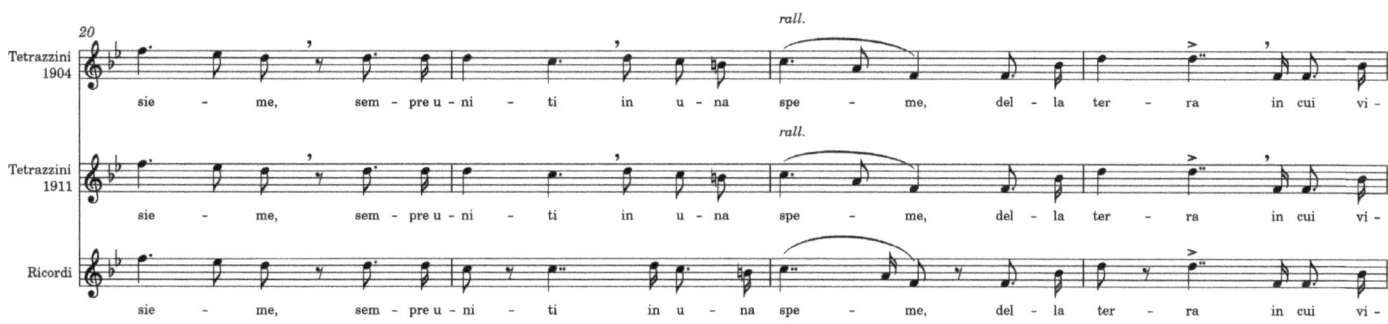

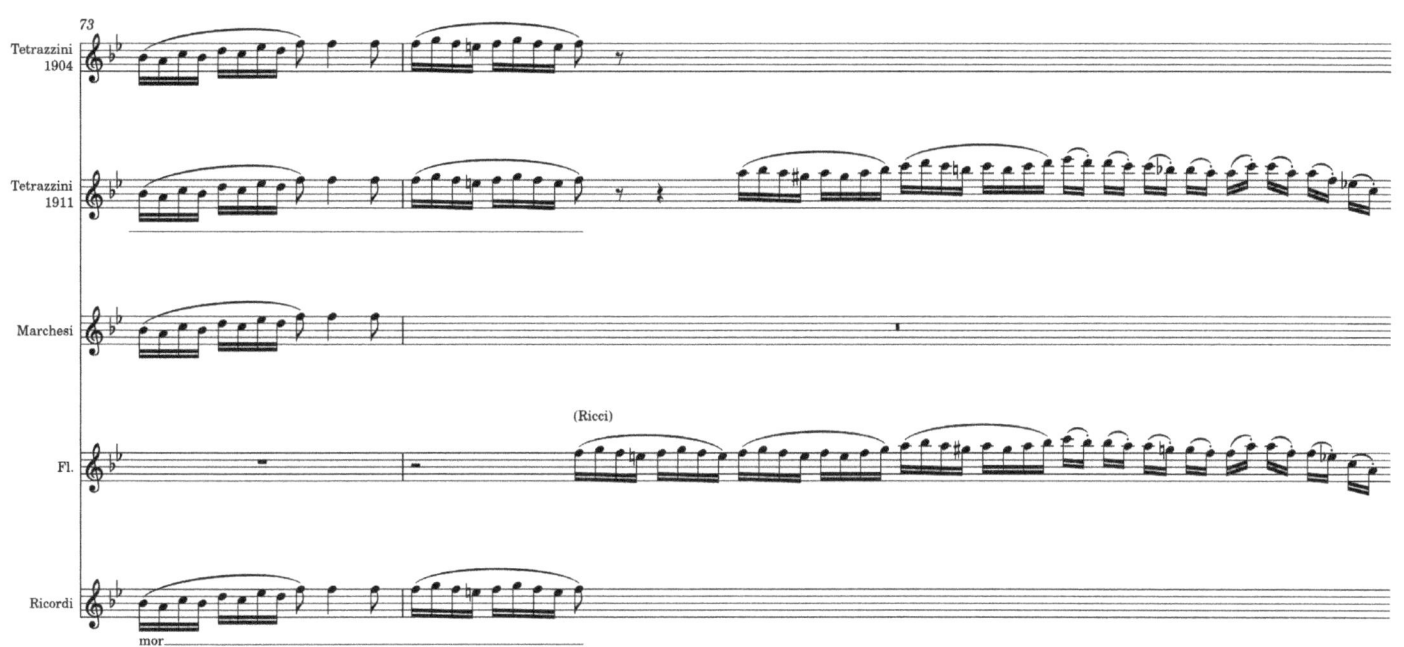
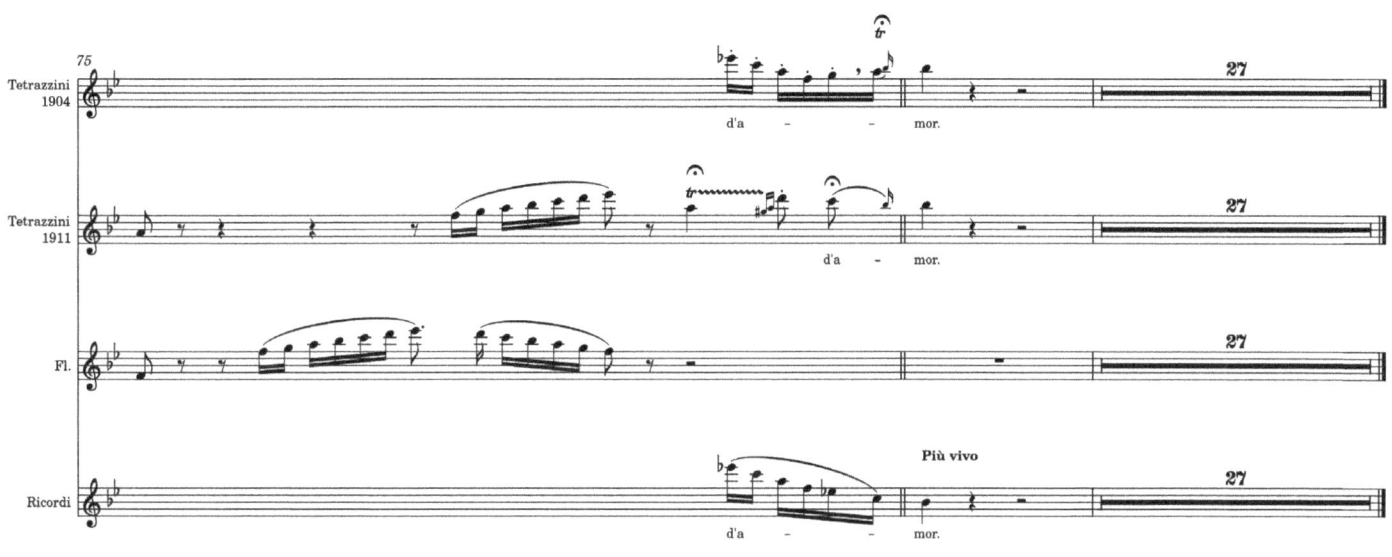

I puritani (1834)
'Vien diletto'

Carlo Pepoli
Vincenzo Bellini

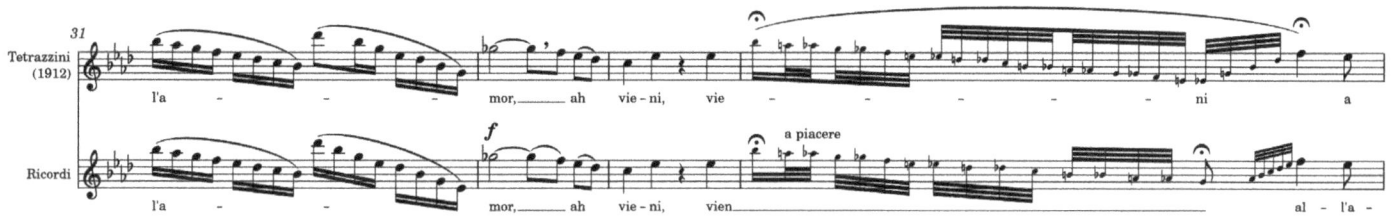

La traviata (1853)
'Ah fors'è lui'
(Scena e Aria)

Fr. M. Piave

Giuseppe Verdi

16
23
Tetrazzini (July 1911)
Tetrazzini (Mar. 1911)
Tetrazzini (1907/8)
Melba (1910)
Sembrich (1908)
Pacini (1905)
Ricordi
Andantino
molto rubato
dolciss.
molto rit.
p
Ah for - s'è lui che l'a - ni - ma so - lin-ga ne' tu - mul - ti, so - lin-ga ne' tu -
34
Tetrazzini (July 1911)
Tetrazzini (Mar 1911)
Tetrazzini (1907/8)
Melba (1910)
Sembrich (1908)
Pacini (1905)
Ricordi
rubato
(stretto)
molto rit.
mul - ti go - dea so - ven - te pin - ge - re de' suoi co - lo - ri oc - cul - ti, de' suoi co - lo - ri oc -

42
Tetrazzini (July 1911)
accel.
cul - ti!... Lui, che mo-de-sto e vi - gi - le al - l'e-gre so - glie a - sce - se, e nuo-va feb - bre ac -
Tetrazzini (Mar 1911)
accel.
cul - ti!... Lui, che mo-de-sto e vi - gi - le al - l'e-gre so - glie a - sce - se, e nuo-va feb - bre ac -
Tetrazzini (1907/8)
accel.
cul - ti!... Lui, che mo de-sto e vi - gi - le al - l'e-gre so - glie a - sce - se, e nuo-va feb - bre ac -
Melba (1910)
cul - ti!... Lui, che mo de - sto e vi - gi - le al - l'e-gre so - glie a - sce - se, e nuo-va feb - bre ac -
Sembrich (1908)
più mosso
molto ritenuto
cul - ti!... Lui, che mo-de - sto e vi - gi - le al - l'e-gre so - glie a - sce - se, e nuo-va feb - bre ac -
Pacini (1905)
accelerando
rall.
cul - ti!... Lui, che mo-de - sto e vi - gi - le al - l'e-gre so - glie a - sce - se, e nuo-va feb - bre ac -
Ricordi
pp
cresc.
f
cul - ti!... Lui, che mo-de - sto e vi - gi - le al - l'e-gre so - glie a - sce - se, e nuo-va feb - bre ac -

48
Tetrazzini (July 1911)
allargando...
ce - - se de - stan - do-mi al - l'a - mor!...
Tetrazzini (Mar 1911)
allargando...
ce - - se de - stan - do-mi al - l'a - mor!...
Tetrazzini (1907/8)
allargando...
(= 50)
ce - - se de - stan - do-mi al - l'a - mor!...
Melba (1910)
ce - - se de - stan - mi al - l'a - mor!... o!...
Sembrich (1908)
ce - - se de - stan-do - mi al - l'a - mor!... o!...
Pacini (1905)
ce - - se de - stan - do-mi al - l'a - mor!...
Ricordi
pp
ce - - se de - stan - do - mi al - l'a - mor!...

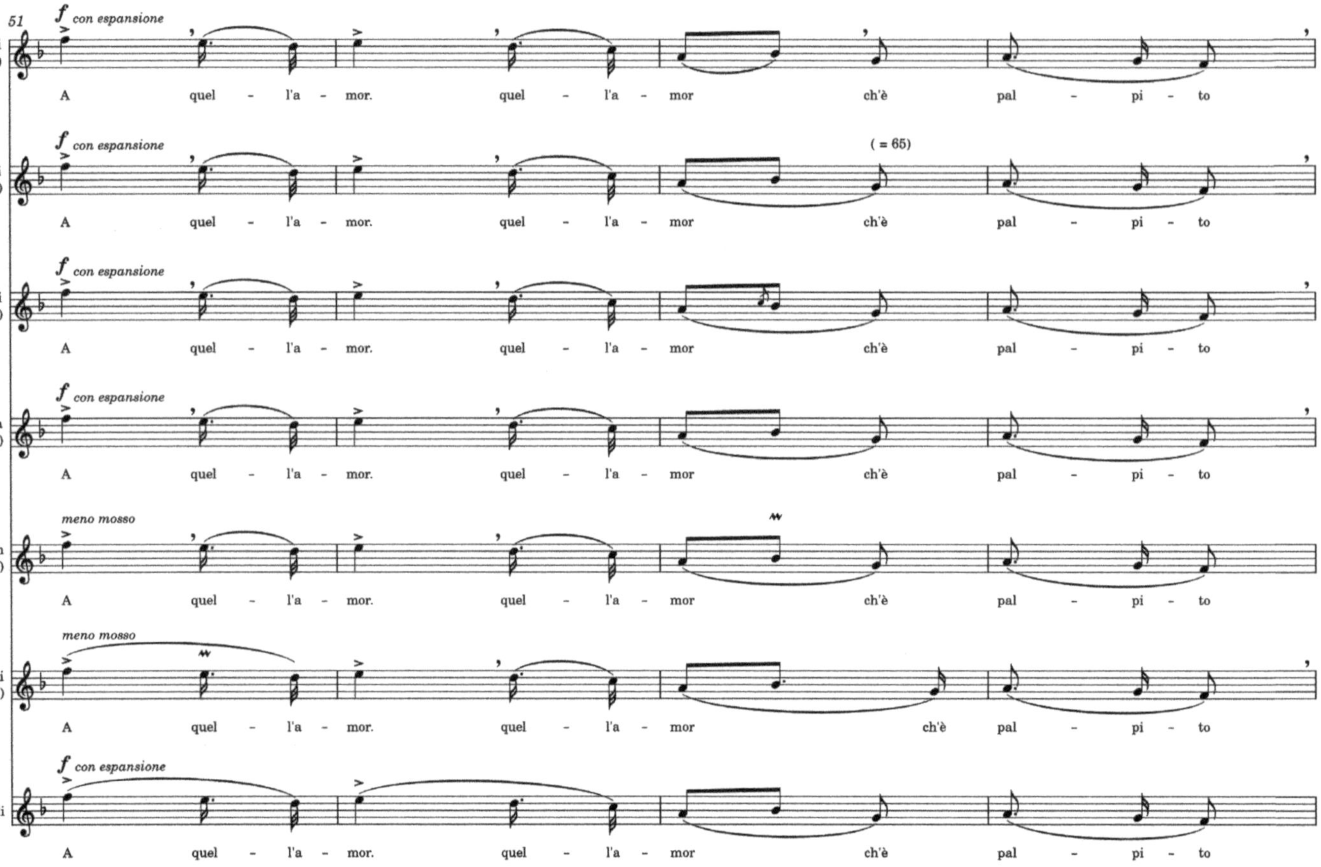
51
Tetrazzini (July 1911)
Tetrazzini (Mar 1911)
Tetrazzini (1907/8)
Melba (1910)
Sembrich (1908)
Pacini (1905)
Ricordi
f con espansione
meno mosso
(= 65)
A quel - l'a - mor. quel - l'a - mor ch'è pal - pi - to

55
Tetrazzini (July 1911)
Tetrazzini (Mar 1911)
Tetrazzini (1907/8)
Melba (1910)
Sembrich (1908)
Pacini (1905)
Ricordi
ritenuto
più animato
del - l'u - ni - ver - so, del - l'u - ni - ver - so in - te - ro,

59
Tetrazzini (July 1911)
mi - ste - ri - o - - so, mi - ste - ri - o - so, al - te - - ro,
Tetrazzini (Mar 1911)
Tetrazzini (1907/8)
Melba (1910)
più mosso
rall. . . .
Sembrich (1908)
Pacini (1905)
Ricordi
63
(libero)
cro - ce, cro - ce e de - li - zia, cro - ce e de - li - zia, de - li - zia al
libero, rallentando
f
leggero

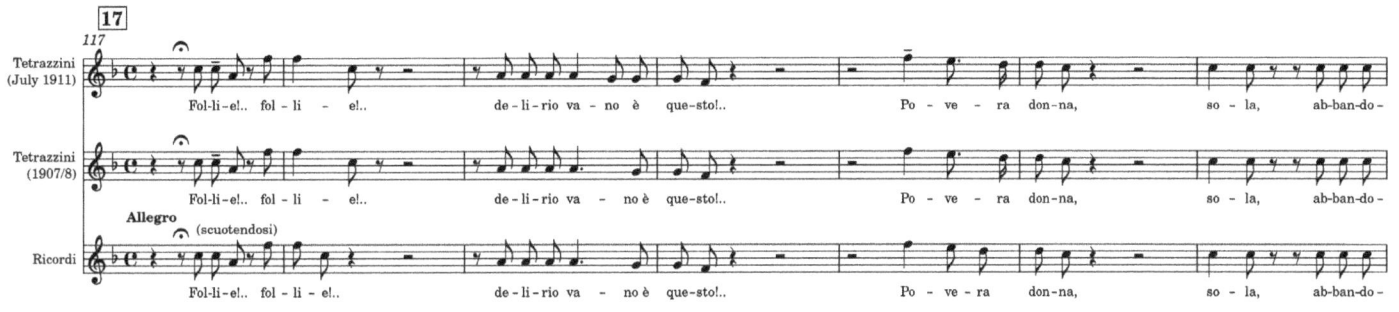
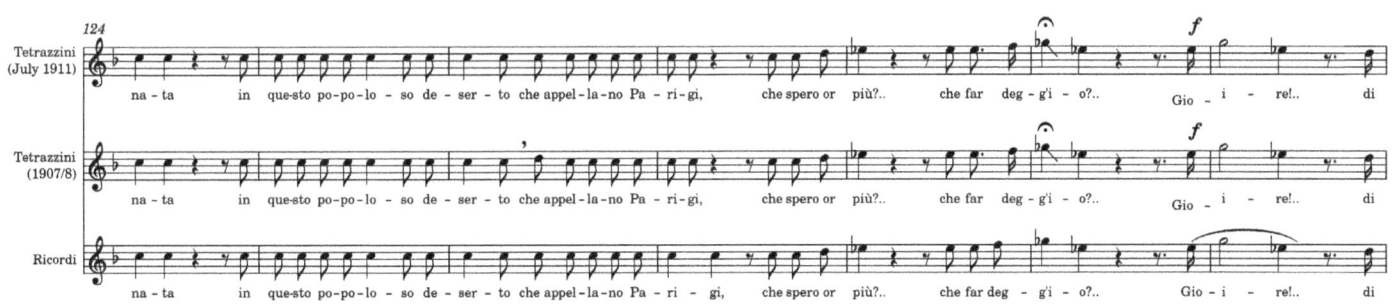

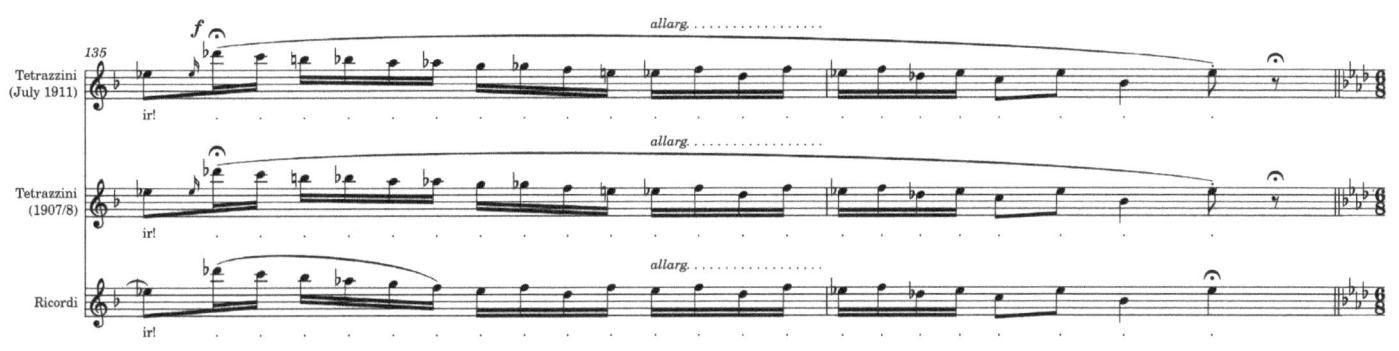

202
Tetrazzini (July 1911)
cer. Nasca il gior-no, o il gior - no muo-ia, sem-pre lie - ta ne' ri - tro vi a a di-
Tetrazzini (Mar 1911)
cer. Nasca il gior-no, o il gior-no non muo-ia, sem-pre lie - ta ne' ri - tro - vi a a di-
Tetrazzini (1907/8)
(. = 98)
cer. Nasca il gior-no, o il gior-no non muo-ia, sem-pre lie - ta ne' ri - tro - vi a a di-
Melba (1910)
cer. Nasca il gior-no, o il gior-no muo-ia, sem-pre lie - ta ne' ri - tro - - - - - vi a di-
Pacini (1905)
cer. Nasca il gior-no, o il gior - no muo-ia, sem-pre lie - ta ne' ri - tro - vi, a di-
Ricordi
con effetto questo ripiglio
cer. Nasca il gior-no, o il gior-no muo-ia, sem-pre lie - ta ne' ri - tro - vi, a di-

209
(tempo primo)
Tetrazzini (July 1911)
let - ti sem - pre nuo - vi dee vo - la - re il mio pen - sier, dee vo - lar, dee vo - lar, dee vo - la - re il mio pen-
Tetrazzini (Mar 1911)
let - ti sem - pre nuo - vi dee vo - la - re il mio pen - sier, dee vo - lar, dee vo - lar, dee vo - la - re il mio pen-
Tetrazzini (1907/8)
let - ti sem - pre nuo - vi dee vo - la - re il mio pen - sier, dee vo - lar, dee vo - lar, dee vo - la - re il mio pen-
Melba (1910)
let - ti sem - pre nuo - vi dee vo - la - re il mio pen - sier, dee vo - lar, dee vo - lar, dee vo - la - re il mio pen-
Pacini (1905)
let - ti sem - pre nuo - vi dee vo - la - re il mio pen - sier, dee vo - lar, dee vo - lar, dee vo - la - re il mio pen-
Ricordi
let - ti sem - pre nuo - vi dee vo - la - re il mio pen - sier, dee vo - lar, dee vo - lar, dee vo - la - re il mio pen-

237
Tetrazzini (July 1911)
dee vo - lar il mio pen - sier, il mio pen -
Tetrazzini (Mar 1911)
dee vo - lar il mio pen - sier, il mio pen -
Tetrazzini (1907/8)
dee vo - lar il mio pen - sier, il mio pen -
Melba (1910)
dee vo - lar il mio pen - sier, il mio pen -
Sembrich (1908)
a tempo)
accel. . . .
dee vo - lar o dee vo - lar o dee vo -
Pacini (1905)
dee vo - lar il mio pen - sier, il mio pen -
Ricordi
dee vo - lar il mio pen - sier, il mio pen -
242
Tetrazzini (July 1911)
sier ah! ah! ah! sier.
Tetrazzini (Mar 1911)
sier ah! ah! ah! sier.
Tetrazzini (1907/8)
sier ah! ah! ah!
Melba (1910)
sier ah! il mio pen - sier.
Sembrich (1908)
lar a [dee vo - lar.]
Pacini (1905)
sier Ah ah pen - sier.
Ricordi
(entra a sinistra)
sier il mio pen - sier.

Rigoletto
'Caro Nome'
Scena e aria

Fr. M. Piave
G. Verdi

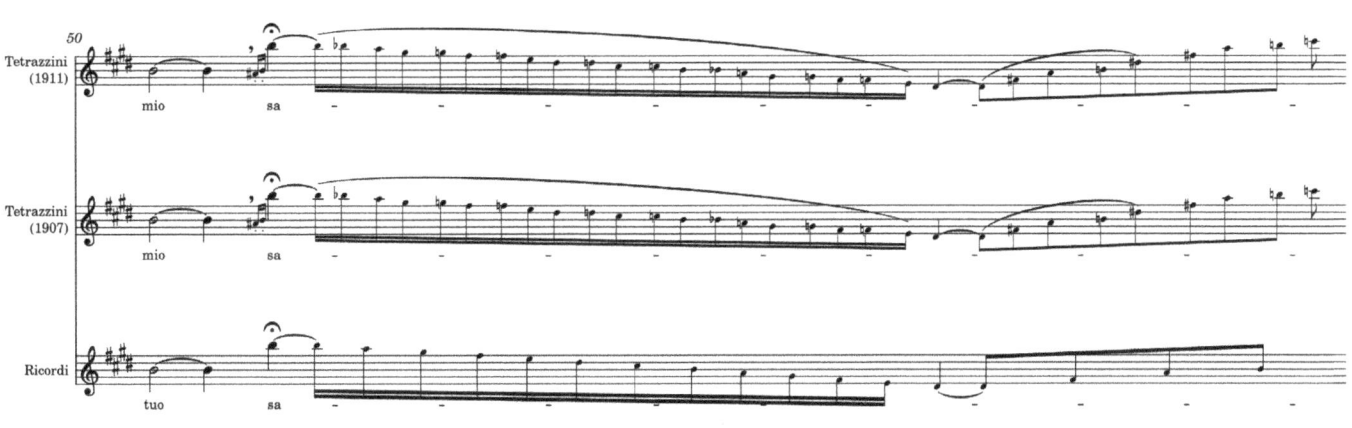

Una ballo in maschera (1859)
'Canzone di Oscar'

A. Somma
G. Verdi

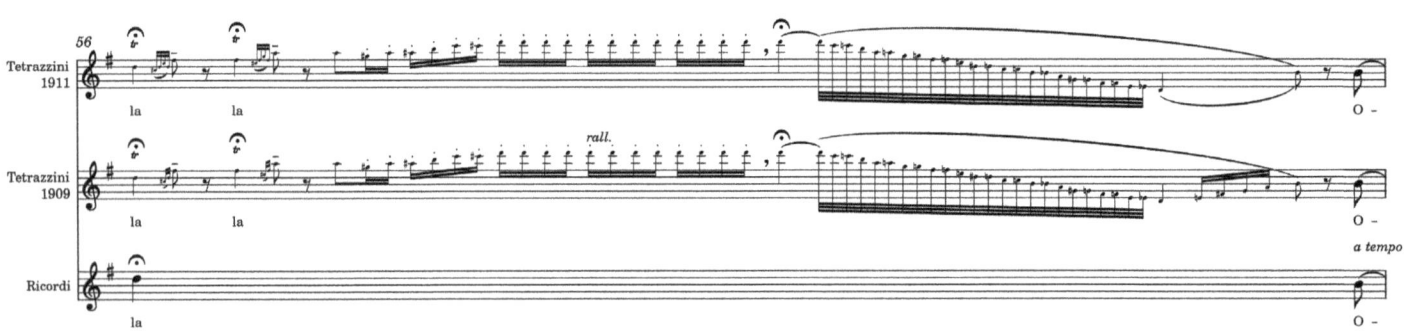

Il trovatore (1853)
'Tacea la notte placida'

Bardare - Cammarano

Giuseppe Verdi

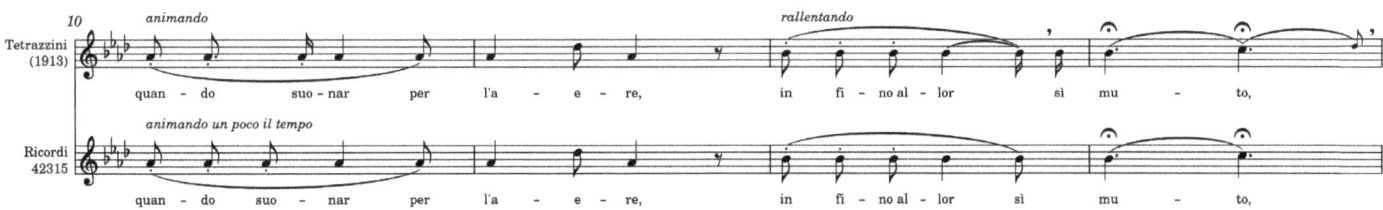
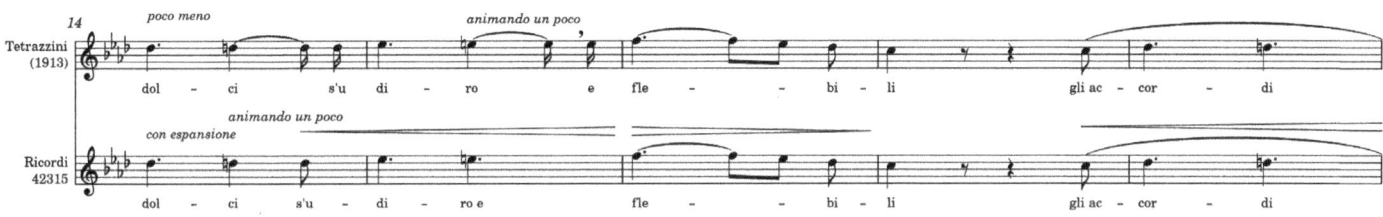
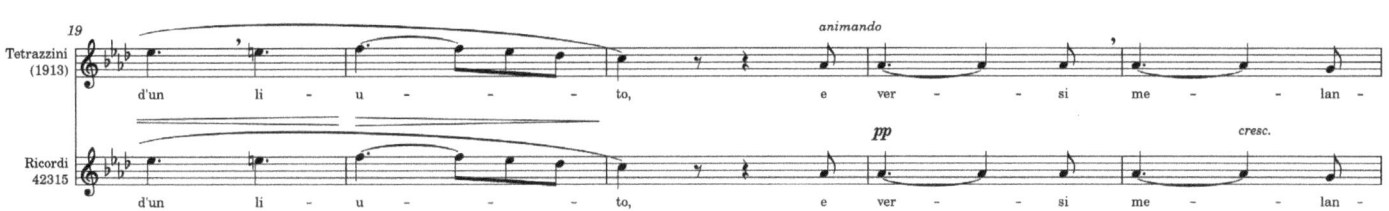
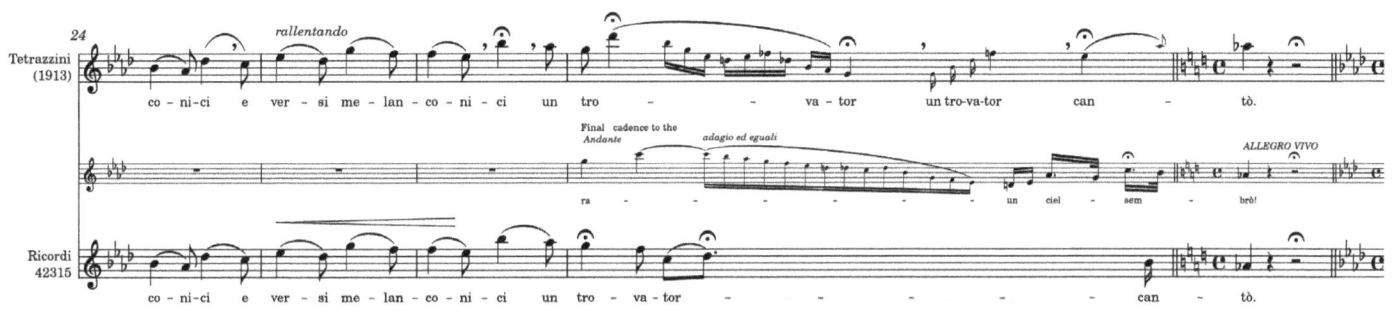

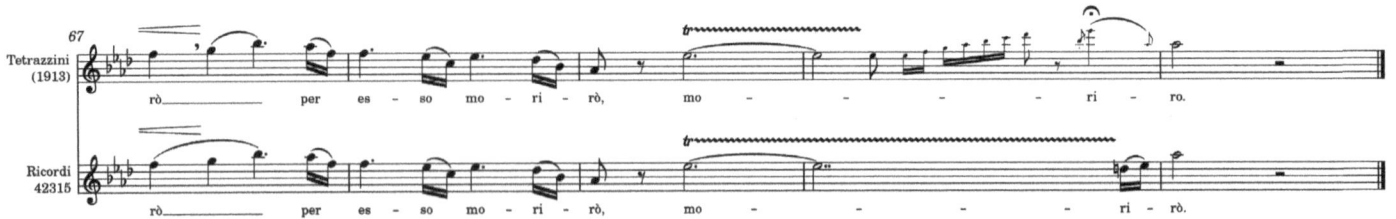

List of Illustrations

Figure 1	shows the spectrogram of Tetrazzini's 1908 recording of 'Ah! Fors'è lui' in Verdi's *La traviata*.	xiv
Figure 2	shows the use of vibrato and portamento in Tetrazzini's 1911 recording of 'Ah non credea mirarti'.	5
Figure 3	shows Patti's use of portamento in her 1906 recording of 'Ah, non credea mirarti'.	5
Figure 4	shows the first four measures of Verdi's 'Ah, fors'è lui' in *La traviata* as sung by Tetrazzini.	6
Figure 5	shows Tetrazzini's use of portamento in the opening bars of Verdi's 'Ah, fors'è lui', recorded in 1911.	6
Figure 6	shows Marcella Sembrich's use of portamento in the opening bars of Verdi's 'Ah fors'è lui', recorded in 1904.	6
Figure 7	shows Nellie Melba's use of portamento in the opening measures of Verdi's 'Ah, fors'è lui', recorded in 1904.	7
Figure 8	shows the two ornamented versions of 'Ecco ridente il cielo' in Rossini's *Barbiere* which García suggests in his *Scuola di Garcia*, Ricordi, pp. 38–39.	12
Figure 9	shows the melodic material given to Rosina in the duet 'Dunque io son'.	20
Figure 10	shows the concertato-like setting in the duet 'Dunque io son'.	20
Figure 11	reproduces the variations to 'Dunque io son' from *Barbiere*, present in M. García's method (1842).	21
Figure 12	reproduces the variations for mezzo soprano to 'Dunque io son' from *Barbiere*, present in M. García's *Hints* (1894).	21
Figure 13	reproduces the variations for soprano to 'Dunque io son' from *Barbiere*, present in M. García's *Hints* (1894).	22
Figure 14	presents the ornamented version sung by Maria Callas in 1956 and 1957.	23
Figure 15	the chart shows the cuts in Tetrazzini's recordings of Rosina's cavatina.	28
Figure 16	shows the cadenza at bar 28 of the Andante.	29
Figure 17	the closing cadenza of the Andante.	30
Figure 18	shows the cadenza traditionally sung before the repeat (B') in the Moderato section.	31
Figure 19	shows the final measures of the aria, where Tetrazzini sings the variants Rossini wrote for Matilde Juva; in the 1911 recording she concludes with an accented trill leading to the top E. Her cadenza was transcribed by Ricci in his *Variazioni-Cadenze*.	32
Figure 20	illustrates how a trill could be executed according to the new, modern habits discussed in García's *Scuola*.	32
Figure 21	the cadenza concluding 'Io son Tatiana', which Tetrazzini recorded in 1907.	34
Figure 22	Tetrazzini adds some modifications to Proch's third variation.	35
Figure 23	the cadenza with which Proch's *Variations* conclude.	36
Figure 24	Tetrazzini's cadenza to Proch's *Variations*.	36
Figure 25	shows the cuts present in Tetrazzini's 1910 recording of 'Bel raggio lusinghier'.	43
Figure 26	presents the cadenza reproduced by Ricci that concludes the Andante grazioso.	44
Figure 27	shows Sembrich's and Tetrazzini's recorded renditions of the initial measures of 'Bel raggio lusinghier'.	44
Figure 28	shows Sembrich's and Tetrazzini's recorded renditions of 'Bel raggio lusinghier' (measures 4 to 9).	45
Figure 29	shows Sembrich's and Tetrazzini's recorded renditions of 'Bel raggio lusinghier' (measures 11–15).	45
Figure 30	shows Sembrich's and Tetrazzini's recorded renditions of 'Bel raggio lusinghier'.	46
Figure 31	shows the traditional cadenzas before the reprise of 'Dolce pensiero'.	46
Figure 32	shows Sembrich's and Tetrazzini's recorded renditions of the final cadenza of 'Dolce pensiero'.	47
Figure 33	shows the motif as Lucia sings it the first time.	52

Figure 34	shows the flute passage inserted in the mad scene as a reminiscence of the meeting between Lucia and Edgardo.	52
Figure 35	shows the reminiscence motif from 'Verranno a te sull'aure' in Marchesi's second cadenza for Lucia's mad scene.	52
Figure 36	shows the last bars of 'Quando rapito', where Tetrazzini reaches the high D, as also noted by De Koven in 1908.	57
Figure 37	shows the change from pizzicato to legato with portamento in the strings at bar 3 in the Larghetto.	60
Figure 38	shows Tetrazzini's small rhythmic modifications and portamentos in 'Regnava nel silenzio'.	61
Figure 39	shows Tetrazzini's rendition of the cadenza that concludes the Larghetto of 'Regnava nel silenzio'.	61
Figure 40	shows Tetrazzini's changes in the Moderato.	61
Figure 41	shows Tetrazzini's coloratura in the closing measures of 'Regnava nel silenzio'.	62
Figure 42	shows the changes made by Tetrazzini in the initial measures of 'Ardon gl'incensi'.	65
Figure 43	shows Tetrazzini's own changes in 'Ardon gl'incensi'.	65
Figure 44	shows the arpeggio and the four-note figure echoed by the flute with which Tetrazzini opens the cadenza.	66
Figure 45	shows the closing cadenza sung by Tetrazzini: in 1911 Walter Osterreicher plays a longer arpeggio.	66
Figure 46	shows Tetrazzini's use of appoggiaturas in the opening recitativo 'Ah! Tardai troppo'.	68
Figure 47	shows the fermata with which the recitativo closes, as sung by Tetrazzini and her senior colleagues.	69
Figure 48	shows the fermata that concludes the first section: while Marchesi suggests two possible cadenzas, Tetrazzini does not sing any.	70
Figure 49	shows Tetrazzini's small modifications in the reprise of the aria.	70
Figure 50	shows an example from García, Volume II, p. 16, regarding 'Come per me sereno' from Bellini's *La sonnambula*.	77
Figure 51	shows an example from García, vol. II, p. 36, regarding the use of a half-breath before the reprise in *La sonnambula*.	78
Figure 52	shows the same example as that in Figure 51 from García (p. 36). Now the half-breath can be found placed on the 'ah' (penultimate measure).	78
Figure 53	shows an example from 'Ah! Non credea mirarti' on which García writes 'variante della Malibran' (vol. II, p. 39).	79
Figure 54	shows García's suggestion as to how to prevent excess of ornament in a cadenza by dropping the fermata between the two dominant chords (vol. II, p. 51).	80
Figure 55	presents the variants sung by Maria Malibran as reported by Maria Merlin in 1840.	80
Figure 56	shows the modifications sung by Jenny Lind in Bellini's 'Vien diletto'	81
Figure 57	shows Tetrazzini's modifications in *La sonnambula*, 'Ah! non credea mirarti' (measures 119–20, p. 314, Ricordi, 2010) compared to Patti and Lind.	85
Figure 58	*La sonnambula*, 'Ah! non credea mirarti' (Ricordi, 2010, bb. 132–33, p. 315).	86
Figure 59	*La sonnambula*, 'Ah! non credea mirarti' (Ricordi, 2010, measures 134–135, pp. 315–16).	87
Figure 60	shows Tetrazzini's rendition of the closing cadenza with cello obbligato in *La sonnambula*, 'Ah! non credea mirarti', (measures 144–145, p. 316 in Ricordi, 2010).	87
Figure 61	*La sonnambula*, 'Ah non giunge', Ricordi, 2010, b. 272, p. 334.	88
Figure 62	shows the closing measure of Heinrich Proch's *Variations* 'Deh torna mio bene'.	89
Figure 63	shows the final cadenza of 'Charmant Oiseau' from David's *La perle du Brésil* (Paris: Launer, [n.d.]), p. 263.	90
Figure 64	shows the first variant sung by Emma Nevada in Paris, as was published by Heugel in 1885 (p. 311).	90
Figure 65	shows the second variant sung by Emma Nevada in Paris, as was published by Heugel in 1885 (p. 313–14).	91
Figure 66	shows the cuts present in Tetrazzini's 1912 recording of 'Sovra il sen'.	93
Figure 67	shows the fermata of 'Come per me sereno' as was sung by Tetrazzini, compared to those of García and Marchesi.	94
Figure 68	shows Tetrazzini's rendition of the cadenza preceding the Allegretto brillante in *La sonnambula*, 'Come per me sereno', Ricordi, [1869], reprint 1971, p. 24, measure 11 after rehearsal mark number 21. For this example, the earlier edition was preferable, since the critical edition includes a different passage for the cadenza (Ricordi, 2010, b. 58, p. 29).	94

List of Illustrations

Figure 69	shows the different rendition of the central cadenza in *La sonnambula*, 'Sovra il sen la man si posa' (measures 119–20, pp. 35–36 in the Ricordi 2010 edition).	95
Figure 70	shows the modifications sung by Tetrazzini in *La sonnambula*, 'Sovra il sen la man mi posa', Ricordi, [1869], reprint 1971, p. 27, measure nine before rehearsal mark number 25. The critical edition differs from the one then published by Ricordi (Ricordi, 2010, bb. 98–106, pp. 33–34).	96
Figure 71	shows Tetrazzini's variant in *I puritani*, 'Vien diletto' (Ricordi, 2015, vol. I, measures 222–23, pp. 420–21).	96
Figure 72	*I puritani*, 'Vien diletto', Ricordi, 2015, measures 276–77, p. 427.	97
Figure 73	shows Tetrazzini's variants in the reprise of *I puritani*, 'Vien diletto' (Ricordi, measures 252–65, pp. 425–26).	97
Figure 74	shows Tetrazzini's rendition of 'È strano...' compared to Regina Pacini's.	117
Figure 75	shows the first measures of 'Ah! Fors'è lui' in Tetrazzini's recordings compared to those of Melba, Sembrich and Pacini.	118
Figure 76	shows the small interventions in Tetrazzini's rendition of 'Ah! Fors'è lui' compared to those of Melba, Pacini and Sembrich.	119
Figure 77	shows the different cadenzas sung by Tetrazzini, Melba, Sembrich and Pacini to 'Ah! Fors'è lui'.	119
Figure 78	shows the descending chromatic passage before the reprise, that Tetrazzini used to sing in 'Ah! Fors'è lui'.	120
Figure 79	shows the second descending chromatic passage typical of Tetrazzini, compared to those of Melba and Pacini.	120
Figure 80	shows the last chromatic passage Tetrazzini used to sing in 'Ah! Fors'è lui'.	121
Figure 81	shows how Tetrazzini conveys Violetta's sense of hysteria thanks to the repeated high Cs.	121
Figure 82	shows the final measures of 'Ah! Fors'è lui' featuring Tetrazzini's top Es.	122
Figure 83	shows Tetrazzini's modifications in the opening measures of 'Caro nome' in Verdi's *Rigoletto*.	124
Figure 84	shows Tetrazzini's cadenza to 'Caro nome' in Verdi's *Rigoletto*.	125
Figure 85	shows Tetrazzini's small modifications in the 'Canzone di Oscar' from Verdi's *Un ballo in maschera*.	126
Figure 86	shows modifications sung by Tetrazzini in the repeat of the 'Canzone di Oscar'.	126
Figure 87	shows the cadenza sung by Tetrazzini in the 'Canzone di Oscar'.	126
Figure 88	shows the ascending scale which concludes 'Tacea la notte placida' as sung by Tetrazzini.	127
Figure 89	shows Tetrazzini's modifications in the closing measures of 'Mercé dilette amiche' from *I vespri siciliani*.	127

Select Bibliography

Abbate, Carolyn, and Roger Parker, *A History of Opera* (New York: Norton, 2012).

Adamo, Maria Rosaria, and Friedrich Lippmann, *Vincenzo Bellini* (Turin: ERI, 1981).

Anfossi, Maria, *Trattato teorico-pratico sull'arte del canto / A Theoretical and Practical Treatise on the Art of Singing* (London: Published by the Authoress, [1837]).

Artists' Vocal Album (Boston: White, Smith & Co., 1887).

Aspinall, Michael, 'Il cantante nelle interpretazioni delle opere rossiniane', *Bollettino del centro rossiniano di studi*, 1 (1970), 11–21.

Aspinall, Michael, 'Rossini, il bel canto e Adelina Patti', *Musica*, 119 (2000), 58–61.

Balthazar, Scott L., 'The Primo Ottocento Duet and the Transformation of the Rossinian Code', *Journal of Musicology*, 7 (1989), 471–97.

Barblan, Guglielmo, *L'opera di Donizetti nell'età romantica* (Bergamo: Ed. del centenario, 1948).

Basevi, Abramo, *Studio sulle opere di Giuseppe Verdi* (Florence: Tipografia Tofani, 1859).

Beghelli, Marco, 'Per Fedeltà a Una Nota', *Il Saggiatore Musicale*, 8.2 (2001), 295–316.

Beghelli, Marco, 'L'emblema melodrammatico del lamento: il semitono dolente', in *Verdi 2001: atti del Convegno internazionale = proceedings of the international Conference, Parma, New York, New Haven, 24 gennaio-1 febbraio 2001* (Historiae musicae cultores; 96) (Firenze: L.S. Olschki, 2003), pp. 241–80.

Beghelli, Marco, and Raffaele Talmelli, *Ermafrodite Armoniche, Il contralto nell'Ottocento* (Varese: Zecchini Editore, 2011).

Beghelli, Marco, 'A Ritroso: Indizi Nella Divulgazione Extrateatrale per il recupero della prassi esecutiva verdiana', in *Fuori dal teatro. Modi e percorsi della divulgazione di verdiercorsi della divulgazione di Verdi*, ed. by Antonio Carlini (Venezia: Marsilio, 2015), pp. 247–64.

Bellini, Vincenzo, *Tutti i libretti di Bellini*, ed. by Olimpio Cescatti (Turin: UTET, 1995).

Bellini, Vincenzo, *Vincenzo Bellini: verso l'edizione critica. Atti del convegno internazionale, Siena, 1–3 giugno 2000*, ed. by Fabrizio Della Seta and Simonetta Ricciardi (Firenze: Olschki, 2004).

Berlioz, Hector, *Autobiography of Hector Berlioz*, trans. by Rachel (Scott Russell) Holmes and Eleanor Holmes, 2 vols (London: Macmillan & Co., 1884).

Bigio, Robert, 'Albert Fransella: The Paganini of the Flute', *Pan*, 12 (June 1994), 19–25.

Cambi, Luisa, *Vincenzo Bellini. Epistolario* (Milan: Mondadori, 1943).

Capra, Marco, '"Effekt, nicht als Effekt". Aspekte der Rezeption der Opern Verdis in Italien des 19. Jahrhunderts', in *Giuseppe Verdi und seine Zeit*, ed. by Markus Engelhardt (Laaber: Laaber Verlag, 2001), pp. 117–42.

Capra, Marco, *Verdi in prima pagina* (Lucca: Libreria Musicale Italiana, 2014).

Castel-Blaze, *L'Opéra-Italien de 1548 à 1856* (Paris: Castil-Blaze, 1856).

Celletti, Rodolfo, *A History of Bel Canto* (Oxford: Clarendon Press, 1996; first Italian edition 1983).

Celletti, Rodolfo, *Il canto* ([Milan]: Vallardi, 1989).

Cesari, Gaetano, Alessandro Luzio, and Michele Scherillo (eds), *I copialettere di Giuseppe Verdi* (Milan: Commissione, 1913), https://archive.org/details/icopialettere00verd.

Chamier, Daniel, *Percy Pitt of Covent Garden and the B.B.C.* (London: Edward Arnold, [1938]).

Chorley, Henry F., *Thirty Years' Musical Recollections*, 2 vols (London: Hurst and Blackett, 1862).

Chusid, Martin, 'A Letter by the Composer about "Giovanna d'Arco" and Some Remarks on the Division of Musical Direction in Verdi's Day', *Performance Practice Review*, 3.1 (1990), 7–57.

Cinti-Damoreau, Laura, *Méthode de chant composée pour ses classes du Conservatoire* (Paris: au Ménestrel, 1849).

Colas, Damien, 'Improvvisazione e ornamentazione nell'opera francese e italiana di primo Ottocento', in *Beyond Notes: Improvisation in Western Music of the Eighteenth and Nineteenth Centuries*, ed. by Rudolf Rasch (Turnhout: Brepols, 2011).

Cone, John Frederick, *Adelina Patti: Queen of Hearts* (Portland: Amadeus Press, 1993).

Cook, Nicholas, 'Performance Analysis and Chopin's Mazurkas', *Musicae Scientiae*, 11.2 (2007), 183–207, https://doi.org/10.1177/102986490701100203.

Crivelli, Domenico, *L'Arte del Canto* (London: published by the author, [n.d.]).

Crutchfield, Will, 'Vocal Ornamentation in Verdi: The Phonographic Evidence', *19th Century Music*, 7.1 (1983), 3–54.

Da Costa, Neal Peres, *Off the Record* (Oxford: Oxford University Press, 2012), https://doi.org/10.1093/acprof:oso/9780195386912.001.0001.

Delibes, Lèo, *Lakmé, Opéra in trois actes, poème de MM. Edmond Gondinet et Philippe Gille* (Paris: Heugel, 1883).

Duey, Philip, *Bel Canto in Its Golden Age* (New York: King's Crown Press, 1951).

Dyer, Richard, 'Puccini, his Sopranos, and Some Records', *Opera Quarterly*, 2.3 (1984), 62–71.

Edgcumbe, Richard, *Musical Reminiscences, Containing an Account of the Italian Opera in England from 1773* (London: J. Andrews, 1834).

Elliott, Martha, *Singing in Style, A Guide to Vocal Performance Practices* (New Haven: Yale University Press, 2006).

Embellished Opera Arias, ed. by Austin Caswell, vols VII–VIII (Madison, WI: A-R Editions, 1989).

Fabian, Dorottya, *A Musicology of Performance: Theory and Method Based on Bach's Solos for Violin* (Cambridge: Open Book Publishers, 2015), https://doi.org/10.11647/OBP.0064.

Fabian, Dorottya, 'Commercial Sound Recordings and Trends in Expressive Music Performance', in *Expressiveness in Music Performance* (Oxford University Press, 2014), pp. 58–79, https://doi.org/10.1093/acprof:oso/9780199659647.001.0001.

Freitas, Roger, 'Towards a Verdian Ideal of Singing: Emancipation from Modern Orthodoxy', *Journal of the Royal Musical Association*, 127.2 (2002), 226–57.

Gaisberg, Fred W., *The Music Goes Round* (New York: The Macmillan Company, 1942).

García, Manuel, *Scuola di Garcia, trattato completo dell'arte del canto*, 2 vols (Milan: Ricordi, [1842]).

García, Manuel, *Treatise on the Art of Singing*, ed. by Albert Garcia (London: Leonard, [1924]).

García, Manuel, *Hints on Singing by Manuel Garcia, Translated from the French by Beata Garcia* (New York: Ascherberg, 1894).

Gartioux, Hervé, *La réception de Verdi en France, Anthologie de la presse 1845–1894* (Weinsberg: Galland, 2001).

Gattey, Charles Neilson, *Luisa Tetrazzini the Florentine Nightingale* (Portland: Amadeus Press, 1995).

Gossett, Philip, 'Verdi, Ghislanzoni, and *Aida*: The Uses of Convention', *Critical Inquiry*, 1.2 (1974), 291–334.

Gossett, Philip, *Divas and Scholars. Performing Italian Opera* (Chicago: Chicago University Press, 2006).

Gothard, John, *Thoughts on Singing* (Chesterfield: Pike, 1848).

Hepokoski, James, 'Under the Eye of the Verdian Bear: Notes on the Rehearsals and Première of Falstaff', *Musical Quarterly*, 71.2 (1985), 135–56.

Huebner, Steven, 'Lyric Form in Ottocento Opera', *Journal of the Royal Musical Association*, 117.1 (1992) 123–47.

Kauffman, Deborah, 'Portamento in Romantic Opera', *Performance Practice Review*, 5.2 (1992), 139–58 https://doi.org/10.5642/perfpr.199205.02.03.

Klein, Herman, *The Reign of Patti* (London: T. Fisher Unwin, 1920).

Kreuzer, Gundula, *Verdi and the Germans* (Cambridge: Cambridge University Press, 2010).

Lablache, Luigi, *Metodo completo di canto* (Milan: G. Ricordi, 1842; facsimile edition with an introduction by Rodolfo Celletti Milan: Ricordi, 1997).

Lablache, Luigi, *Method of Singing* (Philadelphia: Ditson, [n.d.]).

Lamperti, Francesco, *Guida Teorico-Pratica-Elementare per lo studio del canto dettata dal Prof. Francesco Lamperti per le sue Allieve del R. Conservatorio di musica di Milano* (Milan: Ricordi [1864]). English translation: *The Art of Singing* (New York: Schirmer, 1890).

Lawton, David, 'Ornamenting Verdi's Arias: The Continuity of a Tradition', in *Verdi in Performance*, ed. by Alison Latham and Roger Parker (Oxford: Oxford University Press, 2001), pp. 49–78.

Leech-Wilkinson, Daniel, 'Listening and Responding to the Evidence of Early Twentieth-Century Performance', *Journal of the Royal Musical Association*, 135.1 (2010), 45–62, https://doi.org/10.1080/02690400903414822.

Liebling, Estelle, *The Estelle Liebling Book of Coloratura Cadenzas containing Traditional and New Cadenzas, Cuts, Technical Exercises, and suggested Concert Programs* (New York: Schirmer, 1943).

Limansky, Nicholas E., 'Luisa Tetrazzini: Coloratura Secrets', *Opera Quarterly*, 20.4 (2004), 540–69, https://doi.org/10.1093/oq/kbh076.

Manén, Lucie, *Bel canto: The Teaching of the Classical Italian Song-Schools, Its Decline and Restoration* (Oxford: Oxford University Press, 1987).

Marchesi, Mathilde, *Variantes et points d'orgue* (Paris: Huguel, 1900).

Martin, George W., *Verdi in America* (Rochester: University of Rochester Press, 2011).

Martland, Peter, *Recording History: The British Record Industry, 1888–1931* (Lanham: The Scarecrow Press, 2013).

Matsumoto, Naomi, 'Manacled Freedom: 19th-Century Vocal Improvisation and the Flute-Accompanied Cadenza in Donizetti's Lucia di Lammermoor', in *Beyond Notes: Improvisation in Western Music of the Eighteenth and Nineteenth Centuries*, ed. by Rudolf Rasch (Turnhout: Brepols, 2011), pp. 295–316.

Merlin, Maria de las Mercedes, *Memoirs of Madame Malibran*, 2 vols (Philadelphia: Carey and Hart, 1840).

Monelle, Raymond, 'The Orchestral String Portamento as Expressive Topic', *Journal of Musicological Research*, 31.1–2 (2012), 138–46, https://doi.org/10.1080/01411896.2012.680878.

Montemorra Marvin, Roberta, 'Verdi's Tempo Assignments in "I masnadieri"', *Revista de Musicología*, Del XV congreso de la Sociedad Internacional de Musicología: culturas musicales del mediterráneo y sus ramificaciones, 16.6 (1993), 3179–195.

Ott, Karin, and Eugen, *Handbuch der Verzierungskunst in der Musik, Band 4, Die Vokalmusik im 19. Jahrhundert* (Munich: Ricordi, 1999).

Pennino, John, 'Tetrazzini at the Tivoli: Success and Scandal in San Francisco', *The Opera Quarterly*, 8.2 (1991), 4–26.

Petrobelli, Pierluigi, and Roger Parker, *Music in the Theater, Essays on Verdi and Other Composers* (Princeton: Princeton University Press, 1994).

Philip, Robert, *Early Recordings and Musical Style* (Cambridge: Cambridge University Press, 1992).

Pleasants, Henry, *The Great Singers, from the Dawn of Opera to our own Time* (New York: Simon & Schuster, 1966).

Poriss, Hilary, *Changing the Score: Arias, Prima Donnas, and the Authority of Performance* (Oxford: Oxford University Press, 2009).

Poriss, Hilary, 'A Madwoman's Choice: Aria Substitution in "Lucia Di Lammermoor"', *Cambridge Opera Journal*, 13 (2001), 1–28.

Powers, Harold S., '"La solita forma" and "The Uses of Convention"', *Acta Musicologica*, 59.1 (Jan.-Apr., 1987), 65–90.

Pugliese, Romana Margherita, 'The Origins of Lucia di Lammermoor's Cadenza', *Cambridge Opera Journal*, 16.1 (2004), 23–42, https://doi.org/10.1017/S0954586704001776.

Radic, Thérèse, *Melba the Voice of Australia* (St. Louis, MO: Magnum Music-Baton, 1986).

Raposo, Jessica Ann, *Defining the British Flute School: A Study of the British Flute Performance Practice 1890–1940*. Unpublished doctoral thesis, University of Columbia, July 2007, https://doi.org/10.14288/1.0100743.

Ricci, Luigi, *Variazioni-cadenze tradizioni*, 4 vols (Milan: Ricordi, 1937).

Rockstro, William Smyth, *Jenny Lind: A Record and Analysis of the 'Method' of the Late Madame Jenny Lind-Goldschmidt*, ed. by Otto Goldschmidt (London: Novello 1894).

Rognoni, Luigi, *Gioacchino Rossini* (Turin: Einaudi, 1977; first published 1968).

Rossini, Gioacchino, *Lettere inedite e rare di Gioacchino Rossini*, ed. by Giuseppe Mazzatinti (Imola: Galeati, 1892).

Rossini, Gioacchino, *Tutti i libretti di Rossini*, ed. by Marco Beghelli and Nicola Gallino (Turin: UTET, 1995).

Senici, Emanuele, 'Per una biografia musicale di Amina', in *Vincenzo Bellini: verso l'edizione critica. Atti del convegno internazionale, Siena, 1–3 giugno 2000* (Firenze: Olschki, 2004), pp. 297–314.

Senici, Emanuele, ed., *The Cambridge Companion to Rossini* (Cambridge: Cambridge University Press, 2004), https://doi.org/10.1017/CCOL9780521807364.

Smart, Mary Ann, 'The Silencing of Lucia', *Cambridge Opera Journal*, 4.2 (1992), 119–41.

Stark, James, *Bel Canto, A History of Vocal Pedagogy* (Toronto: University of Toronto Press, 2003).

Stendhal, *The Life of Rossini* (*La vie de Rossini*, 1824), trans. by Richard N. Coe (New York: Criterion Books, 1957).

Sutherland, Edwards, H., *The Prima Donna: Her History and Surroundings from the Seventeenth to the Nineteenth Century* (London: Remington and Co., 1888), https://archive.org/details/primadonnaherhis02edwa?q=adelina+patti.

Taruskin, Richard, 'The Pastness of the Present', in *Authenticity and Early Music*, ed. by Nicholas Kenyon (Oxford: Oxford University Press, 1988), 137–206.

Tetrazzini, Luisa, *My Life of Song* (London, New York, Toronto and Melbourne: Cassell, 1921).

Tetrazzini, Luisa, *How to Sing* (New York: George H. Doran, 1923).

Thomas, Ambroise, *Mignon, Opera in Three Acts, with Italian and English Text Translated and Adapted by Theodore T. Barker* (Boston: Olver Ditron Company, 1881).

Toft, Robert, *Bel Canto: A Performer's Guide* (Oxford: Oxford University Press, 2013).

Donizetti, Gaetano, *Tutti i libretti di Donizetti*, ed. by Egidio Saracino (Turin: UTET, 1996).

Vellutini, Claudio, 'Adina Par Excellence: Eugenia Tadolini and the Performing Tradition of Donizetti's *L'elisir d'amore* in Vienna', *19- Century Music*, 38.1 (2014), 3–29, https://doi.org/10.1525/ncm.2014.38.1.003.

Verdi, Giuseppe, *Verdi: lettere inedite: le opere verdiane al Teatro alla Scala (1839–1929)*, ed. by G. Morazzoni and G. M. Ciampelli (Milan: Libreria editrice milanese, 1929).

Verdi, Giuseppe, *Giuseppe Verdi nelle lettere di Ernrnanuele Muzio ad Antonio Barezzi*, ed. by Luigi Agostino Garibaldi (Milan: Fratelli Treves, 1931).

Verdi, Giuseppe, *Letters of Giuseppe Verdi*, ed. by Charles Osborne (New York: Gollancz, 1971).

Verdi, Giuseppe, *Interviste e incontri con Verdi*, ed. by Marcello Conati (Milan: Emme Edizioni, 1980).

Verdi, Giuseppe, *Tutti i libretti di Verdi*, ed. by Luigi Baldacci (Turin: UTET, 1996).

Volioti, Georgia, and Aaron Williamon, 'Recordings as Learning and Practising Resources for Performance: Exploring Attitudes and Behaviours of Music Students and Professionals', *Musicae Scientiae*, 21.4 (2017), 499–523, https://doi.org/10.1177/1029864916674048.

Weinstock, Herbert, *Rossini* (New York: Limelight Editions, 1987).

Zicari, Massimo, *Verdi in Victorian London* (Cambridge: Open Book Publishers, 2016), https://doi.org/10.11647/OBP.0090.

Zicari, Massimo, 'Expressive Tempo Modifications in Adelina Patti's Recordings: An Integrated Approach', *Empirical Musicology Review*, 12.1 (2017), 42–56, http://dx.doi.org/10.18061/emr.v12i1-2.5010.

Zicari, Massimo, 'Expressive Tempo Modifications in Early 20th-Century Recorded Performances of Operatic Arias', *Music&Practice*, 5 (2019), https://doi.org/10.32063/0507.

Zicari, Massimo, 'Identità stilistica e capriccio: Luisa Tetrazzini nelle registrazioni discografiche', *Rivista italiana di musicologia*, 40 (2020), 153–209.

Index

Abott, Bessie 64
Albani, Emma 53, 65, 94
Alboni, Marietta 42, 130
Arditi, Luigi 52
Argonaut, The 54
Arimondi, Vittorio 15
Arnoldson, Sigrid 33
Athenaeum, The 13, 100, 102–103

Bad Homburg 42
   Kursaal Theatre 42
Badiali, Cesare 19
Barberini Nini, Marianna 103
Barbier, Jules 33
Barone, Clement 35–36, 83, 89, 91
Barrientos, Maria 91
Bartoli, Cecilia 133
Basevi, Abramo 99, 116
Battistini, Mattia 15
Bazelli, Giorgio 82
Beethoven, Ludwig van 17, 40
   Pastoral Symphony 40
bel canto xii, xiii, xv, xvi, 1, 3, 7–11, 14, 43, 49, 55–58, 73, 75–76, 81–82, 85, 97, 99, 101–102, 104–105, 107–109, 114, 128–133
Bellincioni, Gemma 132
Bellini, Vincenzo 10, 14, 25, 49, 73–77, 79–86, 88, 92, 94, 96–97, 99, 101–102, 128, 131–133
   Beatrice di Tenda 76
   Il pirata 77
   I puritani 1, 73, 81, 83, 96–97, 133
   La sonnambula xvi, 1, 4, 49, 73, 76–83, 85–89, 94–97, 131, 133
   Norma 41, 76, 133
Bellinzaghi, Giovannina 101
Benedict, Julius 7, 25–26, 37
Berlendi, Livia 33
Berlioz, Hector 11
Birnbaum, Theo 9

Bishop, Henry 25
Bizet, Georges 49, 105
   Carmen 1, 49
   Les pêcheurs de perles 1
Boccabadati, Augusta 69
Boccabadati, Luigia 69
Boccabadati, Virginia 69
Bologna 23, 51, 68, 132
Borghi-Mamo, Adelaide 19, 29–30
Bosio, Angiolina 18–19, 24, 103
Boston 15, 33, 42, 89, 128
Boston Evening Transcript 128
Bottesini, Giovanni 47
Brambilla, Teresa 51, 69
Bruno, Elisa 93
Brussels 18
Buenos Aires 3, 15, 33, 49, 68, 82
   Teatro San Martin 15, 33, 49, 68, 82

cabaletta xvii, 39, 41, 43, 49–50, 56, 58–59, 61, 63, 67, 81, 83–84, 88, 91–93, 95–97, 99, 101–103, 110, 115–116, 120, 127–128
Cabel, Marie 33
Caccini, Giulio 10
cadenza xi, xii, xvi, xvii, 3, 7–8, 11, 13–14, 19, 28–32, 34, 36–37, 42–47, 51–57, 59–61, 63, 65–70, 77, 79–80, 83–96, 102, 104, 111, 113, 118–120, 122–127, 133, 135
Callas, Maria 22–23, 93, 130, 133
Calvé, Emma 64, 91
Camden, New Jersey 1, 7, 28, 36, 43, 64, 88, 91, 123
Cammarano, Salvatore 101
Campanini, Cleofonte 82, 105, 110, 113
cantabile xvii, 58, 60, 63, 67, 83–84, 91–94, 103, 111, 116, 118, 122, 127–128
Carafa, Michele 40
Carpi, Fernando 55, 106
Carré, Michel 33

Caruso, Enrico 8, 54, 104
Castil-Blaze 11
cavatina 11, 15–19, 24–25, 27–28, 38, 40–43, 47, 49–50, 56, 58, 67–68, 77, 79–80, 103, 116
Cesari, Pietro 15, 49, 82
Chicago 15, 33, 42
Child, Calvin G. 64
Chorley, Henry F. 13, 100, 102–103
Cilea, Francesco 133
   Adriana Lecouvreur 133
Cincinnati 42
Cinti-Damoreau, Laura 19, 30, 81, 93–95, 135
Colbran, Isabella 38
Coleoni Cori, Benedetta 50
coloratura xi, xii, 3–4, 7–8, 10, 18–19, 25, 30, 32–33, 42, 47, 49, 54–59, 62, 69, 76, 97, 104–107, 109, 112, 116, 128, 132–133

Daily Mail 131
David, Félicien 25, 89–90
   La Perle du Brésil 25, 89–90
Davison, James W. 25, 100
De Belocca, Anna 23
De Candia, Giovanni Matteo (Mario) 102
declamato 10, 17, 39, 63, 73–74, 81, 96, 99–100, 105
De Koven, Reginald 56–57, 111
Delibes, Léo 25, 37
   Lakmé 25–26, 37
De Luca, Giuseppe 55, 74
de Lurieu, Gabriel 89
de Murska, Ilma 53
Dereyne, Fely 33
Dixon, Sydney W. 64
Donizetti, Gaetano 10, 23, 49–52, 54, 56, 58, 62, 64–65, 67, 69, 73–76, 99, 101–102, 104–105, 107, 132–133

Fausta 51
La figlia del reggimento 49
L'elisir d'amore 49, 99
Linda di Chamounix xvi, 1, 49, 67
Lucia di Lammeroor xi, xvi, 1, 3–4, 49–58, 64, 67, 88–89, 97, 105, 107, 133
Lucrezia Borgia 23–24
Maria Padilla 75
Marino Faliero 51
Rosmonda d'Inghilterra 50
Sancia di Castiglia 50
Donzelli, Domenico 74–75
Duprez, Gilbert-Louis 74

Elias, C. 15
Ercolani, R. 15
Evening Standard 130
Evening World 109, 118, 120, 129

Faccio, Franco 103
Ferrani, Cesira 132
Fétis, François-Joseph 74–75
fioriture 11, 13, 15, 19–20, 24–25, 41–43, 50–51, 55, 102
Florence 2–3, 23, 38, 50–51, 103, 107
Fodor Mainvielle, Joséphine 23
Fransella, Albert 49, 63–64, 66
Frezzolini, Erminia 86, 102
Fucito, Salvatore 8

Galli-Curci, Amelita 36–37, 69, 89, 91
Galliera, Alceo 22
Galvany, Maria 36
Garbin, Edoardo 104
García, Beata 20
García, Manuel 9–12, 18–23, 32, 40, 50, 74, 76–80, 93, 96, 101, 131
Gassier, Josefa 31
Gazzetta Musicale di Milano 51, 74–75, 99
Gazzetta privilegiata di Venezia 38
Gerster, Etelka 69, 82, 110
Giordano, Umberto 132
Giraldoni, Eugenio 15
Giulini, Carlo Maria 22
Global and Commercial Advertiser 113
Globe, The xv
Gobbi, Tito 22
Goethe, Johann Wolfgang 33
    Wilhelm Meisters Lehrjahre 33
Goldoni, Carlo 49
Gounod, Charles 25, 64
    Faust xv, 1, 108
    Roméo et Juliette xv
Granchi, Almerinda 102
Gravina, Giovanni 82
Grisi, Giulia 41–42, 97
Guadalajara, Mexico 33

Guckeisen, August 103

Hammerstein, Oscar 109–110, 129
Hanslick, Eduard 24
Harmonicon, The 40
Hempel, Frieda 36
Herz, Leo 101
Horne, Marilyn 133
Hugo, Victor 73
Huguet, Giuseppina 127

Ivanoff, Nicola 102

Juva Branca, Matilde 18, 31

Kallez, Emilia 50
Kark, Friedrich 36
Klein, Hermann 42, 86, 116–117
Köln 103
Kurz, Selma 81

Lablache, Luigi 13
La gazzetta privilegiata 38, 80
Lamperti, Francesco 8, 10, 14, 75–76
Lehmann, Lilli 8
Le Ménestrel 51
Leoncavallo, Ruggiero 114, 132
Liebling, Estelle 19, 37, 43, 89, 104, 122
L'Illustrazione italiana 103
Lind, Jenny 31, 55, 81, 85–86, 107–109, 130
London x, xv, xvi, 1–3, 7, 9, 15, 18, 23–27, 37–38, 40–43, 50, 53, 55, 63–64, 81, 83, 85, 99–100, 102–103, 105–106, 108, 112–113, 116–117, 123
    Covent Garden x, 2, 25, 42, 55, 76, 79, 82, 85, 106–109, 113, 117, 129–131, 133
    Drury Lane 18, 78–79, 81
    Her Majesty's Theatre 23, 40, 52
    Royal Albert Hall 68, 113
    Royal Italian Opera 18, 42, 53
Lorenzini, Carlo 99
Löwe, Sophie 75–76
Lufsky, Marshall P. 91
Luppi, Oreste 55, 107
lyric form 58, 63, 84, 114, 122

Malatesta 25, 27
Malibran, Maria 19, 23–24, 29–30, 41, 78–81, 85, 94, 130, 133
Mancinelli, Luigi 94
Mancini, Giambattista 10
Marchesi, Mathilde 9, 19, 29–30, 43, 45, 52–54, 60–61, 64–70, 77, 81, 88–89, 93–94, 96, 104, 122, 135
Marchisio, Barbara 19, 30–31, 43, 81, 95
Marcoux 25, 27
Mariacher, Michele 15
Mascagni, Pietro 50, 114, 132
    Cavalleria Rusticana 132

Maurel, Victor 104
Mazza, Adelaide 50
Mazzucato, Alberto 20, 74–75, 99
McCormack, John 25, 57, 82, 106–107
Melba, Nellie 6–7, 9–10, 30, 37, 43, 51–56, 62, 64–65, 71, 86, 88, 104, 108–109, 113–114, 130–131, 135
Merlin, Maria 80
messa di voce xiv, 4, 7, 110, 113, 118, 124, 127, 131, 133
Mexico City 33, 37
Meyerbeer, Giacomo 25
    Dinorah 1
    Il crociato in Egitto 77
    L'Africaine 3
    Les Huguenots 1
Michailova, Maria 91
Michotte, Edmond 17–18
Milan 2, 9, 17–18, 22, 33, 51, 99, 101, 103–104, 132
    Teatro alla Scala 22, 38, 51
Monteverdi, Claudio 10
Montevideo 68
    Politeama 68
Moore, Thomas 37
Moriani, Napoleone 74
Mount-Edgcumbe, Richard 38
Mozart, Wolfgang Amadeus 10, 40, 76, 106, 132
    Così fan tutte 40
    Die Zauberflöte 1, 108
    Don Giovanni 1, 3, 40, 76, 106
    Le nozze di Figaro 1
Mugnone, Leopoldo 15, 132
Muir, Kenneth 9
Munich 2, 18–19
Musical Courier 57
Musical Times, The 26, 53, 55, 107, 113
Muzio, Claudia 104

Naples 17, 38, 50–51
    Teatro San Carlo 17
Nasolini, Sebastiano 38
Nevada, Emma 89–91
New York xv, xvi, 3, 7, 24, 26, 37, 42–43, 56–57, 86, 109, 112–113, 117–118, 123, 129
    Academy of Music 24, 42
    Manhattan Opera House 3, 26, 56–57, 86, 109–111, 129, 131
    Metropolitan Opera House 43, 64
New York Daily Tribune 108, 110, 130–131
New York Press 113
New York Sun, The 109
New York Times, The 3, 24, 109–110, 133
Nilsson, Christine 52–53, 108, 110
North 54

Novara 50

Oesterreicher, Walter 49, 64, 66, 89

Pacini, Giovanni 13
   Niobe 13
Pacini, Regina 36, 81, 89, 94
Pagliughi, Lina 9
Paisiello, Giovanni 100
Palazzesi, Mathilde 51
Pall Mall Gazette 52
Pandolfini, Angelica 132
Panizza, Ettore 25, 55, 82, 106
Paris 24, 33, 37, 51–53, 67, 90–91, 100, 102
   Comédie Française 37
   Opéra Garnier 51
   Théâtre Italien 50, 100, 102
Parma 51
   Teatro Ducale 51
Partington, Blanche 26, 54–55, 105–106, 130
Pasta, Giuditta 13, 40–41, 76, 94, 130, 133
Patti, Adelina 10, 18–19, 24–27, 29–30, 32, 37, 42–44, 47, 54–56, 65, 68–69, 76, 85–86, 94, 97, 100, 102, 104, 107, 109–110, 112–113, 129–131, 133, 135
Pavia 50
Pepoli, Carlo 73, 83, 101
Persiani, Giuseppe 50
   Ines de Castro 50
pertichini 39, 43, 60, 63, 84, 92, 115
Petersburgskie Vedomosti 54
Philadelphia 37, 42
Piave, Francesco Maria 114–115
Piccolomini, Marietta 100, 104, 108, 130
Pini-Corsi, Antonio 104
Pinkert, Regina 94, 97
Pitt, Percy 7, 15, 27, 43, 49, 63, 68, 83, 127
Polacco, Giorgio 105–106
Pons, Lily 19
portamento xi, xii, xv, 4–7, 60–61, 71, 75, 117, 123, 125–128, 131–133, 135
Proch, Heinrich 25–26, 35–36, 89, 91
   Air and Variations 25, 35–37, 89
Puccini, Giacomo 114, 132–133
   Edgar xiii
   La bohème 3–4, 86, 132
   Suor Angelica 133
   Turandot 133

Radcliff, John R. 53
Reeves, Sims 102
Remorini 40
Ricci, Luigi and Federico 49
   Crispino e la Comare 1, 49
Ricordi, Giulio 103
Ricordi, Tito 17

Riegelman, Mabel 33
Righetti-Giorgi, Geltrude 18, 23
Rio de Janeiro 68
Rode, Pierre 19, 23
Rogers, Walter B. 7, 15, 28, 43, 49, 64, 83, 88, 91, 127
Romani, Felice 76, 80, 83, 103
Romani, Pietro 103
Rome 23, 102
Ronzi de Begnis, Giuseppina 23
Rossi, Gaetano 37–38
Rossini, Gioachino 10, 12–19, 23–29, 31–32, 38, 40–44, 47, 49, 62, 74–77, 100, 102, 104–105, 117, 132–133
   Aureliano in Palmira 17
   Elisabetta, regina d'Inghilterra 17
   Guglielmo Tell 15
   Il barbiere di Siviglia xvi, 1, 11–12, 15–18, 21–28, 31, 38, 47, 97, 105, 113, 129
   La gazza ladra 24
   L'italiana in Algeri 133
   Semiramide xvi, 1, 15, 24–25, 37–43, 47, 133
   Tancredi 23, 38, 77
Rouget, Eugénie 18
Rowling, Sylvester 109, 111
Rubini, Giovanni Battista 14, 79

Saint-Étienne, Sylvain 89
Saint Louis, Missouri 7, 42
Saint-Saëns, Camille 24
Sammarco, Mario 25, 27, 55, 57, 104, 106–107
Sampieri 25
San Francisco 9, 26, 54, 56, 82, 86, 105–106, 111, 129–130
   Alhambra Theater 54, 86
   Tivoli Theater 54–55, 86
San Francisco Call, The 9, 26, 54, 56, 82, 105–106, 111, 129–130
San Francisco Chronicle, The 9
Santley, Maud 107
São Paolo 68
Schmidt, Giovanni Federico 17
Schulhoff, Jules 7
Schumann, Robert 19
Sembrich, Marcella 6, 10, 30, 37, 43–47, 53–54, 62, 69, 88, 110, 114, 117, 127, 131, 135
Shakespeare, William 33
   A Midsummer Night's Dream 33
Sografi, Antonio 38
solita forma xvii, 58, 83, 92, 116, 127
Sontag, Henriette 23–24
Standard, The 15
Stehle, Adelina 104
Stendahl 13

Stendhal 76
stile parlante 10
St. Louis Globe-Democrat 7
St. Petersburg 3, 15, 33, 54, 91
Strakosch, Maurice 24–25
Strauss, Johann II 133
   Die Fledermaus 133
Strauss, Richard 8, 105
Stretponi, Giuseppina 51
stretta xvii, 99, 115, 122
Sunday Times, The xv
Sun, The ix, xvi, 30–31, 85–86, 110, 112, 120
Sutherland, Joan 42, 133

Tacchinardi-Persiani, Fanny 50–51, 67
Tadolini, Eugenia 50–51, 67, 69, 99, 101
Taffanel, Paul 51
Tamagno, Francesco 15, 104
Tbilisi 33, 68
tempo d'attacco xvii, 58, 83, 116, 127
tempo di mezzo xvii, 58, 60, 63, 84, 116, 127
Tetrazzini, Eva 129
Tetrazzini, Luisa 6–10, 14–15, 19, 25–28, 30–37, 43–47, 49, 54–58, 60–71, 73, 77, 82–83, 85–86, 88–89, 91–97, 104–114, 116–118, 120, 127–133, 135
   How to Sing ix, 8, 15, 109
   My Life of Song 49
Thomas, Ambroise 9, 25–27, 33
   Mignon 3, 9, 25–27, 33, 108
Thos, Edoardo 55
Tietjens, Thérèse 41–42
Times, The 18–19, 24–27, 40–42, 53, 55–57, 68, 76, 82–83, 106–108, 112–113, 130
Tomba, Raffaele 49, 82
Toscanini, Arturo 103, 132
Tosi, Pier Francesco 10, 78
Trebelli-Bettini, Zelia 41
tremolo 32, 111, 131
Turin 51, 103

Usiglio, Emilio 49
   Le donne curiose 49

Vaccai, Nicola 9, 51, 73
   Il precipizio 51
Van Hoose, Ellison 54
Van Zandt, Marie 37
Venice 37–38, 80, 102
   La Fenice 37–38, 80, 84
Verdi, Giuseppe 7–8, 10, 14, 23, 25, 49–50, 56, 58, 73–76, 99–106, 108–109, 113–116, 122–124, 128, 130, 132
   Aida 101
   Attila 99
   Don Carlos 103
   Ernani 100–104

Falstaff 103–104, 132
Giovanna d'Arco 103
I due Foscari 102
I Lombardi alla prima crociata 101–102
Il trovatore 1, 101–102, 104–105, 127
La forza del destino 104
La traviata xiii, xiv, 1–2, 4–6, 10, 49, 55–56, 99, 101, 104–108, 110, 112–114, 116, 118, 130
Les vêpres siciliennes 1, 104
Luisa Miller 99
Macbeth 103
Messa di Requiem 103
Nabucco 74, 100–101
Otello xiii, 86, 102, 104, 132
Quattro pezzi sacri 103
Rigoletto 1–2, 49, 55, 86, 102–103, 105–107, 113, 122, 124–125
Un ballo in maschera 1, 3, 104–105, 124, 126
Vernati, Pietro 9
Viardot, Pauline 9, 18–19, 22–25, 100, 102
vibrato xii, xiii, xv, 4–7, 131–133, 135
Vienna 17, 67, 99, 101
voce bianca 3–4, 54, 56–57, 108, 111, 126, 131–132
voix sombre 74
Voltaire 37–38

Sémiramis 37

Wagner, Richard 8, 17, 50, 58, 105, 108, 113, 132–133
   Die Meistersinger 133
Winter, Peter von 40
   Il ratto di Proserpina 40

Zaffira, Giuseppe 33
Zanardini, Angelo 49
Zecchini, Amalia 101
Zeigner Uriburu, Julio 9
Zucchi 25

About the Team

Alessandra Tosi was the managing editor for this book.

Melissa Purkiss performed the copy-editing and proofreading, as well as indexing the book.

Anna Gatti designed the cover. The cover was produced in InDesign using the Fontin font.

Luca Baffa typeset the book in InDesign and produced the paperback and hardback editions. The text font is Tex Gyre Pagella; the heading font is Californian FB. Luca produced the EPUB, AZW3, PDF, HTML, and XML editions—the conversion is performed with open source software freely available on our GitHub page (https://github.com/OpenBookPublishers).

This book need not end here...

Share

All our books—including the one you have just read—are free to access online so that students, researchers and members of the public who can't afford a printed edition will have access to the same ideas. This title will be accessed online by hundreds of readers each month across the globe: why not share the link so that someone you know is one of them?

This book and additional content is available at:

https://doi.org/10.11647/OBP.0277

Customise

Personalise your copy of this book or design new books using OBP and third-party material. Take chapters or whole books from our published list and make a special edition, a new anthology or an illuminating coursepack. Each customised edition will be produced as a paperback and a downloadable PDF.

Find out more at:

https://www.openbookpublishers.com/section/59/1

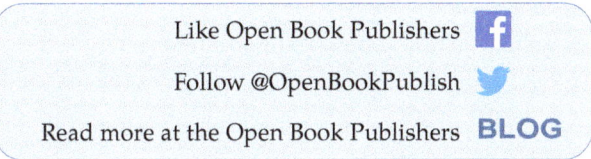

You may also be interested in:

Verdi in Victorian London
Massimo Zicari

https://doi.org/10.11647/OBP.0090

Classical Music
Contemporary Perspectives and Challenges
Michael Beckerman and Paul Boghossian (eds)

https://doi.org/10.11647/OBP.0242

Annunciations
Sacred Music for the Twenty-First Century
George Corbett (ed.)

https://doi.org/10.11647/OBP.0172

 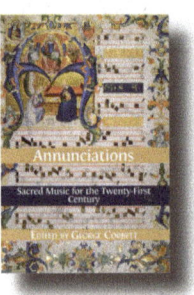

Denis Diderot 'Rameau's Nephew' — 'Le Neveu de Rameau'
A Multi-Media Bilingual Edition
M. Hobson (ed.)

https://doi.org/10.11647/OBP.0098

www.ingramcontent.com/pod-product-compliance
Lightning Source LLC
Chambersburg PA
CBHW061935290426
44113CB00025B/2920